Psychodynamic Music Therapy:
Case Studies

Edited by
Susan Hadley

Barcelona PUBLISHERS

Psychodynamic Music Therapy: Case Studies

Copyright © 2003 by Barcelona Publishers

ISBN: 978-1891278-16-7

Distributed throughout the world by:
Barcelona Publishers
10231 Plano Rd.
Dallas TX 75238
www.barcelonapublishers.com
SAN 298-6299

Cover design:
© 2003 Frank McShane

To my sons
Gabriel Miles Yancy
and
Elijah Kahlil Yancy

ACKNOWLEDGMENTS

There are many people whom I would like to thank sincerely for their part in the process of the development of this book:

First and foremost, the contributors and their clients for their courage and openness in sharing these deeply personal stories. From them, I have learned so much.

Ken Bruscia, for his continued support and encouragement, personally and professionally, and for seeing the value of this book.

Denise (Erdonmez) Grocke, Jane Edwards, Ken Bruscia, and Cheryl Dileo, each for their unique role in shaping my identity as a music therapist. They have been such great models and mentors.

Phyllis Boone, Benedikte Scheiby, and Alan Turry, for helping to shape my identity as a person, through very different musical experiences.

Mary Priestley and Clive Robbins for the inspiration gained through our conversations.

The translators Julia Schaper, Antonietta De Vivo, Annette Dulzin, Jeroen De Backer, Eleonore Hertweck, Kathryn Abbott, and Markus Kaiser, and Tony Wigram for acting as a language consultant to several of the authors. Knowing the challenges involved in such a task, I have a deep appreciation for the work that was done.

My colleague Sue Shuttleworth whose humble, thoughtful, and generous presence has been so appreciated. My close friend and colleague Laurie Jones for her support, encouragement, insight, musicianship, and the inspiring example she offers as a fellow music therapist and music therapy educator.

Cynthia O'Dell, for her thoroughness and her eye for detail.

Joanna (Minchin) Randell for leaving a significant, early, and lasting impression of her wonderful relationship with music and the joy it can bring to others.

My parents, Lillian and Geoff, for their love, for always believing in me, and for providing me with such wonderful opportunities throughout my life. Also, Dad for all the hours of proofreading. My mother-in-law, Ruth, for her love and generosity and who even came for an extended stay to help out with the children.

My family and friends, who have supported me over the years and who have helped me in various important ways: Ruth, Michael, Charles, Megan, Geoffrey, and Susan Sutherland; Peter, Jen, Emma, Thomas, and Sonya Hadley; Lib, Don, Jane, Richard, and Cath Allen; Ros and Pauline (Hadley); Artrice, Carson, and Mika; Brother El Yancey; Kylie Johnston-Leek; Emma Collins; Andrea McCallum; Anne (Owen) McAuliffe; Toni Lalich; Caroline Cusack; Donna Hessing; Nick, Vik, Max, Lexi, Chris, Chris, and Ric Haslam; Tony Meadows; Beth and Ian Dun; Leah Klibanoff; Amy Clarkson; Serena Hughes;

Jo Lawler; Janet and Ted McDade; Linda Bamberger; Flor Capistrano; Sheryl Ogburn; Helen Shoemark; Jane Wheeler; James Spady; Melvin Rogers; Larry Krafft; the faculty, staff, and students in the music department at Slippery Rock University; and, Dr. McKinney, dean of the College of Humanities, Fine and Performing Arts.

My children, Gabriel and Elijah, for bringing me such a healthy balance of saneness and zaniness. And Adrian, for his understanding and willingness to help out with the young boys when he would much rather have been doing something else.

And finally, my husband, George Yancy, who, as a friend, partner, co-parent, and co-intellectual has given love, support, stability, advice, challenging critique, insight, and genuineness throughout this process. With two people both actively engaged in creative endeavors, both needing time and space to realize our dreams, the fact that our relationship is based on mutual respect and understanding is so very important to me. I am also greatly appreciative of the times we spend together talking late into the night, laughing, dancing, and singing.

Contents

Part Two
Adolescents

CONTRIBUTORS

Jos De Backer is professor of music therapy at the College of Science and Art, Campus Lemmensinstituut (Leuven, Belgium) and coordinator for the training course for music therapy. He is head of the music therapy department at the University Centre, Kortenberg, where he works as a music therapist treating young psychotic patients. He also has a private practice. Currently he is undertaking Ph.D. research in the international Ph.D. program in music therapy at Aalborg University, Denmark. He specializes in psychoanalytically oriented music therapy, and has given various papers and workshops in the domain of music therapy with handicapped people and psychiatric patients. He is president of the European Music Therapy Confederation (EMTC).

Jan Van Camp is professor of psychotherapy at the College of Science and Art, Campus Lemmensinstituut and coordinator for the training course for music therapy, Louvain. He is a psychotherapist at the University Centre St.-Jozef, Kortenberg, and a supervisor/psychoanalyst at the University of Louvain. He is coordinator for the European Consortium for Arts Therapy Education (ECARTE).

Dr. Janice M. Dvorkin is an associate professor and coordinator of the music therapy program at the University of the Incarnate Word, San Antonio, Texas, and a licensed psychologist in Texas and New York. She is maintaining a music psychotherapy practice in San Antonio, as well as continuing to present and publish her work using object relations-based music psychotherapy.

Misty D. Erlund is a graduate of the University of the Incarnate Word in San Antonio, Texas. She is a board certified music therapist, currently working with autistic individuals. She has presented her work in music therapy at a state psychiatric setting at regional conferences. She has also presented introductory workshops on music therapy at colleges without music therapy programs. She is concentrating on continuing her education through clinical supervision and beginning her music therapy practice.

Gianluigi di Franco is a musician (vocalist), composer, and music therapist. He was the founder of the "neapolitan" group of music therapy (1986). He has had three years of Freudian group therapy with Prof. P. Perrotti at "Lo Spazio" Centre, Rome. He is the music therapy training program director (ISFOM) in Napoli and in Foggia (ISMEZ) at the Conservatorio "U. Giordano," which was the first recognized course in Italy at a Conservatorio. He is coordinator and supervisor of the music therapy project at the Audiology Institute (Napoli, Faculty of Medicine) and of the music therapy project at the Cardiosurgery for

Children (Monaldi Hospital/Napoli Faculty of Medicine). He was the founder of CONFIAM (the Italian Confederation of Music Therapy Associations) and president for six years (1994–2000). He was also president of the European Music Therapy Confederation from 1998–2001. He has been actively involved in the World Federation of Music Therapy as council member and chair of the commission on publications. He has written and co-edited several books.

Gabrielle Fruchard is a clinical psychologist, music therapist, and practising vocalist. She works principally with adolescents with very diverse social and cultural backgrounds. She has written numorous articles in a variety of journals such as *Revue de Musicotherapie*.

Dr. Denise Grocke (previously Erdonmez) is associate professor and head of music therapy at the University of Melbourne, Victoria, Australia. She co-ordinates the undergraduate and graduate degree programs in music therapy and the graduate diploma in Guided Imagery and Music (Bonny Method). She is director of the National Music Therapy Research Unit and co-founder of the Australian Music Therapy Association, and currently president of the World Federation of Music Therapy.

Dr. Susan Hadley received her bachelor's degree in music therapy from the University of Melbourne, Australia, and her master's and Ph.D. degrees in music therapy and psychoeducational processes from Temple University, Pennsylvania. She has worked as a music therapist with a wide variety of clinical populations including hospitalized children and adults with psychiatric disorders. Her published articles and reviews appear in a variety of scholarly journals and books. She is currently assistant professor of music therapy at Slippery Rock University, Pennsylvania, and is on the editorial board of *Qualitative Inquiries in Music Therapy*.

Dr. Niels Hannibal was educated as a nurse in 1984. He began his music therapy training at Aalborg University, Denmark, in 1994. He received his Ph.D. in 2001. His dissertation research examined the preverbal transference relationship in the musical interaction in music therapy. He received the Spar Nord Foundation Research Prize in 2002 and is now working full-time doing research and clinical work at the music therapy clinic at Aalborg Psychiatric Hospital and teaching at Aalborg University.

Juliane Kowski earned her B.A. in elementary school music, German, and mathematics. Later she obtained a second B.A. as a singer and vocal teacher for contemporary music and jazz. She has performed in both Berlin and New York as a jazz singer. Looking for more satisfying ways to put her musical knowledge to work, she obtained an M.A. in music therapy at New York University in 1998. She worked for three years as a consultant for the Association for Help for Retarded Children, establishing music therapy in home residences for adults with developmental disabilities. Since then she has worked with emotionally disturbed children at a family health and support center in Brooklyn, and has opened her own private practice. Presently, she is working for The New York City Music Therapy Project.

Dr. Mechtild Jahn-Langenberg Ph.D., Dipl.Musiktherapeutin, has been the director of the music therapy department at the University of the Arts, Berlin, Seminar Musiktherapie (postgraduate program, master's degree) since 1995. She has specialized in analytical music therapy with psychosomatic patients (children and adults), qualitative research, and has initiated international symposia since 1994 with this focus. In addition to teaching and training she has a private practice as an analytical music therapist and supervisor.

Dr. Edith Lecourt is a clinical psychologist, psychoanalyst, and music therapist. She is the co-founder of the first music therapy association in France. She is professor of clinical and pathological psychology at the University Rene Descartes (Paris V), where she is co-director of the Institute of Psychology, and responsible for the music therapy training. She has written several books including *Freud et le Somore: Le Tic-tac du Desir, Analyse de Groupe et Musicotherapie*, and *L'experience Musical, Resonances Psychoanalytiques*, and has authored numerous journal articles and book chapters in both French and English.

Dr. Wolfgang Mahns received his Ph.D. in music therapy from Aalborg University, Denmark, and is a qualified teacher and psychotherapist. He is currently the head of the Weiterbildung Musiktherapie fur Musikpadagogen and the chairman of Verein Musiktherapie Rendsburg. He also belongs to the Berlin research group Qualitative Research in Music Therapy. Mahns has worked with children and adults for twenty years and published widely on music therapy in education.

Dr. Susanne Metzner, Diplom-Musiktherapeutin, Kinder- und Jugendlichen-Psychotherapeutin, worked as a social-pedagogue with children, young people, and with mentally handicapped persons in Hamburg. In 1988 she finished her music therapy training and her music studies at the Hochschule für Musik und Theater, Hamburg. She has worked as a music therapist with children suffering from psychosomatic diseases. For ten years she worked with adult patients in psychiatry. There she specialized in psychoanalytically informed music therapy and finished her Ph.D. in 1998. Since 1991 she has been professor at the Institut für Musiktherapie at the Hochschule für Musik und Theater at Hamburg and since 2001 at the Hochschule Magdeburg-Stendal. In her private practice she supervises music therapists. Since 1994 she has been chair of the German Professional Association (BVM).

Dr. Louise Montello is an internationally known authority on music and healing; author of *Essential Musical Intelligence: Using Music as Your Path to Healing, Creativity, and Radiant Wholeness* (Quest Books 2002). A psychoanalyst, certified music therapist, jazz pianist, and composer, she is the founder/director of Musicians' Wellness, Inc., conducts clinical research in the psychology department at NYU, and is director of the Creative Arts Therapy Program at New School University. She maintains a private practice in psychodynamic music therapy and supervision in New York City and Lackawaxen, Pennsylvania.

Simona Katz Nirensztein was born in Florence, Italy, where she graduated in piano and began performing. She continued her career in Jerusalem, Israel, where she completed her artist diploma in piano and chamber music, at the Rubin Academy. For some years she performed and taught, until she developed her interest in the therapeutic use of music. She graduated in music therapy at the David Yellin College, Jerusalem, and since then she has been developing her clinical practice in a psychodynamic approach, working with children and adolescents. A member of the staff of a child mental health clinic in Jerusalem, she is engaged in defining the specific role of music and sound elements in the psychotherapeutic, analytic setting.

Paul Nolan, M.C.A.T., M.T.-B.C., L.P.C., is associate professor and director of music therapy education at the Hahnemann Creative Arts in Therapy Program at Drexel University, Center City Hahnemann Campus (formerly, MCP Hahnemann University) where he has taught for over twenty years. He has a wide range of clinical experiences, a private practice in music psychotherapy, and is a licensed professional counselor in Pennsylvania as well as a performing musician. He has authored several book chapters and articles, serves on several editorial boards, and has presented internationally to a wide variety of health-care groups. His special interests include the relationship between creativity and mental health.

Inge Nygaard Pedersen received her M.A. in music from Copenhagen University in 1981. She then received the Dipl. Music Therapist from

Mentorenkurs Herdecke 1980. She has been associate professor at the five-year music therapy program at Aalborg University, Denmark, since 1982. From 1982 to 1995 she coordinated this program with some short breaks. Since 1995, she has been in charge of the music therapy clinic—a joint treatment and research clinic of Aalborg Psychiatric Hospital and Aalborg University. She also conducts clinical work with a variety of clients including counseling work with people who voluntarily seek out therapy treatment (i.e., who are not referred), clinical work with autistic children and adults, and for the past seven years with all categories of psychiatric patients. She is the co-editor of five books and author of more than twenty-five articles and book chapters, national and international.

Roia Rafieyan, M.A., M.T.-B.C., has been providing music therapy services to adults with significant developmental disabilities and autism for the past fourteen years. She has presented her work at numerous conferences and has a chapter (co-authored with Janice Dvorkin) which appears in *Inside Music Therapy*. She is a past president of the New Jersey Association for Music Therapy. A strong advocate for building inclusive communities, she has, along with the help of equally dedicated friends, created a monthly coffeehouse, the purpose of which is to provide a venue for all people to share their music. She recorded a CD, *Songs from Behind Locked Doors*, and she has recently completed her master's degree in music therapy.

Jacqueline Z. Robarts, M.A., A.R.C.M. (Performer), Cert. Ed., Dip. M.T.-N.R., S.R.As.T. (M.), is research fellow in music therapy, City University, London, where she is completing doctoral research on music therapy with anorexic adolescents. She has received two further research awards since 2000, relating to music therapy with emotionally disturbed and deprived children. She is clinical/research consultant to a PPP Healthcare Medical Trust-funded music therapy project with deprived and traumatized children. A senior therapist and clinical tutor at the Nordoff-Robbins Music Therapy Centre, London, and former head music therapist in a child and adolescent mental health service, Jackie has many years' experience with young people with severe emotional disturbance, eating disorders, and developmental problems, as well as with children with autistic spectrum disorders. In the last eight years, she has also worked with self-referring adults and musicians. She has published chapters and papers on various aspects of music therapy, and lectures widely in the UK and abroad, particularly in the field of child and adolescent mental health.

Penny Rogers qualified as a music therapist in 1982 and has completed three master's degrees: in cognitive neuropsychology; child protection; and more recently systemic psychotherapy alongside trainings in management and clinical supervision. She has worked in all areas of psychiatry and conducted doctoral research into process in music therapy with abused children (while a research fellow at City University, London). She has played a leading role in national organizations for music therapy in the UK. Today Penny is working as clinical specialist, Child Protection for North Essex Mental Health Partnership NHS Trust (a joint health and social services trust serving a population of 1.3 million people). Her post includes both the direct provision of therapy with children and their families in complex abuse cases; the provision of consultation, training, and supervision for professional colleagues; and a lead role in the development of child protection policies both within the trust and across agencies in Essex. She has written extensively about her work with both abused and abusing young people and their families and has lectured both nationally and internationally.

Viola Schönfeld was born in 1959 in Braunschweig, Germany. She received a master's degree for sacred music at the University of Berlin, and a master's degree for music therapy at the Hamburg Academy of Music and Theatre. She first worked as a music therapist at the children's hospital in Wolfsburg and at the "Kinder und Jugendpsychiatrische Praxis" (a special center for child psychiatry) in Uelzen, Germany. Since 1991 she has had her own music therapeutic office. She also works as a therapeutic teacher at the music school of Gifhorn, Germany, and as a music therapist at the academic hospital for music therapy at the "Klinik Gut Wienebuettel/Lueneburg," Germany.

Catherine Sweeney was born in Ireland to a family of musicians. She studied music at Bangor University, Wales, specializing in flute studies and winning the performance prize for her degree recital. She trained as a music therapist at Anglia Polytechnic University, Cambridge, and currently works in the fields of children's palliative care, adult head injury, and learning disability. She lives in Shropshire, England, where she continues to perform regularly both instrumentally and vocally.

Helen M. Tyler completed her music degree and M.Phil. at Reading University, England, and taught music to a wide range of children, from ages two to eighteen. She then trained as a music therapist at the Nordoff-Robbins Music Therapy Centre in London. She is now the assistant director of the Centre, and also works there as a therapist and as a senior tutor on the master's training course. She has a particular interest in music therapy with children with emotional and behavioral problems and has written and lectured widely on this, and other areas of clinical work. She is a member of the WFMT Education and Training Commission.

Dr. Susan Bray Wesley, Ph.D., M.T.-B.C., L.C.P.C., is a member of the graduate faculty for the concentration in adult development at the University of Maine. She maintains a private practice in music therapy and counseling psychotherapy and continues, as a credentialed music educator, to also teach children at the Adams School in Castine, Maine.

PREFACE

The initial inspiration for this book grew out of both a personal and a pedagogical conviction. On the personal side, as a student, client, clinician, supervisor, and educator, I have been drawn to the view that our present is shaped by our past and that in order to make lasting and meaningful change, we must resolve our past conflicts. As a student, I was introduced to a multitude of theoretical perspectives, many involving experiential components. Those that impacted me most deeply were the psychodynamic ones. That my former professor, Dr. Ken Bruscia, has strong psychodynamic leanings cannot be dismissed as an insignificant influence, but the fact that not all of his students have adopted this view presumably indicates that there was something about my own prereflective experiences that brought me to view pathology and health/ wellness within a psychodynamic framework. Furthermore, as a client I have undergone sessions in three models of music therapy: Analytical Music Therapy (Priestley's model), Creative Music Therapy (Nordoff and Robbins's model), and Guided Imagery and Music (Bonny's model). These experiences have given me a profound sense of the potential and potency of psychodynamic music therapy. They heightened my excitement about the possibilities of the work that we can do as music therapists and gave me a real sense of the power that music has in terms of reaching and expressing emotions. This, of course, was not new to me in theory. After all, I have had substantial training in the field. However, these experiences gave me something that none of my other training had—a chance to experience the therapeutic process over an extended period of time from the perspective of the client. Furthermore, they gave me a glimpse of the type of music therapy work to which I would like to aspire. What made these experiences so profound, I believe, is that in each case the method of music therapy I experienced was psychodynamic in orientation. In these sessions, each therapist helped me gain greater self-awareness, resolve inner conflicts, mobilize blocked emotions, find a means of self-expression, change unhealthy emotions and attitudes, resolve interpersonal problems, develop healthier relationships, heal emotional traumas, and experience greater meaning and fulfillment in my life. These are all examples of goals to be achieved in psychodynamic music therapy.

The pedagogical conviction that prompted me to compile a book solely devoted to psychodynamic music therapy case studies is that it is very important for music therapists to undertake advanced training in music therapy. Music therapy is the only creative arts therapy that offers a bachelor's degree. Furthermore, according to the American Music Therapy Association member sourcebook (2001), only 24 percent of the membership in the United States holds a graduate degree and many of these are not in music therapy. It is important, however, to note that holding a graduate degree is not synonymous with being an advanced clinician. Some music therapists have advanced training in a specialized area of music therapy such as Nordoff-Robbins Music Therapy (Creative Music Therapy), Analytical Music Therapy, or Guided Imagery and Music without holding an advanced degree as such, while other music therapists hold graduate degrees without being trained in more advanced levels of music therapy.[1] Although the majority of music therapists in the United States have not been trained to practice more advanced levels of music therapy, I believe that with more exposure to the in-depth work done by music therapists with advanced training, such as the case studies in this book, more music therapists will be inspired to pursue further training. This could only benefit the music therapy profession as a whole.

This book contains twenty-one psychodynamic music therapy case studies using musical improvisation (see the case studies by Sweeney, Tyler, Mahns, di Franco, Kowski, Rogers, Robarts, Dvorkin & Erlund, Schönfeld, Katz Nirensztein, Metzner, De Backer & Van Camp, Montello, Nolan, Rafieyan, Jahn-Langenberg, Pedersen, Hannibal), songs (see Sweeney, Tyler, Kowski, Wesley, Rogers, Robarts, Schonfeld, Montello, Rafieyan), music imagery (see Wesley, Grocke), and music listening (see Fruchard & Lecourt) with children from as young as five years old to adolescents and adults. The length of treatment ranges from a few sessions, spread over a couple of months, to weekly sessions spanning five or six years.

I chose the format of case studies for this book because their engaging narrative flow allows readers to feel as though they are right there, watching the process unfold. Case studies have a personal dimension that profoundly touches those who read them. My students repeatedly express how much they appreciate reading the case studies in *Case Studies in Music Therapy* (Bruscia, 1991) because they feel that through case studies they can more fully understand and appreciate the music therapy process.

The case studies in this book have been organized according to the chronological age of the clients (as indicated) and are divided into three sections: children, adolescents, and adults. Each case study utilizes a uniform format which begins with an introduction that provides information about the approach, client, or condition, followed by background information on the client, a detailed description of the treatment process, and, finally, the authors discuss the case study in terms of various psychodynamic constructs.

Although this book is devoted to a psychodynamic approach, I do not in any way wish to suggest that this is an approach that should be adopted by

---

[1] For a thorough examination of levels of music therapy practice see, K. E. Bruscia (1998a) and B. Wheeler (1981, 1983).

everyone. Psychodynamic music therapy consists of useful constructs, not "absolute truths," which are adopted by clinicians and provide a framework within which to analyze and interpret behavior. This framework provides conceptual tools that are used to enhance our understanding of our clients and their experiences. It is very important that we, as music therapists, use these tools in relationship to the distinctive nuances that each client brings to the therapeutic situation. By applying these conceptual tools to the unique needs of each client, our thinking is informed in such a way that we are able to create innovative ways of using music to help each individual client lead a healthier life within the context of his/her particular issues. Thus, our thinking becomes theory-informed rather than theory-led (Robarts, personal communication, 2002).

I like to think of the psychodynamic music therapist as a "sound spelunker," exploring the depths of the human psyche using musical tools. Not limited to exploration though, the sound spelunker, when entering a space with a fragile foundation, must sometimes reconstruct this space or even construct it for the first time. This text, then, is an excursion through various landscapes, using a variety of tools. Bringing a diversity of perspectives, these highly qualified music therapists innovatively build on psychodynamic theory to develop unique ways of working in music therapy. For each music therapist, the way they work in psychodynamic music therapy depends on the culture of the therapist, his/her training, the clients they work with, the setting in which the work is done, and the kind of supervision they have undertaken.

Finally, as editor, I would like to say that it has been a great experience compiling this book. The process has had its challenges and its delights, all of which have further shaped my identity as a music therapist, scholar, and person. So, it is with a profound sense of gratitude and respect to the authors and their clients that I turn you now to the incredibly engaging stories that follow.

Susan Hadley
Editor
July 2002

Psychodynamic Music Therapy:
Case Studies

Introduction

PSYCHODYNAMIC MUSIC THERAPY: AN OVERVIEW[*]

Susan Hadley

Music is an integral part of human life and aspiration, and as such it is one of our most useful therapeutic tools—at once delicate, versatile and powerful. Like all instruments, it can be abused or prostituted by the ignorant, the careless or the untalented; in the hands of the trained, dedicated and skillful, it can mediate the most fundamental of personal and social experiences.

—J. H. Masserman, M.D.

If the therapist cannot play, then he [she] is not suitable for the work. If the patient cannot play, then something needs to be done to enable the patient to become able to play, after which psychotherapy may begin. . . . It is only through being creative that the individual discovers the self.

—D. W. Winnicott, F.R.C.P.

A Brief Historical Look at Psychodynamic Music Therapy:

Although music therapists only began writing about psychodynamic music therapy in the 1960s and 1970s, music has been linked with psychodynamic therapy from at least the early part of the twentieth century. In fact, there is a comprehensive historical overview of music and psychodynamic thought that appeared in the *Journal of Music Therapy* as early as 1966 (Noy, 1966, 1967a, 1967b, 1967c, 1967d). Although this overview looks at the work of analysts rather than music therapists, there are some notable examples from this overview that warrant a mention here. For example, from as early as 1917, Teller emphasized the role of music in weakening the censors, making it

---

[*] I am very grateful to the insightful comments made by Jackie Robarts and Ken Bruscia on an earlier version of this chapter.

possible for unconscious content and wishes to appear in the form of fantasies. In 1921, Ferenczi actually incorporated musical activities in his sessions (piano playing and singing) in order to understand his patients' problems better. In 1951, Racker described music as nonthreatening because it "represents the good object, which loves and therefore is loved." In the mid 1950s, Masserman addressed the National Association of Music Therapy about the benefits, limitations, and dangers of music in the practice of dynamic psychiatry. In 1957, Kohut described music in terms of its impact on the id, ego, and superego in terms of 1) allowing catharsis for primitive impulses, 2) it being a form of play, thus constituting an exercise in mastery, and 3) being an aesthetic experience. Furthermore, he stated that "the therapeutic efficacy of musical activity at each level of functioning of the psyche depends upon the capacity of music to repeat an emotional conflict in a medium that is relatively free from conflict" (Kohut, 1952). And, in 1960, Friedmann linked music with primary process thinking.

By the 1960s, music therapist Florence Tyson was pioneering the application of psychodynamic principles to music therapy practice in the United States. She proposed that by using a psychodynamic orientation to music therapy that "the patient is not only helped to discover strengths, but to deal with the manifestations of deeper unconscious problems as they arise" (Tyson, 1981, p. 20). She recognized the importance of relatedness in human life and saw the role of the therapist as not one of pure analyst, but more of an "ally and active supporter who helps the patient to learn, to mature, and to grow emotionally by working through problems on a more realistic level" (Tyson, 1981, p. 20). Also in the 1960s and 1970s, Juliette Alvin was using psychoanalytic concepts in her writings on music therapy.[1] The analytic concepts found in her work include the use of free improvisation as a means of self-projection and free association; the use of music to evoke the personality functions of id, ego, and superego; the use of music to penetrate ego defenses; the interpretation of musical responses as ego defenses (Alvin, 1974); the use of instruments as a means of projection onto an intermediary object (Alvin, 1977); the interpretation of musical responses in terms of sexual symbolism and psychosexual stages; regressional techniques in music therapy (Alvin, 1981); and she proposes a relationship between music and dreams/altered states of consciousness.

In the early 1970s, Helen Bonny was developing her method, Guided Imagery and Music, utilizing psychodynamic principles of therapy. Bonny's method uses music to evoke altered states of consciousness to explore and resolve unresolved conflicts (Grocke, 1999). At this same time, Mary Priestley, along with colleagues Peter Wright and Marjorie Wardle, was developing her method, Analytical Music Therapy. By creating innovative ways of interpreting

---

[1] See "Free Improvisation Therapy" in K. E. Bruscia (ed.) *Improvisational Models of Music Therapy* (1987), chapters 5–8.

unconscious processes as manifested through musical improvisation, Priestley formed a crucial bridge between psychoanalytic theory and music therapy (Hadley, 2001).

Other influential early contributors to the development of psychodynamically oriented music therapy include Nordoff and Robbins (1971, 1977) for their research on improvisational music-making as the creative medium of the therapeutic relationship, including working musically with the child's "resistiveness" (i.e., defenses); Even Ruud (1980) in terms of his exploration of music therapy and its relationship to various treatment theories, including psychoanalytic; Rolando Benenzon (1982) in terms of his work on music therapy in child psychosis; Kenneth E. Bruscia (1987) in terms of his articulation of the symbolic significance of various musical elements in a psychodynamic framework in his Improvisation Assessment Profiles and more recently his pivotal book *The Dynamics of Music Psychotherapy*; Edith Lecourt in terms of her pioneering work as both a psychoanalyst and music therapist in France; and, Johannes Eschen in terms of his fundamental role in the early training of European music therapists in analytical music therapy.

Continuing in this tradition, the purpose of this book is to present a broad spectrum of the clinical work done in psychodynamic music therapy. Currently, in the music therapy literature, there is no such text. There are texts devoted to a single psychodynamic approach, such as *Music Therapy in Action* (Priestley, 1985); *Essays on Analytical Music Therapy* (Priestley, 1994); and, *Analytical Music Therapy* (Eschen, 2002). There is also *The Dynamics of Music Psychotherapy* (Bruscia, 1998b), which focuses on a broad spectrum of psychodynamic music therapy, but specifically in terms of how transference and countertransference unfold in music psychotherapy. Being solely devoted to case studies in psychodynamic music therapy, *Psychodynamic Music Therapy: Case Studies* will make a very good companion to *The Dynamics of Music Psychotherapy*.

Over the last twenty years, there has been a growth of music therapists working from a variety of psychodynamic theoretical orientations, with many developing innovative approaches using improvisation, songs, music imagery, and music listening, and this book is a testament to the quality of work being done. The reader will note that the authors vary in the degree to which they adhere to a psychodynamic paradigm. Some of this variety is due to the differing degree and types of trainings of the therapists themselves in terms of using music "as" or "in" therapy (Bruscia, 1998a, pp. 214–215). All, however, illustrate the significant impact that psychodynamic theory has on the practice of music psychotherapy.

What Is Psychodynamic Therapy?

Psychodynamic therapy is an outgrowth of traditional psychoanalytic psycho-therapy. It is a continually growing field and is cited in the *Handbook of Psychotherapy and Behavior Change* (Bergin & Garfield, 1994) as the most dominant specific theoretical orientation used by psychotherapy clinicians and educators, trailing only those labeling themselves as eclectic, with the majority of eclectic clinicians reporting that they use psychodynamic concepts (p. 468). Psychodynamic psychotherapy has been defined as "an approach to diagnosis and treatment characterized by a way of thinking about both patient and clinician that includes unconscious conflict, deficits and distortions of intra-psychic structures, and internal object relations" (Gabbard, 1990, p. 4). This def-inition covers a variety of strands of analytic thought including drive theory, ego psychology, object relations theory, self psychology, and Jungian theory. Psychodynamic treatment techniques have evolved from free association and the couch to include various domains of observation and varied techniques of intervention, including play and the creative arts. Furthermore, there has been a widening scope of patients worked with, including children and nonverbal clients.

In order to provide greater detail about the scope of psychodynamic therapy, five major domains of psychodynamic thought will be described:[2] 1) traditional Freudian drive (or id) psychology; 2) ego psychology and its emphasis on defenses, adaptation, reality testing, and defects in the development of each; 3) object relations theory and its emphasis on relationships and their internalization, distortion, and repetition; 4) self psychology and its emphasis on differentiation and boundary formation, personal agency, authenticity, and self-esteem; and, 5) Jungian theory. Although these areas are being delineated separately, many theorists draw from one or more domains to differing degrees, making it difficult to classify them in one or other category. Therefore, certain key aspects of the work of various theorists will be delineated (concentrating on those most referenced in the following case studies) in order to describe each domain. However, this is not to delimit any one theorist to a particular domain.

Drive Psychology

Centered on his theory of infantile sexuality, Sigmund Freud viewed instincts and their associated taboos as central in organizing the personality. He believed that instincts were biologically based, but take the form of psychological wishes that are embodied in conscious or unconscious fantasies. He understood psychic

---

[2] For a more comprehensive description of the first four, see Pine (1985, 1990).

life as organized around conflict and its resolution. As such, the central issues in drive (or id) psychology include the drives/urges themselves, social and internalized taboo, and the conflict resulting from these, the development of defenses, anxiety, guilt, defensive failure, and symptom formation, and how these are repeated in the transference (Pine, 1985). Therefore, for Freudians, psychoanalysis centers on the analysis of resistance and transference. For case studies drawing from psychoanalytic theory see Jahn-Langenberg and Nygaard Pedersen.

As a self-professed Freudian, central to Jacques Lacan's thought is the primacy of drives. Combining psychoanalysis with poststructural thought, Lacan also emphasizes the central role of language in the understanding of the self (Plottel, 1985). He articulates three planes in which humans function—the imaginary, the symbolic, and the real. For example, I can never "see" myself, just an image of me, which is an example of the imaginary plane. However, this image is inscribed in my memory as "I am me." This is an example of the symbolic function. The real is what is neither symbolic nor imaginary. For example, a physical act that I perform is real. As soon as I speak about the act, however, it becomes symbolic. It is within the symbolic realm that one distinguishes subject and object, self and other. With access to language, the infant enters the symbolic world, which results in alienation, experienced as the separation of infant from mother, and the splitting of the subject into the different "subject-positions" of I and you (Elia, 2001, p. 9). Lacan writes about a mirror phase that the child goes through (6–18 months) in which the child "sees" its self and "puts its self on." That is, "The 'I' shapes itself before objectifying itself as an ego in the dialectic of identification with the imago of the double and before language assigns it the function of subject in the world of the universal" (Lacan, 1966, p. 94). When the child is able to recognize its own image in the mirror, s/he has a notion that s/he is an "I." The further development of the understanding of the self is mediated through language and through social relationships. Lacan holds that the unconscious is structured like a language and that the real can only be manifested through a symbolic operation (Plottel, 1985). See De Backer and Van Camp's case study, which draws on Lacan's thought.

Ego Psychology

Ego psychology grew out of drive psychology following Freud's development of the tripartite system of the mind: the id, the ego, and the superego. Observing how individuals successfully adapt in order to deal with adversity and to creatively and constructively make something out of conflict, ego psychologists view the individual in terms of their capacity to defend against drives (Pine

1985). Whereas in drive psychology the ego's function is to provide a safe balance between the ongoing conflicts between drives and societal rules, and therefore only has a defensive function, in ego psychology it is believed that there are ego processes, such as memory, perception, and motor coordination, that have their own energy, separate from the id (Prochaska, 1984). Ego psychology is based on the writings of Hartmann (1958), Erikson (1950), and Rapaport (1958). Hartmann describes what he refers to as conflict-free spheres of the ego. Not denying the importance of drives and conflicts around their gratification on personality development, ego psychologists believe that equally important is the individual's striving for adaptation to reality and mastery of the environment (Prochaska, 1984). Furthermore, ego psychologists believe in the ongoing development of the personality well past the psychosexual stages of Freud. Erikson (1950) felt that not all problems could be reduced to repetitions of unconscious conflicts from childhood and proposed stages of development that cover the span of one's life. These include issues of trust, autonomy, initiative, identity, industry, intimacy, generativity, and integrity. In summary, issues of identity, intimacy, and ego integrity are central concerns of ego psychology.

Object Relations

Object relations theory has come to refer to "internal mental representations of self and others [the objects] (Sandler and Rosenblat, 1962) in varying experienced and ideal forms, bound together by affects (Kernberg, 1976), memories and behavioral expectancies and having a determinative influence upon current functioning" (Pine, 1985, pp. 60–61). It is the object relationship, as experienced by the child, that is internalized and carried around in one's memory, and then is repeated in new relationships.

Although Freud wrote about the "object" as that through which satisfaction is achieved, it was the writings of both M. Klein (1948) and Fairbairn (1952) that were instrumental in the development of an object relations theory, with Fairbairn first coining the term "object relations theory" (Pine, 1985, p. 59). Both worked with an intrapsychic rather than intrapersonal object relations theory and saw a tie between objects and drives. Klein discussed early drive processes in terms of the incorporation and expulsion of good and bad objects, while Fairbairn purported the object-seeking rather than pleasure-seeking nature of drives (Pine, 1985). For both theorists, the quintessential object relation was that with the primary caretaker. For case studies drawing on Kleinian theory, see Tyler and Schönfeld.

Furthering the development of object relations theory, Winnicott is best known for his concept of transitional object/transitional phenomena. He maintains that the infant forms an affectionate attachment to a "not me" object or experience. In this relationship, the infant assumes rights over the object/phenomenon. To us it is external, but not to the infant, although it is not from within either. The transitional object/phenomenon is symbolic for something else. After the object/phenomenon has served its purpose, it gradually loses meaning for the child. This relationship details the infant's journey from the purely subjective to objectivity (Winnicott, 1971). Winnicott describes individuals in terms of their inner world and outer reality and that there is an intermediate area of experiencing that accommodates both inner and outer reality, keeping them both separate and interrelated (Winnicott, 1971). In fact, he states:

> We experience life in the area of transitional phenomena, in the exciting interweave of subjectivity and objective observation, and in an area that is intermediate between the inner reality of the individual and the shared reality of the world that is external to individuality (1971, p. 64).

Winnicott believes that this intermediate area of experiencing is a place where we are imaginative. It is this intermediate area that both joins and separates infant and mother. This is illustrated in Winnicott's view of the mirror role of the mother. Influenced by Lacan, Winnicott sees the mirror phase as important, but proposes that the mother's face functions as a mirror. By looking at the mother, the infant sometimes sees his/her own self when the mother is reflecting what the infant is experiencing, and when she is not, the infant sees the not-me object. This intermediate area is the space in which the infant and object relate, interact, and play. Play is central to Winnicott's theory. Through playing, the child expresses his inner or personal reality (Winnicott, 1971). Of relevance to the interactive nature of music therapy, Winnicott views psychotherapy not only as a form of playing but as the *joint creation* of the client and the therapist. He asserts that if a client cannot play then it is up to the therapist to help to create a safe environment in which the client can be brought to a state of being able to play, before psychotherapy can be done. As Winnicott understands the intermediate area of experiencing as a space in which one is imaginative, symbolic, playful, etc., he views the arts and creativity as essential to the health of individuals (Winnicott, 1971). Winnicott's views are widely embraced by music therapists. For example, see the case studies of Sweeney, Tyler, Mahns, di Franco, Kowski, Rogers, Robarts, Dvorkin & Erlund, Schönfeld, Katz Nirensztein, Fruchard & Lecourt, Metzner, Nolan, and Rafieyan.

Also within the object relations school, Wilfred Bion is best known for his concepts of the "container-contained" and "maternal reverie" (or "alpha function") whereby the mother is able to contain her infant's anxieties and unbearable feelings ("beta elements") by "holding them in her mind" and giving them back in a transformed state (as "alpha elements") that the infant can then take in ("introject"). This allows the infant to internalize her *and her capacities* as a mother who can contain the infant's unbearable feeling states. This relationship operates primarily at a presymbolic level, and is formative to intra-psychic structure (Bion, 1962a, 1962b; Robarts, this volume). In therapy, therefore, the therapist (symbolically the mother) must "not only absorb the [client's] pain without being transformed by it—i.e., yielding to the infant's projections, identifying with them and responding reactively in turn—but must also delay them, sort them out and act upon them by relating to the infant's specific needs" (Grotstein, 1985). Further developments of this concept include the projection of the client's *valued* aspects of himself onto the therapist (Alvarez, 1992). Bion's concepts of alpha function, alpha elements, and beta elements belong to a complex "grid" of the dynamic interpersonal structuring of the mind. He believes that experience begins as a beta element, a raw stimulus that meets the sense organs head-on. However, the sense organ experiences the beta element through the alpha function, transforming the beta element into an alpha element that is able to be comprehended, unlike the raw beta element (Grotstein, 1985). When this process is not working appropriately, it is difficult for the person to make sense of what is or is not real. Of particular relevance to music therapists, Bion stresses the need to move beyond the language barrier so as to approximate experience before language. He feels that words limit experience and rob it of meaning. Thus, he describes the arts as a superior way to understanding a client's inner state (Grotstein, 1985). For case studies drawing on the work of Bion, see Rogers and Robarts.

Instrumental to object relations theory, Mahler emphasizes the funda-mental importance of the separation-individuation process and how self and object representations are attained. She saw this process as beginning with a state of symbiosis with the mother, to growing awareness of separateness, to development of one's own unique characteristics (Bergman & Ellman, 1985). That is, the infant grows from a state in which there is no differentiation between self and object, to a stage in which the object is only dimly perceived as outside and separate, to the attainment of a unique attachment to the object, and finally to "a stage of loving in which a positive image can be maintained even in the face of anger and frustration and in which the capacity for concern for the other takes the place of the demand for omnipotent control" (Bergman & Ellman, 1985, p. 245). However, this view of early infantile states as being "undifferentiated" and "chaotic" has been challenged in the last three decades by research on parent-infant communication. Studies showing the sophistication and precise interpersonal timings of the infant's emotional communications provide strong evidence that the infant brain is prewired for communication, and that the social nature of the self is inborn (Schore, 1994; Stern, 1985;

Trevarthen, 1979). Modern infancy research and affective neuroscience (Damasio, 1999; Schore, 1994) have thus brought about a paradigm shift in psychodynamic thinking that has particular significance for music therapists, given the quasi-musical characteristics of early communication and empathic interpersonal relations that continues throughout the lifespan (Robarts, 1994, 1998). This convergence of thinking about the growth of the personality (and particularly primitive mental states) and its significance in clinical practice (with adults as with children) is best described in the seminal text *Live Company* by Anne Alvarez (Alvarez, 1992). Alvarez's synthesis of contemporary object relations theories, ego- and self-psychology, informed by contemporary infant developmental and neuroscience of the emotions, embraces a deeply aesthetic perception and understanding of the nonverbal realm of experience that is the familiar territory of music therapists (Robarts, personal communication, 2002). For case studies drawing from Mahler, see Metzner and Rafieyan; for those drawing on Trevarthen, see Rogers and Robarts; and, for those drawing on Alvarez, see Robarts.

Although not considered as belonging to the object relations school, with increasing frequency object relations theorists are drawing on John Bowlby's work on attachment, separation, and loss, with its emphasis on the importance of mother-child relations[3] (or primary caretaker-child relations). Like Stern and Bion, Bowlby views human behavior as cooperative rather than individualistic. He believes that maternal care in infancy and early childhood is essential for mental health and compares it with the role of vitamins in physical health (Hamilton, 1985). Bowlby maintains that attachment behavior is instinctual and that the infant develops a complex repertoire of behaviors in order to main-tain proximity with his/her caretaker to ensure survival and protection from predators. He maintains that we have a tendency to orient toward the familiar and away from the strange. The way in which we respond to the novel (or strange) reveals the degree and qualities of the primary attachment that have been internalized. For case studies drawing on theories of attachment, see Rogers, Katz Nirensztein, and Nolan.

Utilizing concepts that resonate with both object relations and self psychology, although aligning himself with neither solely, psychoanalyst and infant developmental researcher Daniel Stern's work centers on "intersubject-ivity": "the sense of self-and-other [as in object relations], [with] its starting place the infant's inferred subjective experience [as in self psychology]" (Stern, 1985, p. 26). According to Stern (1985), there are four different senses of the self: 1) the emergent self (0–2 months), where the infant seems to experience through what he calls amodal and crossmodal perception (that produces a unity

---

[3] Although many psychodynamic theorists emphasize the mother-infant relationship, it does not necessarily have to be the mother, but a significant primary caregiver.

of experience through the senses). Stern refers to the basic form of early emotional communication as "vitality affects" (1985, p. 54), that is, dynamic, kinesic forms of feelings ("surging," "fading away," "fleeting," "explosive," "crescendo," "decrescendo," "bursting," "drawn out," etc.) that cannot be separated from the vital processes of life—breathing, getting hungry, falling asleep, etc.; 2) the core self[4] (2–6 months) where the infant experiences self with other, experiencing self-agency, self-coherence, self-affectivity, and self-history; 3) the subjective self (7–15 months) where there is a deliberately sought sharing of experiences; and 4) the verbal self (16 months and on) where the child now has language and the capacity for symbolic play along with the tools to distort and transcend reality (Stern, 1985). Stern (1977) maintains that the basic patterns of behavior learned in the first six months serve as a prototype for all later interpersonal exchanges. Furthermore, it is the "free play" and the dynamic qualities of "vitality affects" between mother/primary caregiver and infant that are crucial in the infant's first phase of learning. Also, Stern describes an "affective attunement" between "mother" and infant that serves to regulate the infant's state of attention, excitation, and affect. This is a mutual intersubjective sharing of feeling state and "occurs largely out of awareness and almost automatically" (Stern, 1985, p. 145). It involves a process of internalization of interactional schemas that then generalize. Stern (1985) refers to these schemas as representations of interactions that generalise (RIGs). He states that "it is important to note that what is initially internalised as a schema is not the object itself or alone, nor the action itself, but rather an interaction between the infant and the object, that is, an active 'object relation' in the form of a sensori-motor schema" (p. 98). So, with each new interaction, one brings to it a history, in the form of a representation of a former interaction, which then affects how the new interaction is received. Most significantly (and especially applicable to music therapy), Stern and other researchers in this field have described the importance of interpersonal timing and the role of temporal organization for social and cognitive development of the infant.[5] Stern's views are also widely embraced by psychodynamic music therapists. For example, see case studies by Rogers, Robarts, Schönfeld, Katz Nirensztein, Metzner, and Hannibal.

Self Psychology

Self psychology emphasizes the subjective states/experiences of a person with respect to self-definition in relation to the other. Like object relations theory, self

---

[4] Trevarthen (op cit.) maintains that the infant's communicating self with other begins much earlier than eight weeks.
[5] For its relevance to music therapy, see Pavlicevic, 1997; Robarts, 1994, 1998.

psychology is centered largely on infant-caregiver relationships, but the primary concern is the integrity of the self and promoting the development of the self (Muslin, 1985). Although Kohut, with his insistence on "prolonged empathic immersion into the *experience* of the self" is recognized as the founder of the psychology of the self (Muslin, 1985), self psychology draws on the work of Mahler in terms of boundary formation or differentiation of the self from the other; G. S. Klein in terms of personal agency or the ability to live life as an active agent; Winnicott in terms of authenticity, that is, in respect to his distinction between true and false self; Stern in terms of the importance of the relationship of self with other in the early stages of development; and, Kohut in terms of the search for esteem, from early life through death, through the self-selfobject relationship (Pine, 1990, p. 38). Kohut (1971) believes that the infant has inherent needs to be mirrored and to idealize. Therefore the infant needs "others as objects that reflect the developing self that the self can idealize as models" (Prochaska, 1984, p. 44). The functions of the primary caregiver are to be the admirer, approver, or echoer of the developing self, which allows the child to experience unconditional confirmation of his/her worth (Muslin, 1985). This must be internalized in order to develop self-esteem. Thus, the stunted self is not able to internalize adequately certain functions due to the failures of the selfobjects to provide what was needed. Therefore, by using the therapist to develop parts of the self, the focus of therapy, according to Muslin (1985), is to meet the clients' needs for confirming, admiration, and echoing (mirror transference); for firm ideal, support, or guidance (idealized parent imago transference); or to experience the parental self as essentially the same as the client's own (twinning transference). The focus of therapy, therefore, is on self-selfobject transferences, relationships that reflect the held back development of the self in relationship to a selfobject. For case studies drawing on the work of Kohut, see Schönfeld and Katz Nirensztein.

Jungian Theory

Although beginning his career embracing Freud's concepts, Carl Jung later de-emphasized the roles of sexual instincts (or id) and superego. Instead, Jung developed a different system of personality made up of the conscious, personal unconscious, and collective unconscious. He saw the ego as the center of the conscious and the aspect of the psyche that provides one's sense of identity. Within the conscious, Jung describes two attitudes: the extrovert (outward flow of the libido) and the introvert (inward flow of the libido). Furthermore, he describes four functions of the psyche: two rational (thinking and feeling) and two irrational (sensation and intuition). The personal unconscious contains repressed desires, memories, and emotions of a personal nature, while the collective unconscious is a universal life drive, the same for all humans. He describes two parts of the collective unconscious: instincts (unconscious modes of action) and archetypes (unconscious modes of understanding). Jung described three ways of accessing the unconscious: through word association, dreams, and active imagination. For him, symbols were important modes of expression and could integrate the conscious and the unconscious. The major archetypes include the persona, the shadow, the anima, the animus, the old wise man, the earth mother, and the Self. Unlike Freud, who views development in terms of childhood psychosexual stages, one of Jung's major contributions to psychology and psychotherapy is in terms of his views on the continuing development of the adult, unique and separate from childhood conflicts. He believed that psychological problems concern both the past and the present. He felt that the process of individuation was a primary concern for adults. He saw this process as one moving toward "wholeness" or "integration," where the conscious and the unconscious become balanced. Furthermore, he encouraged his patients to pursue this process essentially independently, bringing material to him that was more obscure and needed further analysis (Storr, 1988, pp. 190-201). In music therapy, Jungian concepts were utilized in the early developments of Priestley's Analytical Music Therapy and Bonny's method of Guided Imagery and Music. Operating within the framework of Jungian theoretical assumptions are the case studies of Wesley, Montello and Grocke.

Summary

Therefore, as can be seen from the above and based on those delineated by Bruscia (1998b, p. xxii), the basic common assumptions of psychodynamic music therapy are:

- Human behavior, broadly construed, is determined by the psyche.
- Human beings interact and relate to the world with varying levels of consciousness (unconscious, preconscious, and conscious layers).
- Human beings develop unique patterns of relating to the world that are based on interactions/relationships experienced in the past with members of the family of origin/their surrogates.
- Human beings use these patterns of relating repeatedly, either by replicating past relationships in the present or by generalizing a basic pattern of relating from one person to others in the present.
- Both client and therapist bring to the therapeutic relationship their own unique patterns of relating to the world, based on their own pre-dispositions and life experiences (transference, countertransference, and defenses).

Psychodynamic Constructs[6]

In this section, some of the main constructs used by the authors in this book to discuss their work will be described briefly. These are defenses, transference, and countertransference.

Defenses

Defenses are patterned ways of responding to situations based on painful past interactions and relationships. Defenses are a normal and necessary part of psychic development because they help to contain some of the overwhelming anxiety that would otherwise be caused by the awareness of threatening feelings, thoughts, impulses, and memories. However, if defenses become too strong they can effect one's life activities. Defenses include projection, introjection, identifi-cation, withdrawal, denial, isolation, intellectualization, avoidance, repression, suppression, and specifically in the therapy situation, resistance.

Transference

Transference is the reliving of a significant relationship from the past in the present. Providing a broad and inclusive definition of transference, Bruscia states:

> A transference occurs whenever the client interacts within the ongoing therapy situation in ways that resemble relationship patterns previously established with signifi-cant persons or things in real-life situations from the past. Implicit is a replication in the present of relationship patterns learned in the past and a generalization of these patterns from significant persons or things and real-life situations to the therapist and the therapy situation. Essentially, the client re-experiences in the present the same or similar feelings, conflicts, impulses, drives, and fantasies as she did with significant persons or things in the past while also repeating the same or similar ways of handling and avoiding these feelings, persons, and situations (Bruscia, 1998b, p. 18).

Transferences can be positive or negative relationship patterns. They may originate from parental sources, significant nonparental relationships, or

---

[6] For a more thorough examination of these constructs see K. E. Bruscia's *The Dynamics of Music Psychotherapy*, Gilsum, NH: Barcelona Publishers (1998b).

nonhuman sources, and may be conscious, preconscious or unconscious (Hadley, 1998, p. 250). The object of the transference may be the therapist or, in music therapy, may be a musical instrument or musical interaction. Depending on one's theoretical orientation, different types of transferences are focused on. It is important to note that distortion is a process inherent in transference, whether it is of what happened in the past or what is happening in the present.

As transference may be conscious or unconscious, it is not in bringing them into awareness that is key. Rather, it is through understanding and managing transferences that, as therapists, we gain greater understanding of the client's problems and needs.

Countertransference

Countertransference, simply stated, is the therapist's reactions to the client. Again, Bruscia (1998b) provides a broad and inclusive definition:

> Countertransference occurs whenever a therapist interacts with a client in ways that resemble relationship patterns in either the therapist's life or the client's life. Implicit is a replication in the present of relationship patterns in the past, a generalization of these patterns from one person to another and from real-life situations to the therapy situation, the casting of the client and/or therapist within the past relationship, and a reexperiencing of the same or similar feelings, conflicts, impulses, drives, and fantasies through identification (Bruscia, 1998b, p. 52).

Like transferences, countertransferences can be positive or negative and may be conscious, preconscious, or unconscious. Countertransference reactions can enhance or inhibit therapeutic outcomes, depending on the therapist's awareness and understanding of them and ability to use them to facilitate the therapeutic process. Integral to this is the therapist's participation in ongoing supervision.

REFERENCES

Alvarez, A. (1992). *Live Company: Psychoanalytic Psychotherapy with Autistic, Borderline, Deprived and Abused Children*. London: Routledge.

Alvin, J. (1974). "Music as a Means of Projection and Protection." Paper presented at the conference of the British Society for Music Therapy, Birmingham, England.

Alvin, J. (1977). "The Musical Object as an Intermediary Object," *British Journal of Music Therapy,* 8 (2), 7–12.

Alvin, J. (1981). "Regressional Techniques in Music Therapy," *Music Therapy,* 1 (1), 3–8.

American Music Therapy Association (2001). *Member Sourcebook.* Silver Springs, MD: AMTA.

Benenzon, R. O. (1982). *Music Therapy in Child Psychosis.* Springfield, IL: Charles C. Thomas Publisher.

Bergin, A. E., & Garfield, S. L. (1994). *Handbook of Psychotherapy and Behavior Change.* Fourth edition. New York: John Wiley & Sons, Inc.

Bergman, A., & Ellman, S. (1985). "Margaret S. Mahler: Symbiosis and Separation-Individuation" in J. Reppen (ed.), *Beyond Freud: A Study of Modern Psychoanalytic Theorists.* Hillsdale, NJ: The Analytic Press.

Bion, W. R. (1962a). "A theory of thinking," *International Journal of Psycho-Analysis,* 43, 306–310.

Bion, W. R. (1962b). *Learning from Experience.* London: Heinemann.

Bruscia, K. E. (1987). *Improvisational Models of Music Therapy.* Springfield, IL: Charles C. Thomas Publishers.

Bruscia, K. E. (1991). *Case Studies in Music Therapy.* Phoenixville, PA: Barcelona Publishers.

Bruscia, K. E. (1998a). *Defining Music Therapy.* Second edition. Gilsum, NH: Barcelona Publishers.

Bruscia, K. E. (1998b). *The Dynamics of Music Psychotherapy.* Gilsum, NH: Barcelona Publishers.

Damasio, A. (1999). *The Feeling of What Happens: Body and Emotion in the Making of Consciousness.* London: William Heinemann.

Elia, N. (2001). *Trances, Dances, and Vociferations: Agency and Resistance in Africana Women's Narratives*. New York: Garland Publishing, Inc.

Erikson, E. H. (1950). *Childhood and Society*. New York: W.W. Norton.

Eschen, J. Th. (2002). *Analytical Music Therapy*. London: Jessica Kingsley Publishers.

Fairbairn, W. R. (1952). *An Object Relations Theory of the Personality*. New York: Basic Books, Inc., Publishers.

Ferenczi, S. (1921). "The Further Development of an Active Therapy in Psychoanalysis." In *Further Contributions to the Theory and Technique of Psychoanalysis*. New York: Basic Books, Inc., Publishers (1952).

Forinash, M. (2001). *Music Therapy Supervision*. Gilsum, NH: Barcelona Publishers.

Friedman, S. M. (1960). "One Aspect of the Structure of Music," *Journal of American Psychoanalysis*, 8, 427–449.

Gabbard, G. O. (1990). *Psychodynamic Psychiatry in Clinical Practice*. Washington, DC: American Psychiatric Press.

Grocke, D. (1999). "The Music Which Underpins Pivotal Moments in Guided Imagery and Music." In T. Wigram & J. De Backer (eds.), *Clinical Applications of Music Therapy in Psychiatry*. London: Jessica Kingsley Publishers.

Grotstein, J. S. (1985). "Wilfred R. Bion: An Odyssey Into the Deep and Formless Infinite." In J. Reppen (ed.), *Beyond Freud: A Study of Modern Psychoanalytic Theorists*. Hillsdale, NJ: The Analytic Press.

Hadley, S. (1998). "Transference Experiences in Two Forms of Improvisational Music Therapy." In K. E. Bruscia (ed.), *The Dynamics of Music Psychotherapy*. Gilsum, NH: Barcelona Publishers.

Hadley, S. (2001). "Exploring Relationships Between Mary Priestley's Life and Work," *Nordic Journal of Music Therapy*, 10 (2), 116–131.

Hamilton, V. (1985). "John Bowlby: An Ethological Basis for Psychoanalysis." In J. Reppen (ed.), *Beyond Freud: A Study of Modern Psychoanalytic Theorists*. Hillsdale, NJ: The Analytic Press.

Hartmann, H. (1958). *Ego Psychology and the Problem of Adaptation*. New York: International Universities Press.

Kernberg, O. (1976). *Object Relations Theory and Clinical Psychoanalysis*. New York: Aronson.

Klein, M. (1948). *Contributions to Psycho-Analysis, 1921–1945*. London: Hogarth.

Kohut, H. (1952). "The Psychological Significance of Musical Activity," *Music Therapy 1951*. Chicago, Ill: National Association for Music Therapy, Inc.

Kohut, H. (1956). "Some Psychological Effects of Music and Their Relation to Music Therapy." In E. T. Gaston (ed.), *Music Therapy 1955*. Lawrence, KS: Allen Press.

Kohut, H. (1957). "Observations on the Psychological Functions of Music," *Journal of American Psychoanalysis*, 5, 389–407.

Kohut, H. (1971). *The Analysis of the Self*. New York: International Universities Press.

Lacan, J. (1966). *Écrits*. Paris: Edition, du Seuil.

Masserman, J. H. (1955). *The Practice of Dynamic Psychiatry*. Philadelphia: W. B. Saunders Company.

Muslin, H. L. (1985). Heinz Kohut: Beyond the Pleasure Principle, Contributions to Psychoanalysis." In J. Reppen (ed.), *Beyond Freud: A Study of Modern Psychoanalytic Theorists*. Hillsdale, NJ: The Analytic Press.

Nordoff, P., & Robbins, C. (1971). *Therapy in Music for Handicapped Children*. London: Gollancz.

Nordoff, P., & Robbins, C. (1977). *Creative Music Therapy: Individualized Treatment for the Handicapped Child*. New York: John Day. [Revised edition in preparation.]

Noy, P. (1966). "The Psychodynamic Meaning of Music—Part I," *Journal of Music Therapy*, 3 (4), 126–135.

Noy, P. (1967a). "The Psychodynamic Meaning of Music—Part II," *Journal of Music Therapy*, 4 (1), 7–23.

Noy, P. (1967b). "The Psychodynamic Meaning of Music—Part III," *Journal of Music Therapy*, 4 (2), 45–51.

Noy, P. (1967c). "The Psychodynamic Meaning of Music—Part IV," *Journal of Music Therapy*, 4 (3), 81–94.

Noy, P. (1967d). "The Psychodynamic Meaning of Music—Part V." *Journal of Music Therapy*, 4 (4), 117–125.

Pavlicevic, M. (1997). *Music Therapy in Context: Music, Meaning and Relationship*. London: Jessica Kingsley Publishers.

Pine, F. (1985). *Developmental Theory and Clinical Process*. New Haven, CT: Yale University Press.

Pine, F. (1990). *Drive, Ego, Object, and Self: A Synthesis for Clinical Work*. New York: Basic Books, Inc., Publishers.

Plottel, J. P. (1985). "Jacques Lacan: Psychoanalyst, Surrealist, and Mystic." In J. Reppen (ed.), *Beyond Freud: A Study of Modern Psychoanalytic Theorists*. Hillsdale, NJ: The Analytic Press.

Priestley, M. (1985). *Music Therapy in Action*. Second edition. St. Louis, MO: MMB Music, Inc.

Priestley, M. (1994). *Essays on Analytical Music Therapy*. Phoenixville, PA: Barcelona Publishers.

Prochaska, J. O. (1984). *Systems of Psychotherapy*. Second edition. Pacific Grove, CA: Brooks/Cole Publishing Company.

Racker, H. (1951). "Contribution to the Psychoanalysis of Music," *American Imago*, 8, 129–163.

Rapaport, D. (1958). "The Theory of Ego Autonomy: A Generalization," *Bulletin of Menninger Clinic*, 22, 13–35.

Robarts, J. (1994). "Towards Autonomy and a Sense of Self: Music Therapy and the Individuation Process in Relation to Children and Adolescents with Early

Onset Anorexia Nervosa." In Ditty Dokter (ed.), *Arts Therapies and Clients with Eating Disorders*. London: Jessica Kingsley Publishers.

Robarts, J. (1998). "Music Therapy and Children with Autism." In C. Trevarthen, K. Aitken, D. Papoudi, & J. Robarts (eds.), *Children with Autism: Diagnosis and Interventions to Meet Their Needs*. Second edition. London: Jessica Kingsley Publishers.

Robarts, J. (2002). Personal communication, July 2002.

Ruud, E. (1980). *Music Therapy and Its Relationship to Current Treatment Theories*. St. Louis, MO: MMB Music, Inc.

Sandler, J., & Rosenblatt, B. (1962). "The concept of the Representational World," *The Psychoanalytic Study of the Child,* 17, 128–145.

Schore, A. N. (1994). *Affect Regulation and the Origin of the Self: The Neurobiology of Emotional Development*. Mahwah, NJ: Lawrence Erlbaum Associates, Inc.

Stern, D. N. (1977). *The First Relationship: Mother and Infant*. Cambridge, MA: Harvard University Press.

Stern, D. N. (1985). *The Interpersonal World of the Infant: A View from Psychoanalysis and Developmental Psychology*. New York: Basic Books, Inc., Publishers.

Storr, A. (1988). *Solitude: A Return to the Self*. New York: Ballentine Books.

Teller, F. "Musikgenuss and Phantasie," *Imago,* 5, 8–15.

Trevarthen, C. (1979). "Communication and Cooperation in Early Infancy. A Description of Primary Intersubjectivity." In M. Bullowa (ed.), *Before Speech: The Beginnings of Human Communication*. London: Cambridge University Press.

Trevarthen, C. (1999). "Musicality and the Intrinsic Motive Pulse: Evidence from Human Psychobiology and Infant Communication," *Musicae Scientiae,* August, 155–215.

Tyson, F. (1981). *Psychiatric Music Therapy: Origins and Development*. New York: Creative Arts Rehabilitation Center.

Wheeler, B. (1981). "The Relationship between Music Therapy and Theories of Psychotherapy," *Music Therapy: Journal of the American Association for Music Therapy,* 1 (1), 9–16.

Wheeler, B. (1983). "A Psychotherapeutic Classification of Music Therapy Practices," *Music Therapy Perspectives,* 1 (2), 8–12.

Wigram, T., & De Backer, J. (1999). *Clinical Applications of Music Therapy in Psychiatry.* London: Jessica Kingsley Publishers.

Winnicott, D. W. (1971). *Playing and Reality.* London: Tavistock Publications.

Part One

Children

Case One

"COULDN'T PUT HUMPTY TOGETHER AGAIN": SYMBOLIC PLAY WITH A TERMINALLY ILL CHILD

Catherine Sweeney

ABSTRACT

This chapter gives an overview of the development and ethos of the children's hospice movement in Britain. It presents a case study of some short-term work with a young boy in the terminal stages of a brain tumor and looks at the way in which he used embodiment within symbolic play to express and come to terms with his illness and his impending death.

INTRODUCTION

In Britain today there are an estimated twenty thousand children suffering from life-limiting conditions. The majority of these children have metabolic disorders or neuromuscular degenerative conditions, with only approximately 20 percent suffering from cancer.

The children's hospice movement is a recent development, which began less than twenty years ago. The first children's hospice was founded in Britain, and although the movement has spread throughout the world, Britain remains very much at its forefront. The first hospice, Helen House in Oxford, was founded in 1982 by Mother Frances Dominica, the Superior General of the Anglican Society of All Saints. She began a close friendship with Jacqueline and Richard Worswick when their daughter Helen developed profound and multiple disabilities following an operation to remove a brain tumor in 1978, when she was just two years old. Out of this friendship was born the idea of a small unit, akin to a family home, which would provide care for up to eight children with life-threatening illnesses or disabilities.

At present there are twenty-two operational children's hospices in Britain with a further fifteen hospices planned. These figures reflect a remarkably rapid development in the children's hospice movement, when one considers that five years ago there were only half a dozen open. They are individually planned, but all offer support to children with life-limiting or life-threatening illnesses, and their families. Many childhood terminal illnesses can have a long-term prognosis where deterioration occurs over many years and may involve profound physical and cognitive damage. Therefore the children's hospices offer respite care as well as terminal care and bereavement support. Remaining true to the original vision of Helen House, they are all small units, with none having more than eleven beds. Each child has his/her own room and the hospices also provide some family rooms or flats [apartments], so that parents can stay with their child if they wish.

The hospices seek to engender a home-away-from-home environment, with high levels of staffing (usually one-to-one) and a noninstitutional approach. Most hospices have a wide range of facilities, including a swimming pool, computer room, soft-play area, music room, multisensory room, and art or play room. Some have nondenominational chapels where funerals can take place, and most have at least one temperature controlled room where the bodies can stay after death until the time of their funeral.

The provision of music therapy in children's hospices throughout Britain began in 1994 with the foundation of a charity called Jessie's Fund in memory of a young girl named Jessica George who died of a brain tumor at the age of nine. Jessie's parents started a fund to raise money to send Jessie to America for alternative treatment when her tumor failed to respond to conventional radiotherapy. Her parents are both professional musicians and their friends gave numerous concerts for what came to be known as Jessie's Fund. Unfortunately, Jessie's condition deteriorated quickly and she did not live long enough to have the treatment. Five months after diagnosis she died at a children's hospice in Yorkshire.

Although Jessie was only at the hospice for a week before she died, the one thing that she and her family really missed there was music. After her death, her parents decided to use the money raised to start a fund to provide music therapy in children's hospices.

Jessie's Fund equips hospices with instruments, runs training courses for nursing and care staff in music-making, and gives hospices initial funding for a part-time music therapy post over three years. By the end of 2001 there were sixteen children's hospices throughout Britain with part-time music therapists.

This case study is based in one of the two children's hospices in which I work. I set up the post there at the end of 1997 and work there one day a week. Although most of my work is with children who are staying for respite or terminal care, I also offer music therapy as a day-care provision and a few children and their families access music therapy on a weekly basis.

As the majority of the children at the hospice have conditions that leave them with profound and multiple disabilities, much of my work involves using music to promote relaxation and pain management, and to provide these very damaged children with a means of nonverbal communication. With more able children, however, my work has a psychodynamic orientation.

Initially I found some difficulties working psychodynamically within the hospice. I was viewed as someone who was going to entertain the children with music and "cheer them up." The hospice itself can seem almost fiercely cheerful with its bright colors, large toys, and happy pictures. While this can be reassuring to families and children who may have had fantasies of a children's hospice as a gloomy place with rows of dying children lying in beds, it also means that difficult and negative emotions can seem strangely out of place.

I first had to establish a space for what Kuykendall (1998) terms "shadow": an accepting space where children and families could bring their difficult and dark emotions that conflicted with the cheerful surroundings. In order to establish myself as someone willing to work in this way I undertook education work with the staff to explain the function and processes of psychodynamic music therapy. I was aware that because children came to stay for up to two weeks at a time and because I would be working just one day a week, I would need the support of the staff to be able to work in such a way.

In such a friendly home-away-from-home atmosphere it took some time to establish the music room as a private space, where staff, parents, or other children cannot come and go as they please while I am working, or interrupt a session to show visitors around or to inform me of a phone call.

The other problematic aspect of working within a psychodynamic framework at the hospice is the irregularity of sessions. As only a small number of children come for regular sessions, I see the majority of the children on a very infrequent basis. They have sessions with me while they are staying for respite care and therefore these sessions need to be viewed as "one-offs." It may be months or even years before I see them again, or they may die in the meantime. There is little opportunity to work through a therapeutic process and I cannot offer the safety of a regular therapeutic space.

Due to these constraints, much of my psychodynamic work at the hospice takes place under the guise of play. As children naturally use play to explore and make sense of their world, working through play is a nonthreatening way of dealing with difficult issues and expressing emotions associated with them.

Working in this way with a terminally ill child in music therapy gives him/her the opportunity to explore different scenarios and emotional states without the need to acknowledge verbally that he/she is actually experiencing them. The children that I work with often have limited verbal capacity due to either physical or cognitive disabilities associated with their illness. Even children with language can find words too threatening, too precise a vehicle with which to address profound and emotionally charged issues around their impending death, and they often show resistance to acknowledging issues verbally. This resistance occurs when the child is not consciously aware of his/her situation, or when he/she has learned that open communication about his/her illness cannot be borne by his/her family and others around him/her.

Much has been written about children's awareness of death and the means by which they communicate it (Kübler-Ross, 1969, 1981; Bertoia, 1993). While Kübler-Ross (1981) notes that children as young as three are aware that they are going to die and can talk about it, most communication by children about their impending death is at either a symbolic verbal level or a symbolic nonverbal level. In the case study discussed here, all of the material fell into these latter categories.

The distancing process involved in symbolic musical play is an important aspect of music therapy with this client group. When a child explores his/her situation through musical play, the instruments that he/she uses and the music that he/she creates form transitional objects (Winnicott, 1971) through which communication of unconscious material occurs. These transitional objects may represent people and situations around the child, or can be used to express an aspect of the child him/herself through a kind of embodied musical play. In my experience, roles taken on in musical play are already familiar to the child, such as Disney characters, animals, or role models from television or films. Communicating through these various characters is less threatening than direct self-expression and reduces the level of resistance within the therapeutic encounter. Children often revisit characters and scenarios over long periods of time, even when there are significant breaks between sessions, reassimilating experiences and emotions according to their needs and abilities.

In the case study I have chosen, a five-year-old child appeared to choose a single instrument to represent his situation and to communicate the knowledge and emotion of his illness, and employed nursery rhymes to facilitate an understanding of his dying.

BACKGROUND INFORMATION

At the turn of the twenty-first century, active treatment of cancer is far more successful than it was even ten years ago, with some cancers, such as leukemia, seeing an increase in survival rates from 4 percent in 1962 to 90 percent today.[1] And yet, apart from accidents, cancer still accounts for more deaths in children aged between one and fourteen than any other illness. Brain cancers account for approximately 15 percent of pediatric cancers, with an average of three hundred children developing brain tumors each year in the United Kingdom.

Matthew was born in 1993 and was by all accounts an extremely lively child, who was able to read and count to beyond a hundred before he started school. Shortly after his fifth birthday his parents began to notice a subtle change in his coordination. The staff at Matthew's school had also seen a slight problem with his balance when playing ball games, and they reported that he had some impairment in his attention span and that he had been falling asleep in class. Matthew's parents decided to send him for tests to identify the problem, and in August 1998 he was referred to the consultant pediatrician.

His first NMR scan revealed a highly malignant tumor of the brain stem. Its size and position were such that although doctors recommended treatment, they could give no guarantee that it would be effective.

Shocked and terrified by the news, Matthew's parents agreed to a course of radiotherapy. The course lasted for six weeks, followed by a further six weeks spent waiting to see if it had shrunk the tumor. When at last the results came, they showed that the treatment had been ineffective in reducing the tumor or even in arresting its growth. Further treatment was offered, but chances of survival were deemed to be extremely slim. At that point, the family made the decision not to pursue further treatment and were encouraged to look around their local children's hospice.

At the end of November the family first visited the hospice. I was not there that day, but the following week I heard reports of an engaging young boy with

---

[1] Statistics from St. Jude's Children's Research Hospital, Memphis, Tennessee, 2001.

a mischievous sense of humor and some eccentric habits. With the growth of his tumor, and the resultant steroid treatment, Matthew was reported to have developed some challenging behaviors. These included pinching bottoms, stealing shoelaces, and covering people with stickers from a large collection that he kept with him. At times he could be aggressive toward others, which upset his parents as they felt that this was so unlike his normal character. Matthew spent that first visit energetically exploring the hospice, which he termed a "Fun House." This unusual naming of a hospice was typical of Matthew's determination to enjoy life, but also represented a defiance of his situation.

I met Matthew the following week. I had the impression of a very strong character, who on only his second visit seemed to have organized the hospice in the way that he wanted it and who had most of the staff at his beck and call. He appeared unable to focus on any activity for long and was very restless. He was testing the boundaries of this new environment, pinching the bottoms of new people that he met and showing some aggressive and demanding behavior. Some of this behavior was quite regressed and seemed to stem directly from neurological deterioration, such as his increasing fascination with urine and feces. Yet he had an awareness of his own behavior and on our first meeting he told me that he was allowed to be as naughty as he liked because he was "poorly."

On the other hand, I was presented with a young boy who seemed to be really struggling with his situation. He was suffering from nausea, his balance was poor, his eyes squinted because of his tumor, and he was increasingly unable to hear and keep up with what was going on around him. Matthew's speaking voice was gradually becoming louder as he was unable to hear himself speak, so that he tended to shout at everyone. As a means of self-preservation in the midst of his failing abilities, Matthew blamed this problem on everyone around him. According to him, we were all inexplicably moving faster and talking quieter just to annoy him. He was having difficulty managing to play the computer games that he loved and was losing some of his intellectual sharpness.

TREATMENT

I was asked to assess Matthew for music therapy and, after speaking with his parents, offered him an individual session. His parents informed me that Matthew seemed unaware of how ill he was and had never asked about dying, although they would be open and ready to communicate with him if he initiated it.

Later that day, Matthew had his first music therapy session. The music room in the hospice is quite small, with a good selection of instruments including a piano, guitar, metallophone, drums, cymbal, and many small percussion instruments. Matthew immediately made himself at home in the music room and began to explore several instruments at once. I noticed again how he was flitting from one thing to another, almost as if he was afraid of staying still, which seemed to be an attempt to mask the deterioration of his abilities. When asked how he would like to spend the session, he said that he wanted to sing. However, he immediately asked me to join him at the piano and "singing" turned out to mean playing piano duets. I was unsure as to whether this misplaced terminology was due to Matthew's deteriorating capacity to use words, or simply a five-year-old's inability to differentiate between vocal and instrumental music.

We played a lot of "songs" during that first, long session, all in a cheerful, childish style. Matthew was very much the leader in these improvisations, organizing me in the natural way that he organized everyone in his life. Matthew used eye contact and physical gesture to give me instructions as to how to play or how to finish playing. He showed an ability to communicate through the music he played, with an awareness of turn-taking and musical humor. Despite Matthew's ability to engage in reciprocal play, I felt as though I was not being perceived musically as a separate other. It was as if I was being used as an extension of Matthew's physical body with no individual input into the improvisations apart from my role in following his instructions.

He was very structured in the way he approached these improvisations, which were all of roughly equal length and clearly demarcated. There was a short break after each "song" during which Matthew gave it a title. He named the first one "Myself," and in many ways it did seem to reflect his personality: full of dotted rhythms and flamboyant, confident gestures that covered the whole range of the piano. Its energy and scope belied the physical fact of Matthew's deterioration, which did not seem to be addressed. Other titles included "the weather" and "friends," but he did not elaborate verbally on any of them.

These "songs" showed none of the anger or frustration that I might have expected from a young boy who was deteriorating so rapidly. Indeed, all of the improvisations sounded quite similar and undifferentiated. They seemed to embody an attempt to remain in an innocent, childish world of happy events and people, where nothing nasty or frightening occurred. I was aware that Matthew's negative emotions were perhaps being projected through "naughty" but childish behaviors such as bottom pinching, biting, and kicking.

After Matthew had finished all of his piano songs, he moved to an alto metallophone which was on the floor, instructing me to stay at the piano. He told me that we would play another song and began to play with the by now familiar dramatic flourishing of his arms. Again, Matthew's music sounded cheerful and untroubled.

As we played, I suddenly felt overwhelmed by a deep sense of sadness and loss. I turned to look at Matthew and saw that he had carefully removed the top bar of the metallophone and laid it on the floor without interrupting his improvisation. I realized that the effect of the removal of the bar was to handicap both him and his music. I wondered if this was Matthew's attempt to reflect the physical situation that he was experiencing. I changed my accompanying music to acknowledge this change in affect even though Matthew's cheerful physical stance and music remained unchanged.

Matthew looked up briefly in acknowledgment but did not stop playing. After about another minute, he removed the next highest metallophone bar, again without ceasing his playing, thus further restricting himself. This continued until approximately half of the bars from the metallophone were lying on the floor. I felt very moved by this visual communication from a young boy who was gradually dying from the top down and losing his abilities as he did so.

Although he could not speak about his experience of dying, or even directly express it in his music, it appeared that Matthew could use the alto metallophone to communicate the knowledge of his deterioration.

As soon as this improvisation ended, Matthew jumped up and cheerfully said good-bye, leaving the room before any of the material could be addressed. After this session, I was left having to hold and process Matthew's unmanageable feelings. I felt irrationally annoyed that he had skipped out of the room so lightly after playing, leaving me to replace the bars of the metallophone and to try to digest the material that he had communicated. It appeared that at this time Matthew needed to use me as a container for the awareness of his situation that he was as yet unable to assimilate. While Matthew could openly admit that he was "poorly," he was not ready to accept that he was dying.

Although he visited the hospice several times with his family after this, Matthew was often not there on the day I worked. On a few occasions when Matthew was in the hospice on the day that I was there, he chose not to come for a session, either because he did not feel well enough (at this stage he was suffering debilitating "headaches in his tummy" which made him very inactive) or, alternatively, because he felt very well and preferred to be outside playing. I felt some frustration at not being able to follow up on the first session, which had been so intense, but felt that he would return when he needed to.

Matthew's other session with me took place three months later, just three weeks before he died, and ten days before his final visit to the hospice. We began with musical games where Matthew controlled my playing. He was taking the role of conductor, giving me nonverbal instructions as to how to play: pointing at me to tell me to start playing, and controlling the speed and volume of my playing through physical gesture. I was constantly directed to play fast and lively music and felt that here I was being used as a kind of transitional object, a vehicle for the music that he would have liked to play. Matthew was quite weak at this stage and was not capable of the sustained physical effort needed to play that he had managed three months earlier. He therefore needed to use me to express the energetic and healthy aspect of himself that he had lost.

After this initial activity, Matthew again chose to play the alto metallophone, instructing me to accompany him on the piano. As in his first session, he began by removing the top bar a short time into the improvisation and went on to dismantle the instrument from the top down. The music itself was calmer and more introverted than it had been the previous time, with less drive and flamboyance. Again, I accompanied his playing by musically reflecting the emotion that I felt. This time, however, I felt less overwhelmed than I had in the previous session. On reflection this could partly be explained by the familiarity of Matthew's actions, but there was also a sense that he had less need to project the emotion but could now survive its assimilation.

During this improvisation, Matthew did not stop when half of the metallophone bars were lying on the floor as before, but continued until all of the bars had been removed. As we looked together at the metallophone frame lying on the floor, stripped of its bars, I was struck by how like a small coffin it looked. Both the shape of the box and the material it was made from, unpainted wood, seemed suddenly, shockingly, coffin-like. Matthew then asked me to help him as he carefully placed all of the discarded bars and the beaters inside the shell of the metallophone.

As we worked, I asked Matthew what had happened to the bars and he replied that they had got stuck inside the box. I wondered if that was a frightening place to be stuck, but he told me very seriously that they were happy in there. It seemed as though the coffin box could be a place of refuge for all of the worn-out, broken bars that could not play any more, and for the beaters that no longer had anything to resonate against.

Matthew seemed tired after all of this activity, and so we sat in silence for some time. He then asked to sing the nursery rhyme "Humpty Dumpty." I played it on the piano while we both sang. In a child's language and symbolism he seemed to be acknowledging the fact that he was now, like the metallophone, irreparably broken. There was no means of restoring him to health, despite all of the traumatic medical interventions he had experienced and the desperate wishing of his parents. In the end, not even the concentrated efforts of a king's entire army could repair one cracked egg.

Humpty Dumpty sat on a wall,
Humpty Dumpty had a great fall,
All the King's horses and all the King's men
Couldn't put Humpty together again.

Matthew then chose to finish the session by singing "Twinkle, Twinkle Little Star." Having worked through an experience of dying and accepting it without fear, he then seemed to be able to contemplate what things might be like after death.

> Twinkle, twinkle little star,
> How I wonder what you are.
> Up above the world so high,
> Like a diamond in the sky.
> Twinkle, twinkle little star
> How I wonder what you are.

Unlike the previous session, when I had been left with Matthew's unmanageable feelings as he skipped out the door to play computer games, I felt that he had completed a process of integration of knowledge about his death. It seemed as though he had come to an acknowledgment and an acceptance of his fate via a journey of symbolic play and children's rhymes.

That was the last time I saw Matthew. He visited the hospice once more for day care, but was extremely poorly. He died peacefully on May 11, 1999, at home in bed, with his mother, father, and sister around him.

DISCUSSION AND CONCLUSIONS

The course of Matthew's therapy was not untypical of children's palliative work. Several aspects of the therapy were significant: the unusual structure of his therapy in terms of timing; the use of instruments in symbolic play; the role of countertransference; and the function of nursery rhymes.

Temporal Aspects

Working with people close to death can be challenging when one is used to working within a process involving regular therapeutic encounters. With this client group temporal boundaries of engagement can be more fluid than with others. Aldridge (1996) has differentiated linear time (chronos) and creative time (kairos), pointing out that much interaction within music therapy takes place within the latter. Bunt (2001) notes that for people close to death who no longer have a daily routine of work or school, the chronological delineation of time becomes less important and they tend to inhabit the world of kairos.

The physical condition of clients can also impinge on the therapy space, and sessions may need to be altered due to external factors such as medication, nausea, tiredness, and pain. Therapeutic meetings therefore often take place in an ad hoc fashion without significant prior arrangement. In this case study, each of Matthew's two sessions provided a space where he was free to explore both fantasied and real scenarios. Milner (1952) sees temporal boundaries in psychoanalysis as a kind of picture frame within which an altered reality, a creative illusion, can develop, and notes that it is this illusion that facilitates an adaptation to the world. Despite the sporadic and limited nature of his engagement, Matthew approached the sessions in a linear way and completed a process of integration and adaptation within them. For a child of five with deteriorating memory, this was astonishing. It made me realize that my wish for consistent sessions did not originate in Matthew and that he simply did not need the security of a regular encounter.

The Use of Instruments in Symbolic Play

Matthew used the vehicle of an instrument as the transitional object of communication and exploration of his illness in his two sessions. The metallophone was employed in a directly symbolic way. It became a character that was given voice within the drama acted out within our improvisations. Bunt (1994) suggests that an instrument can become a bridge—a "field of play" within music therapy. Here Matthew was using one specific instrument to embody his physical being. The physicality of the metallophone meant that it could be used and reused within representational play, allowing Matthew to make sense of and assimilate his experience.

The Role of Countertransference

Although Matthew knew that he was very ill, he could not integrate that with a cognitive understanding of his death. Speaking about drawing with children suffering from leukemia, Bertoia (1993) notes that even though children have an inner awareness of their prognosis, they may not be able to understand it in the context of their own experiences. Therefore, she suggests that providing opportunities for creative self-expression can be an important means of developing insight with terminally ill children due to the ability of creative arts to access unconscious expression.

Initially, Matthew's knowledge about his dying was split off and unassimilated. The music that he played held nothing of the emotion attached to this knowledge. It was only through his embodiment of an instrument as a transitional object that I could gain insight into his inner world and he could come to understand and express what was happening to him. In the first session the feelings to do with this understanding were projected and my initial insight stemmed from a countertransference reaction, which had nothing to do with the music that he played. In the second session, Matthew seemed to be able to process this emotion without the need to split it off into me. This was then borne out by his request to sing nursery rhymes that dealt directly with these issues.

The Function of Nursery Rhymes

Nursery rhymes form a modality of interaction for children and are learned and sung from a very young age. Yet they often contain disturbing imagery of violence and death. As such, they have a useful function for children as familiar containers for frightening material.

Matthew's choice of "Humpty Dumpty" perhaps charts his physical fall from health, which must have seemed quite sudden to him. The nursery rhyme is to do with the hopelessness of broken things and the uselessness of interventions. In "Twinkle, Twinkle," the image is more hopeful. The bereaved siblings that I work with often refer to their brother or sister as a star in heaven, and it is an image that young children seem comfortable with. Matthew's choice of this nursery rhyme reflects a hopeful and calm approach to his fate.

FINAL THOUGHTS

Matthew's engagement in music therapy was sporadic and because of this our work together could be said to have lacked a process. As issues were not dealt with in a direct way verbally, one can never be sure of Matthew's awareness of death. However, the way in which he used these two short sessions suggests that he had explored profound existential themes using the transitional phenomena of children's play and had come to an acceptance of his fate.

REFERENCES

Aldridge, D. (1996). *Music Therapy Research in Practice and Medicine: From Out of the Silence.* London: Jessica Kingsley Publishers.

Bertoia, J. (1993). *Drawings from a Dying Child: Insights into Death from a Jungian Perspective.* London: Routledge.

Bunt, L. (1994). *Music Therapy: An Art Beyond Words.* New York: Routledge.

Bunt, L. (2001). Collaborative Research into Music Therapy and Cancer Care. Seminar, Musicspace, Bristol, UK.

Kübler-Ross, E. (1969). *On Death and Dying.* New York: Macmillan.

Kübler-Ross, E. (1981). *Living with Death and Dying.* New York: Macmillan.

Kuykendall, J. (1998). Oral Presentation, Master Class for Help the Hospices, London.

Milner, M. (1952). "Aspects of Symbolism in Comprehension of the Not-Self," *International Journal of Psychoanalysis*, 34, 181–195.

Winnicott, D. W. (1971). *Playing and Reality.* London: Tavistock.

GLOSSARY

NMR: Nuclear Magnetic Resonance. A scan which uses magnetism to build up a picture of internal organs.

Case Two

BEING BEVERLEY:
MUSIC THERAPY WITH A TROUBLED
EIGHT-YEAR-OLD GIRL

Helen M. Tyler

ABSTRACT

This case study follows the music therapy process of Beverley, an eight-year-old girl diagnosed with moderate learning difficulties. She had been referred to music therapy because of her aggressive and disturbed behavior at school which was preventing her from learning and fulfilling her potential. The weekly music therapy session became a place where Beverley could explore her feelings in a safe, nonjudgmental environment through fantasy play and musical improvisation. Understanding Beverley's outward play as a representation of her inner world enabled the therapist to survive her potentially overwhelming attacks and to find the real child behind the "acting out" behavior. This in turn helped Beverley develop some insight into her difficulties and enabled her to lead a more fulfilled life, emotionally, socially, and intellectually.

INTRODUCTION

It is a well-established fact that children's development and learning are affected by pressures such as family conflict, financial strains, illness, or the loss of a parent through separation, divorce, death, or imprisonment. In the final pages of "Good Wives," written in the 1860s, Louisa M. Alcott's character, Jo March, expresses her dream of opening a school in the large family home, Plumfield, for "poor little forlorn lads who hadn't any mothers." When challenged by her family that a school for poor children would not be profitable, she replies:

> Rich people's children often need care and comfort, as well as poor. I've seen unfortunate little creatures left to servants, or backward ones pushed forward, when it's real cruelty. Some are naughty through mismanagement or neglect, and some lose their mothers. Besides, the best have to get through the hobbledyhoy age, and that's the very time they need most kindness and patience (Alcott, 1994, p. 338).

The issues which Alcott tackles through the pupils of Plumfield are astonishingly wide-ranging, including overeating, running away, bullying, theft, fighting, murder, and imprisonment, but each episode comes back to the overriding need for a child to have someone reliable to "feed, nurse, pet and scold them" (1994, p. 337). Today, we might translate this in terms of the need for emotional and physical nurturing, unconditional acceptance, containment, and boundaries. Dickens, too, expressed his concern for society's neglected children through literature, in the stories of Oliver Twist, Nicholas Nickleby, and David Copperfield. The Victorian philanthropist, Thomas Barnardo, put all his missionary zeal into the rescue, care, and education of destitute children through the founding of his "Dr. Barnardo's Homes." Although moral and spiritual teaching was a priority, Barnardo's vision went beyond this:

> Little cottages should arise, each of them presided over by its own "Mother". . . . The girls should be of all ages, from the baby of a few months or weeks to the growing girls, some of whom would be nearly out of their teens. There, family life and family love might be reproduced and gentle modest ways would be made possible. . . under the influences of godly women (Wagner, 1979, p.80).

There are echoes of Alcott and Barnardo in Docker-Drysdale's account of the setting up of the Mulberry Bush School for emotionally disturbed children in 1948. She writes:

Therapy in child care is concerned with the content of the total life situation in the place, including waking and sleeping, eating and drinking, working and playing and so on (Docker-Drysdale, 1993, p. 57).

In the same post-war period Axline was drawing up her principles of non-directive play therapy to address the emotional needs of difficult children and so free their minds to work and develop to their full potential.

A teacher whose mind is beset with anxieties, fears and frustrations cannot do a satisfactory teaching job. A child whose emotional life is in conflict and turmoil is not a satisfactory pupil (Axline, 1989, p. 133).

The link between emotional difficulties and learning was also acknowledged by Nordoff and Robbins, who recognized that music therapy addressed more than simply musical needs. In a rationale for their pioneering work in the special education department of Philadelphia they wrote:

It is the music therapists' role to supplement the educational and classroom activities of the teacher with a programme aimed at providing special experiences that have central psychological significance for the children, and which can be therapeutic for their whole development. The strengthening of ego-function, the liberation from emotional restrictions and the alleviation of behavioural problems all make for happier, more fulfilled children who can participate more fully in their school life and derive greater benefit from it (Nordoff & Robbins, 1992, p. 139).

Winnicott, in his dual role of pediatrician and psychoanalyst, saw the child as part of its family and society. His case studies of work with children reveal his concern for the child within the context of home, family, and the wider world while his theory of play expresses many of the principles that he drew from his analytic work with both children and adults.

It is play that is the universal and that belongs to health: playing facilitates growth and therefore health; playing leads into group relationships; playing can be a form of communication in psychotherapy; and, lastly, psycho-analysis has been developed as a highly specialised form of playing in the service of communication with oneself and others (Winnicott, 1999, p. 41).

Like psychoanalysis, the music therapy session provides a place for a child to play, in every sense of the word, and a safe, accepting environment in which to explore "communication with oneself and others." The framework of the therapy gives the security and consistency of time and place, while the shared language of musical improvisation offers a medium for expressing unsounded feelings and thoughts. In this chapter I hope to show how the "highly specialised form of playing" which takes place in the music therapy room can make a significant difference even to children like Beverley, facing the most intractable of life situations.

BACKGROUND INFORMATION

Beverley was referred to the Nordoff-Robbins Music Therapy Centre in London by her school—an inner-city primary school for children with moderate learning difficulties and behavioral problems. The school was in an area of social deprivation with poor housing and a high crime rate. All the background information that I had about her came from her class teacher, Peter. I did not ever meet Beverley's mother, but Peter visited her to explain about the music therapy program and to obtain consent for Beverley to attend. This was necessary as her mother also had learning difficulties and could not complete the usual consent form without help. As a child, she too had been a pupil at the school Beverley now attended, but was described by Peter as being "not as bright" as her daughter. Beverley's father did not live with the family, and at the time of the therapy was, in fact, in prison. There were two other children in the family and the mother had recently had two pregnancies, which ended in miscarriages. Home life was said to be chaotic, with various boyfriends coming and going. Because of the instability of the family there were concerns for the children's safety, and social services were monitoring their well-being. Beverley's grandmother lived nearby and was able to help out when things were difficult by having Beverley to stay. This provided a safety net. The unpredictability of Beverley's life showed in her appearance when she arrived for her Monday morning music therapy session. Sometimes she looked unkempt, grubby, and neglected while on other occasions she was smartly dressed with new clothes.

TREATMENT

Peter had referred Beverley initially because of poor peer relationships and aggressive outbursts in school. He felt that she had ability, but was not achieving as well as she could in class because of her emotional difficulties. She came with three other girls from her class for group music therapy where the aim was to encourage positive relationships, cooperation, and sharing through musical activities. However, although she was obviously motivated to take part in the music-making, Beverley found it impossible to share the instruments or the attention of the therapists with the other children. She would become distressed, claiming that the others were "picking on her" and would rush out of the room. As her presence became increasingly disruptive and detrimental to the progress of the rest of the group, her group therapists suggested that she should transfer to individual therapy. This was agreed, and after a planned ending with the group, Beverley began therapy with me on a one-to-one basis, work which was to last two years.

Early Sessions—Preacher and Pop Singer

Beverley made the change from group to individual therapy willingly and seemed delighted to have all the instruments to herself. The room contained a piano, side drum, bongos, a cymbal, a metallophone, windchimes, and a selection of small percussion instruments. My first impression of Beverley was of a graceful, well-coordinated girl with a great deal of physical energy. She was rarely quiet or still, restlessly moving around the room, often dancing and singing into an imaginary microphone. Her speech was muddled and unclear, with a lack of grammatical structure, and her tendency to change from one topic to another added to the sense of confusion. In the early sessions, she played the percussion and I accompanied her on the piano. Her musical tendency was to "run away" from me, so that if I matched her playing precisely, she would invariably change tempo or meter. She also sang, revealing a flexible and wide-ranging voice, which was generally so loud that it drowned out my accompaniment. She often interrupted the music suddenly, saying it was time to go, or rushing out to the toilet, finding it hard to stay in the room for the full half-hour. Her lack of containment was apparent, as was her need to control our interactions and the environment. Each week she would rearrange the instruments and the furniture in the room, often putting them behind the piano so that I could not look at her directly when she was playing.

As Beverley settled into the new relationship, she began to use the sessions to act out a variety of scenes which mixed fantasy with reality. They were usually highly dramatic with a sense of energy and excitement. I would accompany her singing, acting, and dancing wherever possible, but she was quite controlling of my participation, shouting at me to "cut the music," "you be quiet," or "shut the piano!"

I would generally comply with Beverley's musical demands to meet her omnipotence in the way that Winnicott identifies as vital to a child's emotional development.

> The good-enough mother meets the omnipotence of the infant and to some extent makes sense of it. She does this repeatedly. A True Self begins to have life, through the strength given to the infant's weak ego by the mother's implementation of the infant's omnipotent expressions (Winnicott, 1984, p. 145).

Clear boundaries, however, were necessary in other areas. For example, Beverley would want to take my shoes off or braid my hair. I felt that this kind of closeness would not be helpful to the therapy, so I would state clearly, "I'm keeping my shoes on" or "My hair's fine like it is." I would also monitor my countertransference response to her frequent commands for me to "stand up," "sit down," or "go in the corner." If I began to feel despised or abused by Beverley I would reply firmly that I would stay on my chair and allow her to experience the frustration of not being able to control me. I wanted to demonstrate that it was possible to have a relationship which was based on respect, not on domination or bullying.

Beverley would generally take on another persona in the sessions, imitating well-known pop stars or a boxer or wrestler, famous from a television show. Another figure who often dominated the sessions was a hell-fire religious preacher. When she took this role her excitement could turn to near hysteria, with her singing transforming to shrieking or screaming. There was often a feeling of disassociation, bordering on the psychotic, when she became deeply involved in her fantasy. I would match her emotional intensity with strong playing, and found that the music could organize her responses and keep her in touch with external reality. Her innate musicality would draw her to complete a phrase at a cadence or to wait for me to give her a musical cue. Although her words were hard to understand I would catch short phrases which seemed significant and sing them back to her. I would also frequently introduce a refrain, such as, "We're singing together on Monday" or "This is Beverley's song" to try to keep a connection. Here is a transcription of part of a session in the fourth month of therapy.

Beverley begins by telling me that "we're making a little bit of music, a little bit of sound, we're making a show." She instructs me to sit and watch her while she sings into a drum beater "microphone." She sings unaccompanied.

B: This is my song, this is my friend, this is my friend, this is my friend.
      I played the drum in music, I played the drum and drumpet [sic].
      And the rain is falling down.

I then sing back to her, unaccompanied, the essence of what she had sung.

H: That was your song, a song about a friend,
      You played the drum in music
      And the rain was falling down.

This structure is repeated for a second verse, both of us listening attentively to the other, but when I extend the words and sing "Beverley and Helen are singing together" the connection between us is suddenly lost, and she begins to scream and gyrate like a pop singer. She moves to the back of the room and flings herself at the wall, still singing/screaming. At this point I go to the piano, feeling that she needs some containment and grounding. I sing and play with strength.

H: This is Beverley's song, she's singing in music today,
      Beverley's song, she's singing in music today.

Beverley waits till I've finished my phrase then joins in, with the same tune, extending it. I can only make out a few of the words:

B: My name is Beverley, take me, and see.
      You can sing, you can cry.

Again I reflect back to her the words which seem important, "crying and singing." Her singing becomes more intense and passionate, with the phrases lengthening, Beverley allowing me to support her musically. Just as it feels as if we will come to a satisfying ending together Beverley suddenly switches to her "preacher" persona.

B (*shouting*):   Alleluya! Amen! Cut the music!
                God is Bible,
                My name is Bethlehem Jesus.
                Remember me for the discipleship.
                Young woman! (*to me*) You better rise up.

Beverley then prowls round the room like a boxer, punching the air and muttering "the death of Jesus" and "the blood of Jesus." She throws herself at the wall dramatically and falls down groaning. I sing "Poor Beverley, she's hurt," at which she jumps up and commands me:

B: Stand up! Close your Bible, turn to chapter 3.
      (*Then more softly and prayerfully*)
      The God is my shepherd, she made me lie down in green pastures.
      Thou anoint my head with oil and my cup runs over.
      They threw me in the path of the shadow of death—no evil.
      You want to listen to my prayer. Just close your eyes.
      Father, we bless you tonight, I want to go away,
      Shepherds, just leave me alone.
      Thank you for your old mum and your school,
      Thank you for your music therapy. Amen.

This session illustrates Beverley's sudden changes of mood and subject and the muddling together of home, school, and music therapy with images from the Bible and a church service. It also shows how structure, both in the music and in the poetry of the 23rd Psalm, which she was quoting in the above extract, could help her become more coherent and expressive.

In her dramas Beverley generally took the role of a powerful male adult, often threatening me and attacking me verbally. Her characters were unpredictable, suddenly becoming angry and losing control. In this way she made me experience her own unarticulated feelings of vulnerability and powerlessness. An example of this comes from a session in the sixth month of therapy. In this part of the session we are speaking, with no music.

B: Shut the music! (*Threatening gesture*)
H: You want me to shut the piano. (*I shut it*)
B: What you doing to my wife? (*Throws beater at me*)
H: Somebody's very angry. (*Beverley hangs her head*)
      Somebody's sad? (*Beverley pushes me*)
B: You told me what to do, I don't even tell you, Helen.
      You keep on picking on me.
H: I keep on picking on you so you're getting angry with me?
B: I didn't tell you what nothing.
H: I kept telling you what to do. . .
B: Yes, man.
H: And you got angry. . .
B: Yes! If you do it one more time. . . (*threatening gesture*)
H: And now you really want to hit me.
B: Yes! If you do it one more time I'll GET THE WOLF PACK!
H: And now you're shouting at me because you feel really cross.
B: If you do it one more time, YOU'LL FEEL THE BANG!

At this point Beverley rushes out of the room but I call her back, saying that I want to listen to her. She then goes on to say that the "Wolf Pack" will whack me and throw me through the window. I continue to reflect verbally how I think she is feeling and despite her agitation, she at last seems to recognize that I am hearing her. She then comes very close to me, wanting to take a hairclip out of her hair to put in mine and saying, "Shall we get married?" Her mood has changed from aggression to intimacy and then, just as quickly, as though discounting what has gone before, she shouts exuberantly, "Let's have a party!" and starts dancing. At this point I begin to play music for her dancing, and this then leads into a shared "good-bye" song. There was a sense of relief in having survived the confrontation and all the feelings it stirred up, while being able to make music together at the end of a stormy session was an affirmation of the reality of our developing relationship.

Winnicott says that children's play is "inherently exciting and precarious" and can lead to a high degree of anxiety. He suggests that the precariousness derives from "the interplay in the child's mind of that which is subjective (near hallucination) and that which is objectively perceived (actual or shared reality)" (Winnicott, 1999, p. 52). The "near-hallucination" refers to the dreamlike state of children playing which can conflict with the reality of the situation. This seems to describe Beverley when she became deeply engrossed in her fantasy play. Her anxiety was apparent, and she needed constant grounding by the reflections which I offered her, whether musical or verbal.

Another feature of Beverley's fantasy play was its punitive nature. The preacher, in particular, threatened blood and death, and most of her characters were aggressive and violent. Kalsched (1996, p. 118) writing about the archetypal figures who appear in dreams, refers to "gigantic, fantasised beings" which are "of two types, malevolent and destructive on the one hand, benevolent and protective on the other." The man who promises salvation but also threatens punishment and death is surely an example of this, expressed in play, not in a dream. It was important that I could withstand these attacks and not retaliate, nor make myself into a victim.

As our relationship developed, Beverley began to show a strong emotional reaction to breaks in the therapy, either planned holidays or sessions which were missed through illness or problems with school transport. After six months of therapy there was to be a four-week holiday break. Beverley comes into the room saying "I missed you." I take that to be a confusion of tenses (meaning "I'm going to miss you"). I begin to talk about the break, but she immediately drowns me out with loud drum and cymbal playing. She finds it too close for me to reflect her feelings so directly. She then begins to proclaim in a deep voice, half-singing, half-chanting:

B: My name is Sunkanan. The Bible says you ought to believe in the drum.
      I want to bring up my mum, my wife, my sister, and Helen, all my family.
      You're gonna miss her tonight, I'll miss you tomorrow.
H: (*singing*) I'll miss you next week. . .
B: Bye, see you Helen, I'll miss you tomorrow. (*leaves the room*)

She goes out of the door and sings "pop style" outside. Again, it seems that she
cannot tolerate me expressing her feelings for her.

H: (*calling to her*) Beverley, where are you?
B: (*marches back in*) I'm doing my exercises. Alleluya! (*exercises vigorously
      to marching music*)

Then, another mood change as picking up the drumbeater "microphone" she
begins to sing. I accompany at the piano.

B: You're my wife. I'm gonna sing a song for Mother's Day.
      [This had been the previous day]
      You can touch me, you don't touch me.
      Your mum is dead, your Nan is crying for yourself,
      And I am pregnant, I am pregnant.
H: Your mum is dead, your Nan is crying and you are pregnant.
B: My mum is dead, you're gonna miss me tonight,
      You pray for me tonight, say good-bye to me.
H: A sad song, for Mother's day, you're gonna miss me.
      No music next Monday.

At this point Beverley cuts across the mood of shared sadness, screaming and
running around. I stay very still, and, when she is quieter, ask her if she would
like to come and sit at the piano by me. Unusually, she agrees, and we have a
brief turn-taking exchange before leading into a familiar good-bye song, which
we sing calmly. As Beverley leaves she asks me three questions.

"Are you my friend? What's your name? Let me see your teeth."

These questions seem to reflect her growing awareness that she can trust this
relationship, I am a real person, and I can, like her, be strong and show my teeth.
However, I am also behaving like an unreliable or absent mother, in leaving her
abandoned for the holiday.

Middle Period—The School Game

After this break, Beverley introduced a new scenario in which she was a teacher, and the instruments were pupils. She gave them the names of children in her class, so it felt as though they had come to join us, almost as though going back to group music therapy. The "children" were invariably badly behaved, and therefore Beverley could vent all her anger on them. Typical phrases were: "Don't you swear at me or you'll get a whack on the head," "Don't even hit anybody," and "I HATE it!"

After the long summer holiday at the end of the first year of therapy Beverley came back to sessions concentrating on the school game. In the first session after the break she allows me to join in, telling me to play "relaxing" music and ordering the children to "just relax and listen to the music while your feet grows." Here, despite her restlessness and constant criticism of the children, she accepts that I had something to give her through the music even though she cannot stay with a quiet mood for long.

When characterizing the instruments, the drum was usually "the winner," the "best behaved," while the wind chime, erratic and hard to control, was the naughty one. The cymbal too was frequently sent out of the room for being noisy and indeed, the session sometimes ended with no instruments left in the room. This made explicit Beverley's need to be the only one. It also seemed that she could now symbolize her feelings, rather than needing to act them out by leaving the room herself. The instruments represented the parts of herself which she found difficult to manage, and in bringing their conflicts into our session, she was enabling us to work on the issues together.

Klein, in describing her psychoanalytic play technique sessions says:

> The variety of emotional situations which can be expressed by play activities is unlimited: for instance, feelings of frustration and of being rejected; jealousy of both father and mother, or of brothers and sisters; aggressiveness accompanying such jealousy; pleasure in having a playmate and an ally against the parents; feelings of love and hatred towards a newborn baby or one who is expected, as well as the ensuing anxiety, guilt and the urge to make reparation. We also find in the child's play the repetition of actual experiences and details of everyday life, often interwoven with his phantasies (Klein, 1991, p. 43).

The symbolic use of the instruments was part of Beverley's exploration of relationships. All her issues—low self-esteem, rivalry with her peers, lack of self-control, and aggressive outbursts—could be contained and worked on during the sessions. For example, I developed a song about "trying to be good—

it's really difficult," reflecting on the struggle of "the other children." At about this time I discovered that Beverley's mother was pregnant, although it was not known when the baby was due. This made sense of some of Beverley's play, in which she would throw herself to the floor, writhing and groaning as though giving birth. I also wondered whether she had been present during her mother's previous miscarriages. It seemed even more significant that she frequently brought material relating to jealousy and the need to be special.

Ending—Becoming Beverley

Gradually the school game developed and there was generally a calmer, more constructive atmosphere, Beverley decided that each person, including me, could choose a song to sing. Those that were good would get a prize (a drum beater or a shaker). For the first time, she actively wanted me to play with her, accompanying the songs, rather than controlling me or just tolerating my participation. The songs ranged from nursery rhymes such as "Old MacDonald had a Farm" and "Three Blind Mice" to "When I'm 64" and "Waltzing Matilda," songs enjoyed by any nine-year-old. Beverley allowed herself to become one of the children in the class, and let go of the punishing super-ego figure of the teacher. At the same time she was able to accept me as a benevolent figure.

She also began to take pleasure in dancing to my accompaniment on piano or drums, no longer avoiding my gaze but experiencing my full attention. She was now able to accept my praise and value her own worth, wanting me to give her "a prize." A more childlike quality came into her voice in contrast to the forced and strident sound of earlier sessions.

Beverley was developing her musical skills and, what was more important, the self-control to use them. I brought a xylophone into the session, and she immediately picked out the children's song "Twinkle, Twinkle, Little Star," correcting herself when she miss hit a note, and looking very pleased with her achievement. Having worked at an unconscious level for the first eighteen months with the music as a supportive accompaniment, it seemed that she was now able to experience it in the here and now. Free association and the dream-like state had been replaced by a purposeful and intentional involvement in the music therapy sessions.

Beverley's baby brother was born sixteen months into her therapy, an event which she seemed to take in her stride. Shortly after this she announced that the instruments were too small and gave several other indications that she was moving into a new stage of maturity. I began to consider finishing the therapy and in speaking with Peter, her teacher, I learned that she was showing improvement in all areas, with an increase in her concentration span and a leap forward in her reading and writing. Peter and I both felt it was time to draw her therapy to an end, at least for the time being, with a planned ending. Beverley was well aware of the forthcoming ending and was able to join me in counting down the weeks to finishing.

The final sessions were, in Beverley's typical style, acted out in the context of a school leavers' ceremony. In it, she announced that she was leaving and going to another school, that it was sad but she would have to say good-bye. She told all the children to "be good for Helen" when she had gone and everyone would get a prize. Then she improvised a "leaving song" and allowed me to watch her, support her, and sing with her, as we both expressed sadness at the parting. Nevertheless, there was a celebratory feel to her final song and dance, as though she knew this had been an important achievement.

DISCUSSION

An interesting aspect of Beverley's treatment is that the point at which she began to use her musical ability in a more intentional and focused way, in the playing and singing of known songs, was the time when I began to think of terminating the therapy. I felt that the further development of her creative abilities through singing, dancing, or acting was not my primary task. My hope was that the insight she had gained through the therapy would facilitate her in experiencing these activities in other settings. This was a situation I had experienced with other children in therapy, for example, Joe, a twelve-year-old boy with Asperger's syndrome about whom I have written elsewhere. Our stormy and often chaotic music therapy sessions eventually became more ordered and productive and we mutually felt an ending was appropriate. With Joe, leaving therapy coincided with him giving away his toys to his younger brother and starting to have "proper" piano lessons rather than the free musical play of the therapy sessions. It was as though he recognized that music therapy had addressed the angry, fearful, and omnipotent infant part of himself, and that it had helped him to contain and manage it. This was made explicit in our final session when he told me that his dog was getting out of control so perhaps he could send it to live with me (Tyler, 1997, p. 231).

This might lead the reader to the conclusion that the psychotherapeutic function of the sessions with Joe and Beverley outweighed the musical therapeutic dimension, but this could be as a result of what Ansdell has termed "the music therapist's dilemma." He says "Whilst musicians have a limited vocabulary for musical 'objects' and techniques they have almost none for musical *experience*—arguably the starting point for music therapy" (Ansdell, 2001, p. 2). In describing Beverley's music therapy I am aware that it is more straightforward to transcribe words and actions than to convey the essence of the musical interaction. However, moment-to-moment in the therapy I was making musical decisions and monitoring my responses with my "internal supervisor" (Casement, 1985, p. 49). There were endless choices to be made, such as to play or not to play, to sing or speak, to match Beverley's music or be separate musically, to build up or draw back, to increase the musical tension or relax it. The choice of instrument, the key, mode, meter, tempo, and dynamics all had to be decided at every moment of each session. As Pavlicevic (2001) writes, "the powerful flexibility and shifting nuances of improvised clinical music can resonate with, and sound, the child's totality" (p.20). In order for this to happen, the therapist must be finely attuned to the child on all levels.

Aiding this process for me was the discipline of recording every session on either audio or video and listening back to the tape, making detailed notes or an "index" of the session using the method devised and advocated by Nordoff and Robbins (1977, p. 92). This careful study of the weekly session tape helped me to grasp the complex musical self-portrait that Beverley presented to me, with its many forms and facets and this, combined with regular supervision, enabled me to recognize and nurture Beverley's authentic voice.

I began this chapter with thoughts about the care and treatment of disturbed and distressed children. The poignant image of the motherless child was evoked by Victorian authors and philanthropists wishing to raise awareness of the plight of such children to improve their lot. Throughout Beverley's therapy I did not meet her mother or have any more than the minimum of information about her, but the maternal figures she presented to me were generally weak, ill, pregnant, or abused, and in need of prayer. All the power was situated in the male figures who dominated the sessions with their physical or verbal bullying. Beverley's recognition of me as a person who could be strong but not persecuting and who could withstand her assaults without retaliation gave her the strength to find her authentic self. In her role-play as a teacher she explored issues of control and power, and through the school game, eventually allowed herself to be the child Beverley for the first time. Being Beverley, a child who could sing, dance, laugh, cry, love, and hate, without the need for concealment behind another persona, was the achievement of the therapy.

REFERENCES

Alcott, L. M. (1994). *Good Wives.* (First published 1869.) London: Penguin.

Ansdell, G. (2001). "Music Therapist's Dilemma," *British Journal of Music Therapy,* 15 (1), 2–4.

Axline, V. M. (1989). *Play Therapy*. Edinburgh: Churchill Livingstone.

Casement, P. (1985). *On Learning from the Patient*. London and New York: Routledge.

Docker-Drysdale, B. (1993). "Consultation in Child Care." In *Therapy and Consultation in Child Care*. London: Free Association Books.

Kalsched, D. (1996). *The Inner World of Trauma*. London and New York: Routledge.

Klein, M. (1991). "The Psychoanalytic Play Technique." In J. Mitchell (ed.) *Klein: Selected Letters*. Harmondsworth, UK: Penguin Books.

Nordoff, P., & Robbins, C. (1977). *Creative Music Therapy*. New York: John Day. (Out of print. New edition forthcoming: Gilsum, NH: Barcelona.)

Nordoff, P., & Robbins, C. (1992). *Therapy in Music for Handicapped Children*. (First published 1971.) London: Victor Gollancz Ltd.

Pavlicevic, M. (2001). "A Child in Time and Health," *British Journal of Music Therapy*, 15 (1), 14–21.

Tyler, H. (1997). "Music Therapy for Children with Learning Difficulties." In M. Fawcus (ed.), *Children with Learning Difficulties—A Collaborative Approach to Their Education and Management*. London: Whurr Publishers Ltd.

Wagner, G. (1979). *Barnardo*. London: Weidenfeld and Nicholson.

Winnicott, D. W. (1984). "Ego Distortion in Terms of True and False Self." In *The Maturational Processes and the Facilitating Environment*. London: Karnac Books.

Winnicott, D. W. (1999). *Playing and Reality*. (First published 1971, London: Tavistock Publications.) London: Pelican Books.

Case Three

SPEAKING WITHOUT TALKING: FIFTY ANALYTICAL MUSIC THERAPY SESSIONS WITH A BOY WITH SELECTIVE MUTISM[*]

Wolfgang Mahns

ABSTRACT

In this case study, analytical music therapy with an eight-year-old Turkish boy with selective mutism is described. Within fifty individual sessions, and regular discussions with parents and teachers, he was gradually able to rediscover his vocal expression. In this child therapy it is shown that the whole spectrum of symbolic interactions (music, drawing, playing) is needed. Institutional aspects (special school) are discussed, as well as cultural aspects, and reflections on the function of music, musical instruments, and improvisation in a child therapy approach.

---

[*] This article was first published in Isabelle Frohne (ed.) (1999): *Musik und Gestalt— Klinische Musiktherapie als Integrative Psychoherapie.* Göttingen: Wandenhoeck & Ruprecht. The German title is: "Die musiktherapeutische Behandlung eines achtjährigen mutischen Kindes."

INTRODUCTION

In recent years, therapeutic treatment has been introduced into various schools (comprehensive schools, special schools, and regular primary schools) in Hamburg, Germany, to enhance traditional approaches with special programs for dealing with learning and behavioral disorders. The methods employed include play-, client-centered, and music therapy and can be viewed as a balanced combination of pedagogy and therapy in order to both prevent having to send students to special-needs schools and to provide full-time therapeutic treatment for psychological needs. One thing is common in all cases: the knowledge that educational institutions in the future need to be more demanding not only in terms of improving the quality of methodological and didactic practices, but also in terms of possibilities for improving the quality of diagnosis and treatment of children with emotional/behavioral disturbances and meeting the psychosocial needs of these students.

The justification for therapeutic treatment within schools can be shown simply by the fact that referral for therapy through medical insurance or regional educational consulting centers for those in lower socioeconomic groups is rare or given far too late. Consulting or preventive teachers and therapists within schools can respond much more quickly, because they are available as a starting place right "in the field." Furthermore, an interaction with their teaching colleagues is possible without any of the misunderstandings that so often arise between the different service providers of psychosocial care for disturbed children and adolescents in educational settings.

For a number of years now, I have been working as a music therapist in a school in Hamburg for children with learning difficulties. In addition to providing music education, I spend a few hours per week providing individual sessions in music therapy. In arrangement with my colleagues, selected children that are applicable for these sessions are treated in a separate therapy room. This room offers the needed protection/privacy as well as the possibility to make lots of noise. The acceptance and understanding for my work has grown over time in this school.

From my point of view, music therapy is a psychoanalytically oriented treatment for children and adolescents who experience disturbances in perception, behavior, school attendance, or physical activities. I try to give them the opportunity to express their concerns and needs through therapeutic play and discussion. Furthermore, I try to help them to increase their expressive ability and to understand their unconscious motivations.

Music offers a way to this understanding. Using instrumental as well as vocal and movement improvisation with the children, music provides a variety of rich experiences and layers of emotional expression. In such improvisations, the work with the spontaneous, unplanned, and the unforeseen is where the special value of music therapy lies. Even before the expression can be verbalized, the reaction is already being expressed through a different medium, which also means that it allows the client to express feelings that have usually been impossible to verbalize. Other forms of symbolic expression that I incorporate into sessions include painting, puppet play, and other similar activities.

When working with children, one needs to particularly consider the following. A child's disturbed interaction, often seen in various neurotic symptoms, is accompanied by the problem of differentiating between inner and outer worlds (fantasy and reality). Often these children are able to express their emotions, anxieties, and needs, despite the most extreme troubles faced within their family environments. This expression acts as a "transitional object" to facilitate the pain (Winnicott, 1971, p. 13ff). This can become symbolized and overcome through art, music or play. A child that faces the loss of a relationship and is not able to express this pain, for instance, is in a terrible situation and has only one option: to flee into a psychological manifestation; a neurotic symptom, so to speak. By using music, play, and art, and by relearning the ability to claim objects, these symptoms can be transmitted into symbolic expression. These therapeutic treatments have great success in healing.

The use of music therapy with children is not about using set music for a set purpose. Such an understanding of music and of therapy suggests it be used as a substitute for medication or surgery. Rather, it is more like preparing a field for symbolic actions, allowing rigid boundaries to flow freely again. Using only one form of symbolic expression, i.e., musical improvisation, is not very effective from my experience. For specific emotional layers it seems to be more effective to use concrete therapeutic forms of play or art therapy, to build a tower with woodblocks or to paint a fantasy picture. The child feels the resistance of the material which needs to be overcome or has the pleasure of a finished relatively imperishable product. The musical improvisation, on the other hand, offers the opportunity to intensify a feeling or produce a sense of achievement without making mistakes. Unconscious feelings are thus sounding in the flow of time. The created musical shape can be explored in terms of inner states and ambivalences. These connections are further intensified through exploration and then the extensive clinical material is documented.

BACKGROUND MATERIAL

"Osman"

This case study examines the music-therapy work I conducted with a Turkish boy named Osman.[1] I worked with him for nearly two years, while he was visiting our special school. He did not speak at all. An examination in the audiology department of the university hospital found no organic cause. Selective mutism was the diagnosis. It was suggested that Osman's parents should bring him to an educational consulting center, where in the safe, anxiety-free environment of play therapy, he may speak. The parents refused to follow this advice, but Osman's social worker suggested trying music therapy.

Before I discuss the process of the sessions in detail, the symptomatology, history and diagnostic picture of selective mutism will be explained. I will also outline my plan for the therapy. Finally, after describing the music therapy treatment, I will illuminate the progress Osman made in music therapy and discuss possible reasons for this.

Symptomatology

Osman did not speak. The eight-year-old Turkish boy *could* speak, his parents knew, but in school he did not speak. The first time I met him was in his first grade music class. He participated as long as he did not need to produce any loud sounds. He did not sing or play any brass instrument, as this would be very close to singing. Whenever the class was singing a song, it did not seem to reach him at all, although his eyes and mouth would twist. When children in the class were laughing, it was very hard for him not to do so, and when he cried, it happened without any noise at all. It looked as though he wanted to punish himself or his environment.

Osman was the main topic in staff meetings. He was making people feel insecure, sad, and even aggressive. The question was, should he really be in this school at all, or should he visit another school for speech disturbances or even for children with developmental delays? It was absolutely unclear what he was able to do or was not and whether he could follow the lessons or not. Also his classmates had ambivalent feelings toward him—partly aggressive, partly indifferent. It even seemed as if Osman's silence weakened the rules of interaction. All that was important in terms of communication in school lost its significance (questions and answers, encouragement and admonishment, praise and punishment). This symptom of not speaking was not only examined in

---

[1] His name has been changed for purposes of confidentiality.

relation to his social context at school; it had consequences both socially and for Osman's educational development.

Anamnesis (Case History)

I gathered information about Osman's life from various resources: reports from his preschool and the special school, an opinion from the audiology department of the university hospital in Hamburg, as well as discussions with his social worker and a visit with his family. The usual first interview (a personal history) was not feasible, as Osman would not express himself verbally.

When Osman began individual music therapy sessions he was about eight years old. He had two sisters, three and four years older than he. His father was fifty, his mother thirty-five years old. Both parents had moved to Germany to work and save money to enable their siblings to have a better life when they returned to Turkey in the future. Mr. G. was quite disappointed that he had produced only girls at first, but his son finally arrived three years after his second daughter, and he was very proud. Immediately after Osman's birth, the family moved to Germany. Osman learned to speak quite late, when he was four years old. He realized that most other children around him were speaking in a different language. He tried to communicate with them, but this was very difficult, as even his sisters could not assist him at all, because they did not leave the house except to go to school.

It was during this period of his speech development that a traumatic event occurred. He was hospitalized for six weeks due to dizzy spells and sudden fevers. Because the hospital was far away from their home, Osman did not have many visitors. His mother reported that each time they had to leave it was very difficult for him. She recalled that after the stay in the hospital he acted very differently. Incidentally, the results of the medical examination remained unclear.

Both parents were working, but they arranged their shifts so that one of them would always be at home. Mr. G. can be described as warmhearted and very close to his children, especially to Osman. However, he was not often at home, doing shift-work and a lot of overtime. His wife, in complete contrast to him, showed very little emotion. Her face had hard features; she looked as if she had worked her entire life. The housework was done completely by the two sisters, while the mother took care of Osman. Osman enjoyed the advantages of the typical gender-specific conditions of his Turkish upbringing. However, what deviated from the typical model was that Osman was exposed to physical and sadistic punishment when he pushed the limits. Even more unusual was that the punishment was received from his mother, and the comfort from his father.

The family of five lived in a two and a half room flat. The larger room was used as a kitchen, the smaller one as a living room. This was where the two girls slept. Beside it was the half room, which served as the parents' bedroom, and in which Osman also had a mattress. The living conditions were extremely poor. No luxury goods could be afforded, as the majority of the money was supposed to go back to Turkey. Even toys, dolls, cars, etc. were hardly found anywhere. Admittedly, they did purchase a large color television, a video camera, and a variety of electrical devices as status symbols of great worth that would be taken with them when they returned to Turkey to live.

The onset of Osman's silence was a visit to a public school. Before regular primary school, children should go to a preschool. He reacted with panic at the thought of another separation. His whole body trembled as his mother left him at the preschool. He responded to this completely strange world by being shy and hiding. He even attempted to go back home with his mother when she left. As soon as he recognized his hopelessness, he gave up. His mother always accompanied him to school, but as soon they entered the building, he refused to talk at all. He did not speak to anyone; not to the teachers or the children. Various attempts to integrate him into the group, verbal and nonverbal, were totally unsuccessful. He had to repeat the preschool class, but when no progress was seen at all, he was transferred to the special school. In a small group setting of ten children with a very warm and caring social pedagogue[2] he began to feel more comfortable.

His nonverbal communication skills developed well in this new learning environment. He enjoyed playing and enjoyed listening to stories. His drawings were very expressive. This talent was nurtured by the social worker. From that point on, whenever he drew a picture, he expressed his moods, feelings, and fears in an imaginative manner.

In place of getting a personal history from Osman, I asked him to draw me a picture with a definite theme, the theme being "My Friend" (picture 1).

The drawing depicts a young boy with his hand held high, in his right hand a knife, which is pointing toward a cloud directly overhead. In the cloud is his name. There are various possible interpretations of this picture. It could be that Osman was representing himself, a cloud over him, to equally protect him and to stand between him and others. The knife as phallus symbol is expressive of wishes, aggression: pushing through the silence, or being in conflict with others. Another detail would allow for a different interpretation: The cloud at his mouth could be seen as a "call" in comic-style technique, so that we could assume that he indeed has a friend, whom Osman wants to call, to get in contact with him. Most likely both definitions are realistic. "I am my best friend," and "A friend is out there calling my name." More likely, the ambivalence of his silence seems to

---

[2] In Germany, a social pedagogue, unlike a social worker who is involved with more administrative duties, is involved in different practical activities like working with emotionally disturbed children in homes, schools, or in consulting centers.

be saying: I would like to talk, but that is impossible as I have to show my teeth for that. And that is dangerous.

Picture 1

Diagnostic Picture

In the biographies of mute children, there is almost always an occurrence of an early separation, or a deprivation, that leaves them destabilized. In addition to the initial loneliness, there is wider environmental damage. The development of a personal vocabulary is blocked, due to a lack of encouragement; a younger or older sibling may have grown up with preferable treatment. Additional demands, such as achieving at school, inhibit language for formulating thoughts, thus leading to repression, because at the basis is a self that is not fully developed and has not been assimilated (Dührssen, 1982, p. 184ff). "The starting point lies in the Epoche, in the affective meaningful sound, and not the articulated word making a connection between the infant and his environment" (Ibid, p. 189).

The deprivation experience, or rather the demands generally placed on children with particularly sensitive personality structures, can lead to a reaction of mutism, sometimes acute and dramatic, sometimes gradual and insidious. Only seldom will a person be faced with complete silence ("totally mute"). "In the majority of cases, verbal communication is refused in significant groups, while generally, in the context of the family, at least a certain amount of speech contact is maintained" (Ibid, p. 184). I speak here of "selective mutism" or "partial mutism." Mutism is in no way, as is often misconstrued in lay circles, a defiant reaction of the child. That is why the earlier term of "chosen silence" is misleading. Innate adverse factors rarely play a role. Rather, the mute child experiences a number of unfavorable factors, which together prevent him/her from communicating with others.

These general statements about the disorder of mutism are pertinent to Osman's case. Several unfavorable factors were interacting with each other. His mother was unable to give him the love and warmth he needed. One can assume that she could not understand the extent of his fear of loneliness and separation. Furthermore, she had taken over the role traditionally inhabited by the father in a Turkish family. So, as the only male child, contradictory expectations were requested from him. On the one hand he was the "prince," whom everyone served, yet on the other hand he was a disappointment to his family because he did not behave appropriately for his age.

It is important not to forget the difficult conditions facing a Turkish family living in Germany. The parents saw their roots in Turkey. They come from there and would return there to live. In the meantime—for more than ten years—they continued to maintain their traditions and cultural practices in the midst of an atmosphere of hatred toward foreigners. The Turkish children attending school, however, were able to understand the difference between them and their schoolmates. They usually had no chance to compare the differences to their parents. They had to adjust their behavior, educational practices, and language in some ways in order to survive their German school experience. Often they felt as though they could not understand and fulfill expectations in the school situation. Because their parents usually could not help them to understand, this failure to learn could result in psychosomatic or neurotic disorders.

When Mrs. G. reported that the reason Osman did not speak at school was because he was ashamed, this indicated a fear of appearing inadequate. However, the underlying problem lay more deeply. When he "punished" his teachers and schoolmates with silence, he was actually meaning to punish his mother. However, his anger over his mother's aggression toward him, over his failure to fulfill his wishes, could not be pointed directly toward her. This was forbidden by the taboo of the "good mother." So, Osman redirected his aggression toward the hostile school and anyone who gave him an obvious reason to do so, by speaking another language. Admittedly this anger was not expressed as outward aggression, rather it appeared at first as a mute reaction.

Therapy Plan

The ability of music therapy to include nonverbal expression seems to offer alternative healing prospects to those who are mute. This is not just because the mute person is provided with an alternative language. This would not produce a lasting result, just as when one gets a stutterer to sing. Other forms of symbolic expression (art, dance, music, play, etc.) are much more suitable in order to create a bridge between inner and outer worlds, between experience and action, between fantasy and reality. Winnicott speaks about these transitory phenomena, which take on great significance in overcoming the separation experience (Winnicott, 1971, p. 12). Therefore, music therapy with Osman must include the following guidelines:

1. He must have individual music therapy. Only in a one-to-one situation would Osman be able to overcome his fears, and to abandon parts of himself with the added value of being able to take it back if it caused him undue anxiety or felt too premature.
2. Along with musical expression, children frequently benefit from playing with toys, and above all Osman's passion for drawing should be involved. In this way one can engage the transitional phenomena through various modes.
3. At least two to three years of therapy are essential, because such a deeply embedded disturbance as mutism can only be resolved gradually.
4. The school environment, more specifically the special school, even with its clearly defined boundaries, is not always favorable. In Osman's case, however, it is exactly what is indicated, because the silence occurred at school. This had consequences for his educational progress. Furthermore, it allowed for the possibility of support by his teacher.
5. The supportive therapy room, particularly important in providing the entitled anonymity, is especially necessary in the therapy with Osman. In this way he would be able to make important progress within therapy while still not reconciling with the public.

I planned on having individual therapy sessions for forty minutes per week for a period of at least two years. Discussions with his teachers and parents would also take place on a regular basis. Osman would be informed of this involvement of those around him. In addition to the usual variety of musical instruments available in the music therapy room, cloth puppets, building blocks, and a small oven were also provided to meet additional needs a child may have. In Osman's particular case, a variety of diverse drawing and painting materials were also always available. After speaking with Osman's teacher, it seemed important, at least in the beginning, that he be picked up from his classroom and brought to the therapy sessions. In this way, the adjustment to the new environment would not be so drastic, as compared with him walking over by himself.

I had never had a client who was mute, let me make myself clear, so I had great expectations on all sides: When will he start to talk? I have to clarify the expectations I had at that stage, even though they were unconscious. I also must say that I did not feel that using the "ISO-principle" (Altschuler, 1948; Benenzon, 1983, p. 165) would be appropriate in this case. That would entail beginning in the same state of the absolute speechlessness. That would reduce opportunities for experiencing the normal external world as it is.

TREATMENT

I worked with Osman in music therapy for almost two years, for a total of fifty sessions, one session per week. The beginning of the treatment focused on exploring the therapy room and its possibilities. Osman remained rather passive, especially when it came to the musical instruments. His main focus was still on drawing, which I accompanied with piano music. I saw my main function as accompanying Osman in his activities inside and outside of the music therapy room. Now and then, I reassured Osman that in music therapy he would not be forced to do anything he did not want to do. I knew that he would not speak, but was sure that he had his reasons. Sometimes it was a bit confusing to have a silent individual in front of me: to suggest, to inform, to show feelings, but at the same time realizing the intense feelings inside of him: the anger, the sadness, and the rage. I tried to understand his actual needs and wishes without language. But then I had the idea of using gestures for yes/no, with thumb up for yes and thumb down for no. Thankfully, Osman utilized this new option imaginatively. Through a combination of both symbols he even created a gesture for "I don't know."

During the third session Osman discovered a candle and matches that I kept in the cupboard for festive events. He lit one match after another and let them fly through the room like rockets. Because of this, I moved the following session outside, where we lit a small bonfire. With this significant action he showed me how much fire he had inside, the desire for a warm center, for a mother that would understand his feelings. Playing with fire can also refer to the unresolved Oedipus complex: a desire for his mother that could not be satisfied because she could only show her hard side.

The music therapy room has the theme "beat and be beaten." The following occurred during the fourth session: Osman found the animals and puppets and started to throw them around, pull them, and finally beat them up. "Osman, shall we make some music?" I asked, as the puppets lay scattered and he was taking a rest. He nodded, and walked in the direction of the bass drum and the bongos. I accompanied him on the piano, and expressed the pain I experienced during his outbreak of rage. When we finished I said: "That sounded like you beat someone up." Osman did not react; instead he took a pencil and a piece of paper and started drawing. The drawing showed a person crying (picture 2).

He drew with a lot of pressure, which nearly forced the pencil to break. By using the agreed upon gestures, I found out that it was about his mother.

Picture 2

Viewing the three scenes in combination (beating puppets, beating drums, and drawing his mother crying), one could conclude that this was a representation of a real experience. I had discovered through conversations with his parents that he had received physical punishment by his mother due to his aggressive actions and because of his temporary mutism. The tears of his mother are therefore ambivalent. In one way it could show her helplessness in terms of his not fulfilling her expectations. Alternatively, he probably projected himself into the picture: as the person who was beaten.

In the seventeenth session, after about half a year, Osman decided to build a cave in the therapy room. He had done this several times before, most often with the piano at the center of his cave. Tables, chairs, and a climbing board, with hung blankets, functioned as walls. He chose not to build a door. On the piano he placed some flowers, so the whole cave was very comfortable. I was to make music in the cave, but he did not want to enter the "living room." Instead he painted a series of pictures: either at the table, or on drawing paper on the floor. While I played the piano, I sang and explained to him what I saw in his pictures. He drew dragons, snakes, and sometimes a little child in the middle of all these beasts (picture 3). In this session, the cave was built with more tables and was darker inside. A few bongos, the portable cassette recorder, paper, and markers were inside. I carefully asked him: "Osman, what do you think about allowing me to enter the cave with you?" He thought about it for a little while, then raised his hand with pleasure to symbolize the yes sign.

Inside the cave he painted more pictures that provided additional information about his inner conflicts. On the bongos, we played at times mysteriously, at other times wild music. I continued to comment on his pictures and he would agree or disagree with it.

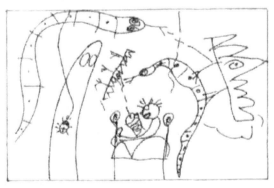

Picture 3

This first picture (picture 3) shows an ill person in a bed, surrounded by dragons, snakes, a ghost, and a spider. It looks ominous in regards to how the snakes spread their poison. The two dragons seem to come to help him out, by grabbing the snakes with their claws.

In the next picture (picture 4) a giant snake surrounds both a child and a dragon, attacks the child with its poison, but is hit by the dragon and is dripping with blood.

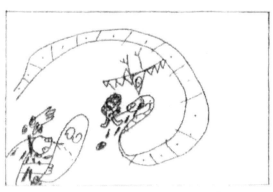

Picture 4

The third picture (picture 5) finally shows the snake lying in its own blood, the child walking on it celebrating in triumph.

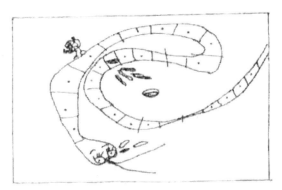

Picture 5

After this picture, Osman left the "cave," took a cymbal out of the cabinet, and started playing a rhythm. I took a rattle and joined him, singing, "We are celebrating, because the snake is beaten." He finished by throwing the cymbal on the floor and kicking it.

It was apparent that by overcoming his inner conflicts through his art he experienced an obvious release, the snake symbolizing his mother. In my conversations with Osman's parents, his mother never seemed to understand, although the teachers stressed it again and again, the importance of not forcing him to speak. Osman's mother, however, suggested draconic actions, through an operation, like tongue correction, or in an educational way, through beating. I tried to be understanding of her feelings of helplessness, but also asked her to please be patient with her son.

In the following weeks, Osman experienced very extreme feelings. In one session, he left the therapy room in total chaos, flooding the floor with a container of water. This manifested punishment fantasies in me; these probably mirrored the expectations that Osman directed toward me. In the very next session (19), for the first time, I experienced Osman tenderly embrace his favorite animal, a big monkey. Right after that he threw him straight across the room again. I tried to support this action with a matching phrase on the piano. I also loudly cried: "Ouch, ouch, you hurt me," whenever he beat or threw the monkey. Some of what Osman did to the monkey had been done to him. In this musical-scenic play I was a kind of "substitute-I" that expressed the pain that Osman was not able to express. At the end of this session, Osman climbed up onto the instrument cabinet and gave me signals to come over and catch him. Osman enjoyed this game so much that he wanted it to be repeated over and over again. I was pleased by the fact that Osman obviously developed more and more trust in me catching him—and symbolically, too.

Some major changes occurred in his pictures at this time. Superman replaced the dragon to protect the child from the bad snake. The child was now lying in bed or in a kind of prison. The musical part of this experience now involved vocal sounds by Osman. He placed microphones and bongos on a table, and from this elevated place he produced electrically supported sounds. He stretched himself to appear bigger, and, lost in the protection of the microphone, he had no fear of his own voice.

The twentieth session, after eight months of working with Osman, marks a significant turning point. It was hard to understand his suggestions and demands that day. "Osman, sometimes it is not easy to understand what you want me to do. Don't you think it would be easier to tell me what you mean?" Osman did not react at first. We improvised, beginning with a calm mood and becoming disturbed by wild drum rolls once in a while. After we finished, I asked him if he wanted to draw a picture. He nodded.

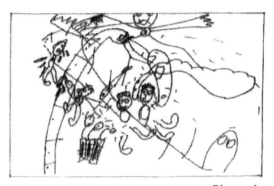

Picture 6

His picture (picture 6) showed two people in the center, a small and a big superman fighting a snake, a dragon, and a ghost. One object was puzzling to me. Through questioning, I found out that it was a bomb. I asked: "Osman, do you think that something dangerous will happen, like a bomb blowing up, if you start talking?" He reacted very impulsively. He scrunched up his picture, and held it in his hand undecidedly. "What would you like to do with that picture?" He found an empty coffee can in the cabinet and put the picture inside of it. I named it the "secret can" from then on. That seemed to please him. From then on all his pictures went in that can. Everything that held value for him had a safe place.

The following session (21) began somewhat unusually. Outside there was some bulky refuge lying out. Osman discovered this large amount of trash that was waiting to be taken away by the maintenance staff. He literally dragged me outside and indicated that he wanted to examine the trash. He examined the different heaps and quietly whispered what he discovered. He took some things like markers, chalk, and a comic with him. On the way back, I recognized that his whispering got quieter. The closer he got to the school, the less intense his talking became. Back in the therapy room I asked him if his treasure should stay here or go home with him. He signified that it should remain here.

In the following sessions, Osman redefined his activities. The drawing activities decreased and the musical activities increased in the therapy room. Except for some clearly understandable whispered statements he was still not talking. I did not pressure him at all about the big event of him talking for the first time. In the twenty-fourth session, on the way from the classroom to the therapy room, Osman went into the secretary's office and wanted to make a phone call. So we talked to each other on the phone, Osman using the secretary's phone, and I from phone in the principal's office. A small conversation took place; a little question and answer game or, rather, an amusing vocal improvisation. More important than anything was the hanging up and calling again procedure. In this play, was I the friend from Osman's first picture who is calling him? In any case, Osman had rediscovered and dared to show his voice "publicly."

This event spread through the school like wildfire. Everybody took an interest in it as if it were a miracle. It was very important that he did not get too much attention now, because that would completely destroy all of the hard work. Also, the relationship between Osman and his mother seemed to improve. One day he proudly presented his warm, colorful, handmade sweater from his mother. She had given him something that would keep him warm and wrapped up during the cold winter.

Osman drew the last picture during the twenty-seventh session (picture 7). It depicted a house with a straw roof and smoke coming out of the chimney. Outside of the house Osman was raising the Turkish flag. For the first time there were no animals, dragons, snakes, or supermen. Maybe this was a sign that his fears had diminished and his ego-strength had developed. Through the connection with his country he may also have been saying: I am at home. I am a Turk in a German school, in an environment that at first was full of danger, threat, and discomfort, but here I can also have the feeling of being "at home." Following that picture I put on a cassette of Turkish pop music for him, which I had in my cupboard for working with foreign children. At first he was surprised, but then he smiled, gave the bongos to me, and grabbed himself a guitar. We were now a Turkish band. All we needed was an audience and a few belly dancers.

Picture 7

From then on, Osman often asked if his friend Olaf could join the session. Such a desire often plays a significant role in therapy with children. It sometimes functions as a defense in response to the intensity of the relationship between therapist and child—someone should come between the two. Maybe this was the case for Osman. But it soon became apparent that the addition of Olaf to the therapy helped in achieving the next therapeutic step. Olaf was proof for all the things that Osman and I experienced. Besides, Olaf was an object for Osman to dominate and to rule. He was also someone who, spontaneously and without questioning, followed my directions and suggestions and, therefore, motivated Osman to do the same. In particular, the music activities took longer. When Osman was sad, we played sad music. When words like "Gypsy," "dried flower," "watered flower" or "travel" were mentioned, we played music using the therapeutic technique of "associative improvisation" (Eschen, 1983, p.41 ff).

Then, a sudden end to music therapy with Osman occurred because the family decided to leave Germany and return to Turkey. The last session was a long prepared for celebration for three—Osman invited Olaf. The final piece of music was a lengthy improvisation based on a melody made by Osman with the words "bella, bella, bella." Osman imagined that he was a Gypsy and traveled throughout the world. Once in a while, the Gypsies celebrated a fest and sung their "bella, bella, bella." Osman and I sang out as loudly as possible. I played the piano and Osman played the drum. Olaf preferred to stay in the background with his rattles. I was very impressed with how Osman was using his voice during the improvisation. I was not sure what the meaning of the words bella, bella were. I was not aware until I looked them up in a Turkish dictionary that they meant "misfortune, evil." Of course, separation is always a bit sad, however the music did not sound sad at all.

The music therapy treatment with Osman ended with a last visit with the family. Everybody was there, between cartons and suitcases. It was very surprising for me that the evening ended in a three-hour festive dinner. Mr. and Mrs. G. were very grateful of my efforts, and even invited me, and my family, to visit them in one of their apartment houses in Izmir, Turkey.

DISCUSSION AND CONCLUSIONS

In the fifty sessions, Osman was given the chance to play through and experience various forms of symbolic expression of situations that until now he had missed out on in his development. I will take the opportunity to talk once again about my first visit with the family. This visit was a little difficult. First of all, there was the language barrier. Second, I got the feeling that Mrs. G. did not understand much of it and could not relate to it emotionally. She strongly believed that Osman was bad and that the teachers should just be tougher, like they are in Turkey. The atmosphere relaxed somewhat when Mrs. G. brought out the photo album. This provided an opportunity to talk about a lot of other things. She indicated that she felt that the basis of Osman's silence was because he was embarrassed at school. Other photos were of his hospital stay and of Turkey.

Osman was in the room the entire time. He was mostly silent, without even reacting to what was said. His mother and sisters continuously encouraged him to talk, without any success. He was stuck in an inner conflict. This was usually a place where he talked. To him, I was part of the "enemy" world. After a while, he tried to get some attention. He threw some cars through the air, turned the television on and off, turned the volume completely up, and filled his mother's tea with spoonfuls of sugar until the cup overflowed. Mrs. G. set no limits. It was easy to see her anger in her facial expressions and her gestures, but she simply ignored her son. From this, I came to understand the reason for his silence: a deep-rooted wish to express his enormous anger and his strong desire to be acknowledged and to be given clear limits. I tried to explain again to Mrs. G. that Osman would not be forced by us to speak. She seemed to feel that Osman had made a positive connection with me. The very last comment I heard from her was the following: "Take him with you; take him home with you. You can keep him!" What does it take for a mother to say that she wants to give her son away!

Osman had to struggle with several separation experiences: his stay in the hospital, the fact that his mother was working most of the time, as well as the move to the German school. In addition, a sensitive child like Osman had greater difficulties dealing with living in two worlds: Turkey at home and German at school. Furthermore, it is important to realize that he was not given the chance at home to resolve this difficulty he had with these transitions. His mother did not have a sense of a child's need for toys as vehicles for understanding. Playing, according to her, was just a stage before becoming an adult. And this stage should be squashed quickly, even if it hurts. Thus, Osman's relationship to his toys at home and to the things in the therapy room made sense: erratic and destructive, without respect. It was probably a lifesaver that he discovered drawing as a way to express himself. Other transitions in the process from fantasy to reality were also seen: making a fire, using a microphone, using the telephone, playing hide and seek, and building a cave. His progress in individual music therapy was predictably difficult. The trust given to me increased when given the possibility to play and express things symbolically. In this way, it was possible for him to trust his voice again.

I would now like to comment about the function of music therapy in Osman's case. In the beginning, the idea of making music seemed to be dangerous for him. The first improvisations were simply to indicate the beginning and the end of a session. In addition, the musical accompaniment that I offered him as background music for his activities was significant. This gave a kind of "musical foundation" which made my presence known, holding him in the activities without any pressure or expectations of him. For Osman, drawing was a more concrete way to explore his fantasies. Through an improvisation, music can certainly intensify an emotional state, and the picture completed this for him.

Through improvisation, things were expressed in the outer world that he was not ready to express verbally. In one improvisation, which I later named "beating up," the sound was dramatic, and this was also reflected in his drawing. Perhaps the music here had the effect of encouraging, stimulating, and allowing him to "talk" about his experiences and feelings; in his case, through pictures. Through this multimodal approach to music therapy (music-speech-music; play-music-drawing, etc) it is possible to examine similarities and differences in the transformation process. One example of this was when wild music followed a "nice" story.

Another function of the music was the specific appeal of the different musical instruments. Of course, it took Osman a long time before he chose brass instruments. Relatively early on, he discovered the rattles and the bongos and bass drums. The rattles fit with his desire to walk around, so of course he chose them first. They were his companions. The bongos and the bass drum allowed him to be wild and to show his impulses and the real fire inside him. These sound pictures were usually very short. They had more of a cathartic function. To perform longer lasting music with piano accompaniment was not appropriate for him.

In music therapy with children instruments are often used as toys. This was true for Osman. Tone bars were used as construction blocks; sticks as knifes, swords or guns. His growth process went hand in hand with the act of rising up on the table and extending the microphone stand. But more than anything,

Osman had a preference for the toylike character of the bongos; perhaps for him it was like the puppet. He carried it through the room, beat it up, threw it on the floor, picked it up, and touched it gently. Furthermore, the bongos were the only instruments he allowed into his cave. This important role of the instruments was further captured when he expressed his first vocal sounds through the microphone.

Just as one can identify and connect with a musical instrument, naturally one can also feel threatened by an opponent while fighting against it. In one situation, in Osman's fantasy, the cymbal was dressed up as a snake and was therefore seen as an enemy that needed to be beaten. Therefore, in addition to their traditional functions, instruments can be objects of play. They can be filled with life because of their outer appearance and what they are made of. When this is the case, the sound experience may be subordinate.

In the whole spectrum of symbolic interaction (music, drawing, and play), sound was the very last form that was recovered and was only important later on when a third party was involved. I was particularly touched by the gradual development of the voice: from the sound over the microphone, to the childlike whispering on the telephone, to the loudly given orders to his friend Olaf. Finally, Osman's singing voice was an incredible discovery. He was able to understand and reproduce melismatic Turkish quarter-tone music, as well as to build bright sounds from the piano into his melodies.

During the course of the therapy with Osman the music-making became more and more central. To summarize, I will list the different functions of music in Osman's treatment. It is very interesting to see that music found its place in the final phase, when Osman was already using language:

- Structuring the sessions
- Wrapped in a sound (musical nourishment)
- Intensifying emotions being experienced in the moment
- Adding sounds to certain impulses
- Identification and argument with the musical instruments (toylike qualities)
- Contact and dialogue

I would like to end this case study with some statements about the end of Osman's therapy: Osman's contact with his same aged peers is considered to be normal. He is not bothering anyone with silence or aggression. On the other hand, he is not yet able to understand the limits of his power, so he sometimes gets into trouble with stronger classmates. Had it not been for the sudden end to therapy, due to the return to Turkey, the sessions would have been continued for a while. The goal would have been to stabilize his condition and include him into a group setting, where he would have learned group processes having to do with confrontation and agreement.

How the new environment, the different treatment of students in Turkey, and the lack of understanding will influence his further development is difficult to predict. Maybe he will resort to selective mutism in stressful situations. However, I hope that he became stable enough through the treatment he received in the special school, the individual music therapy sessions, and his understanding teachers to handle other problems better. His rapid development through music therapy lead me to believe that his chances are good. In addition, his parents now have a far more positive attitude toward him. They bought him a bicycle right before they left. Osman showed it to me on one of my home visits and, for the first time, I saw a glimpse of being proud of her son in Mrs. G.'s eyes, as he was circling around, waving and smiling at us.

REFERENCES

Altschuler, I. M. (1948). "A Psychiatrist's Experience with Music as a Therapeutic Agent." In O. Sullivan & M. Schoen (eds.), *Music and Medicine*. New York: Schumann.

Benenzon, R. O. (1983). *Einführung in die Musiktherapie*. München: Kösel.

Dührssen, A. (1982). *Psychogene Erkrankungen bei Kindern und Jugendlichen*. Göttingen, Zürich: Verlag für Medizinische Psychologie im Verlag Vandenboeck & Ruprecht.

Eschen, J. Th. (2002). "Analytical Music Therapy—Introduction." In Johannes Th. Eschen (ed.), *Analytical Music Therapy*. London and Philadelphia: Jessica Kingsley Publisher.

Winnicott, D. W. (1971). *Playing and Reality*. London: Tavistock Publications Ltd.

Case Four

MELODIC SONG AS CRYING/ RHYTHMIC SONG AS LAUGHING: A CASE STUDY OF VOCAL IMPROVISATION WITH AN AUTISTIC CHILD

Gianluigi di Franco

ABSTRACT

This study presents a dynamic music therapy approach to an autistic child. It provides a conceptual distinction between psychodynamic and dynamic music therapy. From a methodological point of view, the focus is on a vocal approach to the autistic behavior on the one hand and on the emotional aspects happening inside of the client/therapist relationship on the other hand.

INTRODUCTION

I would like to explore the concept of "psychodynamic music therapy," the central focus of this book, which stems from the work I have been involved in for twenty-three years as a music therapist. I will do this in order to contribute to the general discussion about this. In terms of terminology, I think it is useful to consider distinctions between "psychodynamic music therapy" and what I call "dynamic music therapy."

Obviously, it is fundamental to define the meaning of "psychodynamic." We can generally say that "psychodynamic" is a term derived from the original Freudian psychoanalytical root. From this psychoanalytic root, various modifications were developed: some of them transformed the basic concepts created by Sigmund Freud and others followed them more strictly. For example, there are the post-Freudians, but there are also professionals in the field who were inspired by the original psychoanalytical root, but definitively changed the methodological approach to form a "new psychotherapy." For example, I am referring to the speculations of Carl Jung, Wilhelm Reich, Carl Rogers, and others. For this reason, when we use the term "psychodynamic" we take it to be inclusive of many concepts: on the one hand, the historical Freudian psychoanalytical perspective, and, on the other hand, the myriad of perspectives derived from that perspective.

When we talk about a psychodynamic approach, then, we cannot avoid referring to some basic concepts:

a.   The personality structure refers to the dynamic relationship between the conscious, preconscious and unconscious;

b.   The structural aspects of the psyche—id, ego, and superego—basically characterize human behavior and all the internal psychic connections.

Obviously, these two fundamental premises indicate several dynamic implications for music therapy:

1.   Regression, as a defense mechanism, can be more or less structured, but it facilitates a process of going back to the past, implying an emotional memory. This process, facilitated through music, involves psychological reactions mostly focused on projective identifications;

2.   If we place regression inside of the music therapy relationship as a central aspect of the methodological approach, and if we say that music is a way to get in touch with the inner world of

the other, it is then necessary to discuss the emotional reactions between the therapist and the client;

3.   Emotional reactions between the therapist and the client originating from the client's needs and passing through the music (by listening or by playing) lead us to think about other psychodynamic concepts such as "transference/countertransference." Since the concept of transference/countertransference was created within a verbal psychotherapeutic relationship rather than passing through music, I prefer to talk about the emotional investment the client has toward the therapist in music therapy as "emotional aspects" and the emotional reactions of the therapist toward the client as "counteremotional aspects."

I have delineated all of this in order to outline three main points:

1.   We need to give attention to the level of work that gives importance to the emotional "milieu" of expressing things through music in order to address the client's needs, one which implies a sort of dynamically oriented way of observing the events happening in each session. It is essential to pay attention to the growth occurring within the therapist/client relationship process that progresses both from one session to another, and, like in Chinese boxes, one inside of another.

2.   We need a different terminology in which it is possible to show a close connection with a psychodynamic framework, while maintaining a comfortable distance, in order to show that the body of psychodynamic methodologies and techniques already clearly defined can be uniquely applied to other related fields. This is why the title "dynamic music therapy" is effective in defining the use of psychodynamic terms and concepts applied to the music therapy experience with music and through music, more than "psychodynamic music therapy" which seems to me to be more focused on using concepts coming from a verbal psychodynamic perspective. What is important is to place emphasis on methodological observation derived from a deeper level of relationship between the conceptual values of the psychodynamic perspective and the specific musical content developed within the music therapy relationship.

3.   Attention should be given to the fact that it is usual within verbal psychotherapy for the boundaries between the therapist and the client to be clear, so that the client within this defined

context can "transfer" his emotions onto the therapist in order to get a more stable "contractuality," from which we derive the psychodynamic term "transference." However, within the music therapy nonverbal relationship, especially with those with communication disorders and mental health problems, the client does not have direct consciousness of therapy as therapy; the client knows that he will begin a musically based activity. Within this activity it is important to create an "alliance" that will facilitate our music therapy project to address the client's problems, while using his/her way of expressing, with the view to obtaining positive results. The music therapy relationship with these features does not give the client the chance to put his emotional energy within an already defined and recognized setting, but rather one that is being established, and, thus, it is possible for the client to make an emotional investment within the growing music therapy relationship: this process is a dynamic one. But is this investment made directly in the therapist or is this investment made directly in the music or is it made through the music in order to more easily make an investment in the therapist? I feel that I cannot call this investment "tranference." The client is emotionally investing, but he is investing in many different ways and in many different directions. That is why I prefer to call this process, made by the client toward the therapist, "emotional investment" and the one eventually made by the therapist toward the client "counter-emotional investment." Obviously the work of observing these processes is fundamental in terms of understanding how to manage the different aspects of the musical production, in terms of one's own behavior as the therapist toward the client, in the process.

BACKGROUND INFORMATION

General Information

A. is an eight-year-old boy with a diagnosis of primary autism, which led him to receive various treatments, including music therapy. In an interview with the client's family (Feb. 5, 1999), I learned some additional details regarding the client and the family context.

In particular the parents told me:

- A. was not independent (he was not able to eat by himself; he was not able to go to the bathroom without the help of an adult; and so on)
- A. was not able to express himself through verbal language, just through some gestures
- It seemed as though A. was not conscious of time (for example, he was not able to understand which day of the week it was)
- A. has not established relationships with children of the same age
- A.'s birth was an emergency Cesarean and he was born a little premature (eight months and ten days)
- A. began to make musical babbling sounds around six months old, saying MA-MA, LA-LA
- After eight months of age it appeared as though A. was unable to remember anyone except his mother; it seemed that the isolated behavior of being touched by his mother's voice had the effect of calming him down.
- A. was in the habit of waking up during the night every two to three hours
- At around thirteen months of age A. started to spin some objects around
- During the first few months, A.'s parents used to sing lullabies to him and embrace him a lot. Then he adopted a bizarre behavior, when he refused the physical contact of even his parents
- A. does not like loud sounds at all
- Since birth, A. has had various different instruments in his room: keyboards, bongos, castanets, maracas
- A. liked two different kinds of music: one was more focused on melody and while he listened to this kind of music he became sad and sometimes would start to cry; the other one was a more structured pop song which he listened to as background music
- A. liked TV jingles, too, and became really excited and started to move around when he was listening to them
- A. also liked sets of keys as sound objects and hated puppets and shaving foam

When the parents came for the interview, A. was still having psychomotricity[1] twice a week, which he had had since he was six months old, and speech therapy twice a week, which he had had since he was one year old.

Music Therapy Assessment

From a methodological point of view, after interviewing the client's parents, I tend to conduct an assessment with the client in order to evaluate the following areas:

- Reactions to different musical stimuli
- Reactions to the different instruments the client will be exposed to
- Reactions to having one parent as an observer inside of the music therapy room or not
- Reactions to my presence in the room
- How I react to his reactions/lack of reactions
- Motor and gestural abilities and how these are used in the space and how they are related to the persons who are there

Listed below are the results of this initial assessment:

A.   Musical Aspects

1.   A. reacts through facial expressions when he is listening to the music, but he does not respond actively;

2.   A. shows a peculiar sensitivity while listening to melodic fragments, crying a little;

3.   When the musical stimuli are not particularly melodic A. shows interest in touching and exploring the instruments more like objects for their shapes than for their sounds; furthermore, he likes to let the objects fall down;

4.   When A. was invited to explore the keyboard, the only reaction he had was to make some clusters and some simple sequences of different notes, but no more than two or three notes; during this experience he started to make some bizarre vocal sounds.

---

[1] In Europe PSICOMOTRICITA is a method developed by Aucotourier—a French pioneer—who worked with children in such a way that gives value to psychomotor attitudes.

B. Behavioral Aspects

1. When the therapist did not give him a direction, A. automatically gravitated toward objects, exploring them in a primary way (similar to a two- or three-month-old baby);
2. A. did not respond to the therapist's directions at all;
3. A. rarely established eye contact. A few times, however, he was able to look in the eyes of the therapist for a few seconds, smiling briefly;
4. A. moved a lot in the space and within this motor activity some stereotypical movement patterns emerged, e.g., fast flapping like a butterfly; sometimes he tried to leave the room;
5. A few times when the therapist made a clear simple prompt, A. started to show a kind of indirect predisposition to become involved in the relationship.

After these observations, I decided to begin individual music therapy treatment with him, twice a week, with a small instrumentarium, but representative of the different instrument families. I introduced my treatment plan to the parents explaining that because A.'s diagnosis indicated a severe problem, and also because the assessment of him confirmed this reality, the music therapy treatment could not be clearly defined. Because A. had some indirect reactions in the assessment, the plan was to meet him for three months and evaluate his progress in the evolving process, after having established a more stable relationship.

C. Treatment Goals

1. To engage the client by using his selective sensitivity to musical stimuli and to specific micro-patterns introduced during the assessment, particulary the melodic ones;
2. To involve the client, through the musical patterns he prefers, in order to develop a more mutual relationship with the therapist from an emotional point of view; all that in order to give an expressive and communicative orientation to his gestures, such that his behavior can be more understandable from the external environment.

D.   Musical Techniques

In order to achieve the above goals the following techniques were utilized:

1. *A warm-up period* of the session based on listening to melodic music in order to facilitate the emotional involvement of the client;

2. *Improvisation* initiated by the therapist in order to involve the client indirectly, basically focusing on the keyboard on which melodies, which are central to his musical sensitivity, could be more easily reproduced and so that they could eventually have harmony added. All of this was done in order to imitate and re-create some brief patterns of the client's expressions without making the relationship space too crowded; trying to be present musically at this level and also respecting the space between one short musical production and another;

3. The approach of the therapist to the client was *semi-directive*. More specifically, the therapist allowed space for the client to initiate, and then worked with this material. Furthermore, the therapist controlled the client's attempts to escape from the setting, not in a destructive manner, but in a playful noninvading containing way.

TREATMENT

I began meeting with the client twice a week for forty-five minutes. During the first twenty sessions, however, he continually attempted to leave the room. The problem steadily decreased and finally vanished completely.

Following the assessment, I tried to establish a relationship with the client based primarily on the following aspects, keeping in mind the particular features related to his autism:

- To *welcome* the client and to *invite* him into the music therapy room;

- To *sit on a chair close to the keyboard*, which was the instrument during the assessment period to which A. was most attracted. This behavior by the therapist did not imply playing necessarily. From a relational perspective, the aim was to create an atmosphere similar to a container in which the client could start to place his things. During this phase, the therapist's anxiety was obviously increased because he really did not know what the client would do. Furthermore, from a methodological perspective, the therapist was trying to be more focused on himself, so that when the client made a sonorous/musical production he would be more ready to respond creatively. If the attention of the therapist had been focused only on the client, the client would have felt that the therapist's behavior was too compulsive, making the relationship space full of unnecessary material, which would lead the client to become worried and anxious. That is why, from a dynamic perspective, my goal was first to wait for him, putting myself in the position of someone who is apparently not waiting for someone, in order to facilitate his approach to me;

- To *react following the client's bizarre musical expressions*, trying to reinforce his behavior by immediately imitating the patterns introduced by him and bringing in a little variation. This was not only in order to *reinforce him*, but also to *observe* how he would involve himself more within the relationship in response to a musical production made by someone different from him; that is, a kind of indirect answer to my answer. At this level, it was really useful to evaluate the progress of the treatment process to see whether A. was tranforming some aspects of his behavior in other ones; for example, his facial expressions were becoming less frozen as was seen in the way he began to have brief periods of eye contact with me, and when he sometimes laughed at some of the movements I was making while creating the music. He also began to *reduce* some of his stereotypical movements. He began to produce more distinct behavior. He also began to be more connected to things happening around him, mostly in terms of facial expressions and movements. More specifically, the task was to understand the extent to which the client caught the short variations introduced by the therapist in his answers;

- After the first six months of treatment, I introduced a new approach: *to use the melodic aspects of the client's musical production*, which was facilitated by sequences of two or at most three chords on which he could develop a simple melodic structure. This was very important in letting him feel more comfortable and close to me, in that he felt safe and in the position to make something more improvised, yet connected to the patterns I had started to introduce. During this stage I was using what I had observed during the assessment period, which suggested the use of minor chords. It was in response to minor chords that he had shown himself to be more fluid in his behavior, starting to cry a bit. During this period of time, however, he did not cry, but he was close to me, and was responding more to my indirect invitations. The chords were like a canvas on which he started to paint, sometimes shapes obviously discernable to me and sometimes not. But this stage was really useful from a psychodynamic perspective because I felt that he was slowly entering the relationship with me, and also with himself, giving the impression that he was making more meaningful contact with his inner world. This phase continued for approximately six months;

- *To improvise starting from different melodic patterns*, trying to connect them in a kind of composed "here and now song," in which the client participated more closely with the therapist and waited increasingly for the creation of the song. In this stage of the process, he gave me the chance to understand that he was very able to tranform his behavior into emotions, in that he appeared more and more emotionally able to listen to the developing minor song. Furthermore, I felt increasingly in the position of the mother at a counteremotional level. From a containing perspective, I was symbolically embracing him, because he was asking to be embraced. I started to sing and the more I developed the melody the more he established a truly engaged form of eye contact which was maintained for over twenty minutes.

Many interesting dynamics occurred within this process. I will describe some of these dynamics using notes made after observing a video recording of one of our sessions:

- The "mother" role was not the only one that was emerging inside of me as he was becoming closer to me, but also the "father" role increasingly emerged as I was singing. The more I sang, the more I went into the high and low frequencies of my vocal expressive attitude;
- The client's reactions, from an emotional point of view, were to cry first silently and then after a while with sounds, as if he was asking me something. It was as if he were waking up after a long dream or after a long period of time where his memory had been empty. That is why he showed me his willingness to express his emotions, but also the huge need to be embraced in his tragedy to discover in some way *who* he was;

- The client's reactions, from a behavioral point of view, were more focused within the relationship after his contained crying. After the melodic composed song induced his crying, I introduced a pause within which he appeared very calm and without need of escaping from the room or getting away from me. Soon after, I introduced a rhythmic pattern with the sung melody that was more divided rhythmically, which helped him to slowly get out of this strong embrace. He started to follow the directions I was giving him; for example, I began to challenge him within the musical improvisation, starting at that specific moment, and not before, to also give him directions verbally. At that moment his emotional and behavioral reactions were musically focused on making a melodic connection to my chords. I was asking him: "Please, can you give me an answer?" or "Why have you stopped, can you please go on?" He was always reacting to my questions, being in some way orientated to them. At the end of this very important session, within the evolving process, for the first time A. followed my verbal direction: "A, the time is finished; you have to go away. We'll meet again next week!" He gave me the feeling that he understood what I verbalized. As soon as I spoke to him, he stood up and he went away.

DISCUSSION AND CONCLUSIONS

From this case, it can be seen, from a methodological standpoint, that I followed a plan of treatment based on elements derived from the assessment period, while also following the dynamic reactions of the "closed" child's behavior, trying to adapt myself at the counteremotional level through musical language. Obviously, the use of music, within the dynamic music therapy approach described in this clinical case study, can offer great opportunities for reaching clients with comunicative disorders such as autism.

In this case, medical indications implied an "extrema ratio" function (meaning that as we do not have many possibilities for positive therapeutic results with this kind of client, we try music therapy as a last chance). Furthermore, this case shows that when working with clients with severe comunicative problems, which few professionals are trained to deal with, music and the music established in this kind of relational context assumes special importance. It does not mean that a verbal psychodynamic approach cannot be applied to various disorders; rather, at this level, because it can require more time to obtain results, it can be considered less efficient. From this standpoint, it appears that the epistemology and methodology behind a musical approach to the client's needs really involves life choices that are linked to the personality structures that the therapist exposes, intending the therapy as a process with its own development.

At this level, we can consider that this kind of therapist creates a kind of projective identification of his own need toward the "screen" which the music therapy process offers him; furthermore, he passes through the process of helping others and increasingly is creating his own process and his own existential therapy.

REFERENCES

Anzieu, D. (1975). *Il lavoro psicoanalitico nei gruppi*. Roma: Armando.

Benenzon, R. O. (1977). *Musicoterapia en la psicosis infantile*. Buenos Aires: Paidos.

Benenzon, R. O. (1981). *Music Therapy Manual*. Springfield, IL: Charles C. Thomas Publisher.

Bruscia, K. E. (1987). *Improvisational Models of Music Therapy*. Springfield, IL: Charles C. Thomas Publisher.

Bruscia, K. E. (1993). *Definire la Musicoterapia*. Roma: Ismez.

di Franco, G. (1995). "Il grido Universale." In G. di Franco & R. De Michele *Musicoterapia in Italia*. Napoli Idelson.

di Franco, G. (1995). "Voices as Means to Express Emotions" *3rd European Arts Therapies Conference Proceedings*, Hartforshire University, Hatfield, UK.

di Franco, G. (1999). "Music and Autism: Vocal Improvisation as a Containment of Stereotypes." In T. Wigram & J. de Backer (eds.), *Clinical Applications of Music Therapy—Developmental Disability, Paediatrics and Neurology*. London: Jessica Kingsley Press.

di Franco, G. (1999). "Music Therapy: A Methodological Approach in Mental Health Field." In M. Heal & T. Wigram (eds.), *Music Therapy Health and Education*. London: Jessica Kingsley Press.

di Franco, G. (2001). "Le voci dell'emozione: verso una pragmatica della musica come terapia," *ISMEZ*, Roma.

Lecourt, E. (1994). *L'experience musicale/Resonances psychanalytiques*. Parigi: L'Harmattan.

Segal, H. (1975). *Introduzione all'opera di Melanie Klein*. Firenze: Martinelli.

Winnicott, D. W. (1990). *Gioco e realtà*. Roma: Armando.

Case Five

GROWING UP ALONE:
ANALYTICAL MUSIC THERAPY WITH
CHILDREN OF PARENTS TREATED WITHIN A
DRUG AND SUBSTANCE ABUSE PROGRAM

Juliane Kowski

ABSTRACT

In this case study, I will present my work as an analytical music therapist with a group of eight- to twelve-year-old children who attended an afterschool program at a family health and support center within a drug and substance abuse program in Brooklyn, New York. The children, who were seen once a week for forty-five minutes over a period of eight months, are emotionally disturbed and exhibit behavioral problems; some exhibit tendencies of attention deficit disorder or post-traumatic stress disorder. I will discuss the ways in which I have adapted analytical music therapy methods and techniques, developed by Mary Priestley, to this population. I will use musical examples to explain the methods and techniques that I employed within a framework of structure and free-flowing improvisation. Furthermore, I will describe an "improvisational attitude" and the consequent challenges that arise for the music therapist.

INTRODUCTION

I was hired to develop music therapy at a family health and support center within a drug and substance abuse treatment center in Brooklyn, New York. The children were picked up after school by counselors who supervised their homework; they attended dance, music, and art therapy sessions while their parents received therapy or other services provided by the center. I worked with the children, who were divided by age into two groups, once a week for forty-five minutes for twenty-seven sessions in total. I will describe the group music therapy with the older children aged eight to twelve. Eight to ten children attended the group.

Before I explain my work, I would like to describe my theoretical background. I am a humanistically-oriented music therapist. I use a client-centered approach, which means that I rely upon the client for direction within the therapeutic process. I believe in the concepts of self-actualization and peak experience that are elaborated upon in the writings of Carl Rogers and Abraham Maslow. The analytical music therapy [AMT] music therapists Mary Priestley and Benedikte Scheiby are the main influences on how I understand and practice AMT. I have been in training and supervision with Benedikte Scheiby for the past five years and I have developed an eclectic, dynamic style that allows for my techniques to evolve with the circumstances. I work with individuals, groups and families, and am always challenged by AMT. In this case study, I will focus on the therapeutic process itself and my own evolution within the process, rather than on the results of the process.

Priestley's writings have helped to guide my work with children. She offers some interesting thoughts in "Essays on Analytical Music Therapy" about what she calls "Preliminary Music" with so-called "normal" children even though she declares herself too inexperienced to write in-depth about how AMT works with children. She writes:

> Children are acting out their fantasies in this way all the time, working them through in play. It is only when they get trapped in them and cannot develop any further that their learning and behavior suffers and they need help. Therefore the analytical music therapist's aim with a child-patient is to restore to her, or introduce to her, the ability to involve herself in the important "work" of self-healing play, together with the freedom to use her natural curiosity and creativity (1994, pp. 275–276).

Reflecting on when music therapy with children ceases to be analytical, Priestley writes:

> . . . I would say it is when the use of words becomes wholly superfluous because of the child's lack of comprehension due to mental handicap. But even when there is no inter-pretation by the therapist because the child is already working and playing in a self-healing way, the analytical music therapist's exploratory approach will influence the way he helps to shape the movement of the therapy. With his assistance, the child will be led into controlling his environment in a creative way. As Winnicott (1971) wrote: "To control what is outside, one has to *do* things, not simply to think or to wish, and *doing things take time*. Playing is doing" (p. 47). And analytical music therapy can provide an opportunity for such playing (1994, p. 284).

Grounding myself in AMT, and adapting its techniques to the needs of these children, has provided a basis for analytical in-depth work in conjunction with music that maximizes therapeutic potential. Under normal circumstances these children have very little control over their lives. Under my guidance, within the framework of AMT, they had an opportunity to work and play creatively, to control how and what things were done.

BACKGROUND INFORMATION

Ninety percent of the children at the center were of African-American background; 10 percent were Hispanic. Some lived with their parents, others had been separated temporarily until the parent graduated from the program. Many had been in and out of foster care or spent time with relatives. Most had one or more siblings. Due to histories of drug and substance abuse the parents were mandated to attend this program in order to keep their children.

The children lived with issues such as neglect, emotional and/or physical abuse, lengthy separation from their parents and homes, exposure to drugs and, as a consequence, meddling with the law and being involved with legal authorities. They trusted hesitantly, had poor communication skills, and harbored lots of anger and frustration. Their frequent inappropriate behavior resulted in constant problems at school and within the program.

I worked with these children over a period of one school year. I met regularly with the program director, dance therapist, and counselors to coordinate goals, and to share thoughts about the therapeutic process and the children's progress. It took time to establish trust and to lay the foundation that would enable us to reach the goals set by the team.

Working within AMT with this population in a large group setting required an improvisational attitude. Many challenges arose which forced me to adapt more traditional AMT techniques; however, there were moments in the music and in the verbal processing that demonstrated AMT at work with this population.

TREATMENT

In this case study, I will use two sessions to describe my work with these children. In the first example, near the beginning of treatment, I am using the AMT techniques: the holding technique and patterns of significance. In the second example, near the end of treatment, I am using the therapeutic technique of songwriting. In each example, I will discuss my work in terms of transference, countertransference, and resistance.

Therapeutic Goals:

Throughout my work with this group of children, the main goals were:
- Acknowledgment and expression of feelings
- Anger management
- Increasing self-esteem
- Developing communication skills
- Helping with conflict resolution.

Example 1: Free-Flowing Improvisation

Session 5

Description

"What are our Christmas wishes?" suggested itself as a theme after we had sung several Christmas songs and I suspected that this direction might be a fruitful avenue of pursuit. Choosing this theme corresponds with the AMT technique, "Patterns of Significance." This technique involves the therapist and the client(s) choosing a theme that characterizes a significant event in the client's life. They improvise music together and process verbally afterwards. "This technique is used to discover the inner patterns and feelings surrounding significant events in life" (Priestley, 1975, p. 141).

Priestley recommends using this technique with individuals who are post middle-aged adults, however I was nonetheless able to adapt it successfully to my work. When adapting it, I tried to provide a common musical basis for interaction and to develop therapeutic musical and verbal interventions for a group setting.

Sometimes, at the very beginning of the session when the children could not settle down, I asked them to just play what they felt and how they perceived these beginnings. They played and called it "chaos." This was a recurring theme, an undercurrent in their lives that I felt I could substitute for a specific "significant event." We did this repeatedly and it helped them to settle down, to expel the chaos, organize, and contain themselves. They grew more aware of how this "chaotic" musical interaction inhibited their ability to communicate.

When I initiated the improvisation with the title: "What are our Christmas wishes?" I felt a heavy mood come over the group and I could only imagine what these children might miss at a time when other families celebrate. The choice of this theme included a significant risk that I might touch upon something that would be very difficult to process within the group setting. So, I made sure to keep some time available afterward to process with a child alone if necessary. Christmas was obviously a difficult time for these children. In the following sessions, they initiated more thematic playing. Some even wanted to play alone. Issues such as neglect, loneliness, and the longing for a healthy and harmonious family surfaced.

Seven children, whom I will call Andy (cymbal), Bert (kid's djembe), Carl (snare drum), Dan (triangle), Eva (buffalo drum), Fanny (small conga drum), and Gladys (marimba phone), picked instruments. I prohibited the use of the big floor drum because I was afraid it would dominate the music. I encouraged everybody to express what they felt and to listen to the other group members.

G. started playing the marimba phone very quietly. F. responded and went along with G. on the small conga drum looking at G. briefly and then down to the floor. A., at first grinning and looking at C. for reassurance, hit the cymbal once pretty hard. I started playing the guitar, strumming D minor, A minor (picking up the pentatonic scale of the marimba phone: F G A C D), establishing a holding environment. I tried to send the signal that I was there to hold (using the AMT "holding technique"[1]), protect and encourage them, and not to stop them unless somebody acted in a destructive manner.

E. started playing the buffalo drum in a 4/4 rhythm, joining the girls. I felt that they were really trying to get together and to support each other. B sat quietly and scratched away on his drum. I could not tell yet if he was with the group or if he was demonstrating resistance. A. picked up on B.'s scratching and made screechy sounds on the cymbal. C. laughed. E. gave C. an angry look and her playing became louder. The rhythm became more intense, like strong heavy footsteps in 4/4. I was not sure whether to intervene or to let this dynamic play itself out. C. picked up E.'s stronger buffalo drumbeat on the snare drum. G. established a melody that she repeated over and over again.

Transcription:

An image elicited from the music of G. sitting all alone on Christmas Eve crying out for her mother arose in my mind. I supported her with gentle strumming on the guitar and gave her a reassuring look. B. picked up the rhythmic pattern of G.'s melodic playing as if he were joining her, although he avoided looking directly at her. Others followed this rhythm. For a short time the group developed a strong musical message. I looked at D. He sat there, seeming spaced out, holding on to his triangle, swinging it back and forth, not playing it. Where was he? Neither the group nor I seemed to reach him. Meanwhile the group sounded as if they had composed their own little "Klagelied" (German word for wailing song) until C. started hacking away on the cymbal, purposefully

---

[1] In my work with these children I often used the "Holding Technique," which is described by Priestley as follows: "This technique is also sometimes called "containing." Its purpose is to allow the client to fully experience her emotions right through to its climax through emotional sound expression while being held emotionally by the musical matrix of the therapist" (1994, p. 38). I played D minor and A minor at the beginning to establish a musical container, holding the children musically, allowing them to express their feelings. I then switched to playing sliding chords in half steps symbolizing tension in order to follow the more chaotic character of the music, but also to give the boys the opportunity to express their feelings in a holding environment. I used this technique in almost every session to provide containment.

destroying the unity. The girls stopped playing and the other boys joined C. The group had split.

I accompanied the boys' emerging power by playing sliding bar chords moving in half steps on the guitar. The 4/4 rhythm fell apart. The boys played a loud, angry sounding chaos. They were laughing, looking at me for reassurance. I kept following them, "telling" them that it is OK to play chaos. Perhaps chaos is what they had experienced at Christmas? I tried to encourage them to vent their feelings. They kept laughing. I felt their anger very much, and their resistance as well. They were hiding behind that musical chaos. Their laughter seemed to protect them from feelings that really hurt deep inside. The girls withdrew.

I raised my hand to initiate the end. I wanted to give the boys some space for their male energy, but also to return to the girls with their female energy that was obviously quite different. I encouraged a few seconds of silence in order to let the music settle in, but the boys were unable to calm down so I moved on to verbal processing. These 2½ minutes of music had passed so quickly.

I asked G. what she thought of the music. She said that she had liked the first part more. I asked her why and what she had tried to say musically. She replied, without looking at anybody, that her wish had been to be with her whole family for Christmas. The room got very quiet. I responded that her wish was entirely normal and that Christmas should be celebrated with the whole family. I acknowledged her sad feelings and uncertainty over whether her wish would come true. I also let the group know that she had demonstrated a lot of courage by sharing her thoughts musically and verbally.

I asked the group if anybody shared these feelings and if they had heard these feelings in her music. F. said that G.'s melody had made her feel sad and that she had played along with her. I asked her what she was trying to say and she said that she did not know, but that she wanted to be happy. The boys started giggling again. I was feeling the group falling apart anew. What could I do to keep them together?

I mentioned to A. that by scratching his cymbal he had demonstrated that he had not wanted to join the girls at the beginning. He replied that that was girls' stuff and not for him. I asked him how he had tried to express his wishes for Christmas. He said that he had wanted to have fun and I told him that that also was a viable wish.

I asked the group how they felt when they were together musically for a moment, and what it had sounded like. F. said that it had sounded sad, like a sad Christmas song. E. supported her, nodding. A. and C. started giggling and talking again. I felt angry; the "teacher" was arising in me. I felt powerless to handle the situation. It seemed that whenever we were getting somewhere we had to stop.

I decided to ignore the troublesome boys to some extent and asked D. why he had not played at all. D. said he had not known what to play. I asked him what he had wished for. Very quietly he said that he had wished that no bad stuff would happen. B. and C. laughed loudly. I asked them to explain their response to what D. had to say. They kept giggling, enjoying the attention. B. said that D. never participates. I said that D. was probably shy and that the group needed to help him to feel more secure.

I decided to get back to the music and asked C. what he thought about the second part of the music when the girls had not played. C. said it was fun to play like that. I tried to dig deeper by asking him to describe the character of the music. C. said that it had been fast and happy. I passed this on to A., asking him what he thought. A. said that he thought that the music was very strong, happy and wild. I asked who else agreed with this description. G. said it had sounded like guns and that that was why she had stopped playing. E. agreed with a confirming facial expression. F. said that she had felt scared.

A. and C. laughed again and acted as if they were proud of what they had accomplished. I felt I needed to react, to let them know that I think that everybody has a right to express their feelings and that we ought to respect each other. I also acknowledged what the girls were feeling and why they had stopped playing. I mentioned that I might have heard anger in the chaotic part and I wondered if others were feeling the same. I could tell that I had hit a nerve. A wall of resistance sprang up. I repeated myself, stating that I did think that it would be very normal to feel angry because one had not had a nice Christmas. The boys began to hit the drums randomly. Were they trying to stop me? I asked for their attention, struggling with the bad feeling of having lost them. They refused to pay attention and I knew that I had to wrap this up.

I acknowledged everybody's active participation as well as the importance of listening. I realized that this was only Session 5 and that I should not expect too much from these children at such an early stage. I did not want to scare them off. I wanted to give them some time to process individually before we had to end the session so I suggested that we continue exploring these Christmas themes next time around.

Feelings of sadness, anger, abandonment, and loneliness surfaced in subsequent sessions related to Christmas. I heard stories from children who received no gifts, saw sad eyes talk about missing family members and celebrations. Unfortunately, I was usually aware that we would probably be unable to work through these issues and feelings sufficiently to bring about real and profound change. There was simply not enough time, too many children bearing heavy burdens, and the constant interruptions caused by the ever-present and powerful resistance emanating from several of the boys.

Discussion of Session 5:

As transference, countertransference, and resistance are integral to my work, let me first provide descriptions of each as I understand them.

Transference

Priestley describes transference as follows:

> Freud referred to the phenomenon of transference as "wrong association," as he recognized that some of his patients were regarding him with emotions that were relevant to previous relationships in their lives, usual parental. . . .The therapist, however, does not react in the way that earlier object—whether parent or parent substitute—did in her early life, and his response and interpretations enable the patient to liberate herself from her repetition compulsion and begin to experiment with new ways of acting and responding (1994, p. 77).

Countertransference

The following is a clear and simple definition of countertransference: "Broadly speaking, countertransference describes the emotions that the therapist develops toward the client in response to the client in sessions" (Pavlicevic, 1997, p. 166). Priestley describes it further:

> The therapist may find that either gradually as he works, or with a suddenness that may alarm him, he becomes aware of the sympathetic resonance of some of the patient's feelings through his own emotional and/or somatic awareness. Often these are repressed emotions that are not yet available to the patient's conscious awareness. . . (1994, p. 87).

Resistance

Austin and Dvorkin describe resistance in psychoanalytical terms: ". . . a paradoxical phenomenon regularly encountered in the course of insight oriented psychotherapy" (1998, p. 423). Priestley's work with resistance is based on the classical psychoanalytical model. She described how levels of resistance surface in music and are used diagnostically in work with psychotic patients. I found the following definition by Bruscia to be useful for my description and analysis of the resistance that occurred in my work. "Like defenses, resistance is healthy when it serves to protect the client from a harmful or premature lifting of repression and it is unhealthy when it prevents the client from benefiting the most from therapy and living a full life" (Bruscia, 1998, p. 41).

Transferences in Session 5

Transference was continuous within the group. The neglect and abuse that normally occurred in the children's lives was reflected unconsciously in the music and expressed as constant chaos. They came from chaotic situations; they had no consistency in their lives, no limit setting, and no stable parental love. They were abused. In return they needed to do the same to the group, and to me. Perhaps this familiar pattern made them feel safe. The music helped to translate this transference, to bring it alive and into awareness.

When I started working on this case study I listened once again to all of my recordings. I found it shocking how chaotic most of the sessions had been. Many began with children yelling at each other, laughing, and cursing. It usually took me a long time to focus their attention. I had this picture in my head of wasps flying around the room frantically trying to sting each other. I had to find ways to break through the resistance and chaos, to show them different ways of interacting, to create a comfortable place for them without the chaos.

In this session, my role shifted, or was two-dimensional. For the girls, I took on the role of the "good mother," providing them with a supportive shoulder, embracing their sadness and encouraging them to express it. I chose the guitar as a harmonic instrument of soft presence in shape and sound. I strummed D minor and A minor, providing a holding musical container that represented the "good mother." I chose the minor mode as a response to the open, sad sounding melody that had developed. For the boys, I was sometimes the "bad mother" who neglected them and upon whom they therefore projected a message of anger and frustration.

I struggled during the moments of interruption and obvious resistance. I felt powerless, anxious, and at times angry. Was it all their anger that I felt, or was it my own anger that had been triggered by them that I needed to work on?

In supervision I learned that I did experience some of their anger expressed in the music or verbally, sometimes to a point where I felt tense physically. I had to keep my focus, to accept that it was not my own anger, to take a deep breath, pause, and relax and then to go on. To reiterate, it seemed that the children, especially the boys, had to "transfer" their "abuse" onto me because that was the method of relating that they knew and understood.

I had to look at my own memories, my past. Before my present incarnation as a music therapist I had been a schoolteacher and I had to discipline the children. I remembered feelings of inadequacy. I struggled with the idea that their expressions of anger had not been directed at me personally, but at that point in my life I lacked the training to properly evaluate this dynamic. I am now able to comprehend it intellectually, but still need to revisit this issue in supervision.

The girls brought in different dynamics by choosing to express their sadness. In some sessions they joined the boys in the musical expression of anger although they often needed encouragement, which implied to me that they were normally afraid to bear the consequences of expressing their true feelings. Over time, I learned how to flow with this resistance and what the resistance symbolized for these children.

Countertransference in Session 5

My own countertransference emerged. At times I wondered, "Am I a 'good enough mother' for them?" These feelings stem from my own personal struggle as the mother of two little boys. I always want to be the perfect mother and have had to learn that there are limits, to accept my weaknesses, and to let go of my overly high expectations.

There were times when the children's verbal or musical actions mirrored their feelings of low self-esteem and inadequacy. When projected by the music these feelings made me, the therapist, feel inadequate. Often I was unsure how and why I ended up feeling this way. I am aware that this explanation might sound diffuse and leave the reader dissatisfied, but, e-Countertransference, as Priestley calls it, is a very difficult countertransference to describe or analyze in measurable terms.

Working with Resistance

Resistance occurred verbally and musically in this session with these children. Their resistance protected them from getting hurt where they had been hurt before, i.e., a healthy form of resistance. I observed verbal resistance when the children were laughing, interrupting, and opposing during moments that opened up issues that addressed family life, home, holidays, and parental love. Whenever musical or verbal interventions touched their vulnerability, the children responded with healthy resistance, banging aggressively on drums, cymbals, and triangles. It was not always clear to me whether these were expressions of pure pain or resistance. Sometimes they played their resistance in raps and blues in such a way that they used funny words and metaphors to represent serious, sad issues. I had to find ways of working with their resistance in order to keep them protected. At times, I just let them play or state their resistance. There is a method, explained by George J. Thompson (1983), called "verbal judo," which I tried to incorporate into my work, based upon the idea that in order to break resistance one has to go with it. This can be done verbally as well as musically. I allowed them to play "chaos" which sometimes resolved the tension, and gave them ways to work together.

When A. "resisted" at the beginning of our musical example by hitting the cymbal like a warning after G initiated the soft, sad melody on the marimba phone, he needed reassurance from his friends. He needed to couple up with B. and later with C. He clearly stated in his music: "Not me! I am not going there." He was not ready to expose himself and/or his feelings. He was protecting himself. He showed healthy resistance. The children have needed this type of self-protection in order to survive their worlds. To do away with it, they would have to go through an extensive learning process in which they would have to be taught how to meet their needs. I sent a message of sympathy to him by letting him be, and to the girls by joining and staying with their music at the beginning.

Giggling and laughing are very common resistance behaviors. Unfortunately, this behavior often led to group conflict. Children who felt laughed at shut down, and it sometimes took a substantial amount of negotiation by the therapist to enable both sides to express themselves. That is why I would identify this as unhealthy resistance. It obstructed the therapeutic process for individual children, as well as for the group as a whole.

How do I work with this resistance? When A.'s "resistance" first surfaced, I focused my musical response on the girls, hoping to draw them out. I tried to encourage them not to back down through facial and body expression. Later, when A. and C. coupled up, I let the group take responsibility. When E. gave C. an angry look I decided not to intervene, but to let things flow until a moment of musical and emotional togetherness developed. When C.'s cymbal smashing, a sign of resistance, interrupted us once again I was hesitant, not knowing what to do. The girls stopped and the boys kept on. I did not want to end the music entirely. I felt that perhaps the boys had a different message to convey, or needed to explore their resistance, so I went with them. In retrospect, I feel certain that it would have been a mistake to stop them. They needed to express their anger even though they were not able to acknowledge the feeling. I pointed out, in the discussion that took place during verbal processing, how unhealthy resistant behavior can hurt others' feelings and prevent them from sharing any issues in the future.

The children stated their resistance in the music by expressing emotions, but they were usually unable to connect these expressions to their thoughts afterwards. Often there was a disconnection between what had been expressed musically and what was said verbally. Some children played very repetitive motifs, melodies, and rhythms demonstrating resistance. Others stopped precipitously or refused to play at all. Sometimes the tempo, or a sudden change of tempo, indicated resistance.

In summary, the children often expressed healthy resistance in order to prevent a premature and potentially harmful lifting of repression at this early stage of therapy. Unhealthy resistance surfaced when the children acted very disruptively and prevented the most basic exchange of ideas or feelings. At times, this unhealthy resistance triggered feelings of annoyance and anger in me. I had to address this issue over and over again in supervision, to look carefully at my own anger. Reacting in the moment required an ability to identify the type of resistance and to apply suitable interventions. When I felt overwhelmed, I often just took a deep breath, spoke to myself, and went on. Resistance is a very big issue in my work with these children and a constant field of battle.

Example 2: Song Writing

Session 25

Description

In this session I started talking about termination. We improvised on the emotional issues involved with saying good-bye. At the last session I suggested that the group create a rap with the title "Good-Bye." I split the group in half and asked a few boys to write the lyrics and the other half to create the music.

Here are one boy's lyrics. I call him U. and chose his lyrics because he was leading this group and his lyrics were most significant.

It's Hard to Say Good-Bye

It's hard to say good-bye
Why?
Because it seems like the person
You say bye to gonna die
Some people will cry when they say bye,
Just be strong and say "Hi"
Just be like me
And don't cry
Act like as if you was gonna see the person again and say bye

Chorus: It's hard to say good-bye

Afterward I acknowledged U.'s courage and ability to put his thoughts and feelings into rhyme. The group had supported him nicely by providing a tight rap rhythm. They had worked independently, but as a group, on a piece of music communicating their ideas.

I asked the children what they thought about what U. had to say. One of the boys (W.) said: "He is right, we just say bye and know that we see you again some time." I had to explain that I would not be coming back and that only the accidental chance of running into each other remained. I could tell at this point that they were hoping for some reassurance that this was not in fact the end. I shared with them how I felt saying good-bye and that I would miss them. They wanted to know exactly why I had to leave, and once again an angry dynamic surfaced. The group started acting out, children were laughing, screaming at each other. When I mentioned that my two little boys needed attention too, some children quieted down a bit. We ended the session with a long "good-bye" song wherein everybody again expressed what they had to say. I realized afterward that it would have taken years of trust and relationship building with them in order to process their feelings in a more profound manner.

Discussion of Session 25:

Transference

I again took on a role of an adult in their lives who had abandoned them. I accepted and understood their feelings of anger. I thought mentioning my own responsibilities as a mother of two boys helped them in accepting my parting.

Countertransference

When the children played the rap and this boy rapped his own words, tears came into my eyes. Their good-bye pains were completely conflated with my own feelings. How well they had learned to not allow themselves to feel the pain of saying good-bye. Here I was "abandoning" them, a presumably recurring phenomenon in their lives. And I, too, could relate to their feelings. My mother worked full time during my childhood and was an elusive presence.

I had also to face my own feelings of guilt and responsibility. I tried to find a good replacement for myself to help alleviate some of these feelings. I used supervision to take a fresh look at other partings in my past. I live an ocean away from my own family. Being separated and saying good-bye to them over and over again has spurred a whole set of personal issues. While attempting to "rescue" these children, I needed to attend to my own neglected inner child, to concentrate on these issues in order to enable myself to feel and understand the countertransference that surfaced repeatedly in my work.

Resistance

Again the children expressed a lot of anger, sadness, and healthy resistance when acknowledging any feelings of pain. Some children laughed paradoxically while playing and singing. Some looked rather sad. It was a strange dynamic in the room. I wanted to help them to experience the feelings of a real good-bye, but I understood and accepted the denial that allowed protection.

Other Challenges

Lastly, I would like to mention another challenge that arose in this work, the cultural gap between the children and myself. I had to learn about their values and cultural upbringing, which are very different from mine. Many of these children grew up in religious homes, where music is always an important aspect of their lives. Many of them have such a good feel for rhythm and bring a natural understanding of the blues, gospel, jazz, and rap into the work. I suspect I did not feel much resistance to me, even though I am a white person, because I brought music, and because I knew their music. The underlying issues of whether I understood or could accept the way in which they were brought up, the way they interacted, remained. I feel that music can really be a wonderful bridge between cultural groups. The implication of these cultural issues for music therapy is a topic unto itself and should be discussed and researched separately. I can only refer to the writings of Joseph Moreno (1988), who contributed much to my understanding of cultural issues arising in my work with these children.

DISCUSSION

This case study has shown how AMT techniques can be utilized, with adaptations for a group setting, with this population. Through this work, it became clear to me that these techniques were essential for in-depth work. They helped the children to become more aware of their feelings and conflicts, to develop better communication skills and to express their feelings appropriately.

My method fluctuates between free-flowing improvisation and structure. Structure is absolutely necessary in this work. It gives the children a feeling of belonging, containment, and safety. The structure was provided by the use of pre-composed songs, and creating blues and raps. It offered a musical container in which the children learned how to express themselves. The free-flowing improvisations usually had a theme to begin with. When less structure was provided, the children had to learn how to express themselves appropriately.

The challenges I faced in this work were varied. I had to learn to develop an "improvisational attitude," by which I mean that I had to dispense with rigid plans and be willing to let the session flow in a more spontaneous and extemporaneous fashion. Every session was different and often started out in chaos. Children came in with a whole spectrum of energies after a long day at school. It often felt as if everything was out of control, which was very difficult for me because I like to be in control. There was no way to prepare or to have a plan. I had to find ways to ground them. I solved this problem by drumming and chanting at the beginning of the session which then developed into a natural way of inquiring about their day and how they felt. They often responded by saying that they felt either happy or sad. The children did not seem to know subtle shades of feelings and I believe that the music helped them to better express these nuances.

Over time, I developed a typical session structure: 1) Hello, 2) Drumming and chanting, 3) Use of precomposed songs/songwriting (blues or rap), 4) Free-flowing improvisation, and 5) Good-bye.

I often wished that I could see some of the children individually in order to meet their needs more effectively. So many issues arose that never had a chance to be sufficiently processed within a group setting, both musically and verbally. Statements of resistance too often interrupted moments of deep musical connection. On the one hand, the group's dynamics did not always support a real therapeutic outcome, and yet, on the other hand, the group setting protected children from being overly exposed. They had a chance to model and to learn from each other, to develop a strong bond and community that might be of help in times of distress and loneliness.

CONCLUSIONS

I will end now with some thoughts and conclusions about some of the positive outcomes for the children and myself. Music therapy came to be a special time for the children, a safe place where they were allowed to express what they had been suppressing. They probably showed affection toward me because I was one of the few adults in their lives who did not yell at them and who treated them with respect and love. Music is clearly a meaningful medium of expression for them, since they bring a rich, strong musical background with them. All of them were talented and music gave them a field of immediate gratification as well as a base for practicing their communication skills.

For this kind of work, my organizational strengths and love of control seemed not to do me any good. I had to learn to improvise constantly, to feel comfortable having no plan and to let go. I learned to enjoy that side of the work. It is delightful to experience the spontaneity of a child. Slowly, I was able to "go with the flow," to read body language, to react quickly to very subtle express-ions, and to turn them into meaningful therapeutic events.

These children contributed immensely to my understanding of how AMT works. I had never wanted to work with children on the verge of adolescence because I was afraid of the challenges, but I have become convinced that this work can be very gratifying and fun. It was a joy to see them grow and change, and it has motivated me to seek work with this age group in a public school system in the near future.

REFERENCES

Austin, D. & Dvorkin, J. M. (1998). "Resistance in Individual Music Therapy." In K. E. Bruscia (ed.), *The Dynamics of Music Psychotherapy*. Gilsum, NH: Barcelona Publishers.

Bruscia, K. E. (1998). "The Dynamics of Transference." In K. E. Bruscia (ed.), *The Dynamics of Music Psychotherapy*. Gilsum, NH: Barcelona Publishers.

Kowski, J. (2002). "'The Sound of Silence'—The Use of AMT-Techniques with a Non-Verbal Client." In J. Th. Eschen (ed.), *Analytical Music Therapy*. London: Jessica Kingsley Publishers.

Moreno, J. (1988). "Multicultural Music Therapy: The World Connection," *Journal of Music Therapy*, 25 (1), 17–27.

Pavlicevic, M. (1997). *Music Therapy in Context*. London: Jessica Kingsley Publishers.

Priestley, M. (1975). *Music Therapy in Action*. St. Louis, MO: MMB Music.

Priestley. M. (1994). *Essays on Analytical Music Therapy*. Phoenixville, PA: Barcelona Publishers.

Robbins, A. (1994). *A Multi-Modal Approach to Creative Art Therapy*. London: Jessica Kingsley Publishers.

Scheiby, B. (1998). "The Role of Musical Countertransference in Analytical Music Therapy." In K. E. Bruscia (ed.), *The Dynamics of Music Psychotherapy*. Gilsum, NH: Barcelona Publishers.

Thompson, G. J. (1983). *Verbal Judo: Words as a Force Option*. Springfield, IL: Charles C. Thomas Publisher.

Wigram, T., & De Backer, J. (eds.) (1999). *Clinical Applications of Music Therapy in Psychiatry*. London: Jessica Kingsley Publishers.

Winnicot, D. W. (1971). *Playing and Reality*. London: Tavistock Publications.

Yalisove, D. L. (1997). *Essential Papers on Addiction*. New York: New York University Press.

Case Six

THE VOICE FROM THE COCOON:
SONG AND IMAGERY IN TREATING TRAUMA
IN CHILDREN

Susan Bray Wesley

ABSTRACT

This case describes a four-month course of treatment for a ten-year-old boy with a life history of physical, emotional, and sexual abuse. The treatment included singing, and music relaxation experiences based on a modified form of the Bonny Method of Guided Imagery and Music. By providing access to the sound of his own voice and creating a small repertoire of imagery skills, the patient was able to demonstrate initial signs of self-monitoring and self-control over explosive behavior.

INTRODUCTION

This chapter describes one case from a project examining whether therapeutically based music interventions increase treatment efficacy for inpatient children at a psychiatric hospital when including ambient sound as a contributing psychological stressor. The purpose of psychiatric hospitalization is to stabilize, mediate and regulate, or change behavior. To that end, the interventions discussed, in the case which follows, were compliant with the hospital purpose but were unlike the traditional interventions used on the unit. Through the use of song and modified Bonny Method of Guided Imagery and Music, the patient demonstrated elementary acquisition of behavioral regulation by attending to his body's cues related to his trauma history and auditory triggers.

BACKGROUND INFORMATION

The Setting

The setting of the study was The Acadia Hospital in Bangor, Maine. The hospital contracted for six hours of music therapy to serve children both in outpatient and inpatient treatment programs. Music therapy techniques employed with these children included large group music/movement, small group improvisation, and an evening lullaby time (inpatient only).

The Ambient Sound Environment

Trauma literature is rich with information about what can/may trigger flashbacks and assaultive or withdrawal behaviors. Many of these triggers are sensory. After working on the unit for eighteen months, and experiencing such auditory assaults as doors slamming, overhead pages and codes in the midst of quiet-time, carpet scrubbers, vacuums, turbo carpet drying fans, shouts, and cries of distress and rage (all being part of that ambient sound space), a study with a focus on auditory triggers seemed logical to me. Seeing so many children (and staff as well) in a state of tension and operating almost from a startle mode piqued my curiosity about how much the ambient sound of the unit could be contributing to patients' behavior.

I felt I was on the right track when I further investigated what the research literature said, or more important did not say, about sound/acoustics relative to the impact of the design of healthcare facilities on patient outcomes. In particular, the 1998 meta-analysis of research on healthcare design for healthcare facilities, conducted by the Center for Healthcare Design, identified only twenty-five studies referencing noise and music, out of the 78,761 titles that were examined for other design concepts such as way-finding and color (Rubin, Owens & Golden, 1999).

The most powerful affirmation for me, however, came through some of the neurological research literature associated with trauma. Several researchers have documented that brain cells can be "recruited" for particular purposes as a result of strong interactive experiences; in other words, extra cells might be recruited for hearing rather then for seeing. Furthermore, deprivation or alteration of needed experiences can produce a range of deficits. It made sense that trauma could interrupt emotional development leading to deprivation or alteration of sensory experiences by shutting down, so to speak. Therefore, if auditory stimulation triggered flashbacks for some patients, primitive or developmentally delayed behaviors might result. This was what I believed I was seeing in several children and one in particular.

The Patient

Bruce was a ten-year-old boy admitted for hospitalization. He was removed from his parents early in his life due to severe physical and emotional abuse and neglect. He also had been subjected to repeated sexual abuse. During one of his foster-care placements, he again incurred sexual abuse by yet another caregiver. Bruce's behavior became increasingly uncontrollable, assaultive, and destructive.

He was given the diagnosis of post-traumatic stress disorder with dissociative features at the time of his admission. On the unit, Bruce became immediately known for "that look." It was described by staff as "wild, terrified eyes," and became the cue for a major meltdown which often led to a net restraint on his bed or a papoose and medication.

Bruce arrived in the late summer and joined the weekly song/movement group with the rest of the milieu. Sessions are forty-five-minutes long in a large group format. All the children (census of twenty) are expected to attend unless they are in visits, with clinicians, or unsafe. Bruce was extremely quiet and rigid in both posture and presence, but when he began to sing his affect softened. He had a rough, but potentially strong, boy soprano voice. Bruce did not attend the two sessions following his first session, because he was either asleep from medication or in restraint. The next couple of times that he did attend, he was only able to maintain appropriate behavior for a short time and would have to leave due to his silliness. I also tried to include him in the small group music improvisation sessions but, once again, Bruce's attendance was minimal. Because of assaultive behavior earlier in the day, he was often medicated and sleeping, restrained, or room-based. In many ways, Bruce was typical of most of the children on the unit in that his diagnosis of trauma was based on a history of severe abuse and neglect.

It appeared to me that Bruce was one of the patients who might benefit most from auditory interventions based on what might be auditory triggers. My hypothesis was based on reports from his staff and clinician that his symptom of "the look" was the only available cue for when he would go into a major bout of assaultive and dangerous behavior. They also believed that his triggers were not visual, or at least visible, since there appeared to be "nothing going on in the room" when he decompensated. In addition, I noticed that he liked to sing, was good at it, and perhaps there was an auditory connection to his trauma, as well as possible therapeutic interventions.

TREATMENT

Bruce's treatment consisted of two phases after his music therapy assessment. The first phase was twelve weekly forty-five-minute sessions held in the evenings. These sessions focused on active music-making for energy release and raising self-esteem, and relaxation skill development. The second phase consisted of daily twenty- to thirty-minute sessions planned for eight weeks. The focus of these sessions was to increase Bruce's awareness of his behaviors that were stimulated by sounds generated basically from the unit milieu, and to increase his experience with therapeutic music exercises that could be used autonomously when Bruce recognized his anxiety being triggered.

Music Therapy Assessment

Bruce's formal assessment was based on a modified form of the Multimodal Psychiatric Music Therapy assessment by Cassity & Cassity (1998), after which he was introduced to a series of music activities. The activities, after the formal assessment, included Bruce's exploration of various percussion instruments and singing in order to assess such skills as ability to keep a steady beat, identification of basic rhythm instruments, and comprehension of music elements like dynamics, tempo, and melodic direction. Bruce agreed that he would like to continue to meet with me once a week to use music for "getting his sillies out" and for relaxation techniques.

Treatment Plan and Process—Phase 1

Bruce's treatment was designed for forty-five-minute sessions once a week during the 5:00-7:00 evening shift and began the week following his music therapy assessment. Bruce's goals included demonstration of confidence in singing; identification of specific moods or emotions through the selection and playing of instruments; and relaxation using music and imagery. The goals were intended to help Bruce develop conscious awareness of his auditory triggers and how he could use music to interrupt the violent thought process that sprang from such triggers. This plan was followed for twelve consecutive weeks. My approach to each of Bruce's sessions depended on his psychological and emotional availability on any given evening or day, due to his overall volatility.

Session 1—Bruce's first priority was to build a song list and to sing as he built it. Bruce chose traditional children's songs like "This Land Is Your Land," "This Old Man," and "Bingo." He became relaxed and laughed at "silly" words as he sang. I introduced him to the song "Don Gato." It is in a minor key and is about a cat that falls off a roof and supposedly dies, but then springs back to life when carried by the fish market. The song is usually sung fast but Bruce asked to slow it down and his affect became pensive. I asked Bruce to name some "feelings" and he said sad, upset, angry, and mixed-up. Then I asked him about what he did when he felt these. He described coping skills, not his behavior. He said self-time-out for upset; deep joint compression for angry; and blanket wrap for mixed-up. He had nothing to say for sadness. I noticed, too, that all the coping skills he provided isolated him from others and focused on "containing through pressure" any potential explosion resulting from feeling upset, angry, or mixed-up. Perhaps his inability to articulate clearly about what he felt during any of the emotions he named was a defense. If it was, it was quite unconscious. Having observed his "wild eyes," and looks of terror when he entered a bout of assaultiveness, I had no doubt that he had few, if any, words to describe what indeed was coursing through him at those times.

Bruce was quite willing to work with me. Perhaps his lack of resistance to my meeting with him, even at the start, had to do with the quiet space and the one-to-one interaction. We used a well-lit office with several windows at the end of the corridor. It was carpeted and not cluttered and I had many instruments nearby which Bruce found intriguing.

Session 2—Bruce asked to use the large elastic band with me. He said that he had too much energy and wanted to "tug and pull." So we did, to some hammered dulcimer jigs. Then he asked for the drums and "pounded." At this point, Bruce asked about relaxation to music and if he could try it. I showed him a bag filled with large colored scarves and asked if he wanted to use any for a cover or pillow or blanket. He chose red and green. After a breathing exercise, I played Respighi's "The Nightingale" using a voice-over that included clouds, birds, a big tree, and Bruce sitting on a big rock. I chose a setting that would be familiar and grounding to Bruce. He liked being outdoors and had talked about his backyard from time to time. His comment at the close of the session was that he felt calmer and liked the use of the colors and music.

Bruce chose red and green, the colors of "stop and go" or "heat and growth," and unprompted, he had asked to try the relaxation.

Session 3—Bruce asked to do only the relaxation exercise. He chose a red scarf and explained that it would be his cape. I used new-age music infused with bird and stream sounds and suggested that he begin in his backyard again and let his imagination wander with the music. During the music, he reported, "a bear with cubs is playing around and catching something in a stream." There was a gap in his comments and then he saw "a couple of birds—blue jays" and then nothing.

Bruce used the music for imaging, without my guiding, without difficulty. Bruce chose red again and requested only the relaxation with music and imagery activity. The bear cubs (siblings) were with the mother and they were all at play but also "catching" something in the stream—perhaps this was something to nourish. The possibility that Bruce might feel at some level as if he was being nourished occurred to me briefly, but his reference of missing his brothers, from an earlier conversation, made me wonder if he was recalling a playful time with his siblings.

Session 4—Bruce chose hand drums and tambourines for improvised conversation and then wanted to sing. I asked Bruce if he had ever heard himself sing. He said no and added that he did not think he was a very good singer. I felt sad that Bruce did not know that he had a good voice. I wondered if that could be a reason that he had no named behavior or coping skill for sad. When he sang, his affect always brightened and that felt like a clue to some possible sense of security deep inside to which he might learn to connect. I felt more strongly that Bruce had "learned" the coping skills of choice on the unit, but none of these addressed sadness or ways of dealing with self-comfort, unless he was to "talk" to someone.

Session 5—Bruce began with a lumi stick accompaniment to recorded music followed by a song and Bruce playing the Omnicord. He asked to do the relaxation next followed by the elastic band. However, before we settled into the relaxation, we were interrupted for his evening medications. Shortly after the nurse left, I noticed a very distant look on Bruce's face, and I became aware of some commotion in the hallway. Then he looked right at me and asked if he could leave in order to go and use a coping skill in his room—"I feel unsafe." My reaction to the session was one of anger and affirmation. I was angry about the interruption, but the observation of Bruce's complete shift of attention and affect affirmed my belief that his auditory system was hyper-alert and affirmed the reality that our safe container could be easily invaded.

Session 6—There was a scattered and somber feeling as Bruce had difficulty deciding what activity to start with. After wandering around the room, he asked to sing. His first choice was "Don Gato" and then "Silent Night," followed by two more Christmas songs (it was two weeks until Christmas). Then Bruce asked for the elastic band and we did some relatively energetic tugging. When I offered the possibility of doing some imaging, he became very ambivalent and said no. It felt like the session was a rebound to Session 5 and we were back into the "getting to Trust you" stage. Considering his choices to sing and tug/pull it felt as if Bruce was struggling with a loss.

Session 7—I suggested to Bruce that he try his hand at composing lyrics. I wanted to assess his emotions or moods through a story line. He chose dinosaurs for the subject. Although a primitive and potentially aggressive subject, Bruce's dinosaur was a colorful (purple, green, blue, and yellow) plant eater by the name of Stevie. Stevie was "long" and "liked to eat leaves and ivy." When I prompted the thought of a carnivorous dinosaur by asking "But does he eat the ants?" Bruce became very playful and exclaimed "No, I said PLANTS." I noted that purple is the "mixed-up" color resulting from blue and red, sometimes considered "dragon fight" colors or colors of separation from the parents. Green was again included and perhaps as a sense of "re"-newal or potential like spring or the "go" of a traffic light. Then the colors of blue and yellow combine to make green but were named separately. Depending on the shade of blue, it can represent an engulfing maternal connection. Yellow can be interpreted as related to solar or masculine. My assessment was that Bruce was beginning to connect, albeit unconsciously, through his musical experiences, to additional means of expression and communication. Through my various trainings in color interpretation, my interpretation was that the yellow of the masculine was combining with the blue of the maternal and perhaps Bruce's courage was growing to connect with his own young masculine nature within a nurturing environment of the music with me.

Session 8—Twenty minutes into the session, after playing a drum, bells, and triangle, Bruce suddenly asked to leave to go to his room to use a coping skill. It was three days after Christmas and the milieu was chaotic. Bruce's affect that night was flat and his day had been uneventful. His lack of interest in the session felt odd. It was, however, another opportunity for me to encourage his decision-making process about coping skills that he could choose to keep him safe. It was also another opportunity for me to observe that with a highly stimulating environment (holiday visits, toys, candy, and "vacation-like" schedule), Bruce was seeking less stimulation not only in his instrument choices, but also overall in a shorter session.

Session 9—Holidays were over and Bruce requested an imagery session and chose a lapis blue scarf. He asked to be wrapped up in it like the "blanket-wrap coping skill." I called it his cocoon and used a voice-over about the image of a cocoon being warmed by the sun and held securely by its wrap while connected firmly to the limb of a big tree. The music was new-age piano music with nature sounds. It supported the concept of gentleness and security. Bruce drew a picture of his cocoon. From that session on Bruce referred to the "cocoon wrap" as a favorite place. With this comment, it felt as if he had made another connection. He integrated the use of music, a safe image, and a unit skill as a "cocoon wrap" and it was completely his. The color choice of lapis blue can be interpreted as resting in the arms of a kind and gentle mother figure.

Session 10—Bruce began by playing lumi sticks to an upbeat recording. Then he requested the music and imagery relaxation. His colors were blue and green. He wanted to lie in the "grass" and have the "sky" above him. I used a ten-minute cut from a minimalist new-age CD (wind sounds included) with a voice-over that encouraged the stability of being supported by the earth in his grassy place and watched over by the bright blue sky. He stayed with that image and drew a "grass and sky" picture. The colors of bright green and lapis blue can be interpreted as healthy choices and the fact that Bruce designated them to be the grass and sky and he would lay in the grass was a grounding choice. The drawing of his imagery showed that he could attend for over ten minutes to a positive image. His affect was positive and pleasant throughout the session.

Session 11—Bruce asked for the music and imagery with "the music I used last time." He chose the lapis blue cloth, asked me to roll him up cocoon like, and off he went for the ten-minute cut. When the music ended, he went directly to drawing. I had put out black paper for this session, as an introduction to the concept of brightness even in darkness, and Bruce did not question it. He drew stars in the sky, a tree, and a critter emerging from the cocoon. His cocoon and the emerging critter were rusty brown; however, on black paper it looked red. This did not seem to disturb him. His affect was positive and his demeanor quiet. He showed no signs of anxiety or tension building. The choice of a blue wrap and the resulting red cocoon and critter felt congruent with my sense of his inner struggle, red sometimes representing anger. Perhaps his awareness of his unconscious anger/rage was becoming conscious. Bits of starlight were shining on the cocoon, as it emerged under the night sky. The tree was only an outline, and although its roots appeared important since the ground bulged, the trunk ended definitively with a line drawn across the top with the canopy like a spiked head of hair coming out of the top, simply sketchy green strokes. The canopy's growth appeared to be stunted or at least delayed.

I had a growing concern about the frequency and the possible dependency Bruce might be having on me. I was providing the music and some image suggestions and of course the breathing exercise. I decided it was time to increase my effort in guiding and encouraging Bruce's awareness and use of his singing voice. My biggest concern was that if Bruce was discharged at anytime soon, would he be more or less vulnerable to the auditory onslaught of the "normal" world? When the auditory triggers caught his attention, instead of the assaultive responses he had learned from his inner voice that said "survive at any cost," perhaps he could sing to calm himself.

Session 12—I suggested to Bruce that we make a tape so that he could have a "sing-along" anytime he chose. He was fine with the idea and we used his song list to select tunes. His reaction to his own voice was "that's me?" He was very pleased and even chose to add simple percussion instruments to his singing. Bruce's reaction and sense of pride in his first efforts to construct his own tape were powerful. He sat taller, smiled, and even asked to run the tape machine. At the end of this session I decided to redesign his treatment plan and process.

Treatment Plan and Process—Phase 2

Bruce's psychiatrist and clinician were in full support of an increase in music therapy sessions. The schedule was for daily thirty-minute sessions for eight weeks beginning in the first full week of February. Bruce's new goal was to practice consistent grounding and self-affirming music exercises. Bruce received a residential placement and left after four weeks.

Session objectives were to demonstrate competence in (1) singing with his tape, (2) relaxation using music and imagery, and (3) drawing his imagery for concretization. Time and location for sessions was midafternoon in Bruce's room. Bruce missed only three of the possible sixteen sessions, due to assaultive behavior, over the four weeks.

Session 13—Bruce sang with his tape for the first ten minutes and then chose blue and green cloth for his imagery. At the close of listening selection, Bruce drew himself positioned between the green and blue colors of the cloths he chose. He titled the picture "Cocoona." This appeared to be a reinforcement of sessions 9 and 10, but the drawing was more chaotic and scribbled in appearance—much like a description of the auditory environment. Although Bruce's door could be closed for our sessions, the transmission of sound was far greater than in the therapy room, due to the proximity of his room to the general activity on the unit.

Session 14—Bruce sang using his headset and tape, but only for a few minutes, and then asked me to sing with him. After two songs, he was ready for the relaxation exercise. The picture he drew afterward, "Dream World," showed a tree similar, but not the same, in design from an earlier cocoon picture. This tree was solid and appeared to be very firmly planted. The canopy, although still very stunted, was now colored in with firm strokes. Two birds were flying nearby and the round blue cocoon was suspended in space. It appeared that Bruce was feeling unsure about just where he was and that although the comfortable blue color of the cocoon could be taken as positive, the fact that the cocoon was unattached and in midair conveyed a sense of being ungrounded and a lack of security. The change of location and time seemed to be reflected in his picture.

Session 15—Bruce sang only three songs and then asked to move to the relaxation. I suggested a very tactile image of a sandy beach and the ocean. Bruce said he knew what it felt like to walk in the sand and wade in the water, and also talked about how bright the sun could be shining off the water. This seemed as if it could be the next positive image that could "ground" him, and the more grounded or concrete to his experience Bruce could be with his images, the less likely he would be to dissociate. I chose Respighi's "The Nightingale" which offered sounds that can be interpreted as reflective, like sun reflecting off the water. It appeared to be an appropriate shift because Bruce placed himself standing next to a palm tree in his drawing that day. He called the picture "Palm Tree." His palm tree had no coconuts like some children draw. It was simply a "palm" tree. The canopy offered more protection/shade than his cocoon picture trees and it was one of only three pictures in which Bruce drew himself. The representation was a stick figure, but this was the first time he placed a likeness to his human form in his drawings.

Session 16—Prior to the session, Bruce's one-to-one staff approached me to let me know that Bruce was to have a family visit (foster family) and had asked his staff to ask me if his session could be adjusted. I agreed. Bruce sang two songs and then asked for the relaxation. He chose a royal blue scarf "to be underwater." He asked for the headset, instead of the boombox, since noise in the hallway had increased. (I reminded him of the time, but he did not want to end the session at that point in spite of the visit.) The music for this imagery was Respighi's "Venus." Bruce's picture was of a turtle under the water and his imagery storyline was that he was on a raft on the water and dived in. He saw white and purple crabs and lobsters. He was swimming and then noticed three or four sea turtles swimming above him, so he swam up to join them. He said that the water felt good, but that it was hot coming up into the boat. He also said that he got some seashells and sand. He drew a green turtle under dark blue water. The perspective was as if looking down into the water. He called the turtle Harry and the picture simply "Sea Turtle." Bruce's descriptions and multiple images of creatures appropriate to the environment conveyed a sense of his feeling at home and, as he described the coming up into the boat as hot, I wondered if it felt like being a "fish out of water." His visit was an "out of the routine" event for him and his desire to continue the music therapy session as planned rather than cutting it short felt like a means of acclimating himself, particularly as he included the bringing up of seashells and sand, very tangible images.

Session 17—Bruce demanded, "You sing a couple" and asked that I add/sing a couple of songs for his tape, but he chose only "Michael, Row the Boat Ashore." Bruce appeared fidgety and in a "clockwatching" mode. He chose the blue scarf again and also the use of the headset for the relaxation. The music was new age with nature sounds. His picture was of a whale jumping in the water. Although the color of the ocean he drew was not alarming, the fact that the whale was jumping and he was fidgety implied the possibility of the need for something to surface, and quickly and aggressively. Two hours later as I went by his room I saw he was in a restraint. He asked me if he could have his song tape, which was then placed in a boombox on the desk near him. Staff reported that this had a calming and positive effect on him as he sang along to some songs. The fact that the day before his session was canceled due to his being restrained and medicated after an especially difficult morning, and his fidgety behavior, added to my concern about the impact of his family visit. I also recalled how his desire to keep the session as planned the day of the visit felt to me like his effort to ground himself as much as possible. But now he was in the "net" (restraint), the fish caught, and I reflected on his "fish out of water" and "jumping whale."

Session 18—"Can you play my tape?" Bruce was in a restraint when I arrived. He had had a very assaultive morning, but after fifteen minutes of singing, he asked if the restraint could be removed. I called the staff and Bruce was assessed as being safe. The restraint was removed. The session continued with the relaxation, but no colored scarf. Bruce also chose not to draw. He described the colors and shapes of his imagery as brown, blue, and white ovals, triangles, and rectangles. Reflecting on his drawing from the previous day, the "Jumping Whale" picture used the shapes that he reported (oval, triangle, and white for the whale; blue and rectangle for the ocean) in this session. It felt as if the whale was now broken into shapes or fragmented—triangle/tail and oval/body and the color of the water was blue-green and the rectangular shape of the ocean. What also surprised me was his sun, since this was the only sun he had drawn to date. Its color combination was yellow and brown or ochre, which is a color that can be interpreted as contamination and infection. Bruce also reported the color brown and my sense was that Bruce's earlier assaultiveness and the resulting restraint were a continuation of the previous day's inner events. Brown, the color of feces, ground, and deteriorating matter perhaps was something trying to be eliminated from a deep unconscious.

Session 19—(Rescheduled for the following day due to Bruce being asleep as a result of restraint and medication.) It was poignant that on the following afternoon just as I arrived at his room, Bruce was receiving redirection from staff regarding some unsafe behavior. While one of the "techs" was on his way down the hall to get Bruce's chart to check on the possibility of a PRN, I asked the staff if I could intervene and they gave the OK. I approached the doorway, and as I leaned into it rather casually I started singing "Blue-Tail Fly." By the time I got to the end of the verse, he had joined in singing. At the end of the refrain, he asked me to bring my "stuff" in and sing some more. Bruce settled in to three more songs with his tape and then asked for the "other" music. He chose red and blue scarves this time. The music was again Respighi's "The Nightingale." I asked him to imagine standing on the shore feeling the sand between his toes and to look out over the ocean. Bruce drew two whales leaping out of the water. There was no sun this time and the water was sky blue. The whales were outlined in ochre and both whales' tails were filled in with the blue ocean color. Bruce labeled the picture "Leaping Whales," but talked about it as "two whales mating." My interpretation of this session and this drawing was based on the colors he chose to wrap himself in—red and blue, which sometimes can be interpreted as the colors of the "dragon fight"—separation from the parents/authority. The reference to "whales mating" also raised the question of Bruce's own struggle with sexuality given his early and lengthy abuse, particularly in his family of origin.

Session 20—This was a Friday and I intended to make Bruce's song tape and relaxation tape available for his use over the weekend. So the focus for this session was to evaluate his ability to operate the tape player with headset and for him to identify when he would ask for these as a coping skill. He demonstrated appropriate use of the tape player and identified his feeling to become silly or if he started feeling fearful as key to when he would ask for his tapes. He added that the beach scene would be his choice if he used the relaxation tape. We did a relaxation session for reinforcement of the beach scene and Bruce drew himself lying on the shore. The figure showed was half in the water and half on the sand with a big smile and three birds in the sky. His ocean was sky blue and the sand was the ochre again. This use of ochre seemed appropriate since sand contains such colors, but metaphorically he was caught between the ocean where he previously swam with sea turtles and groundedness of the "sand between his toes." One could also interpret it as the waters of the unconscious where the lower half of his body was drawn and of the conscious as his upper body and head rested on the sand.

Session 21—(Rescheduled for Tuesday due to medication on Monday, although staff reported that he did successfully use the tape and player over the weekend.) When I arrived and asked if he wanted to meet, Bruce replied, "Yup." (He had just come out of a restraint.) He took charge of the session immediately and chose three songs, then asked to use the relaxation tape. He wanted no colored cloth and asked that he use the ocean for his induction. After the music finished, he drew a picture of himself fishing from a sailboat. Three birds flew above in a blue-green sky and his figure smiled while holding on to the fishing pole at the back of the boat. He called the picture "Sunny Day—Caught a Bass." Bruce appeared self-assured in this session. As we discussed the use of the tape, he proudly informed me that he had used it over the weekend. I reminded him that I would be gone a short time, leaving the next day, and that during that break, he should feel free to access his tapes and player just as he had the previous weekend.

Session 22—Severe weather delayed my return, so when I finally got to see Bruce it was evening. He was interested in a few songs and although he appeared sleepy, his affect changed when he noticed an audience—a staff person—was listening, and he brightened considerably.

Session 23—"Can we have a shorter session?" Bruce was very excited about a chess game with a peer. Although I was willing to accommodate his request, just as in a previous session that he had requested to be shortened, once we began to work, Bruce forgot about the time and the session went as usual. He chose two songs and then went on to the imagery. He appeared restless during the music and his drawing was of a turtle on its back floating above the water. The water and sky were the same sky-blue color and the green turtle was in the middle—sandwich-like but not tight. It reminded me of the cocoon in its color and the use of color both above and below the figure was also a theme in Bruce's drawings. He called the picture "Swimmingtime." As we concluded, Bruce told me he had been told that he was going to be discharged on the following Monday. This was big news. I was amazed, but now his antsy behavior made sense. Bruce asked if I could make more tapes for him, especially ones with nature sounds.

Session 24—Bruce was looking particularly sad when I arrived and wanted "his music time." "Jimmie Crack-Corn first," he said and brightened. "Silent Night" followed and then the relaxation tape. He used an outdoor/nature scene for his setting during the seven-minute piece of music. When it concluded he asked if he could just tell me about what he saw and not make a picture. He described the "Titanic" and that he was in a cabin in the bottom looking out at eagles and sea turtles. When I asked him where the ship was, he simply replied, "You know the

Titanic, it sank." Bruce was at the bottom of a sunken ship but saw eagles and a sea turtle. The split between sky creature and sea creature was initially anxiety-producing for me. No land in sight, in the bottom, at the bottom, looking out, yet both creatures are strong and powerful in their own habitat. Bruce had not used the image of an eagle in prior sessions and it was only in the first session that he had seen birds of any type, although he drew them in two of his pictures. The eagle is also a visionary figure and I hoped that it might mean Bruce's "insight" may be submerged in the collective unconscious, but that given time and continued depth-work connecting his voice and imagination as we had been doing, his eagle would emerge like the butterfly from the cocoon.

Session 25—The next day was Friday and this was the final session, since Bruce was scheduled to leave at 6:00 a.m. on Monday. He chose three songs to sing while he played Legos with his roommate. He chose his music for the relaxation session, being quite familiar with the options. He chose not to draw and reminded me that he would like more tapes to take with him. I assured him he would have tapes and the player with headset. Bruce made the choices to share his songs with his roommate, to name his music for the imagery, and to reiterate his desire to have additional music tapes. Although I felt it was too soon for him to go, I did realize that he had demonstrated the skills for choosing and using music through song and relaxation on some occasions as a means of redirecting his negative behavior.

DISCUSSION

The Importance of a Depth Psychology Approach

The 1998 Beech Brook study, "Music therapy with children with severe emotional disturbances in a residential treatment setting," reported that studies demonstrating benefits of music therapy interventions with emotionally disturbed children are abundant, but that there is a lack of literature on music therapy interventions for the most disturbed children, particularly those in residential treatment (Hong, Hussey & Heng, 1998). Although a psychiatric hospital is not considered a residential treatment center, in Maine there are many patients who spend well beyond ninety days on the children's unit because of lack of residential placements or the case becomes mired in the paperwork of bureaucracy. Six- to eight-month hospitalizations for some children are not uncommon nor are multiple readmissions.

Having described and interpreted music, technique, pictures, and images from Bruce's sessions, with attention to the auditory function as both trigger and path for intervention with his behavior, I will briefly discuss my rationale for what I believe were the important elements of Bruce's treatment that increased his consciousness of his "voice."

I acknowledge that the primary modality for psychiatric treatment/therapy in residential care and hospitals is verbal. While language, either written or spoken, has been the mainstay of American communication, this form of language can also be a significant block for those who have no sense of control of their voice. Trauma literature is rich with examples of sensory inputs that can trigger negative reactions in trauma survivors. Although talk therapy might ultimately label or categorize in order to provide meaning for the individual, trauma experienced by children particularly prior to language comprehension remains sensory, symbolic, and primitive. For Bruce, this was certainly the case. His wild, terrified looks when starting a meltdown; his silliness that led to assaultiveness; and his drawings all communicated important information which "talk" could not contain. His choosing of specific music activities, and particularly his relationship to singing with himself on tape, validated my notion that he had much being "said" to him by his inner voice. But the language that the inner voice used was primitive and Bruce was unable to translate its needs and reactions into what the adults in the outer world were asking of him. The more Bruce tried to comply over the decade of his life's experience, the more violations occurred until his behavior/inner voice got him hospitalized.

As the work with Bruce evolved over those four months, he began to speak differently with, and to, his inner voice. He began to demonstrate his sense of self-worth and his desire to be safe. Bruce was not cured, he was not fully in control, but what he had was a growing awareness that he could dialogue with his inner voice and that the behavior could be a conscious choice and not just an automatic or reflexive response to what his ears perceived.

Bruce's family-of-origin history showed a lineage of abuse and neglect. He certainly was living according to the voice he learned from birth and the most likely the voice of his conception, perhaps even "incubated in terror." With a hyper-alert sensory system and only a primitive (brain-stem based) means of communicating rage, fear, and sorrow, his behaviors were assaultive, silly, and self-destructive. As Bruce began to recognize his reactions to some of his auditory inputs, he began to express these emotions through singing, instrument playing, and imagery with supportive music. He also began to release and experience firsthand another way to communicate.

CONCLUSIONS

The following conclusions were included in the memo for Bruce's new psychiatrist.

- Bruce responded well to music therapy through two particular activities, singing and music with selected imagery relaxation techniques focused on "interrupting" then mediating dangerous and assaultive behavior.
- Bruce's song tape contains songs he chose and sang and has been useful as a "sing-along" coping skill.
- Bruce has also been able to de-escalate his potential aggressiveness by singing with staff on a few occasions.
- Bruce used the image of being at a beach or in a cocoon for his relaxation work.
- Bruce would usually draw after the relaxation, in order to concretize the imagery.
- Bruce has his own collection of song and relaxation tapes for use as coping skills.
- Bruce has demonstrated a growth in self-esteem and self-confidence by his ability to now sing informally with one or two peers.
- Bruce received music therapy, not music education or "singing lessons."
- Bruce works well with a logical approach that is collaborative in style.

As fate would have it, although Bruce's tapes and player were packaged for his discharge, the staff failed to look in the proper place and his six-hour road trip to his placement was without music. I received a phone call three days later from his new psychiatrist who requested his tape package after reading his file and my memo. I assured her that there were en route. Nearly a month later, I heard from her again. She said that she had inadvertently phoned my office and after she apologized for the "wrong number" she told me that Bruce was doing well and the tapes were very useful. She may have consciously thought that she had dialed a "wrong number," but I believe "there are no accidents."

REFERENCES

Cassidy, J. W., & Ditty, K. M. (1998). "Presentation of Aural Stimuli to Newborns and Premature Infants: An Audiological Perspective," *Journal of Music Therapy*, 35 (1), 70–87.

Cassity, M., & Cassity, J. (1998). *Multimodal Psychiatric Music Therapy For Adults, Adolescents, And Children: A Clinical Manual.* St. Louis, MO: MMB Music, Inc.

Greenspan, S. I. (1997). *The Growth of the Mind.* Reading, MA: Perseus Books.

Hong, M., Hussey, D., & Heng, M. (1998). "Music Therapy with Children with Severe Emotional Disturbances in a Residential Treatment Setting," *Music Therapy Perspectives*, 16, 61–66.

Rubin, H. R., Owens, A. J., & Golden, G. (1999). *Status Report (1998): An Investigation to Determine whether the Built Environment Affects Patients' Medical Outcomes.* Lafayette, CA: Center for Healthcare Design.

Case Seven

WORKING WITH JENNY:
STORIES OF GENDER, POWER AND ABUSE

Penny J. Rogers

ABSTRACT

This chapter describes music therapy with Jenny,[1] an eleven-year-old with a history of paternal sexual abuse and a familial history of emotional abuse and neglect. In this case study, I consider the constraints of working therapeutically within statutory child protection responsibilities. I particularly consider issues of gender, power, and abuse, where the therapist holds the same gender as an alleged abuser.

---

[1] Jenny was not the client's real name. All factors that could facilitate "Jenny's" identification have been changed to help protect her identity.

INTRODUCTION

Background Context

The case study described in this chapter occurred within the context of a county child sexual abuse project situated within the U.K. The project was jointly funded by two national children's charities and the local health service. The project team was small; just six specialised clinicians. The team was, however, augmented by clinicians seeking placements with the team to develop their own learning or to conduct research. Music therapy provision occurred through the latter context, funded through a grant from the Music Therapy Charity.

The project offered treatment to children who had been sexually abused and their families, including siblings. Individual, group, and family therapy was provided. All treatment was offered after investigation by the statutory authorities; thus many children engaged in treatment were the subjects of child protection plans, and some had experienced the trauma of giving evidence in court proceedings against their abuser(s). Such a legal context places particular constraints regarding issues of consent and confidentiality.

Therapy with these children occurred in a multi-agency context where agencies held differing agendas, stories, beliefs, powers, values and languages about abuse. It was constantly necessary to reflect on how family stories of abuse could be mirrored in the interagency dynamics—often splitting every player in the system against others—and how differing roles impacted our work (Furniss, 1991; Rogers, in press; Summitt, 1986).

Client Referral

Jenny was referred to the project by her social worker, who was responsible for drawing together a child protection plan to support Jenny. The purpose was to allow Jenny a therapeutic space within which she could explore the impact of her past sexual abuse experiences, the subsequent trauma of disclosure, court experiences, and her removal from her family into foster care. The alleged sexual abuser was Jenny's father. Allegations included indecent sexual assault and rape over several years. While there was physical evidence that Jenny had been sexually abused, there was no forensic evidence to link this with Jenny's father and he had not been prosecuted. A court case (application by Social Services for a full care order) had concluded that Jenny had been sexually abused, and that on the balance of probability, the identity of the abuser was her father. Both Jenny's birthparents denied that Jenny had been abused (by anyone). Concerns were raised by a number of agencies about the ability of Jenny's mother to protect her. There was a known history of intergenerational sexual abuse on both paternal and maternal sides of Jenny's birthfamily. These difficulties were compounded by histories of paternal alcohol abuse, maternal depression and domestic violence. Jenny's siblings were all assessed as having behavioral difficulties; the family members were well known to a wide number of agencies. Jenny's family remained (living) together following Jenny's removal into care despite the concern of many professionals for the safety of her siblings. Referral information also stated that Jenny exhibited sexualized behavior. She was a vulnerable child.

At the time of Jenny's referral to the project she had been in foster care for nine months, and this placement was considered stable and secure. The project initially offered Jenny a ten-week group-work program for preteen sexually abused girls. This program is aimed at both the abused child and their care givers. Jenny's foster carers were invited to attend a ten-week carers group, however they only attended the first five weeks of the program and appeared to find it difficult to accept that Jenny's allegations of sexual abuse could be true.

Following Jenny's participation in the group, her group therapist recommended that Jenny would benefit from individual music therapy. She observed that Jenny appeared to be a very vulnerable child, presenting as younger than her years, with little understanding of sexual issues and had demonstrated some "touching muddles"[2] within the group therapy program. Jenny's group therapist suggested that Jenny required music therapy to enable her to explore, within a safe contained space, her stories about her past, issues around her separation from her parents, and her identity.

The referrer also commented that Jenny appeared to have some learning difficulties. To determine the nature of these would require a specific psychological assessment. I was, however, curious as to whether Jenny's apparent learning difficulties might be linked with her traumatic experiences and whether they would change as her emotional health improved (Sinason, 1992).[3]

Confidentiality and the Legal Context

Jenny's therapy took place in the following legal context. Parental responsibility was held by Social Services and Jenny was also the subject of a child protection

---

[2] "Touching muddles" is a term used by the project to describe a child exhibiting sexualized behavior without resorting to pejorative labelling.

[3] During the course of Jenny's therapy, I was (in the context of a court report) to comment specifically on her cognitive abilities. I observed that these could only be assessed by a clinical psychologist, but that she appeared to present as a child of seven or eight years old, rather than an eleven-year-old.

plan. During the course of therapy, reports were requested by the courts to inform decisions regarding contact with her birthparents (who wished her to be returned home), and by Social Services in reconsidering her placement and in connection with her child protection plan. Alongside these constraints, confidentiality was also limited in respect to any new information that Jenny should share in therapy (Department of Health Children Act, 1989). Exploration of the meaning and impact of these constraints were frequently explored both in therapy with Jenny and with other agencies.

Initial Assessment

My first impression of Jenny was of a pleasant and engaging girl; talkative, friendly, and eager to please. She was small, slim, and appeared to be in good physical health. There was no evidence of depression or of any psychotic process occurring. Although at times Jenny was restless and distracted, her levels of concentration clearly fluctuated, and when actively engaged in musical improvisation could be very good. Jenny had good eye contact and initiated speech appropriately. She was skilled at changing the subject if she wished to avoid a particular area of exploration. Jenny reported nightmares and flashbacks consequent to her abuse. While Jenny appeared willing to engage in music therapy, I was curious as to how Jenny would have been able to decline therapeutic input should she have wished to do so.

After my initial assessment with Jenny, I noted how she had quickly expressed conflict about the contact she has with her birthparents: "Sometimes I don't want to talk to them." I also observed that Jenny showed an ability to use the media as a metaphor for exploring emotions and issues. There appeared to be a marked split between Jenny's verbal presentation—where she appeared superficially eager to please, polite, and contained—and her musical presentation—where she expressed considerable anger and rage, was consistently controlling, and musically abusive. This split could demonstrate a contrast between Jenny's internal world—expressing the confusion and hurt she feels—and the external world.

Following Jenny's initial assessment session, I concluded that music therapy could appropriately offer Jenny a containing environment within which she could:

- Explore her confused and conflicting feelings regarding contact with her birthfamily.
- Explore her relationships with others—e.g., foster parents and school friends.

- Explore and express her emotions and memories of her early childhood, including those caused by past experiences of sexual abuse.
- Provide a containing environment in which issues such as safe touching and acceptable and unacceptable behavior could be explored.

THERAPEUTIC APPROACH

I originally trained as a music therapist in the U.K. in 1983. My approach is grounded in the use of free clinical improvisation, using tuned and untuned percussion instruments, in which attention is afforded to transference and countertransference processes. Addressing issues of power is fundamental to my approach. I seek to ensure that an environment of safety and trust is generated for my clients by acknowledging the implicit therapeutic power I hold. Offering careful, empathic listening, a nonjudgmental attitude, respect, a sense of safety of time and space, and a collaborative approach in which I seek to provide a secure base from which the client can begin to explore are key therapeutic tasks.

My approach is informed by additional training (master's degrees) in cognitive neuropsychology; child protection (Tavistock Clinic) and systemic psychotherapy (Institute of Family Therapy); by many years of clinical supervision with leading child psychotherapists, and a practice based within a child and adolescent mental health service. My work has been inspired by psychoanalytically-informed approaches to music therapy (e.g. Priestley, 1994; Odell-Miller; Robarts, 1994; Bruscia; Dvorkin; Austin), alongside influences from social constructionist, narrative, postmodernist, and feminist approaches to therapy. Research and the necessity for music therapy to gain validity within health structures through evidence-based practice is another discourse that has strongly influenced my own personal development. Implicit is my belief that no school of therapy provides the only "truth" (Rogers, in press). Remaining curious is the therapist's principal task, whilst simultaneously acknowledging one's own prejudices and beliefs; in the context of this case study an example would be that sexual abuse can never be condoned. Personal dominant discourses privilege the therapeutic relationship and the function of therapy is to effect change. Within this overall framework, my therapeutic method involves the use of questions that can be generally defined as reflexive (Tomm, 1987; 1988) and are used to create new contexts for thinking about familiar patterns and stories; to expand, amplify, question, and develop the client's own beliefs, stories, and hypotheses.

Music therapy involves conversations (musical, verbal, and nonverbal) that take place between client and therapist. Implicitly, such conversations include some kind of exchange and find links with the interaction between infant and mother as described by Stern (1985) and Trevarthen (1993). This contrasts with the more hierarchical (expert/dummy) interactions that are supposed to take place in psychoanalysis (Hoffman, 1985).

Music therapy is a particularly useful therapeutic modality for work with abused clients as it specifically offers the opportunity to explore and express feelings that the child may find difficult or may be unable to verbalize (Rogers, 1992; 1995a; 1996b). Music therapy is thus suitable for work where the client may have been threatened to not talk about the abuse, is holding a secret, or whose cognitive abilities may make verbal exploration difficult (Rogers, 1995a).

Description of Therapeutic Approach in Context

The therapeutic process is not predetermined, but in my work with Jenny the following therapeutic frame was used. This provided a structure and secure base within sessions. It had the following format:

Initial conversation: Verbal reflection on the previous week.
Jenny would rapidly report on any difficulties at school or in her foster home. Jenny would report "messages" from home—e.g., "my foster parents don't think I should come here" or "I'm a bad girl because I tell lies," etc.

An improvisation: (This might be directed or free)
Typically, Jenny would direct me to the keyboard and would move rapidly around the room playing all of the instruments before settling in one space.

Verbal reflection:
Jenny would describe the improvisation that had just occurred. I might reflect her conversation, or note differences and changes. Questions and reflections might be used.

A further and typically more substantial improvisation:
Jenny would direct and control this, which often resembled musical theater or an operetta. Use of metaphor and symbolism were often essential components.

Final verbal reflection:
Making links with previous and present experiences; noting exceptions and unique outcomes; using circular questions and making links between stories lived and stories told.

The boundaries surrounding therapy were consistent: therapy occurred at the same time and place each week, with the same instruments available (Bion, 1959). Sessions lasted fifty minutes and were largely undirected. Unlike some more traditional psychoanalytically-informed approaches, in my work with abused children, I am sensitive to the potentially persecutory impact of silence and would comment on the potential meanings of such. Breaks in therapy were planned for in advance.

Attention was paid to the necessity to ensure that therapy was not abusive of its power (Gorell-Barnes, 1998).

TREATMENT

Sessions 1–15

A number of themes dominated these sessions. Jenny wished to please; verbally she initially denied that she had been abused and repeatedly said that she had been a bad girl who told lies. Musically, Jenny demonstrate her anxiety to please through her attempts to play musical ditties on the xylophone, short melodic phrases that were reminiscent of nursery rhymes or to engage in turn-taking in which she would attempt to imitate whatever I had played but seemed unable to find her own voice. Throughout, I felt Jenny was unduly anxious about playing a "wrong" note and appeared both to be seeking to attempt to please and/or to placate me by playing what she imagined I might want to hear.

There was little space to think, as Jenny was either talking or playing the instruments, and frequently doing both simultaneously. I hypothesized that the necessity to prevent a space for thinking was used by Jenny as a defense against the emotive and painful emotions such a task might elucidate (Sinason, 1992). I also held a belief that Jenny's apparent wish to please was indicative both of anxious attachment (Bowlby, 1973) and a fear of the consequences of annoying or irritating an adult. Gorell-Barnes (1998) notes that, "Obedience and compliance from an early age often characterizes relationships that are also sexually abusive, as does an inbuilt wish to please, in the context of what will probably be experienced as a failure to do so" (p. 176).

By Session 5, there had been a clear shift and Jenny appeared to have gained some confidence. She no longer sought to please; rather, her wish to control the content of the session and the music had become more marked. Jenny was frequently musically aggressive and quite dictatorial in her manner. She would insist that I played the piano and would direct the manner in which I should play. I was not permitted by Jenny to play any other instrument and if I moved away from the piano this could provoke outraged screams from Jenny (developmentally reminiscent of the temper tantrums of a two-year-old). I frequently felt musically abused as Jenny would play at a considerable volume, so that at times it was quite painful to be in the room with Jenny for the full fifty minutes. My countertransference response was to feel shocked, powerless, abused, and controlled, and my task was to reflect on and contain these feelings (through clinical supervision), recognizing that Jenny appeared to be inviting further abuse and pushing onto me some of the shock and outrage she had experienced (Winnicott, 1965). I was curious about whether there were any other situations where Jenny could assert her own voice or control her environment and hypothesized that this was probably the only context where Jenny could control an adult. Jenny was able to acknowledge this. How had Jenny experienced other's controlling her? Was her obliteration of me a reflection of her own past experiences of being obliterated (Udwin, 1993)?

For many of her first few sessions, I sensed that Jenny was being rehearsed, or primed by her birthparents, in terms of her contributions (a view subsequently shared by my clinical supervisor). She would arrive at her sessions and make careful statements. At the beginning of her second session, Jenny announced that she had been talking to her Mum and Dad on the telephone and told me, "I have not been abused" and "I told lies and was a bad girl; that is why I live with Anna and Jack" (the foster carers). Later I was able to ask Jenny about what others might wish her to say in therapy and she was able to reflect on the difficulties of finding her own voice (mirroring her initial difficulties in finding her own musical voice). I also experienced Jenny as anticipating rejection and seeking to provoke an abusive reaction from me. She appeared to have no trust in my intentions. Thus, it was necessary for the therapeutic process to be slow and for me to acknowledge that generating a trusting relationship would take time and care.

From Sessions 5–14, Jenny improvised a mini-operetta during the sessions. Both the use of this musical form and its performance were controlled by Jenny, who would shout instructions to me whilst playing and singing out her story. The structure of the operetta provided containment (Winnicott, 1961). It was repeated each week for nine sessions, becoming more elaborate and extensive each week, with the details of the abuse that Jenny described becoming more vivid and painful to hear. This operetta was notionally about a "burglar" who enters Jenny's bedroom whilst she is asleep and steals a precious jewel. The burglar is subsequently furious when Jenny tells others of the theft of the precious jewel. This was clearly a metaphorical tale of Jenny's history of sexual abuse, with the burglar being her father; the telling, her disclosure to authorities; and the precious jewel, her virginity/innocence. Jenny remained controlling throughout these sessions. As the story became more extensive and detailed in each session, I was aware that Jenny was testing out my ability to hear about the details of her experiences without condemning or blaming her. The metaphor initially functioned to allow some separation and distance from the painful story of indecent sexual assault and rape being told. In later sessions, Jenny used her own voice in the operetta as she sang out her narrative of being held down and mentally and physically raped. I was aware of my beliefs that Jenny needed another to understand her hurt without condemnation and that to silence or repress this expression would be damaging. I was curious about my growing sense that there was a further story to be told and my counter-transference sense that I was being provoked into a (musically) violent response. I could not help wonder how others had responded and whom I might represent for Jenny.

In verbalising her abuse through the operetta, Jenny was making her experiences comprehensible both to herself and to others. She used her story, told through the operetta, to language her experiences and in doing so, gave her experiences meaning (Anderson & Goolishian, 1988).

Sessions 15–30

These sessions were dominated by the frequent changes in Jenny's living accommodation and her hurt and anger following the breakdown in her foster placement with Anna and Jack.[4] The placement had broken down in response to a court case to which I had contributed a court report. I experienced concern and fury at the inadequacies of professional protection systems; no doubt mirroring Jenny's own. In raising my anxieties about the limits of Jenny's foster placement with Anna and Jack, Jenny was experiencing further trauma regarding yet another loss and repeated moves between temporary placements. A poor, but secure, permanent placement had been replaced by poor, insecure, and temporary placements. Like Jenny, I experienced victimlike and angry feelings toward the perpetrators of her abuse (Kraemer, 1988). Without the support of my clinical supervisor, and the project team, my efficacy could have been damaged. Sexual abuse is a syndrome of power and secrecy that lends itself to splitting and conflicts of proxy (Summitt, 1986). In my conversations with Jenny and other agencies, I paid attention to ensure that I did not become the "good" professional while the absent social worker became the "bad" protector. This facilitated future working together (Department of Health, 1999).

While Jenny was experiencing considerable insecurities in her home circumstances, within music therapy she became less controlling (both musically and nonmusically) and more hesitant. There was a less abusive quality to her improvisations. Jenny no longer had any sort of external secure base. It became a painful reality that her relationship with me was the only constant in her life,

---

[4] Anna and Jack are not the names of "Jenny's" foster parents. Throughout this chapter names have been changed to protect identification and confidentiality.

as she experienced frequent moves between foster carers, changes of school, and even the absence of her social worker (as many of these changes occurred during the summer and her social worker was absent for four weeks on annual leave).

As Jenny's therapist, I was able to advocate her needs with other agencies, providing a vehicle in which Jenny's voice, opinions, and fears could be heard alongside the powerful voices of other agencies involved in determining her future. The necessity to facilitate Jenny's voice in such agendas impacted the therapeutic process in that it was necessary to check on Jenny's thoughts and beliefs about such issues as future contact with her birthparents or the ongoing changes in foster parents. Like Jenny, I experienced a sense of powerlessness in challenging the agendas of more powerful agencies; it is probable that my experiences of abuse and powerlessness mirrored Jenny's own.

Jenny returned to improvising her operetta about the burglar (perhaps this provided some security and familiarity within the therapy sessions). Within the framework of the operetta, it was necessary for me to stay with the repellent raping child and to allow Jenny to explore this (Sinason, 1992, p. 169), and to experience the projected feelings of Jenny's terrible experiences that were forced into me and that she could no longer bear (Sinason, 1992, p. 175). Within this structure, Jenny elaborated on her belief that it was better "not to tell" or to disclose abuse, as the burglar always wins out in the end. On several occasions, Jenny sang that the burglar had killed the little girl for telling and that the little girl's mother would send her away for being so bad. On those occasions, when I managed to musically rescue the little girl before the burglar could kill her, Jenny would ruefully observe that while the little girl was in the hospital and the doctors, nurses, and therapists were trying to make her better, it would not work, as the "burglar would get her in the end" (Session 22) and "the burglar had told her that no one could protect her" (Sessions 22, 23, and 24).

This was an accurate reflection of a reality in which Jenny had not been adequately protected by the authorities; I could not ensure she was protected from frequent moves between unsatisfactory foster placements and Jenny continued to receive abusive phone calls from her father and mother. Jenny no longer had any sort of secure base while the "burglar" (her father) had not been punished for the alleged sexual abuse, through lack of proof and concerns that as a consequence of her perceived learning difficulties, Jenny would not make an adequate witness in court. In this context, music therapy was perhaps the only secure base Jenny had.

The context of "safe uncertainty" (Mason, 1993) allowed space for Jenny to express new stories in the therapy, and Jenny disclosed that her mother had been both complicit and actively involved in her sexual abuse. This disclosure of maternal abuse appeared to fit with my countertransference experiences of being invited to (musically) abuse Jenny and my growing awareness that Jenny's sexualized behavior was indiscriminate regarding gender. Jenny's disclosure of maternal sexual abuse was shared with the authorities (under the Children Act, 1989) and a further investigation by the police occurred. Kraemer (1988) notes the dangers of uncovering sexual abuse for therapists, whereby they may become blamed or scapegoated; it was, thus, necessary to work actively with other agencies to acknowledge the potential for such a dynamic to occur. Actively naming such issues enabled new stories to be created about working together (Department of Health, 1999). Jenny's disclosure of maternal sexual abuse raised issues for consideration, both as a woman sharing the same gender as one of Jenny's alleged sexual abusers and regarding the limited confidentiality of the therapy sessions. It generated feelings of being on an emotional roller coaster (Chu, 1992).

At times during these sessions, my principal task was simply to remain consistent and curious; to provide, both within improvisations and in all other aspects of the therapeutic space, a secure base within which new narratives could be developed. I became aware, through a detailed analysis of these improvisations, that a musical cell (of three pulsed chords) was used to provide a secure base. This cell appeared in improvisations both when I thought that Jenny might be anxious or at other times when I was anxious. Thus, it appeared to be linked with both transference and countertransference anxieties. Through musical analysis of a number of improvisations over time, it became apparent that this cell had been present within my first improvisation with Jenny and while it developed and evolved over time, remained present in subsequent improvisations. Initially I was not conscious of the significance of this musical motif, but this changed as the course of therapy developed. This sequence of three pulsed chords appeared to be unique to my improvisations with Jenny. It is possible to hypothesize that the analysis of the improvisations of another client might similarly identify musical motifs unique to, and associated with, the provision of a secure base within the musical improvisations. The cell was not purely melodic (Carter, 1990), however, but harmonic and rhythmic; thus finding parallels with the work of Lee (1990). Other musical motifs were associated with different dynamics.

In these sessions, Jenny also indicated her difficulties in connecting with and developing a sense of trust. Musically, Jenny was only able to tolerate musical connection when she initiated this. During our early sessions, Jenny had actively sought to be separate from and disconnected to my playing. If our rhythms engaged, for example, Jenny would quickly syncopate her own rhythm to create a dissonant effect, as if too much connection was dangerous. During these later sessions, Jenny was able to remain connected, through pulse, rhythm, or harmonic center, for significant periods of time.

Sessions 30–55

Jenny was found a new, secure, long-term foster placement with foster parents who were highly experienced and were offering to foster Jenny until she reached adulthood (eighteen years of age). They were highly supportive of Jenny's engagement in therapy and, despite living over ninety minutes away from the project, were committed to transporting Jenny to and from her therapy each week. Jenny's improvisations at this time became more playful; she experimented with allowing me to be positioned in different ways and I was no longer constrained to remain solely on the piano. As Jenny came to trust in the therapeutic relationship, she no longer needed to control our musical and verbal conversations. Jenny's musical stories allowed for new resolutions and different meanings to be generated in language about her experiences (Anderson & Goolishian, 1988). Jenny began to explore dilemmas in the "here and now" and to explore how her past experiences affected her new relationships, such as her dilemmas about establishing trust with a new foster father. Jenny had come to question, and tentatively accept, that the abuse was not her responsibility; that she no longer needed to be burdened with secrets and that others would not reject or blame her if they were aware of her past experiences. Much of our work now focused on challenging Jenny's own sexualized behavior, both that which she presented within the therapy room and that which Jenny described as occurring outside. I saw this behavior as "abuse-reactive" and my task was to enable Jenny to consider the impact of such behavior on others. Jenny began to take responsibility for her own behaviors and, following several conversations, agreed to attend a small group-work program for children with touching muddles.

In contrast to her initial musical expressions that were solely of rage and anger, Jenny was now able to express a wide range of emotions during these sessions, ranging from sadness to joy, from despair to delight. Our musical dances took on a variety of forms in the improvisations and Jenny became much more playful and inventive. No longer did Jenny seek to play solely within defined rhythmic and consonant harmonic structures; she developed more individuated self-expression, developing a new sense of self, creativity, and autonomy.

It is of note that during this time, Jenny was moved from a school for children with learning difficulties to a mainstream school. There was a professional view that many of Jenny's learning difficulties had resolved as her emotional health improved.

Therapy ended in a carefully planned way through mutual agreement. The ending was planned three months in advance and Jenny was aware that she could request future referral to the project if she felt that would be helpful. In our final session, I asked Jenny if she could tell me what aspects of our work had been helpful and what aspects had not been; Jenny observed that I was the only person who seemed able to allow her to be distressed and angry without wanting to dry her tears quickly. Both Segal (1986) and Sgroi (1981) comment that the abused child knows only too well what their therapist can bear to tolerate hearing. Jenny observed that she felt safe in her therapy sessions; I linked Jenny's sense of safety with my own. For therapist's working with issues of abuse it is vital that attention is paid to ensuring our own personal safety from potential allegations or abuse (Rogers, 2000). I was interested that Jenny said that she enjoyed using the instruments, as this enabled her to tell her story and express her feelings without words (or languaging them verbally). Jenny also noted that there had been times when she hated the fact that she knew I saw other young people—I was not just hers—and that I continued to challenge her beliefs.

DISCUSSION AND CONCLUSION

The constraints of this paper prevent a detailed exploration of all aspects of Jenny's therapy. The dominant discourse regarding power and powerlessness is briefly discussed.

Abuse, by its very nature, is about power; it occurs within relationships in which one (usually larger, stronger, embodied with more authority) uses their power to exploit another (usually smaller, weaker, embodied with less authority). Therapy, too, embodies a relationship of power; it implies that the therapist holds authority over the client and it is usually presumed (often by both therapist and client) that it should be the therapist who determines what occurs within therapy sessions and what can be spoken of outside the therapy sessions. It is also the therapist who determines where and when sessions will occur. Therapy may be construed as a confidential process—a secret (with the obvious parallel with abuse, which is also maintained as a secret between two unequal parties).

Within music therapy a further dimension may be added to this unequal relationship, that is, the therapist has considerable musical skills and knowledge to use the instruments while the client (as in Jenny's case) may have no musical training and fewer skills with which to musically express themselves. Furthermore, the client may only be offered a variety of tuned and untuned percussion instruments while the therapist uses a piano (a larger, more powerful, and much more complex instrument capable of rich harmonic material).

Jenny's history was pervaded by a lack of self-determination or control in which Jenny was subjected to the wills of others and consequently suffered at their hands. For Jenny to be able to engage in therapy required that she felt she held some power, some authority, and some self-determination within the therapy session. It was necessary for Jenny to experience a relationship with an adult in which she did not feel powerless. Jenny needed to experience a sense of control, in order for her to feel safe enough to explore emotional material, particularly that connected with her own history of abuse. Detailed analysis reveals that not only did Jenny remain in control or in a position of power for much of the time, but that she also sought to actively disempower me; much of her music was experienced as attacking and abusive. It was extremely destructive at times, although even within this, Jenny retained control to the extent that I never had to intervene. Also, Jenny was actually careful not to break any of the instruments. It was necessary for Jenny to provoke in me the feelings of powerlessness and abuse that she had experienced.

Issues of gender were clearly important—I shared the same gender as Jenny's absent mother whom Jenny alleged (within therapy) had been both complicit and active in her sexual abuse. While as therapists we cannot not take gender into account, how we consider gender can take many forms, relating to our social constructions of gender and the theories of gender we embrace. Clinical supervision provided an essential space within which to consider how my gender could lead to reenactments of abuse within the therapy. It helped me to stay with the repellent when Jenny provoked countertransference feelings in me that made me uncomfortable; when she appeared to be provoking me to abuse her musically; when she attempted to sexualize our musical conversations; or, when she anxiously sought to please. Clinical supervision helped me to explore the transference-countertransference processes, providing a space in which I could reflect on other potential stories and generate new hypotheses that informed our work. The provision of clear boundaries and clear messages to Jenny regarding the inappropriateness of her sexualized behavior within sessions without curtailing the space for Jenny to reflect upon and explore the meanings of these behaviors was important. Ultimately Jenny disclosed more of her experiences of abuse and her mother's involvement in her sexual abuse.[5]

Jenny was clearly aware that the apparent power that she held was limited. This was demonstrated through her questioning of the boundaries of confidentiality relating to the therapy sessions and her recognition that, should she disclose new information, her therapist would have responsibilities to inform others and her parents could get into trouble. This had implications not only for them but also for her siblings. Both Jenny and I recognized implicitly that musically I held more power than her; I could effectively dazzle her with musical technique should I have chosen, or could have exploited her positioning

---

[5] It is of note that when challenged by the police regarding these new allegations, Jenny's mother broke down and admitted both Jenny's sexual abuse by her father and her own active participation in this.

of me on the piano to dominate any musical conversations. That I did not, reflected my beliefs in a collaborative and respectful approach.

Issues of power can also be explored in my relationships with other agencies, such as Social Services who held parental responsibility (Summitt, 1986).

CONCLUSION

Therapy enabled Jenny to explore her past experiences of abuse and in languaging her experiences to create new meanings. The use of music therapy as opposed to verbal therapy enabled Jenny to engage within a safe context in which she felt in control. Jenny was able to test out the response of the therapist to the stories she needed to tell and to explore different outcomes to those stories through the use of a musical operetta within which she was able to generate new meanings about her experiences and move forward.

REFERENCES

Anderson, H., & Goolishian, H. (1988). "Human Systems as Linguistic Systems: Preliminary and Evolving Ideas about the Implications for Clinical Theory," *Family Process*, 27 (4), 371–393.

Anderson, H., & Goolishian, H. (1992). "The Client Is the Expert: A Not-Knowing Approach to Therapy." In S. McNamee & K. Gergen (eds.), *Therapy as Social Construction*. London: Sage.

Bion, W. (1959). "Attacks on Linking," *International Journal of Psycho-analysis*, 40, 308–315.

Bion, W. R. (1962). "A Theory of Thinking," *International Journal of Psycho-Analysis*, 43, 306–310.

Bowlby, J. (1973). *Attachment and Loss, Vol. 2: Separation, Anxiety and Anger*. London: Hogarth Press.

Bowlby, J. (1979). "On Knowing What You Are Not Supposed to Know and Feeling What You Are Not Supposed to Feel," *Canadian Journal of Psychiatry*, 24, 403–408.

Carter, A. (1990). "The Role of the Leitmotif in Music Therapy." Unpublished master's thesis, City University, London.

Chu, J. (1992). "The Therapeutic Roller Coaster: Dilemmas in the Treatment of Child Sexual Abuse Survivors," *Journal of Psychotherapy Practice and Research*, 1 (4), 351–370.

Department of Health. (1989). "Children Act" HMSO.

Department of Health. (1999). "Working Together" HMSO.

Furniss, T. (1991). *The Multi-Professional Handbook of Child Sexual Abuse*. London: Routledge.

Gorell-Barnes, G. (1998). "Sexual Abuse in Childhood," in *Family Therapy in Changing Times*. London: Macmillan Press.

Hoffman, L. (1985). "Beyond Power and Control: Towards a 'Second Order' Family Systems Therapy," *Family Systems Medicine*, 3 (4), 381–396.

Kraemer, S. (1988). "Splitting and Stupidity in Child Sexual Abuse," *Psychoanalytic Psychotherapy*, 3 (3), 247–257.

Kraemer, S. (1998). "What Narrative?" In R. Papdopoulos & J. Byng-Hall (eds.), *Multiple Voices: Narrative in Systemic Family Psychotherapy* (Tavistock Clinic Series). London: Routledge.

Lee, C. A. (1990). "Structural Analysis of Post-Tonal Therapeutic Improvisatory Music," *Journal of British Music Therapy*, 4 (1), 6–20.

Mason, B. (1993). "Towards Positions of Safe Uncertainty," *Human Systems: The Journal of Systemic Consultation & Management*, 4, 189–200.

Priestley, M. (1994). *Essays on Analytical Music Therapy*. Phoenixville, PA: Barcelona Publishers.

Robarts, J. Z. (1994). "Towards Autonomy and a Sense of Self," In D. Dokter (ed.), *Arts Therapies and Clients with Eating Disorders: Fragile Board*. London: Jessica Kingsley Press.

Rogers, P. (1992). "Issues in Working with Sexually Abused Clients in Music Therapy," *Journal of British Music Therapy,* 6 (2), 5–15.

Rogers, P. J. (1994). "Sexual Abuse and Eating Disorders," In D. Dokter (ed.), *Arts Therapies and Clients with Eating Disorders: Fragile Board.* London: Jessica Kingsley Press.

Rogers, P. (1995a). "Childhood Sexual Abuse: Dilemmas in Therapeutic Practice," *Music Therapy Perspectives,* 13 (1), 24–30.

Rogers, P. J. (1995b). "European Music Therapy Research: A context for the Qualitative/Quantitative Debate," *British Journal of Music Therapy,* 9 (2), 5-12.

Rogers, P. J. (1996). "A Place for Certainty." [Forward] *British Journal of Music Therapy,* 10 (1), 2-3.

Rogers, P. J. (1996b). "New Directions in Work with Abused Clients." *International Perspectives: AAMT International Report.* Autumn, 1996.

Rogers, P. J. (2000). *Managing Allegations of Abuse by Professionals: Guidance for Therapists.* North Essex, UK: North Essex Mental Health Partnership NHS Trust.

Rogers, P. J. (In press). "Professional Dynamics in the Treatment of Abuse," In J. Trowell & B. Loughlin (eds.), *Messages in Child Protection Research.* Tavistock Clinic.

Segal, H. (1986). "Notes on Symbol Formation." In *The Work of Hanna Segal: A Kleinian Approach to Clinical Practice.* Northvale, NJ: Jason Aronson.

Sgroi S. M. (1981). *Handbook of Clinical Intervention in Child Sexual Abuse.* Lanham, MD: Lexington Books.

Sinason, V. (1992). *Mental Handicap and the Human Condition: New Approaches from the Tavistock.* London: Free Association Books.

Stern, D. (1985). *The Interpersonal World of the Infant.* New York: Basic Books.

Summit, R. C. (1986). "The Child Sexual Abuse Accommodation Syndrome," *Child Abuse and Neglect,* 7, 177-193.

Tomm, K. (1987). "Interventive Interviewing: Parts I and II," *Family Process*, 26, 3–13 and 167–183.

Tomm, K. (1988). "Interventive Interviewing: Part III," *Family Process*, 27, 1–15.

Trevarthen, C. (1993). "The Function of Emotions in Early Infant Communication and Development." In J. Nadel & L. Camaioni (eds.), *New Perspectives in Early Communicative Development*. London: Routledge.

Udwin, O. (1993). "Annotation: Children's Reactions to Traumatic Events," *Journal of Child Psychology and Psychiatry and Allied Disciplines*, 34 (2), 115–127.

Winnicott, D. W. (1961/1986). "Varieties of Psychotherapy." In *Essays by a Psychoanalyst*. Harmondsworth, UK: Penguin Books.

Winnicott, D. W. (1965). "Hate in the Countertransference." In *The Maturational Process and the Facilitating Environment*. London: Hogarth Press.

Case Eight

THE HEALING FUNCTION OF IMPROVISED SONGS IN MUSIC THERAPY WITH A CHILD SURVIVOR OF EARLY TRAUMA AND SEXUAL ABUSE[*]

Jacqueline Z. Robarts

ABSTRACT

This case study discusses the use of improvised song-poems in music therapy with an eleven-year-old girl, a survivor of early trauma and sexual abuse, and illustrates the integrative, healing potential of spontaneously improvised songs. Case material spans fourteen months of this child's individual music therapy within an inpatient child and adolescent mental health setting. The study focuses on musical and psychodynamic processes of containment and transformation in a synthesis of clinical perspectives that is the author's model of "poietic processes in music therapy." The case study also illustrates how the child's defensive modes of expression are worked with musically and psychodynamically toward a more emotionally expressive and authentic sense of self.

[*] Acknowledgment: I would like to thank my clients, young and old, who continue to help me learn how to help them. I would also like to thank Susan Hadley for allowing this case study to be presented in detail.

INTRODUCTION

"What's music therapy meant for anyway? Is it to cheer you up if you're unhappy, or is it to see if you're a happy child?" asks Lena, her words tumbling forth at high speed. Her cheeks are flushed, and eyes bright, as she anxiously surveys the music therapy room—and me. In a slower tempo, I reply, "It can feel like that, can't it. Is that what you think it is?" Wistfully, Lena responds, "No, I think it's to tell if you're unhappy, or if you are . . . ." She falls silent and thoughtful, playing dreamily on a nearby bass metallophone. I accompany her, in tonally rooted harmonies with a gentle pulse. I sing: "Sometimes we're happy. . . . Sometimes we're sad." Lena joins in, and gradually leads the song, expressing her own feelings. As well as reassuring her that she could be happy, the song also invites her indirectly to express the sadness she has inferred in her opening questions. Our song suggests that all kinds of feelings have a place in our music. This is the beginning of our journey together—a music journey. Using metaphors and narratives of destruction, resurrection, and rebirth, her song-poems reveal an intuitive wisdom beyond her years as she begins to explore feelings that are difficult for her to bear in everyday life. Within the security of the musical therapeutic relationship, her sense of despair, anger, and self-disgust surface, and gradually give way to a surer sense of herself, with the hope of a better life.

When a song arises in music therapy, we hear something special. Freshly minted in the moment, song comes from the deepest roots of our being, our embodied self, and enters the creative flow of life. Person means literally "to sound through," and so the voice, with its subtleties of intonation, rhythmic flow, intensity, and texture, carries the essence of each person's individuality. As a bridge between our inner and outer worlds, and in the borderland between conscious and unconscious life, song can communicate our innermost feelings. Whether in a rush of joy or anger, in the turmoil of anxiety or the tranquility of musing and reflection, when a song grows from spontaneously expressed feelings it is in a sense both a container and transformer of feelings, whereby new meanings may be forged. Songs seem designed to communicate something essential and significant, and are at their most powerful when drawing from lived experience. In music therapy, they can become a means of experiential integration, addressing past and present and helping the client look ahead to the future. This has occurred in my work with many clients of all ages, but never more so than with a child called Lena,[1] whose music therapy I describe in this chapter. Lena's spontaneous song-poems were a channel for unconscious feelings and the development of an authentic sense of her self that had been distorted by early trauma and sexual abuse (Young, 1992). The case study of Lena illustrates how songs[2] in themselves provided the containing and transforming function that she needed, by working within the metaphors and the musical forms in which her feelings and thoughts were expressed. By this, I mean unconscious aspects of her self were expressed in metaphors that arose musically and verbally in the music-therapeutic relationship. This permitted therapeutic working within the metaphor and the music, without prematurely "breaking down" all her self-protective defenses by unduly literal interpretations and "bringing to consciousness."[3]

In the music-therapeutic process, musical receptivity and expression, developmental and psychodynamic thinking come together in a synthesis of perspectives that variously take their turns in the foreground of my awareness. In my work with verbal and preverbal children and adolescents, as well as adult patients, I found that a synthesis of musical-dynamic phenomena and psychodynamic processes needed to be brought together to elucidate both the music-dynamic and psychodynamic as one indivisible "poietic" or creative-constructive process immanent in the music-making (Robarts, 2000).

Before discussing these theoretical and clinical considerations in more detail, I shall introduce Lena and describe her early childhood.

---

[1] The child's name and certain details of the family history and events surrounding the therapy have been altered in order to preserve confidentiality, while retaining the salient features of the therapy process.

[2] I have not included a literature review, which would be too extensive for the purposes of this case study. The use of song in music therapy has been reported in a range of clinical and social settings, informed by different therapeutic models and by the personal, cultural, musical backgrounds of the therapists (Bruscia, 1987, 1991, 1998). They include accounts of free improvisational vocalizing and self-composed songs (Aigen, 1997; Austin, 1998, 2001; Irgens-Möller, 1999; Montello, 1998; Nordoff and Robbins, 1971, 1977; Robarts, 1999; Scheiby, 1998; Tyler, 1997). Precomposed songs and songwriting are reported by Diaz de Chumaceiro (1995, 1998), Lindenberg (1995), Martin (1996), Nordoff and Robbins (1977, 1971), Robb (1996). Songs in a wide range of clinical, educational, and social contexts, including child and adolescent psychiatry, are described by Irgens-Möller (1999); Nordoff and Robbins (1971, 1977), Robarts (2000), Tervo (2001), and in various hospital and residential settings (Aasgaard, 2000; Christenberry, 1979; Pavlicevic, 1999; Robb, 1996; Turry, 1999). Detailed clinical accounts of the therapeutic process in the use of improvised song are given by Austin (2001), Dvorkin (1991), Etkin (1999), Turry (1999), Tyler (1997).

[3] I agree with Bruscia's understanding that "Traditional psychoanalytic methods of analyzing verbal exchanges in therapy are not always appropriate or relevant with musical exchanges in therapy" (Bruscia, 1998, p. 389). This is particularly important to bear in mind with significantly emotionally disturbed children and those with a fragile core to their developing sense of self.

BACKGROUND INFORMATION

An attractive, lively child, with wavy auburn hair, Lena was the youngest of three children, the only girl, in a Caucasian family. Her parents had worked in different professions in the public services. Lena's early history reveals patterns of early emotional difficulties and increasing emotional-behavioral disturbance. Lena's mother had not wanted a third child. She breast-fed her baby successfully for five months, but added that Lena was a "difficult baby," often crying, and not sleeping properly in the day from the time she was five months old. She could be soothed, however, by her mother stroking her and singing to her. Developmental milestones were normal. However, at one year old, Lena had several febrile convulsions; thereafter she slept badly at night as well as in the daytime. At two years old, Lena was traumatically separated from her mother for two months, while her mother was hospitalized for some medical investigations. Looked after by her paternal grandparents and her father, Lena was not taken to see her mother at all during this time. Her father was strict and preferred to keep Lena at home rather than risk the disruption of bringing this "difficult child" to see her mother in the hospital. He was a disciplinarian, and did not show affection to his daughter. On her mother's return, Lena clung to her, and showed a high degree of anxiety at any further separations from her mother. A few months after the family was reunited following her mother's hospitalization, and when Lena was two and a half years old, her father committed suicide. There was a history of depression and suicide on the paternal side of the family. The truth about the circumstances of his death was kept secret from the children, only emerging during Lena's treatment at the child and adolescent psychiatry unit. At the age of four, Lena's behavior was described as increasingly difficult and hyperactive; she was referred to an educational psychologist. Lena was also noted to be isolated from her peers at school and did not like physical contact. She occasionally demanded a cuddle from adults, but shrugged off any intimacy unless initiated by herself. She had difficulties in learning to read and write. Assessed as being of average intelligence, she was greatly underachieving educationally, and suffered from low self-esteem. At school, she was given special help. At home, she continued to be a clinging and "difficult" child, always seeking attention. Lena's main solace was several small pets that she kept at home. She loved all animals, wild and domestic.

When Lena was nine years old, her behavior became increasingly disturbed. In the classroom and in other public places she masturbated against or astride furniture or toy animals, shouting explicitly sexual language. Added to this, she urinated and defecated in inappropriate places in her home and at school. She had begun eating cat and dog food, and was often observed crawling on all fours, like an animal. Her bizarre and eroticized behavior was uncontainable in school; there were concerns, too, for her being at home without full-time supervision. The following year, Lena confided in her mother that she had been sexually abused, but no immediate help was sought. Aged eleven years, Lena was admitted to the inpatient child and adolescent psychiatry unit. The reason for her referral was her extreme emotional and behavioral disturbance, and sexually disinhibited behavior. Lena had been abused by her brother and one of his friends; but it transpired that she had suffered much earlier sexual abuse by her paternal grandfather, probably starting when her mother was in the hospital. Psychologists and teachers described Lena as being rather nonchalant and "adult" in her manner, showing little emotion when talking about painful events. When asked if she cried, she said she was crying inside. When talking about her father's death, she said she never cried, even when hurt. Lena's brother and the rest of the family also were engaged in the therapeutic program.

At this point it is worthwhile reviewing all the factors that contributed to Lena's difficulties: maternal ambivalence, resulting in poor emotional attachment; the baby's febrile convulsions; early separation trauma; sexual abuse from a very young age; and the secrets in a family with a history of suicidal depression. There were obvious transgenerational deficits in parenting: in particular, difficulties in expressing feelings, coupled with a weak sense of relationship boundaries in the family. In addition to sexualized and bizarre behavior, low self-esteem, and underachievement in her educational development, Lena displayed many symptoms of post-traumatic stress disorder.

Early Childhood Sexual Abuse and Post-Traumatic Stress Disorder

Sexual abuse in early childhood is a trauma that has a global impact with lasting consequences for the developing child. Lena displayed all the major symptoms of post-traumatic stress disorder (DSM-IV, 1994): dissociative states, persistent symptoms of increased arousal, poor capacity to self-regulate, a distorted development of sense of self, persistent avoidance of stimuli associated with the trauma, numbing of feelings, and persistent reexperiencing of the event (Herman, 1992).

CLINICAL-THEORETICAL PERSPECTIVES

A Musical, Developmental, and Psychodynamic View of Psychic Structure

My main clinical-theoretical influences come from (i) Nordoff-Robbins Music Therapy, (ii) infant developmental psychology, and (iii) object relations theory, particularly influenced by the work of psychoanalytic child psychotherapist, Anne Alvarez (Alvarez, 1992, 1999), Wilfred Bion (1962a, 1962b) and Donald Winnicott (1965/1990, 1971). All are relational models, which emphasize inter-personal experiences as the dynamic "building blocks" of intrapersonal or self-structure; they operate differently from those based on Freudian drive theory. Music therapy augments dynamic relational processes by using music as the primary medium of relationship. Briefly, I shall consider these three strands to my thinking: (i) The concept of the "Music Child" (Nordoff & Robbins, 1977), and its extension in the "Condition Child" (Robbins & Robbins, 1991), elucidating how potentiating the child's innate musicality can help the child (or adult) restricted by psychopathology, or by a fragile or impoverished core of the self. Evidently, Nordoff and Robbins were working within a musical-dynamic relational perspective: a perspective that utilizes to the full the "therapy that lies in music" (Aigen, 1997, 1999; Nordoff & Robbins, 1971; Turry, 1998). In my view, Nordoff and Robbins' account of the interpersonal and resistive (defensive) aspects of the musical relationship reveals some of the inner workings of the musical transference and countertransference, without actually using those terms (Robarts, 1994; Turry, 1998). (ii) From a developmental per-spective, music engages what psychobiologist and infancy researcher, Colwyn Trevarthen describes as the "intrinsic motive pulse," the core motivations of the self and at the root of interregulatory processes of intersubjectivity, emotional and cultural learning (Trevarthen, 1999; Trevarthen and Malloch, 2000). Trevarthen's ideas illuminate Nordoff and Robbins's concept of the Music Child and the principle of innate musicality that is a basic premise of many approaches to music therapy. From this psychobiological and develop-mental understanding of human musicality, we are shown the significance of musical communication in supporting and augmenting interregulatory processes involved in self-experiencing and in the very structuring of the self and self-in-relation-to another. Lastly, (iii) the musical-therapeutic relationship brings into play the internal and musical worlds of both client and therapist. Psychodynamic understanding can help to "map" the complex psychic phenomena that arise within the music and the music therapy relationship, which can be understood through transference and counter-transference. The therapeutic relationship is also a process of symbolization, growing meaning in the real world of self and self-in-relation. Clinical work with some children demands this level of understanding more than with others. With the child who projects anxieties and intense feelings into the therapist, onto the instruments, and into the music space, or, conversely, with the child who is remote and seemingly unreachable, I have found this interplay of clinical-theoretical perspectives useful. It has come together naturally in my clinical work over many years, learning from my clients, but has also been developed by study and supervision with child psychotherapists.

Poietic Processes in Music Therapy: A Synthesis of Musical, Developmental and Psychodynamic Phenomena

Derived from the Greek verb *poiein*, to make or construct, "poietic" describes the creative-constructive processes in Lena's music therapy (Robarts, 2000). Such "building" is a physical, psychological, psychodynamic, and artistic process. In my clinical work, this model of "poietic processes" grounds Trevarthen's concept of intersubjectivity and cultural learning, together with a developmentally informed object relations theory, in creative improvisational music therapy (see Figures 1 and 2). This theoretical perspective has grown gradually over twenty years of music therapy with emotionally disturbed, anorexic, and autistic clients of all ages (Robarts, 1994, 1998, 2000; Robarts and Sloboda, 1994). In brief, the poietic process model spans three "fields" or levels of response: from the neurobiological level of tonal-rhythmic sympathetic resonance in Field 1, where experience is embodied as "procedural memory" (discussed below). This leads to increasingly defined self-expression in musical-aesthetic forms (or gestalts) of Field 2 that, in Field 3, may culminate in metaphors of the child's autobiographical self within the music-therapeutic relationship. I have also indicated the way in which the processes of symbolization may operate in reverse: proceeding from Field 3, the image or metaphor may act as a "container" for working toward the spontaneity of the emergent organizational level of the self (Fields 1 and 2). This can be useful when responses/feelings at Field 1 level are too heavily defended against to work with directly. Offering a structure or image (Field 3) can provide the necessary security in which to access the spontaneity in the authentically emergent organization of self (Field 1). Furthermore, these poietic phenomena may arise either in the musical material, or as a felt image or sensation in the countertransference. I used my listening and countertransference, musically and verbally, to work with the metaphors in Lena's songs, and to sense whether her defenses would be better addressed directly, or indirectly within the metaphor. As will be seen in this case, I usually opted for the latter.

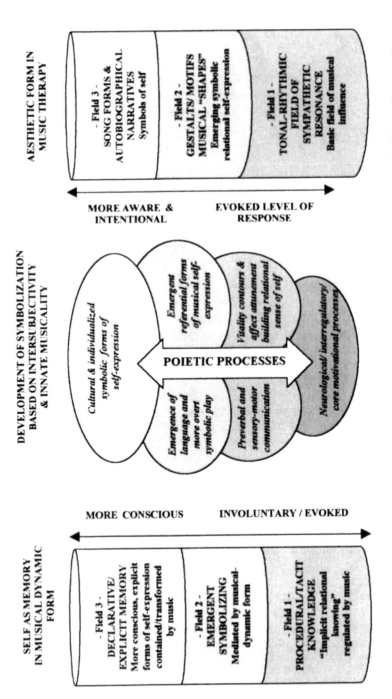

Figure 1: Poietic Processes in Music Therapy: Experiential Integration in Musical Aesthetic Form (Aspect 1): Aspects 1 and 2 (see Figure 2) overlap and inform each other in terms of clinical processes of musical and psychodynamic phenomena. Poietic processes manifest in the space and time of musical-aesthetic form, developmental and psychodynamic phenomena.

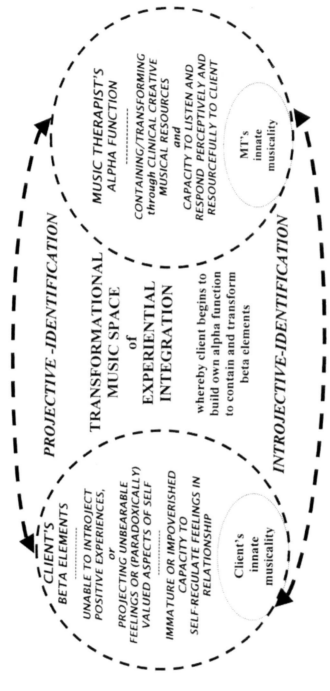

Figure 2: Poietic Processes in Music Therapy: Experiential Integration in Musical Aesthetic Form Informed by an Object Relations Perspective (Alvarez, 1992; Bion, 1962a and b; Robarts, 1994), showing the *bi-directional* nature of the transference, projection and introjection. In music therapy, these processes emphasize musical means of containment and transformation in the transference. The phenomena of innate musicality and the dynamic properties of music link Aspects 1 and 2 of this music therapy model. N.B. This model elucidates the usefulness of the therapist having his/her own therapy and supervision (in their respective functions) to support good clinical practice.

Song and The Procedural Domain of the Preverbal Self

Song can bring forth emotions and images from preverbal and visceral levels, beyond conscious and verbal recall. The preverbal self is the domain of procedural memory, which is the first sense of self, described by Freud as the "bodily ego" (Freud, 1923/1961). Developed in the early intimacy of infant-parent relating, the preverbal self is a social construction of implicit relational knowing (Emde et al., 1991). It continues throughout the life span, undergoing modifications according to life experiences. When the preverbal self is traumatized in early development, the neural "template" of the sense of self and self-in-relation is damaged, with lasting consequences. For the person who has suffered early trauma that has become embodied as part of the body-mind self, and often beyond verbal recall, the power of music and singing can be a healing process (Austin, 2001). The preverbal self (or implicit relational knowing) is thought to function in quite a different way from the verbal self and declarative memory, the storehouse of our experiences that we can search and recollect consciously (Stern et al., 1998). However, in my clinical experience, these two forms of memory or self-experiencing, tacit and explicit, can be bridged by art forms that "speak the language" of the preverbal self. In such cases, music can be used creatively not only accessing the procedural domain of experience, but also in forging new relational experiences at that level, in musical dynamic interplay. These experiences are generally unplanned, and arise spontaneously. This musical model of experiential integration is quite different from the "bringing to consciousness" of the classical psychoanalytic model of internal conflict and repression that is sometimes applied to music therapy.

Avoiding Retraumatizing the Child

In working with abused children, or children who have suffered early trauma in music therapy, the therapist needs to be aware of the impact that the intimacy of musical relationship may bring and the paradoxical feelings in the child that even the slightest display of empathy may trigger. Frequently, the projections of the abused child's terrorized and traumatized self makes the therapist feel like one of the perpetrators of abuse (Rogers, 1992, 1995). This was so in my work with Lena. To avoid retraumatizing Lena, I relied on my musical resource-fulness, alongside psychodynamic understanding of what was happening in the transference, in order to contain her anxieties and projections. It would have been all too easy to sing "happy" songs with Lena to cheer her up, colluding with her defense against feeling her real emotions. My capacity to receive and then hold the intensity of transference feelings along with her projections of sexual, brutalizing experiences was put even more to the test, when her behavior became eroticized within the music therapy sessions. Sexually perverted projections are not easy territory to work with alone. I was glad to have the support of fortnightly supervision. Working within an interdisciplinary team also enabled me to see my work with Lena in the wider context of the treatment program, and learn from their expertise with damaged children.

At this point, it may be useful to consider in more detail the psychodynamic concepts referred to so far.

Containment and Transformation: Psychodynamic and Developmental Perspectives and Their Application to Music Therapy[4]

The concept of containment was developed by Wilfrid Bion (Bion, 1962a, 1962b) from Melanie Klein's original ideas of transference and the related intrapsychic processes of projection, introjection, projective, and introjective identification. To this concept of containment he added the idea of transformation to describe what happens when the mother/therapist receives the projections of infant/client, understands and thinks about it (which he termed "maternal reverie"), and then gives it back in a useful form, that can be felt with less anxiety, and perhaps (at the right time) thought about. This has many parallels with the function of aesthetic form in the music therapy process I describe in this case study. "Containment" is a term that Donald Winnicott also described as "a holding environment." However, there are significant differences between Winnicott's and Bion's concept of "holding" or "containing." Whereas Winnicott's concept emphasizes the mother[5] providing "good enough" care that creates a secure environment—an intermediate space—in which the child can begin to become creative, Bion's idea of containment involves a concept of space, but one that is more internal and communicative. Bion emphasizes not only the mother's receptivity to the child's anxiety, but also her capacity to understand and give expression to the baby's unbearable feelings in a way that the child can take in. If the baby's experiences are intolerable to his immature system, he then projects these feelings (Bion called them "beta elements") psychically into the mother, who then, identifying with the child's emotional state and able to hold them in her mind/feelings and understand them, gives his feelings back transformed by her "understanding" response (for which Bion's term was "alpha function"). Such understanding is most frequently intuitive,

---

[4] For fuller discussion of this rich area of theoretical and clinical perspectives, I refer the reader to *The Dynamics of Music Psychotherapy* edited by Kenneth Bruscia, 1998, although this excellent text does not discuss work with children and adolescents from an early object relations perspective relevant to this case study.

[5] I refer to the mother, with whom the most immediate bonding with her infant has taken place over her nine months' pregnancy, although I recognize that many fathers nowadays are equal or even primary caregivers from their child's early infancy.

and, at a preverbal level, the "transformation" that takes place may be vocal and gestural in form and content, with exaggerated rhythmic and melodic features. Bion used the analogy of the digestive system to describe early mental processes: taking in and giving out. I find this analogy helpful in considering therapeutic work: the way that music is taken in and given out, the aesthetic dynamic forms of music therapy processes that create space and stillness, stability, and the right conditions for feeling and thought. Elsewhere, I have described early object relations in terms of musical introjects and symbolization (Robarts, 1994, p. 234). Regulatory processes in music are the aesthetic creation of a space to think, and, as such, are a form of containment and transformation. The musical aspects of containment and transformation, for instance, might involve phrase length, harmonic texture, pace, or tempo. Is the music too "spicy" or too bland? Is the child responding to a four-measure phrase, or is this indigestible, and would a three-note motif be something the child can take in more easily? The music-psychodynamic aspects of the transference, and particularly defensive phenomena, can be experienced in terms of time and space, intensity; matching or not matching, foreground and background, waiting and listening, or playing and creating interactively.[6]

There is another important consideration, to which I have alluded above, concerning the countertransference of the therapist and the therapist's capacity to hold on to the child's anxieties and incipient or fragmented forms of communication. In working with very disturbed children who have a fragile core sense of self, the therapist may need to be able to hold onto these projected anxieties for much longer than with clients with a stronger ego function (Alvarez, 1992). I have found this to be true with both child and adult clients. Alvarez's theory of deficit and "reclamation" emphasizes that, while therapists need to become "alerters, arousers, and enliveners," they also need to be "capable of being disturbed enough to feel for the patient, and at the same time sane enough to think with him, until the patient's own ego, his thinking self, grows enough to be able to do it for himself" (Alvarez, 1992, p. ix).

A further insight of Alvarez is that severely disturbed children (she refers to borderline, psychotic, abused, and autistic children) may barely have developed "defenses" and these may need to be viewed as a *positive* development when they do manifest. This has particular importance in working with abused and traumatized children, whose self-protective defenses need to be respected and worked with sensitively by the therapist. No amount of therapy will "undo" the fact of sexual abuse, but there are ways to build new meanings

---

[6] For further exploration of the inner workings of improvisational music therapy Bruscia's *Improvisational Models of Music Therapy* (Bruscia, 1987) and Nordoff and Robbins's *Creative Music Therapy* (Nordoff & Robbins, 1977) are classic texts for systematized clinically perceptive musical observations.

and new structures of relating, to enable some healing of the damaged self. Working within the metaphors of Lena's songs enabled the maintaining of her much needed defenses, while at the same time delicately bypassing these same defenses to address her anxieties and nurture her creative capacities. In this way music therapy was able to forge new ways of relating and experiencing herself, while addressing the early trauma of abuse and ongoing difficulties.

TREATMENT PROCESS

Inpatient Treatment Program

At the inpatient child psychiatry unit Lena received a range of therapeutic help, as did her family—but on an outpatient basis, which unfortunately made Lena feel even more rejected. Family therapy, individual sessions with a nurse therapist/key worker, special schooling on the unit, and music therapy were part of her regular treatment, in addition to various children's groups and structured activities that took place on the unit. Weekly ward rounds ensured effective communication among the team members. This was vital as Lena took every opportunity to challenge and "split" the staff on her program of care. She was a deeply disturbed and disturbing child, whose painful feelings were so intolerable that they were readily projected into her carers and would ricochet around the team, had we not been aware of this phenomenon. Supervision was, therefore, an essential part of our teamwork.[7] As there was no full-time child psychotherapist to see the children, the nurses received supervision from a child psychotherapist and family therapist; while I received supervision privately from a child psychoanalytic psychotherapist and consulted a senior music therapy colleague.

Music therapy took place quite near the child psychiatry inpatient unit, in a separate building. The music therapy room was equipped with a grand piano and a wide range of percussion instruments, small and large, including small simple wind instruments, such as birdcalls. With the parents' and/or guardians' permission and, where possible, the child's permission, sessions are recorded on audiotape. The tapes formed a confidential clinical record, enabling reviewing of the musical and other content of the sessions to carry forward as and when necessary from week to week (Nordoff & Robbins, 1971). Additionally, a child might want to listen to the tape, or to record something in a particular way.

---

[7] Recent articles that discuss supervision in detail include Brown (1997), Dvorkin (1999), Frohne-Hagemann (1999), and Rogers (1992, 1995) in relation to working with sexually abused children.

According to how the children used the sessions, my approach to music therapy would sometimes embrace other art forms, such as drawing or painting, puppets, dance, and drama—although not in the case study described here. This use of other expressive arts in the music therapy sessions generally arose out of the child's spontaneous imaginative responses and was developed within the music-based therapeutic process (the musical field of relationship being the vital link in musically supporting and developing the child's feelings and imaginative play).

LENA'S MUSIC THERAPY

Lena's music therapy sessions began shortly after her admission to the unit, increasing from once to twice weekly after the first month, each session lasting forty-five minutes. To transcribe our music adequately would require a vocal, percussion, and piano score, so I present here the words, and describe some of the music within the therapeutic process. The poietic processes model is implicit throughout the case material. It may be helpful to refer to Figures 1 and 2 as a reminder of the underlying principles of the therapeutic process. Lena's fourteen months of music therapy fall roughly into three phases. Phase 1, illustrated below by Sessions 1, 3, 4, and 11, is characterized by listening; songs developing relationship and trust; idealization and self-protective defense; and, symbolic use of musical instruments. Phase 2, illustrated by Sessions 15 and 37, is characterized by anxieties expressed in song poems, later giving way to chaotic and eroticized play; metaphors of the borderland between the unconscious and conscious arising in song; and, symbolic use of instruments. Phase 3, illustrated by Sessions 40, 43–57, and 63 is characterized by beginnings of integration, expressions of sorrow at parting, and hope for the future; and, metaphors of transformation. From hereon in the case study I shall write in the present tense until the Discussion and Conclusion.

Phase 1

Lena's first session is typical of the early months of our work: a hive of activity. Her anxiety shows in her mood, and in her avoidance of shared play and of silences. The detail in this session conveys my feeling of being "flooded" with activity, anxiety, shifts in mood, and general scatter; hovering on the brink of something significant brewing beneath the surface.

Session 1: Containing anxiety; scattered play as a self-protective defense; brief expression of deeper feelings.

Lena darts around the room, examining everything, but never engaging in play. She speaks so quickly that I catch only a few phrases: "Why is music therapy *therapy*? Is it for happy or sad feelings?" I reply that music can be for all kinds of feelings: happy and sad—angry, too. I take care not to infer that she might have sad feelings at this early stage in our relationship. As I speak, Lena has already turned away, and is picking up instruments one after another. I am uncertain that she has taken in anything I have said. Her playing scatters from one instrument to another. At the piano, I play a quiet pulse of major 10ths in the bass register to provide a steadying background. Lena finds a slide whistle, on which she blows slow ascending and descending glissandi. She quickly objects to my accompanying her. She orders me to stop playing and listen to her. She reminds me of a young child who wants her mother's undivided attention. If I let my concentration waver for a second, Lena reasserts her tyranny over me more strongly than before. I feel at once like a puppet on a string, being manipulated by Lena, and a dustbin, a container for feelings that Lena is not communicating overtly to me, or even to herself. In Lena's play, and in my countertransference, I also feel a "lost-ness" and "never-finding-anything-to-be-contented-with." I hold onto these feelings, while I try to help her find herself in some sustained cohesive form of play. In order to hold her attention and focus, it helps to tell her that I am listening to her: "Oh, what was that?" "Could you play that again?" Still more effective are my sudden in-breaths and expressions of interest. This engages her in sustained play, with repetitions of certain formal elements, conveying stillness (and containment) at last.

After a while, Lena approaches me at the piano, but seems anxious. She does not sit down until I have moved to sit at a distance from her. She wants me to listen to her playing, but, as before, does not tolerate my joining her. However, she now seems calmer, less watchful. This represents to me a much healthier "aloneness" than the previous chaotic "scatter." I think of the positive signs of integration or "ego-relatedness" shown by the child's capacity to be alone (Winnicott, 1965/1990). Lena plays a well-known theme from Grieg's Peer Gynt Suite on the black notes (soh-mi-re-doh-re-mi, soh-mi-re-doh-re-mi) but only the first phrase, repeating it endlessly: and then, less successfully, on white notes. This endless string of notes absorbs her interest. I am reminded of the awful gap of her separation from her mother: much of Lena's play, despite her involvement in the predictable, never-ending musical structure, seems to be avoidance, a fear of any space, perhaps filling the gap, so that there is no space for unbearable feelings. After an extensive solo, she suddenly scampers over to the percussion instruments, at the same time telling me to play the piano. I accompany her frantic playing of drum and cymbal, metallophone, trying to match the chaos, while also bringing about some musical organization to steady her playing. At last, we share the basic beat of a sturdy march. Lena plays all the instruments she can at once. The march succeeds in holding her flailing movements in a coordinated rhythmic experience, her feet stamping as she plays. Her mood changes, feelings deepen. The march improvisation slows, as Lena begins to sing a hymn. I harmonize her evolving melody with a few chords here and there. This is tolerated for a few seconds before Lena demands that I stop the music. She then announces, at great speed and quite cheerfully, that two of her pets have died today. Without a pause, she informs me that she is good at singing, and promptly sings a song from her school's Christmas play, in which she had the part of an angel. She wants to know if I think she has "gifts" in her hands. She is now becoming overexcited, wanting to see inside everything, including the piano. I comment (in song) that she seems interested in the inside of things (I hold onto her blithe announcement of her pets' deaths, thinking that perhaps we may venture inside her feelings about them eventually, perhaps linking this with her stopping the music). I remind her of her initial question about music therapy, and a song begins to emerge: "Sometimes we're happy, sometimes we're sad." In this way, the song is acting as a container in which "happy" and "sad" feelings may be encountered in a bearable way. She is beginning to venture inside her feelings, first expressing sadness about her animals' deaths.

In this first session the use of pulse, motif, familiar themes, my listening to her—"taking it all in"—have been fundamental in containing Lena's anxieties, building her trust in our musical relationship. Everything happens in quick succession, like a butterfly alighting on this flower and the next. However, Lena begins to touch on her real feelings, held by the song form with its underlying pulse and harmonies that enhance and seek to deepen the emotional content of her words. She presents me with a rather idealized picture of herself as good, feeling she is rejected because she is less than "perfect" (a theme reiterated in nearly all her songs until the final phase). There are indications of projective identification with me, as she plays the piano, while also perhaps defending against feelings of anger or anxiety, which leads to her excluding me intermittently from her play. There are possible associations of my exclusion with the abandonment Lena must have felt as a little girl. I find the session quite confusing, and overwhelming, and am glad that the music holds my being and thinking as well as Lena. I witness and contain all of this anxiety, acknowledging to myself that this must be how Lena feels and has felt for much of her life. I also realize that there is a great deal of work to be done at many levels in Lena's music therapy.

Session 3: Nursery songs, the "Music House"; symbolic use of the instruments[8] as containers.

Today, Lena arrives in what I now recognize to be her habitual superficially "happy" mood. After playing the Peer Gynt tune rather perfunctorily, Lena abandons the piano, and surrounds herself with musical instruments, creating a "music house" on the far side of the room. This symbolic use of the instruments is to be extended in later sessions, but, in this session, the instruments are arranged to form a physical barrier as much as a "container." She once again demands that I listen attentively to her playing, without joining in myself. From within her barricade, however, she now begins to permit some musical interaction within familiar nursery songs: She requests "Pop Goes the Weasel," "Hickory Dickory Dock," and "Ring a Ring of Roses." These songs emerged in Session 2; they share a similar structure, and the first two feature her beloved animals (although the "weasel" in this song is not actually an animal). Lena jumps up and down like a three-year-old as she plays inside her music house, especially enjoying the dramatic moments in each song. Her physical responses to the music show how efficiently the music regulates her tendency to over-excitement in shared play. By improvising clear phrase structures in music that matches her mood, I can "hold" her feelings, musically transforming them into normal excitement and pleasure. I use an altered diatonic, that brings an emotional "edge" to the traditional concordant harmonic palette. The nursery song structures offer her a certain predictability in which she can begin to trust our relationship. Nevertheless, her use of the songs is also quite defensive and controlling. I sing about her feeling safe inside her music house. I introduced a rondo form (ABACAD, etc) that uses her familiar tunes as a secure base from which she then engages in free vocalizing and improvisational-conversational exchanges. This style of refrain and episodic improvisational play develops in subsequent sessions.

---

[8] Symbolic use of the musical instruments is an aspect of music therapy, revealing pathology, developmental and psychodynamic features; and can evoke associations (from shape, timbre, color, and other characteristics); stories and characterization may also arise from different types of instruments. The transitional qualities, in a Winnicottian sense, have been described in music therapy by Bruscia (Bruscia, 1987), Nolan in relation to work with bulimic clients (Nolan, 1989) and, by Rogers in relation to her work with sexually abused children (Rogers, 1992).

Session 4: A happy/sad song brings Lena in touch with her real feelings, and builds a more trusting working relationship.

Lena wanders around the room rather distractedly. I play the Child's Tune motif (soh-mi-la-soh-mi) in unison, interspersed with close-textured diatonic harmonies. Lena repeats her questions from Session 1: What's music therapy for, anyway? I answer her musings about music therapy leading into a gentle I Ib IV V accompaniment—banal in its predictability, wherein lies its therapeutic value in this instance. It becomes a refrain, to which we return, when the musical development of emotional expression is more than Lena can bear:

We can sing a happy song,   We can sing a happy song,
Cheer us up, cheer us up;   To cheer us up today.

Lena beats a counter-melody on the metallophone, stopping intuitively at each cadence. I repeat the first phrase of the song:

We can sing a happy song,
Cheer us up, cheer us up.

Lena joins in, singing and beating a conga drum and a cymbal so chaotically that her singing is almost inaudible. I offer a contrasting idea (verbally and musically) to steady her beating and to begin to get in touch with her sadness:

We can sing if we're sad.

I deliberately use "we," as a way of indicating there is someone to share the "not happy" feelings, and to avoid referring too directly to her, and triggering her defense against sadness. The melody, previously characterized by ascending intervals, now is inverted as a descending phrase, in a minor key, and in a slightly slower tempo. Lena does not respond, so I sing another phrase:

We - can - sing, if we're sa-a-ad. . . .

This time Lena echoes: We - can - sing, if we're sa-a-ad. . . .

Lena's singing now enters fully into the music's sadder mood, adding her own inflection of the melody. I continue singing and accompanying, to sustain this mood: Sometimes we're sad. . . .

Lena interjects quickly: . . . . or happy. . . .

Spontaneously she continues:

Sometimes we're full of so-r-row	The sky's nice and bright,
Sometimes we laugh with joy, full of joy,	There's happiness in the air.

My music reflects this idea with rippling scale sequences in the upper registers of the piano. I hear a gentle sadness in my music (still in minor key) with slightly increased harmonic tension, thereby holding the two contrasting moods that Lena has expressed. Lena breaks off suddenly from her singing and playing, saying chirpily: Let's start with what you said a minute ago!

I feel that Lena is defending against her own emerging emotions that I have reflected in the music. I decide to revert once more to the safety of our predictable and rather banal "happy" chorus. At this change of mood, Lena is able to join in singing again. The sadness was too much for her to bear getting in touch with. She sings rather wanly: We can be so happy. . . .

She then stops singing and chatters at such speed that I can barely grasp any of it, except that she wants to "get back to the bit about being happy." Her verbal defense against any other feelings is evident; her desperation about being happy rather than thinking about her real feelings is particularly poignant. I concur with a "happy" phrase, hoping to reengage Lena's singing and feelings again rather than her verbal defenses against her emotions.

I sing: Happy, happy day.

I continue in the minor key bridge section of the song, reintroducing the feelings that Lena has seemed to deflect, "split off," and which I am now feeling strongly in my countertransference: Sometimes . . . we feel sad. . . .

This time Lena takes over the song again, expressing her feelings more authentically, with the image of a lonely, upset child:

Sometimes we feel . . .	And lovely shiny faces . . .
like we're small and the world's against us;	Children playing outside,
Some days we feel full of joy	happy and joy
and happiness in the air	Someone sitting on their own, being upset

Lena beats the cymbal and drum sforzando. She stops just as suddenly as she has begun and continues her singing, reverting to the idea of "happiness." She now sings wistfully in response to my delicate, almost imperceptible accompaniment. I have shifted from E major into B minor as Lena sings:

Sometimes we're very happy if it's our birthday
They sing "Happy Birthday" or "Merry Christmas"
It's nice to see the New Year and go "Cheers!"
And Merry Christmas is a good thing.

I briefly play the theme of a carol. However, this is curtailed by Lena guiding me straight back into her improvised song. She says eagerly: "See if we can do that again—I like making things up!" I comply, musically reflecting her wistfulness: Sometimes we're happy....

Lena joins in at the phrase end: ... 'appy....

She continues singing, with a touching lyricism, while I accompany her, marking the pulse and harmonically coloring some of the emotive phrases:

Sometimes we're sad
Sometimes we're mee-dium
Sometimes we're angry
Sometimes we're pleased
with the work we've done
Sometimes we're pleased

with our friends ...
and our animals ...
When you've been naughty,
you don't get nice things
If you're good, you get lovely things,
'cause being naughty is bad

Lena repeats the last line followed by sforzando beating on the drum, cymbal and metallophone, before continuing her song, sweetly:

But if you're like an angel, you get things nicer
And you get lots of cuddles and things like that.

At this cadence, Lena beats the drum and cymbal excitedly, demands a repetition of the "Happy Song," and this time develops it even more expressively. I accompany her slightly allargando, drawing out the vowels in her singing, to create more space for her feelings, relaxing them and deepen them in her singing, as she continues her song:

Sometimes we're happy, sometimes we're sad,
Sometimes we're glad,
Sometimes we're ungrateful,
Sometimes we laugh, sometimes we sad
[here she renders the adjective as a verb]

Sometimes we laugh, sometimes we cough,
Sometimes we laugh, sometimes we... grump,
Sometimes we sulk, sometimes we're sad,
Sometimes we're full of sorrow again.

At the final cadence, with hardly a pause for breath, she begs: "Let's do another one . . . about Jesus . . . I made it up!"

It seems to be a song, that she already knows: one that has captured her imagination. She is impatient with me to get the tune exactly as she remembers it. Lena's paraphrasing is evident, as she uses the song to express her own feelings:

No room for Mary
Long ago two strangers came to town.
They wanted to find somewhere nice for little
Baby Jesus.
When long ago two strangers came to town,
They had to find somewhere,

Somewhere to find and warm a lovely baby
called Jesus Christ.
No room for Mary, no room at all,
But the world came to love
The Child from above
Who was born in a cattle stall.

Lena hums the refrain, before continuing:

Then He was born in Bethlehem,
There was crowds of people outside the cattle
stall;
Jesus was His name.
He is always there, and He grew so big, so big

That no one could believe. . . .
But no room for Mary, no room at all,
But the world came to love
The Child from above,
That was born in a cattle stall.

She hums the refrain again, exchanging phrases this time with my piano accompaniment. She seems deeply contented and calmer than I have yet seen her. She is held in the song, by the song, and in the dialogic singing that has developed quite naturally. In both songs, the song form itself has provided a means of containing and integrating Lena's feelings, allowing her to begin to tune into her real feelings. It has led to a deeper sharing of her feelings. The symbolism of the second song seems strongly connected with her feelings of rejection and being unlovable. In this song, Lena's underlying feelings begin to emerge from the rather false "perfect" self.

Session 11: "Bless my soul"/"Happiness in my hands": A song and piano duet consolidating trust, with a growing sense of autonomy.

Still difficult to engage musically in any sustained shared play, except in her songs, Lena shows me in her own way that she needs a predictable harmonic structure, as well as her habitual "never-ending" motifs. These can sometimes be interspersed with improvisational episodes that are more conversational, less controlled by Lena. Just as she generally takes the lead in her songs, she now demands to learn a well-known piano duet that some children are playing on the ward. There is a sense of her isolation and inability to join in or be accepted easily by other children. Usually played in C major the melody is a "circular" recurring one, over a solid basic I VI IV V I chord progression, which I vary only in the voicings, and in the rhythmic movement within the "vamp." This duet achieves predictability in its repetitive structure, which, I think, is its appeal to all children. Allowing me to point to the keys for her to play, Lena manages to approximate the melody after many repetitions, but gets annoyed and despondent. I suggest she make up a song to the tune, while I accompany her, using the same harmonic frame. She sings about herself, celebrating of the "gift in her hands." There is an obvious identification with me, and that the trustworthiness of her music-making experience has been internalized. She feels good about herself, which paves the way for later work on her abused self:

Bless my soul—she's a lucky girl,
She's got a gift from the piano,
From her head, from her hands;
With this gift she ca-an play,
With her hands she can play,
With her gift in her hands.

She's so happy that she can play . . .
She can play every single thing
Now, now, now . . .
But she can play
Bless my soul, a-aren't I lucky now

She plays freely on the treble keys, in tempo with me, and asks: "How do you make them?" (she means how did I play the accompaniment). "Can I play with the deep part and sing by myself?" Without waiting for an answer, she continues singing:

I can sing, Aren't I lucky, aren't I lucky!
I can sing, I can play, I can play

Playing the piano with me, she sings "doo-doo" to the tune in a contented though excited manner. I celebrate with her:

Oh, she's a lucky girl today,
She can play so well. Oh. . . .

Lena resumes: . . . she's lucky, I'm lucky but . . .

Since when I could not pla-ay,
I had no gifts somehow in my fingers;
How can they pla-ay?
I've got a gift in my hands;
And I did not know how to play
When I first came in

Now I can play piano with my good hands
(she plays)
With my hands I can play.
It's called 'Bless my soul and happiness in
my hands'
Aren't they clever, look!

We both hum, developing a dialogue, which she initially enjoys, then stops suddenly self-conscious. "Good" experiences can be as painful as "bad" ones, when they are unaccustomed; the intimacy of the humming exchanges is suddenly "too much." I quickly move away from the intimacy, to supporting her celebration of her hands, singing: Oh, clever, clever hands, happy. . .

Lena bobs up and down like a two-year-old, squealing excitedly, holding her hands up like a puppy to me: "Kiss my hands, cuddle my hands! I thought I'd never play!"

I hold them gently and sway them in time with her childish body movements, before she resumes the "Bless my soul" song. A coda follows, in which Lena celebrates her newfound ability to play, but conveys the idea of "horrible" feelings being bearable along with the happy ones. Singing about her hands reminds her of the butterfly she has made. This symbol of transformation seems rather apt.

I can pla-a-ay today;
It's raining and horrible, but I can play,
I don't care what the weather's like,
All I'm int'rested in is having a gift.
What can I do today . . . ?
With my little fingers?
I expect they're pleased that the-e-ey can play;
If I never ha-a-a-ad hands,
How could I play?
How could I play without ha-a-ands?
Hands are useful, you know,

Making art and doing art:
I made a butterfly yesterday,
Blue and . . . dark green.

If I had no hands,
How could I work or clap?
How could I play piano?
How could I do my art, or maths, or
Eng-ge-lish, or read?
What could I do, if I had no hands?
How could I sing you a song . . . ?

I punctuate the pause with a few soft 7th chords, seeking to extend this deepening of her self-expression, but she immediately reverts to the refrain of "Bless my soul." Humming the accompaniment to "doo-doo-doo-doo," as if to prompt me, she segues into the final verse:

Hands can play, hands can pla-a-ay,
Hands can play, as you . . . (indistinct)
Hands. . . .

If they've got a gift,
If they've got a gift,
If they've got a gift.

Flushed with pleasure, Lena cadences solemnly with her characteristic sense of musical form. Immediately after the cadence, she dissolves into effusive chatter, telling me about the butterfly she had made at school.

This is an important session in which Lena expresses her feelings freely and much more easily in music with me. As she celebrates her gift, she engages more wholeheartedly in play. Integrating good feelings about herself, and celebrating her other achievements in school as well, there is a positive sense of herself in action—"I did it." I remember Winnicott's words:

> It is in playing and only in playing that the child is able to be creative and use the whole personality, and it is only in being creative that the individual discovers the self (Winnicott, 1971).

Now regarded as the somewhat magical music person who had released this gift in her hands, I am increasingly idealized by Lena, but this is about to change. In subsequent sessions, Lena's anger begins to emerge.

Phase 2

Session 15: Disturbed infantile emotions expressed; symbolic use of the instruments in eroticized play.

Lena has become much more challenging in the sessions. She confronts me with her rage, her self-disgust, and tries to shock me in her infantile ways. The seriousness and trust that have grown in our working relationship in the music are of the utmost importance in the long months ahead. My listening to her, accompanying her songs, is terribly important to her. The following is typical of her songs at this time, when she is identifying herself with feces, animals, and saying that she comes from a pigsty. The song is humorous, self-deprecating, but also full of anger and despair:

The Poo

Once upon a time, there was a poo in the loo,
Brown and chocolate, its mouth looks at you.
It hopped up onto the bog paper[9]
When she got up, she found it on the floor,
Walking around, around and around the store.
She thought it strange to see a poo that could walk.
It had clothes and shoes.
She walked around and around as the poo.

The wee was like rain that nobody's trained,
Anybody see a wee-wee, then they'll be cross.
People threw the loo in the poo and the poo in the loo. . .
Poo-loo-loo-poo-poo-loo. . . .

Babbling but far from happy, Lena becomes increasingly upset and angry. She launches raucously into a children's song, emphasizing its crude innuendos:

Bananas in pajamas walking down the stairs.

Giggling, while looking steadily at me, she sings about sausages and various other kinds of food in pajamas. Her double meanings are intentional. I respond

---

[9] Toilet paper

with a countermelody to hers, in which I half-sing, half-say (in a kind of Sprächgesang):

You want me to know just how you feel	When you feel like a poo.
Even though I can't really know	Weeing all over the place,
How bad it feels, how sad it feels,	Doo-doo-doo-doo. . . .
How angry too	

I babble in a counterpoint to her "poo-loo" babble, and my piano accompaniment adopts a marcato style, with dissonant harmonization to the diatonic cliché, in an attempt to maintain the depth of her feelings of primitive rage. There is also a strong element in Lena's song of wanting to be babylike and cared for, however messy and raging. Thus, the babbling dialogue serves several purposes, and has the character of both babble and scat singing—in this way meeting both the infant and the older child she is. Rather than a "regression," Lena's infant and older self are met musically as one entity, the one accommodating the other, in this way integrating the two emotional realities.

Fewer songs; more primitive, sexualized feelings; fear of separation.

In the ensuing sessions, Lena tests every boundary of our relationship. Setting boundaries and limits on her behavior and ways of using the sessions become the main work of the sessions and a constant challenge to me to get the balance right between firmness and giving her a sense of her autonomy and freedom of expression. I feel she needs to vent her rage and disdain, to put me to the test in every way she can, to confuse me, and to assault me to the extent that she herself has felt confused and assaulted. Can I bear it? Can I take it all on board? In testing me out, she also is challenging her abusers, her mother, herself. Her songs give way to fragmented, chaotic, and angry play. The instruments are used in all kinds of eroticized play: stroking, prodding, pumping them, mouthing and salivating over them. It feels all the more disgusting and perverted, as I can feel the insults almost physically. Her anger and her attempts to denigrate and shock me are sustained for entire sessions, and are extremely difficult to deal with, both clinically, practically (managing tolerable limits of behavior in the sessions), and emotionally. My main function is to sit there and "take it"—by this, I mean all her projections of "mess" and "spoiled/soiled" childhood. Musically meeting her play, interspersed with moments of talking to her quietly, is effective in holding her in the "here and now": in particular, she is able to listen to my acknowledging that she wants me to know how it/she feels, and to make me as angry and despairing as she has felt. Ending sessions requires careful management, preparing her for this from about halfway through the session. She finds it difficult to leave without throwing the instruments everywhere, and becoming aggressive and even more abusive verbally to me. I set firm boundaries about what I will allow in the therapy room, while at the same time interpreting her actions in terms of the feelings and thoughts that impel her.

Session 37: "The Haunted House"—a song that seems to communicate Lena's intuitions (or procedural knowledge) about herself and her family.

Gradually Lena wants to sing again. Her songs carry an instinctive wisdom that seems to come from a deep source. This deeply disturbed child sings with musical sensitivity and almost a religious feeling. This session begins with Lena's characteristic darting around the room. I wonder if she will settle. I punctuate the scurrying movements with a few arpeggiated chords, moving chromatically and then building into a steady pulse on a dominant pedal point as she moves deftly from one instrument to another. After briefly improvising on a nightingale birdcall, Lena offers it to me to play, allowing me to do so only briefly, before moving to a large golden cymbal, which she beats slowly and deliberately with one hand, conducting me with the other. I "obey" with a unison bass register motif of descending octaves in F minor, responding to her absolute concentration, following her beat and her direction, sensing something important is about to emerge. As her song develops, I accompany her, maintaining a steady pulse, harmonically enhancing changes of mood, vocal inflections, and evolving imagery. Maintaining predictability in the music is important to keep Lena feeling sufficiently secure to be engaged, but it is vital not to let the musical relationship stagnate or become superficial. Lena sometimes invents words or uses words out of their normal syntax; sometimes I misunderstand her. The music maintains a creative connectedness between us— and Lena prompts or corrects me, whenever I am not producing quite the effect she wants: "That's how I like it! Keep it deep notes!" She then sings with a purposefulness that I had not encountered before in our sessions:

In the dark wood mist come along the tree,	Dark and misty it may be,
When drag the good new. . . .	No one knows it's full of glee,
In the darkness sky was dark,	Bats are flying in the air,
Owls and witches in the sky	And they seem in despair,
High(er) and high(er) in the sky,	They are flying in the air to-d-a-ay.

She urges me: "Go on!" She listens while I increase the harmonic and rhythmic tensions. The pulse remains a slow 4/4, with a dissonant accent on the 1st and 3rd beats of the bar. The continuity of her creative expression is sustained—a "going-on-being" that holds her steady, instead of either racing on or becoming overaroused. In the 3rd line of the next verse, Lena refers to a ghost "that cannot be perfect." I have a sense of her identifying with this less than perfect ghost, and perhaps indicating identification with her grandfather or her dead father, whose "ghosts" hover over the family. The dramatic narrative continues:

As there's ghosts in the air,	The ghosts are high in the air,
They could almost be,	They seem in despair,
Then there'll be one that cannot be. . . .	There's really . . . despair that you don't know
Pe . . . rfect.	that. . . .

A pause in the song is followed by Lena's command: Deep notes again! As I repeat the opening descending octaves, she nods her approval to me, and resumes singing in Sprächgesang style, inventing words to fit into her rhyming scheme.

The house is haunted	Oh my god!
The ghosts and goolies in there,	Falls through the floorboards . . .
And bogies then there's too,	I've fallen through!
When ladies sneeze and bogies everywhere.	Help! Help!
Maggots and cradgets . . .	Oh dear, she's broken her leg—
Wrigglin' around the house,	she's went to the hospital!
Eating all the rotten wood,	She should not have gone in there, should she?
Eating all the rotten cheese . . . yuck!	Nobody's to go in this house!
It's dangerous in there! (she makes a throat	It's dangerous to go in!
sound and beats the drums erratically)	Bats! Ghosts! Goolies! Except. . . .

There ensues a change of mood that I do not anticipate:

It's morning—still the sun is clean and lovely	And it creaks and creaks forevermore . . .
And the right *(light?)* music playing	With the spirit of evil and spirit of happiness
(Lena conducts me, indicating a gentler mood)	It shines in the daylight too,
The sky shines on the haunted house	and it gets very hard to. . . .
As the house creaks with everything,	

This ends in an out-breath, nearly a sigh. There is a slight pause, in which I continue the pulse and a solemn, hymnlike accompaniment. Lena rejoins me with her next verse and the hymnlike character of the music:

As the world turns by,	(In a) few years' time it's going to be knocked
The house gets rottener and rottener	down
It gets uglier & creepier & ghostlier every day.	Forever and ever and ever more.
And the people that spotted it have no desire	So one day a big bad windy storm—pshoo!
And the people have noticed it	Blow the house to bits . . . and the right notes
since it's been there.	make the next day quiet.

Lena conducts me again, indicating yet another change of mood, this time ethereal. I respond with delicate, poignant music in the treble, aiming to convey the scene, with only the birds singing as a sign of life:

Nothing is left—just a chimney and half a door
The birds perch on what is left in there.
The house is gone;
No people in it.

(In a) few years' time the buildings there are
shops and flats and houses,
Forevermore . . . forevermore . . .
Ends . . . end it!

She says fervently: "That's good! Told you it was good!" As Lena stops singing, her words immediately lose coherence in a fast chatter, as she tries to describe the derelict house—and that "it was true!" I believe her—both in its physical and psychological reality that the metaphor has so powerfully expressed. In the course of a few verses, her imagery has shifted from despairing and imperfect ghosts high in the air, bringing them into a rotting internal world, where the very stuff of house and person is maggot-ridden, and the maggots in turn consume the rot. Her song reveals her unconscious connections between this rotten, haunted house, her falling through its rotten floorboards (the corruption of the family along with her ego/sense of self?), leading to her admission to hospital. An unusually powerful metaphor emerges that seems to represent not only herself but her whole family: the corrupt container, filled with rottenness and unable to hold anything—she "falls through the floorboard, but it was her own fault." Added to her feeling unloved, like so many abused children, she assumes the abuse is her fault. To live in an ordinary world, to lead an ordinary life is something that the abused child longs for.

Coda to "The Haunted House."

Humming the first phrase, Lena tutors me in the melody she would like. Getting the music right is important, but her melody wavers from one key to another, and is not easy to follow, far less reproduce in the form she has in mind. By trial and error, I produce something "good enough," that she accepts, set to a slightly upbeat and syncopated accompaniment. She sings:

The house is forever gone
House is gone forever more.
Danger is nowhere in the world
Bogey Martians have all gone.

We have the joy of the sun;
No badness on the earth.
There is a good-bye today . . .
There's a sun and come and wipe away evil.

She hums the next phrase, before finishing:

Evil has gone . . .
When the house has been blown . . .
The wind has gone . . .

The evil has gone away from the derelict house. That's it. And it's gone . . .
IT HAS GONE!

At the final lines from "There is a good-bye today . . ." she slows to a funereal pace, her voice soaring in each subsequent phrase and a final breathless: "And it's gone." Indeed, it is time for us to end the session. I reflect Lena's final cadence, extending it into "Time for us to go." Lena leaves the room contented. This song has been an experience, with a particular significance at a deep unconscious level for Lena. Created with great self-investment, the song seems to have presented, in a series of metaphors, her autobiographical self, her past, the secrets in the family that have haunted her. Most significantly, the banishing of overwhelming evil, the transformation of shadowy ugliness with which she feels identified, give way to a more down-to-earth, realistic future of ordinary shops and houses—images of normal, ordinary life and contentment.

Phase 3

Session 40: Songs about ghosts, integrations, and transformations.

From Session 37 onward, "ghosts" become the dominant theme in Lena's songs; partly a normal child's interests in "spooky," frightening stories, but also directly relevant to her own life story—the early years of which she cannot have been consciously aware. I believe that everything a child brings to the sessions is of significance. Lena's preoccupation with ghosts, therefore, is not treated superficially, but listened to and responded to in the music. A recurring song indicates that she is getting to know her ghosts, perhaps her father, but not necessarily representing a particular person, but rather the uneasy feelings she has had for so long about so many things:

"The Ghost of the House"

There was a ghost in the house
A very friendly ghost indeed,
He was a ghost who lived in my house for years and years and years.

Yeh, yeh, he's my friend.
Ancient . . .
He used to live in my house and still does.
That was the ghost of the house!

The song falls apart at this point: I sense that she is reminded of her father, his death, and her abusers. This is a strong countertransferential feeling—I can almost see them in the room. Lena diverts to a false, off-key "happiness." She insists on my playing "happy tunes," to which she begins a menacing chant about the ghost "who is a man who has six feet and is bad." She becomes increasingly tense and disturbed, and the song turns into a taunt to one of her abusers: "Pervert! Pervert! He sexually abused me! Sex maniac!" In contrast to her rather adult turn of phrase, she beats the temple blocks furiously as if they are the abuser, repeatedly stabbing the beaters into the "mouths" of the instrument. I support, intensify, stabilize her mood in staccato, close-textured, dissonant, bi-tonal chords. I phrase my accompaniment to give a jagged effect, to complement her raging stabbing movements. I introduce a clear five-note legato motif in octaves, alternating with the dissonant harmonies. I hope that the simplicity of the unison may hold her in the here and now of the musical relationship, and thereby contain the primitive and sexualized feelings. After a time, she stops playing and talks quietly to me, almost in a whisper, but steadily (rather than her characteristic fast chatter) about what happened to her, and how she hates her friends knowing. She begins to reminisce about her family house, the secrets, and more recent happenings involving the death of some of her pets. She tells me she has found a dead fox in the hospital grounds, and has made it a home under the foundations of the music therapy room. In this phase of our work, death is a recurring theme. She plays with death. I am anxious for her safety. These concerns are shared by the team. Lena's "ghosts" trouble her deeply; she tries to find ways of feeling more powerful than them; in music therapy she repeatedly beats them to a pulp. Empowerment, however, does not truly develop until she finds a way of reflecting on her feelings. I support her musically and verbally, creating a music space in which we can reflect on these feelings, calling her back from a dark abyss. Gradually, a steady purposefulness in her playing begins to emerge. She improvises a song about a light in a cave—a theme that recurs in her final session.

Sessions 43–57 and 63 (final): "The Stranger on the Shore."

Healing metaphors continue to develop in Lena's unusual imagination, held by the music and the musical relationship. "The Stranger on the Shore" is sung by Lena to a tune that she claims to know, a tune that resembles "Home Sweet Home," but—in her rendering—pitches all over the place. The song seems to arise from a clear picture in Lena's mind. Could the stranger be her father, one of the ghosts, perhaps her grandfather on the shore, a threatening image, but also one, which nevertheless draws compassion and acceptance from her?

When stranger walks along the shore
And no one knows he's there,
Watching children playing,
Without being seen.
When sea is pounding fiercely,

When he passes slowly by,
"Why me, why me, why me?" he says,
I'm a stranger almost dead
that no one knows.
"Whatever shall be shall be."

This is followed by a more ebullient song: "Down, down, down, down, down, in the mine," apparently inspired by a dream about a school trip, where she had gone down a coalmine, wearing a torch on her helmet to light her way. I respond musically and verbally within the metaphors she introduces. I suggest to her that she now has some light to look into the darkness, as she goes "Down, down, down into the mine." The symbols of the mine—and all its obvious connotations of ego/self/ownership, of going into the unconscious, into the bowels of the earth, and its sources of energy—are taken into our singing together. There is a new expression of relief and a flicker of amazement on Lena's face, that she can now go down into this "mine," without hurting herself, come back up again, take her helmet off, and run off to play with her newfound friends.

The therapeutic work stays within the metaphors that allow her feeling of her feelings, without unduly increasing her anxiety and defenses. It is possible now to talk, if only briefly, about her ambivalent feelings for her father and the circumstances surrounding his death. She begins to talk about herself, her brother, and the rest of the family, expressing her anger and sorrow in words as well as in her music.

Session 63 (final session): Songs of personal sadness, loss, acceptance; metaphors of renewal, resurrection, rebirth.

It is our final session. Lena has a bad cold. After a final rendering of "Stranger on the Shore," Lena sings good-bye to her father. She moves quickly on to sing about her cold. I understand how she still finds thinking about him difficult and confusing. Her feelings shift to losing a friend, who has recently been discharged from the unit. This event helps her bring her sadness into the present situation, and saying goodbye to me. Not quite knowing how to say she will miss me, her song is one of her most forlorn:

When you've got a cold,   Smile with you all . . . .
And you're cold . . .   How you wish you had not
And it's horrible, yes it is,   Just think of horrible cold,
When you're not feeling up to it today; Try to be happy,
When you've got a cold,   When you've got a cold.

Lena requests an "echo." She indicates that she wants me to use the sustaining pedal and play a flowing arpeggio accompaniment (she indicates this by gesture, swooping her arms to and fro over the keyboard). Perhaps she will miss my musical reflecting and sharing of her feelings. However, this time I certainly have not got it right. She complains that I am playing a "different tune," and demands that we start again, this time with an "introduction" and the "right" tune. This is rather difficult, as I am expected to know the tune without hearing it. This seems a useful opportunity to acknowledge my shortcomings. I suggest to her that it must make her terribly angry that we will not see each other any more, and that I do not have the music she wants, but I hope it is "good enough." She nods, feeling understood: "It didn't go like that . . . yeh, now that's it!"

She continues singing:

When the sun is shining everywhere,
The sun is shining, it is shining.
When the sun shines . . .

Easter time is coming again.
Children opening eggs for . . .

Images of resurrection, new beginnings, and hope appear:

When Easter time is here,
Children open Easter eggs.
They open them with a special smile.
All the chocolates eaten up,
Found behind the armchair.
When children smile and their smiling faces,
Easter time has come.

The chicks, the hens, the eggs of them
For Easter time again.
When children smile, the eggs are opened

To be eaten, the Easter eggs,
Children of the Easter time
give a special smile.

On Sunday He has risen,
With Easter Sunday the children wake up,
look around.
They get to know to find out
where the Easter eggs are,
The Easter chicks, the Easter eggs,
the Easter happiness.

She then insists on further verses of her initial woeful song, "When you've got a cold," sounding more and more miserable, before telling me about losing her friend from the ward. Expressing her sadness about her friend seems also to be her way of expressing her sadness at our parting. I have been talking to her about our finishing our sessions for the past two months, since I first was informed of her discharge date. I talk to her about endings, ending our music sessions, and how I feel sad too, but that her song has told us something important: as something ends, something new begins—just as her song says. Lena avers how much she likes her songs and will miss music therapy. She adds that her mother is planning to buy her a piano. It is a sad good-bye, but I sense a feeling of hope and contentment in Lena as she leaves. Lena sums up her progress, saying she is leaving the hospital now "because I feel more sure about myself."

After Leaving the Unit

Lena had responded well to the varied forms of therapeutic help provided on the unit, its continuity and containment. However, she was still not ready for the less structured, wider social environment at home. Her anxiety increased, leading to a resurgence of sexualized behavior. She once again needed full-time supervision that was impossible for her mother to provide. The family refused further outpatient treatment from the hospital. Lena remained on the Child Protection Panel's at-risk register for a further six months, and was eventually found a place at a boarding school, which provided the educational, therapeutic, and structured social setting that she needed. Her musical activity continued there, although not in individual therapy. Life would never be easy for Lena, but she was now much more confident, with a sense of self-worth, and responded well in other areas of her life with the support of her new school.

DISCUSSION

The immediacy of music, and its roots in all of us, draws forth physical, emotional, mental, and spiritual self-expression with a healing potential to transform the old, and mediate the new. In this way, new meaning in life is forged. Lena's improvised songs expressed her feelings about events from her early years. A lonely child, who found life and relationships difficult, Lena felt worthless and unloved. For Lena, songs became a central feature of her music therapy process, and were the only aspect of herself that she seemed to value. They were exclusive to music therapy, in that she did not invent these songs at school or on the unit, needing—or so it seemed—the musical relationship to provide the necessary support and privacy for this.

The Song as Container-Transformer of the Sense of Self

Lena's spontaneous song-poems used metaphors that expressed feelings and images that, in many instances, seemed to arise from beyond her conscious recall. They were brought into expression because the music therapist is a particular kind of accompanist and listener, who also can "digest" what the child is feeling and provide ways of shaping and forming structures that become safe "vehicles" for her senses to be carried into emotional expression. This is the musical-psychodynamic pathway from motivation to meaning (Robarts, 2000). In this way, Lena's songs enabled her to acknowledge her sadness and loneliness, her anger and her joy, as her music began to forge a new sense of her self, developing her confidence to face the future.

The song form thus provided a creative "container-transformer" of Lena's feelings, her sense of self that developed within our musical relationship, in a transitional space created within two "containers": the song form and the musical-therapeutic relationship. My musical accompaniment or companionship served to resonate with her mood, meeting the feelings that words sought to deny or could not articulate.

Music in improvisational music therapy acts as a channel between unconscious and conscious feelings, and one that can meet paradoxical states of being. Music engages many levels of experiencing, and is especially revealing in its sounding of the transference and countertransference. Paul Nolan expresses this most eloquently:

> Music seems to have the capacity to reflect and symbolize the entire spectrum of human experiences, including those that are ineffable and those that contain seemingly illogical juxtapositions of opposites, for example, death and rebirth, within the same experiential time frame. . . . In therapy, projections invite and support transference reactions from the client, which in turn invite and support countertransference reactions from the therapist. In this way, songs can easily become a means for exchanging unconscious processes between client and therapist. This unconscious exchange is further deepened when the song involves simultaneous music-making by client and therapist (Nolan, 1998, pp. 388–389).

The ways in which Lena's preverbal, unconscious aspects of herself found a means of expression in music therapy had particular significance, given the early trauma of her separation from her mother, her subsequent sexual abuse, the death of her father, and the incestuous unboundaried relationships in the family. Here, we see the value of music, and song in particular, in both activating and containing this deepest level of expression of the damaged but still vital core of the self, while avoiding retraumatizing the child with literal interpretations that are not ready to be heard or borne.

Early Object Relations in Music Therapy: Interregulatory Aspects of Containment and Transformation

The containing-transforming action of the musical improvisational relationship with Lena can also be illuminated in terms of the interregulatory attuning to the "vitality affects" of the relationship. In responding to her individuality of musical expression and play, I was providing a musical structure that "held" the evolving sense of self and self-in-relationship (Stern, 1985/2000). Musically being "on the same wavelength" meant I could follow the nuances and subtle shifts of emotion that frequently arose in swift succession in Lena's playing. Equally, I could give her playing a containing, meaningful context through my silent attention. These constitute the musical-dynamic phenomena of early communication/object relations, that I have described as musical introjects in the emergent organization of the self (Robarts, 1994, p. 234). The containing/regulating functioning of early emotional communication is reflected, too, in the developmentalists' terms: "proto-narrative envelope" (Stern, 1977) or "reciprocity envelope" (Brazelton & Cramer, 1991; Brazelton et al., 1974) that are analogous to the psychodynamic concepts of "containment" or "a holding environment" already discussed (Bion, 1962a, 1962b; Winnicott, 1965/1990, 1971).

There were many other aspects of music and the musical relationship that "regulated" Lena's states of overarousal and scattered attention, creating the "holding environment," the safe, creative space in which she could explore her real feelings with me in the transformative (healing) process. I have attempted to report the use of different tonalities, harmonic textures, idiomatic styles, delicacy, as well as directness of musical touch—all of which cannot be described adequately in words. I have described some of the psychodynamic processes within the use of improvised songs. I have tried to take the reader into some of the inner workings of these music-therapeutic experiences. These musical and psychodynamic phenomena are at the vital core of music therapy. Working with Lena was at the beginning of my mapping some of the clinical complexities, helping me ground our feelings in musical expression, while keeping an open channel to her imagination. Lena's songs became a source of empowerment through her own creativity, enabling her to encounter and then say farewell to the ghosts of her past that continued to haunt her present.

CONCLUSION

Music is uniquely endowed, when used creatively and clinically in therapy, to activate or support feelings arising from preverbal (implicit) memory beyond conscious recall. Lena's songs tell her story.

> Words alone, without artistic structure and form are unable to achieve
> the paradox of both containment and expression of some of our more
> shocking and painful experiences (Jennings & Minde, 1993, p. 154).

In this chapter, I have presented a synthesis of clinical-theoretical
perspectives that come together in a model of poietic processes. This model
informs Lena's music therapy, demonstrating how songs acted as containers,
whereby, with the help of both musical form and the evolving form of the
musical-therapeutic relationship, feelings and thoughts could arise safely—yet
richly expressive—from the depths of her being. In this way, songs provided a
healing medium for Lena, expressing her internal world in powerful metaphors,
bringing into greater awareness the feelings and experiences that lay at a
preverbal level, and integrating some of the painful feelings that precipitated
such deep emotional disturbance. Her songs took her on a journey toward a
sounder sense of self, their metaphors containing the feelings of anxiety, anger,
and despair that threatened to overwhelm her. My capacity, working both
musically and psychodynamically, to contain her projected feelings and the
symbolic material arising in her songs developed in the course of Lena's music
therapy to help us both find a way to experience her creative potential that, in
turn, allowed her individuality to flourish.

> Songs are ways that human beings explore emotions. They express
> who we are and how we feel, they bring us closer to others, they keep
> us company when we are alone. They articulate our beliefs and
> values. As the years pass, songs bear witness to our lives. They allow
> us to relive the past, to examine the present, and to voice our dreams
> for the future. . . . They are our musical diaries, our life stories. They
> are the sounds of our personal development (Bruscia, 1998, p. 9).

Lena needed many years to consolidate a more secure and sound sense of
herself. She is now an adult, and has a home and a child. I hope that Lena
and her child sing their songs.

REFERENCES

Aasgaard, T. (2000). "'A Suspiciously Cheerful Lady': A study of a song's life
in the paediatric oncology ward, and beyond." *British Journal of Music Therapy,*
14 (2), 70–82.

Aigen, K. (1997). *Here We Are In Music: One Year With an Adolescent Creative Music Therapy Group.* St. Louis, MO: MMB Music.

Aigen, K. (1999). "The True Nature of Music-Centred Music Therapy Theory," *British Journal of Music Therapy,* 13 (2), 77–82.

Alvarez, A. (1992). *Live Company: Psychoanalytic Psychotherapy with Autistic, Borderline, Deprived and Abused Children.* London: Routledge.

Alvarez, A. (1999). "Addressing the Deficit: Developmentally Informed Psychotherapy with Passive, 'Undrawn' Children." In A. Alvarez & S. Reid (eds.), *Autism and Personality: Findings from the Tavistock Autism Workshop.* London: Routledge.

Austin, D. S. (2001). "In Search of the Self: The Use of Vocal Holding Techniques with Adults Traumatized as Children," *Music Therapy Perspectives,* 19, 22–30.

Austin, D. S. (1998). "When the Psyche Sings: Transference and Countertransference in Improvised Singing with Individual Adults." In: K. E. Bruscia (ed.), *The Dynamics of Music Psychotherapy.* Gilsum, NH: Barcelona Publishers.

Bion, W. R. (1962a). "A Theory of Thinking," *International Journal of Psycho-Analysis,* 43, 306–310.

Bion, W. R. (1962b). *Learning from Experience.* London: Heinemann.

Brazelton, T. B., & Cramer B. G. (1991). *The Earliest Relationship: Parents, Infants and the Drama of Early Attachment.* London: Karnac.

Brazelton, T. B., Koslowski, B., & Main, M. (1974). "Origins of Reciprocity." In M. Lewis & L. Rosenblum (eds.), *The Effect of the Infant on Its Caregiver.* New York: Human Science Press.

Brown, S. (1997). "Supervision in Context: A Balancing Act," *British Journal of Music Therapy,* 11 (1), 4–12.

Bruscia, K. E. (1987). *Improvisational Models of Music Therapy.* Springfield, IL: Charles C. Thomas.

Bruscia, K. E. (1991). *Case Studies in Music Therapy*. Phoenixville, PA: Barcelona Publishers.

Bruscia, K. E. (1998). *The Dynamics of Music Psychotherapy*. Gilsum, NH: Barcelona Publishers.

Christenberry, E. B. (1979). "The Use of Music Therapy with Burn Patients," *Journal of Music Therapy*, 16 (3), 138–148.

Diaz de Chumaceiro, C. L. (1995). "Lullabies Aare 'Transferential Transitional Songs': Further Considerations on Resistance in Music Therapy," *The Arts in Psychotherapy,* 22 (4), 393–357.

Diaz de Chumaceiro, C. L. (1998). "Unconsciously Induced Song Recall: A Historical Perspective." In K. E. Bruscia (ed.), *The Dynamics of Music Psychotherapy*. Gilsum, NH: Barcelona Publishers.

DSM IV. (1994). *Diagnostic and Statistical Manual of Mental Disorders*. Fourth edition. Washington, DC: American Psychiatric Association.

Dvorkin, J. M. (1991). "Individual Music Therapy for an Adolescent with Borderline Personality Disorder: An Object Relations Approach." In: K. E. Bruscia (ed.), *Case Studies in Music Therapy*. Phoenixville, PA: Barcelona Publishers.

Dvorkin, J. M. (1999). "Psychoanalytically Oriented Music Therapy Supervision." In T. Wigram & J. De Backer (eds.), *Clinical Applications of Music Therapy in Developmental Disability, Paediatrics and Neurology*. London: Jessica Kingsley Publishers.

Emde, R. N., Biringen, Z., Clyman R. B., & Oppenheim, D. (1991). "The Moral Self of Infancy: Affective Core and Procedural Knowledge," *Developmental Review*, 11, 251–270.

Etkin, P. (1999). "The Use of Creative Improvisation and Psychodynamic Insights in Music Therapy with an Abused Child." In T. Wigram & J. De Backer (eds.), *Clinical Applications of Music Therapy in Developmental Disability, Paediatrics and Neurology*. London: Jessica Kingsley Publishers.

Freud, S. (1923/1961). "The Ego and the Id." In J. Strachey (ed./trans.), *The Standard Edition of the Complete Psychological Works of Sigmund Freud, XIX.* London: Hogarth Press.

Frohne-Hagemann, I. (1999). "Integrative Supervision for Music Therapists." In T. Wigram & J. De Backer (eds.), *Clinical Applications of Music Therapy in Developmental Disability, Paediatrics and Neurology.* London: Jessica Kingsley Publishers.

Herman, J. (1992). *Trauma and Recovery: The Aftermath of Violence—From Domestic Abuse to Political Terror.* New York: Basic Books

Irgens-Möller, I. (1999). "Music Therapy in Child Psychiatry—A Two-Year Project on a Psychiatric Unit for Pre-School Children," *Nordic Journal of Music Therapy,* 8 (1), 72–75.

Jennings, S. & Minde, A. (1993). *Art Therapy and Dramatherapy: Masks of the Soul.* London: Jessica Kingsley Publishers.

Lindenberg, K. A. (1995). "Songs of Healing: Songwriting with an Abused Adolescent," *Music Therapy,* 13 (1), 93–108.

Martin, S. A. (1996). "I Voice, Therefore I Know I Am," *The Arts in Psychotherapy,* 23 (1), 261–268.

Montello, L. (1998). "Relational Issues in Psychoanalytic Music Therapy with Traumatized Individuals." In K. E. Bruscia (ed.), *The Dynamics of Music Psychotherapy.* Gilsum, NH: Barcelona Publishers.

Nolan, P. (1989). "Music Therapy Improvisation Techniques with Bulimic Patients". In L. M. Hornyak & E. K. Baker (eds.), *Experiential Therapies for Eating Disorders.* New York and London: Guilford Press.

Nolan, P. (1998). "Countertransference in Clinical Song-Writing." In K. E. Bruscia (ed.), *The Dynamics of Music Psychotherapy.* Gilsum, NH: Barcelona Publisher.

Nordoff, P., & Robbins, C. (1971). *Therapy in Music for Handicapped Children.* London: Gollancz.

Nordoff, P., & Robbins, C. (1977). *Creative Music Therapy: Individualized Treatment for the Handicapped Child.* New York: John Day.

Pavlicevic, M. (1999). *Music Therapy—Intimate Notes.* London: Jessica Kingsley Publishers.

Robarts, J., & Sloboda, A. (1994). "Perspectives on Music Therapy with People Suffering from Anorexia Nervosa," *Journal of British Music Therapy,* 8 (1), 9–15.

Robarts, J. Z. (1994). "Towards Autonomy and A Sense of Self: Music Therapy with Children and Adolescents Suffering from Early Onset Anorexia Nervosa." In D. Dokter (ed.), *Arts Therapies and Clients with Eating Disorders.* London: Jessica Kingsley Publishers

Robarts, J. Z. (1998). "Music Therapy and Children with Autism." In C. Trevarthen, K. Aitken, D. Papoudi, & J. Robarts (eds.), *Children with Autism: Diagnosis and Interventions to Meet Their Needs.* 2nd edition. London: Jessica Kingsley Publishers.

Robarts, J. Z. (1999). "Clinical and Theoretical Perspectives on Poietic Processes in Music Therapy with Reference to the Nordoff and Robbins' Study of Edward," *Nordic Journal of Music Therapy,* 8 (2), 192–199.

Robarts, J. Z. (2000). "Music Therapy and Adolescents with Anorexia Nervosa," *Nordic Journal of Music Therapy,* 9, 3–12.

Robb, S. L. (1996). "Techniques in Song Writing: Restoring Emotional and Physical Well Being in Adolescents who have been Traumatically Injured," *Music Therapy Perspectives,* 14 (1), 30–37.

Robbins, C., & Robbins, C. (1991). "Self-Communications in Creative Music Therapy." In K. E. Bruscia (ed.), *Case Studies in Music Therapy.* Phoenixville, PA: Barcelona Publishers.

Rogers, P. (1992). "Issues in Working with Sexually Abused Clients in Music Therapy," *Journal of British Music Therapy,* 6 (2), 5–15.

Rogers, P. (1995). "Childhood Sexual Abuse: Dilemmas in Therapeutic Practice," *Music Therapy Perspectives,* 13 (1), 24–30.

Scheiby, B. B. (1998). "The Role of Musical Countertransference in Analytical Music Therapy." In K. E. Bruscia (ed.), *The Dynamics of Music Psychotherapy.* Gilsum, NH: Barcelona Publishers.

Stern, D. (1977). *The First Relationship: Infant and Mother.* Cambridge, Mass.: Harvard University Press.

Stern, D. (1985/2000). *The Interpersonal World of the Infant: A View from Psychoanalysis and Developmental Psychology.* Second edition with new Introduction. New York: Basic Books.

Stern, D. N., Sander, L. W., Nahum, J. P., Harrison, A. M., Lyons-Ruth, K., Morgan, A. C., Bruschweiler-Stern, N., & Tronick, E. Z. (1998). "Non-Interpretive Mechanisms in Psychoanalytic Therapy: The 'Something More' Than Interpretation," *International Journal of Psycho-Analysis,* 49, 903–921.

Tervo, J. (2001). "Music Therapy for Adolescents," *Clinical Child Psychology and Psychiatry,* 6 (1), 79–91.

Trevarthen, C. (1999). "Musicality and the Intrinsic Motive Pulse: Evidence from Human Psychobiology and Infant Communication," *Musicae Scientiae August Special Issue,* 155–215.

Trevarthen, C., & Malloch, S. N. (2000). "The Dance of Well Being: Defining the Musical Therapeutic Effect," *Nordic Journal of Music Therapy,* 9 (2), 3–17.

Turry, Ann (1999). "A Song of Life: Improvised Songs with Children with Cancer and Serious Blood Disorders." In T. Wigram & J. De Backer (eds.), *Clinical Applications in Developmental Disability, Paediatrics and Neurology.* London: Jessica Kingsley Press.

Turry, Alan (1998). "Transference and Countertransference in Nordoff-Robbins Music Therapy." In K. E. Bruscia (ed.), *The Dynamics of Music Psychotherapy.* Gilsum, NH, Barcelona Publishers.

Tyler, H. (1997). "Music Therapy for Children with Learning Difficulties." In M. Fawcus (ed.), *Children with Learning Difficulties: A Collaborative Approach to their Education and Management.* London: Whurr Publishers.

Winnicott, D. W. (1965/1990). *The Maturational Processes and the Facilitating Environment (Collected Papers)*. London: Karnac Books.

Winnicott, D. W. (1971). *Playing and Reality*. Harmondsworth, UK: Penguin.

Young, L. (1992). "Sexual Abuse and the Problem of Embodiment," *Child Abuse and Neglect,* 16, 89–100.

Case Nine

THE GIRL WHO BARKED:
OBJECT RELATIONS MUSIC PSYCHOTHERAPY
WITH AN ELEVEN-YEAR-OLD
AUTISTIC FEMALE

Janice M. Dvorkin and Misty D. Erlund

ABSTRACT

Elana's parents sought outpatient music therapy in order to eliminate the increasing occurrence of "barking"-type sounds during social events outside the home. Object relations-based music therapy was chosen as the framework for her sessions due to its emphasis on development and increasing expression of emotional perceptions. Over a two-year period (once per week, for thirty- to sixty-minute sessions), Elana developed a symbolic vocabulary to communicate perceptions about herself in the world, to begin to consciously work through the developmental movement from her symbiotic relationship with her mother to separation/individuation, to consciously use musical structures to organize verbal communication, and for emotional expression. In the psychoanalytic literature, this type of approach is usually unsuccessful. However, with the addition of music as a facilitator, Elana's case is only one example of how music increases the overt functioning of children diagnosed with an autistic spectrum disorder.

INTRODUCTION

Over the years, several music therapists have written about their psychotherapy work within an analytic framework. Therapists, such as Edith Lecourt, Mary Priestley, and Rolando Benezon, are among those to use analytic therapy terms to describe their work. Furthermore, Edith Lecourt has written about working psychodynamically with an autistic child, including the mother's involvement and related issues (Lecourt, 1991). This case study, however, is intended to work within an object relations psychotherapy model and focuses on the existence of the first separation/individuation experience for children with autism at the age of preadolescence (ages 9–11 years).

Professionals usually recommend behavioral interventions for individuals diagnosed as having an "autistic spectrum disorder." This case is an example of how viable an object relations approach works with this population. Because object relations theory focuses on the person's ability to relate and interact with their environment and significant others in their lives, it offers the opportunity for autistic children to not only learn expressive language skills, but also to provide ways to develop emotionally. This theory allows the therapist, who works within an object relations framework, to observe different aspects of the patient's level of functioning; that is, how the patient relates to others, particularly in relationship to the therapist. This includes the patient's use of defenses toward the therapist, the patient's perception of the therapist's actions and responses, and the realization that prior beliefs and attitudes toward others are not generalizable. Donald Winnicott initiated the term "good enough mother" (Abram, 1996, pp. 190–216) to define the unique experience the patient has with an object (significant other person) who is able to meet their needs to such an extent that the patient is encouraged to move to a more mature developmental stage. Impediments to emotional and psychosocial growth can be due to the inability of the parent to help the child meet these developmental achievements. However, a neurological disability, such as autistic spectrum disorder, can also be a significant hindrance in a child's emotional development.

A unique factor of music in therapy is its ability to utilize the functioning of other areas of the brain to assist in achieving communication and emotional growth. Music provides nonverbal structure to organize and accompany verbal expression. The stimulation of the limbic system and cortex enables the use of these areas to enhance the undamaged areas of the left temporal lobe (Wernike's area) and thus enables changes in behavior and the individual's perception of others (as they respond differently to the child). The intimacy established by sharing a musical experience allows the autistic individual to experience intimacy without the need for spatial proximity. It is not surprising, therefore, that individuals with autism are responding positively to music in their therapy. Autism has historically been considered a psychotic illness. However, when music is applied to assist in expressive communication, the results are reality-based responses, which are not much different from those of the person who is freely associating in verbal analytic therapy.

BACKGROUND INFORMATION

Elana is an eleven-year-old Hispanic child diagnosed with autism. Following a conference on autism, Elana's mother returned to her home, which is located on the outskirts of an upper middle-class Southwestern rural town, and sought the services of a music therapist (as recommended by a presenter at the conference). Elana's mother sought music therapy services for her then nine-year-old daughter because of her tendency to make a distressing "barking" sound, and the accompanied behavior of positioning herself on hands and knees during social events with peers and family, such as birthday parties and family celebrations.

Music therapy services are provided in Elana's home. Music therapy services, as well as others in this rural area, are sparse. A formal music therapy assessment determined Elana's suitability for music therapy, i.e., how she participated, related, and responded musically. Elana's assessment produced several indicators for a positive prognosis for music therapy services. She was willing to "try out" a variety of instruments and sounds and voluntarily included her own instruments in the session. She indicated an awareness of instrumental mirroring by the therapist and introduced the use of objects (bird puppets, egg shakers, flutes) that served to describe introjects of her primary relationships. The music therapist and her supervisor decided to use a psychodynamic approach due to her symbolic use of musical and inanimate objects to describe her present level of object relations and her inclusion of attempts to express her relationship with her mother during the first session, e.g., she labeled one of two bird puppets the mother bird and followed this action by calling out for her mother. This concurs with object relations theory, in which Scharff and Scharff (1995) explain that the internal object expects all external objects—the bird puppets, other inanimate objects, and other people she comes in contact with—to reflect the perception of the early relationship built with the initial external object. This interaction, seen during the first session, continued throughout the therapy process.

Developmental History

Elana is the unplanned firstborn of two children. She was described by others outside the family as "well behaved" as well as a "snuggler" and in "her own world." Around six months of age, Elana's mother became concerned because Elana was "barely making" the developmental stages suggested for children of her age. She walked alone at eighteen months. Toilet training was initiated at the age of two, but was not mastered until the age of seven for urination and the age of nine for defecation.

Elana attended day care within a private home for nine months. She started public school at the age of three. She was included in a program for children with disabilities. Elana does not have any behavior problems in school, but she has an "incredible delay" in relation to learning ability (although is not diagnosed as mentally retarded). Her special education counseling has included the "circle of friends," which allows for group members to role-play various interactions of "real life."

Summary of Behaviors

Elana has a hard time making friends, but not in keeping her friends. She seems to be in a world of her own, but according to her mother "less and less." Elana has seizures for which she has been prescribed Tegretal. Elana unintentionally harms small pets due to her inability to recognize the amount of pressure she is applying to the animal. If she causes harm, she is "very apologetic." Elana finds humor in cats fighting, and other similar occurrences. In the past, as Elana does not seem to have a fear of oncoming traffic, it was difficult to stop her from running out into the street. She has overcome this, and will now stay near her parents when crossing the street.

TREATMENT

We will now describe the treatment process in terms of the three phases associated with psychoanalytic theories of therapy: 1) establishing rapport, 2) working through, and 3) termination.

1. Establishing Rapport

Establishing rapport included assessing Elana's psychosocial level of development, according to Erickson (Santrock, 2000, p. 35), and her ability to relate, via attending to her progress, or regress, in verbal and musical communication. These constant assessments of Elana's relatedness to the therapist reflected the type of relationship she had with her primary caretaker. In an object relations model, the focus is on this relationship between the patient and the therapist. The information gathered is used to enhance the patient's ability to function, to succinctly communicate, and to problem solve in the areas that the therapy addresses. It is believed, and this is the basis for the ability to do "brief" psychodynamic therapy, that what the patient communicates in the first therapy session are the issues on which the therapy will focus. An example with Elana, seen in hindsight, occurred during the first session (spoken):

Elana:	Happy Birthday for you.
Therapist:	Happy Birthday.
Elana:	For everyone?
Therapist:	What happens at a birthday party?
Elana:	. . . everyone blows all the candles.
Therapist:	What are the candles for?
Elana:	Blowing.
Therapist:	Yeah, to blow out.
Therapist:	What do you like about birthday parties?
Elana:	. . . um.
Therapist:	Are you talking quiet today so no one can hear you?
Elana:	. . . cat. (*sleepily, with a yawn*)
Therapist:	What sound does a cat make?
Therapist:	(*sung*) Elana, you're wakin' up.
Elana:	(*sung*) . . . here comes Santa Claus.
Therapist:	Here comes Santa Claus.
Elana:	(*sung to "Where Has My Little Dog Gone?"*) Where can you be?
Therapist:	Where can you be?
Elana:	Ho, ho, ho . . . climb. You are special.
Therapist:	Is he special to you?

This dialogue led to a repetition of different ideas that Elana had about being special. It is interesting to note that most of the reported barking behavior occurred when she was away from her mother while attending someone else's celebration. Thus, interpretations, which encouraged exploration of Elana's perception of her specialness within her family and social group, were prepared.

Symbolic use of vocal sounds, instruments, and puppets:

In this first phase of therapy, Elana used a variety of objects symbolically, including vocal sounds, instruments, and puppets.

Elana's initial use of music in her sessions consisted of creating disconnected vocal sounds, which appeared to be an effort to speak to the therapist. Her speech was largely incomprehensible, and, at times, sounded as if she was slurring her words or was speaking too rapidly to understand. She seemed to echo the syntax of the therapist's talking or answered "Yah" to the therapist's questions, with an accompanying rising pitch in her voice. This gave her response a similarity in word and vocal affect. Upon offering her the choice to respond with "No," she often answered in the affirmative and then followed this with "No." At first, Elana did not appear to understand the difference, but as she continued working with the therapist, her responses seemed to be more accurate. Elana's responses to her mother's questions about her emotional state were more consistent, in that she would answer "No" to all questions, but her vocal affect expressed her true reactions. For example, Elana would respond with a vehement "No" when her mother asked her, "Are you angry?" However, her vocal affect was almost a shout.

Her initial sessions were composed of her exploration of the different instruments brought by the therapist. The sessions would begin with Elana playing her own instruments and her therapist would point out the similarity between Elana's instruments and the therapist's. At the beginning of the third session, Elana opened the therapist's bag of instruments without acknowledging the therapist. This provided a good example of Elana's tendency to develop a symbiotic relationship with others. In other words, there is no concept of "yours and mine." This infantile tendency was also demonstrated in Elana's use of the "barking sound" during social events as a communication of increased anxiety, an intense desire to leave the situation, and the reason for her distress. It was Elana's belief that her mother would understand this use of this sound. And indeed, her mother did seem to know what she meant because she would come to Elana and they would leave. Her sense of symbiosis with her mother was what allowed her to create this behavior, i.e., her mother would consistently respond by meeting these needs.

Elana used instruments symbolically to represent her family members. At one point, Elana was playing a variety of instruments and she began to talk about "Mommy and Daddy." While most of her words were incomprehensible, the words Mommy and Daddy were clearly articulated. The therapist asked, "Who are Mommy and Daddy?" in order to increase the possibility of understanding what Elana was trying to say. Elana's response was to lightly hit the larger of the bongo drums and say, "Mommy." She followed this by hitting a larger buffalo drum and said, "Dada." She then went on to label the smaller bongo drum "sister" (meaning herself) in the same way. The therapist asked her where her brother was and she responded, "This is Mikey" as she pulled several egg shakers toward her. Interestingly, she represented her mother and herself on bongo drums of differing sizes, demonstrating how she perceived her relationship with her mother. The altering of instruments to describe her parents during later sessions included using two large maracas as "Mom and Dad" and two smaller maracas as "babies."

Elana also symbolically used puppets in her early sessions. In one session Elana said, "C'mon!" in order to encourage the therapist to accompany her with guitar, as she played a variety of instruments. Shortly after the therapist started strumming the guitar, Elana brought a birdcage, with two birds inside, into the music therapy area. Then she went to the living room area to collect her puppets. Two of the puppets resembled the birds in the cage, one green, and the other blue. The other toys that she brought to the session were positioned against the couch in such a way that they appeared to be an audience. First, she placed one puppet bird on each of her hands. Elana moved the puppet birds around the cage, as if they were flying. Then, she handed the therapist a puppet. (While this may be seen as a form of animism, characteristic of an autistic individual, the following interaction may also be seen as an example of maternal transference.) Elana then left the session to convince her mother to come to the music therapy session. After her mother tried unsuccessfully to encourage Elana to return to the music therapy session without her, Elana and mother returned together. Elana directed her mother to wear one of the puppets, instead of the therapist. This "exchange of the baton" was an example of how the therapist was in the role of a maternal figure until the "real" mother was available. Elana continued the session by creating a conversation with her mother using the two birds.

Sometimes, Elana combined the symbolic use of puppets and instruments to express her feelings around separation from her mother. For example, during a session when her mother was away at a meeting, Elana used instruments to depict a "fighting" scene. The instruments, flutes, and the therapist's guitar fought on the keyboard, which created the "battleground" sound. The music was dissonant, similar to the clash of the fighting instruments. When the therapist attempted to improvise sounds that would slow down the degree of aggressive expression, Elana would clearly tell the therapist, "C'mon, faster." It was clear that Elana was quite comfortable with expressing her aggressive feelings in this manner. Her aggressive actions became faster and more intense, with no interruption. Elana played the guitar on the keys of the keyboard, and then tossed it about a foot away. She then moved away from the keyboard and continued telling the therapist about her mother being away at a meeting, through telegraphic language. She said, "Mommy . . . see her eyes." As the therapist attempted to musically mirror this statement, Elana put her fingers in her ears. She continued talking about her mother being away. After Elana's one-sided discussion, she returned to the birdcage, and a bird puppet. She placed what she called the "mother bird" puppet on the cage during the closing song. When the therapist attempted to sing to Elana, using her name, Elana sang with the therapist, but omitted her name in the song. The therapist encouraged Elana to sing what her mother would sing in this song, in the form of the "mother bird" puppet. When no response was forthcoming, the therapist suggested the words, "I'll see you after the meeting." Both in the instrumental improvisation and in the closing song, Elana seemed to use the therapy session (and therapist) for help in problem solving, as she had with her mother.

Elana's relationship with her mother was a major component of the therapy process. During the first few months, Elana acted out a form of rapprochment by leaving the session to make contact with her mother and then return to the session. During the times when her mother was in the session, the therapist modeled ways for her mother to encourage and support Elana's autonomy and acknowledge her as a separate person with unique ideas. Furthermore, Elana's readiness to separate, and the ensuing ambivalence over separating, was a continual issue in her therapy. When Elana initiated separation she was able to exhibit greater tolerance for being apart from her mother than when others insisted that she be on her own.

Elana used lullabies (Diaz de Chumaciero, 1992) as a self-soothing entity or an overt link to her mother. During an early session, Elana seemed to be trying to tell the therapist about her barking and the displeasure expressed by her mother in response to this behavior. The therapist repeated the phrases that were articulate, by musically mirroring them. Following this intervention, Elana curled herself into a fetal position against the wall, on the floor and farther away from the therapist. At this point, her mother entered the session, asking, "What, Elana?" Elana's response was to crawl into her mother's lap and position herself like an infant, and proceeded to sing "Rock-A-Bye Baby."

After the first summer of therapy, Elana's mother informed the therapist that Elana had communicated her distress about the music therapy sessions, during the week, by repeating "No music" to her mother. However, this did not recur. Approximately seven months into the therapy process, Elana's mother reported that Elana's barking had decreased and her expressive verbal language had increased significantly.

2. Working Through

As the therapist learned more about Elana's concerns over the past six months, she would attempt to validate Elana's experience and perceptions by asking her mother about the possible reality of Elana's ideas concerning celebrations of birthdays or achievements. The therapist learned that Elana's birthday celebration often coincided with Valentine's Day (a celebration where others get presents as well). The repeated inclusion of Christmas carols was now seen in light of Elana's realization that there is no unique celebration of her as a separate entity, as well as her strong desire for an acknowledgement of herself as an individual. When this wish was brought to the attention of her mother, the use of the carols reduced significantly. She would bring them back into the sessions when she had a problem that involved her ego functioning or insecurity about maintaining her sense of self.

Elana's concerns about not receiving recognition through birthdays, and other celebrations of her being, induced the urge in the therapist to gratify this want with a birthday gift when her birthday arrived. This experience with projective identification helped the therapist understand the strength of Elana's wish to feel special by having her desire gratified in a concrete manner, e.g. a gift. Elana's need was so great that verbal or musical gratification was not sufficient. In understanding what was occurring dynamically, the therapist was able to feel more comfortable not gratifying Elana's need, but instead helping her to consciously express this need to her family.

During the eighth month of therapy, Elana celebrated her tenth birthday. One week prior to her birthday, she received a wooden flute, or recorder, as a gift from her mother. The following week, on the actual day of her birth, Elana went to search for her new flute by opening the therapist's suitcase of instruments. She was unsuccessful in finding her flute during that session.

During the next few months, she expressed her need to find various objects. In one session, Elana could not find her doll "Susie." She picked up the rainstick, which she called "snow." (The therapist mirrored the sound of the rainstick by strumming the guitar.)

Elana:	. . . put Santa Clause sled
Therapist:	Do they put Santa Clause on a sled?
Elana:	Can we play . . .
	(*in a high voice, different from her usual voice*)
	mother . . . mother . . . story
Therapist:	What would Santa Clause bring you at Christmas?
Elana:	Uhm a . . . Christmas morning. Susie was not. . . .
	But Susie was safe. She had . . . (*whispered voice*).
	(*Elana left the music area to her bedroom*)
Therapist:	Are you going to get Susie?
	As long as she comes back to the music.
Therapist:	(*sung to "Where Has My Little Dog Gone* [Fox, 1985c, p. 86])
	Oh, where, oh, where, can Susie be?
Elana:	Oh, where, oh, where, can she be?
	She be gone.
Therapist:	What were you looking for?

The therapist stood in the doorway and observed Elana walking to the other side of her bedroom. Her vocalization seemed to be intentionally unclear.

Therapist:	(*spoken*) I noticed your words changed. What does that mean?
Elana:	(*she introduced the use of this song independently of the therapist's suggestions, sung to the tune of "Where is*

Thumbkin" [Hart, 1982, p.29])
Where is Susie? Where is Susie? Here I am. Cuz she can.

Elana: (*spoken*) Where is Susie?

Therapist: I don't know. I'd like it if y'all would join the music.
It looks like you're thinking a lot today.

Therapist: (*sung to tune of "Where Has My Little Dog Gone?"*)
Oh, where, oh, where, is Elana
She seems so far away.
Oh, where, oh, where, is Elana
Oh, where, oh, where, can she be?

Elana returned to the music area to continue the music therapy session. Subsequently, Elana transferred the above ideas of loss to another setting. As she returned from her bedroom, she brought several dinosaurs into the music therapy setting. Her facial affect was very sad. She placed the dinosaurs close to the therapist, in between the birdcage and the therapist.

Therapist: What's wrong?

Elana: (*in a high voice, depicting the dinosaurs' voices*) We're sad.

Therapist: (*sung with guitar strum in A minor*) They're sad.

Therapist: (*spoken*) Why are they sad?

Elana: (*in a high voice*) We lost our flute.

The therapist put the ideas presented by Elana into a song. This improvised song alternated between A minor and E minor tonalities, resting mostly in the A minor mode. The chorus was a simple phrase, "They're sad." Toward the end of the session, Elana projected happier feelings on the dinosaurs. Therefore, the music reflected this by changing to an A major and D major tonality. During the transition of these feelings from "sad" to "happy," the therapist alternated tonality between the major and minor, mirroring this lack of resolution of Elana's feelings.

Two weeks later, Elana personalized a song suggested by the therapist ("Where Has My Little Dog Gone?") by changing the lyrics to show her symbolic equivalence of the mother and the flute.

Elana: . . . Mommy . . . does it matter . . .
Oh, where, oh, where can she be? . . .
And I know Daddy and Mother be there
Leaving . . . I know my . . . look at their eyes . . .
Oh, where, oh, where can you be . . .

Elana: (*spoken*) Listen!

Therapist:	I am. Sometimes it's hard to understand.
	Oh, where, oh, where is what?
Elana:	(*in a different voice, depicting the flutes' voices*)
	. . . missing mother . . . oh, there you are . . .
Therapist:	Who do they miss?
Elana:	Their mom.
Therapist:	Who does flute miss?
Elana:	Big Mom.

She sang about the mother and father going away. She pointed to the therapist to sing:

Therapist:	My turn?
Elana:	Yah.
Therapist:	(*sung to the above tune*)
	Oh, where, oh, where did mama flute go?

Elana joined the therapist in singing.

Elana:	(*continued using her own words with the above tune*)
	We want . . . my mama . . .
Therapist:	Mama flute player . . .

She added the rainstick to accompany her change of the tune to a minor mode. The therapist followed her by singing this minor sound:

| Therapist: | Oh, where, oh, where is my flute? (*chorus of song*) |

At this point, Elana sang open vowel sounds, with which the therapist and Elana dialogued repeatedly. The music dynamics grew. The therapist supported this crescendo by adding the guitar. Elana hit the drum louder and louder. The therapist continued singing the chorus. Elana added her own verses, while the intensity of her playing increased. Elana turned to the keyboard in order to play "Oh, Christmas Tree" (Traditional, 1992) by her suggestion. She spontaneously sang this carol to comfort herself.

In the following session, in the tenth month of therapy, Elana played several instruments, including various flutes and fruit shakers. The use of the banana shaker led Elana to sing about monkeys and the food that nurtures them (like a "good enough mother").

| Elana: | (*sung*) I . . . monkey |
| | (*sung to "This is the Day"* [Garrett, 1992, p. 27]) |

	This is the drum
	This is the drum . . . (*bang!*) . . . (*bang!*) . . . (*bang!*) . . .
Therapist:	This is the day (*repeat*)
Elana:	. . . (*sung high*) . . . all day long
	This is the drum
	This is the drum
	. . . all day long.
Therapist:	What did you say?
	What did you say?
	This is the drum.
	This is the drum.
Elana:	(*spoken, almost yelled*) Mommy?!
Therapist:	What made you think of Mommy?
Elana:	(*sung to "Where Has My Little Dog Gone?"*)
	Oh, where, oh, where can she go?
	Oh, what she didn't . . .
Therapist:	(*spoken*) She doesn't what?
Elana:	She . . .
Therapist:	Her game?
Elana:	(*sung*) The game. . . she only . . . I know
Therapist:	Oh, where, Mommy—
Elana:	Do I know she . . . he know . . . oh, where, can she be.
	Oh, where, can my mother be.
	Oh, where can she be? Ah-ah-ah (*in harmony*)

Elana continued the session talking and singing about other subjects until her associations returned to her mother, expressed in a clear, less symbolic manner.

| Elana: | Mom! I miss her. |

The therapist improvised in "A" minor to reflect this first person statement.

Therapist:	(*sung*) I miss you.
Elana:	(*singsong*) Mama!
	Where can she be?
Therapist:	Where can she be?
	I miss her. I miss her.

Elana joins the therapist, using a drum.

| Elana: | (spoken) Mommy? |

Elana played the flute, then the drum. The therapist continued playing the minor chords to support Elana.

Therapist:	(*sung*) Is she not coming to your cry?
	It's gonna be alright
	(*using Elana's words from previous sessions*)
Elana:	(*spoken*) I miss her!!!
Therapist:	(*sung*) Did she go away?
Elana:	(*spoken*) Mommy! I miss you!!
Therapist:	(*sung*) I miss you. Mommy. Please, come here.

Elana walked to the doorway, but this time did not leave the immediate music therapy area. Instead, she called out to her mother from the music area. Her mother joined the session, at Elana's request. Elana used this musical phrase for months after this session. Eventually, this phrase transitioned from singing to spoken words. The music in a minor tonality allowed expression of feelings to be contained.

The issue of separation from her mother was a recurring one for Elana. She is functioning at an earlier stage of development in that she continues to have difficulty with initial separation. This is illustrated clearly in the expression of fear, which evolved from a verbal dialogue about the first day of school and Elana leaving her mother. The focus was on people leaving but "coming back." In response to this theme, the therapist began to sing a song about flying away and coming back. The song "I'll Fly Away" (Brumley, 1992, p. 40) was used as a base for substituting more personal words related to Elana. However, Elana's fear of this situation provoked her to not allow the therapist to sing the part about the person returning.

Therapist:	"Stay right here with Elana (*repeat*),
	'Cuz she's special, too,
	Stay right here,
	Is that true, Elana? (*repeat*)
	Stay right here,
	'Cuz you're special, too,
	Don't fly away"
Elana:	"And—
	When you—
	And Mom and Dad—
	And that's why the children
	Will be happy all day.
Therapist:	(*sings as she strums the zither*)
	Don't fly away, oh Sarah

	Don't fly away, Pretty Bird
	Watch Elana as she plays
	Don't fly away, oh, Sarah
	Don't fly away, Pretty Bird
	Just stay here and watch her play
	Don't fly away.
Elana:	And when they will coming—
	Special children will be—
Therapist:	So if you stay, oh, Sarah,
	Children will be happy
	Is that true?
Elana:	And moms—love them
Therapist:	If you stay, oh, Sarah
	You will love them, too (*repeat*)
	That's how you will know
	Is that true? (*speaking*) Is that right?
Elana:	(*speaking*) Let's sing a Christmas one.
Therapist:	You need a Christmas one?
Elana:	Mommy, you wanna stay?
Mother:	(*softly*) Yes.
Therapist:	She has to take care of something first. She's flying away,
	then coming back, is that true?
Elana:	(*concerned affect*) I want Mommy to come back!

This dialogue was followed by Elana's demonstration of her confusion about her feelings. And her conversation moved quickly from expressing different feelings in different ways. She was unable to follow through with completing any thoughts. Even though Elana and the therapist were actively involved in the song, her mother was listening to the interaction. The increase in her level of anxiety provoked a reaction of insistence upon cleaning up and ending the session.

Elana's ability to increase the clarity in her communication occurred in her use of songs to express dysphoric feelings directly to the person involved. For example, her inclusion of the word "Mommy" in a clear, articulate manner in the good-bye song clearly illustrates this. Previously she would omit or muffle this word when the therapist included it. The therapist and her supervisor agreed that this change indicated an increase in Elana's tolerance for separation from her mother.

3. Termination

Although therapy with Elana has started its third year, she has not reached the termination stage. Indications of Elana's readiness to conclude music therapy would be her ability to express concerns about loss, abandonment, and being autonomous, rather than regressing to a symbiotic stage with her mother. Elana seems to look forward to and be excited about the weekly sessions. She greets the therapist at the door with "Hi" and includes the therapist's name. She then begins to chatter about issues she wants to address during the session (either directly, or symbolically).

Recently, Elana started at a new school and missed a music therapy session. Her mother called the therapist to schedule the next session. As her mother described the present family situation, Elana could be heard singing in the background. Her mother asked Elana if she wanted to talk to the therapist and Elana immediately answered "Yah." Elana stopped singing and took the receiver. She babbled quickly, with the intermittent expression "it's hard."

DISCUSSION

In psychoanalytic theory, symptoms are defined as ways to reduce the discomfort from intolerable anxiety. Elana used "barking" to reduce the increased anxiety she felt at social gatherings. Elana could rely on her mother taking her home from the anxiety-provoking situation when she began to make barking sounds. It enabled her to make her mother return to her immediately and remove her from the distressing environment. Using this way of working also enabled the therapist to understand why Elana was so distressed in social situations, with people she knew. She understood that, due to this type of relationship with her mother, she could rely on her mother to respond consistently to her "barking." Thus, the elimination of the behavior was the result of learning about and fulfilling her emotional needs, and helping her move to a more independent way of seeing herself and her world.

Through the use of music, and eventually through verbal expression, Elana was able to communicate various concerns, moving to a more mature level of functioning. The music enabled changes in these areas to occur with greater alacrity. The music psychotherapist is particularly trained to interpret musical expression, which is used by a person with autistic spectrum disorder until verbal expression is available. An additional aspect of training is the ability to recognize musical expressions of transference and the possibility of resulting countertransference within the therapy process, and respond both musically and verbally.

Transference and Countertransference in Musical Communication

Object relations theory describes transference "as the expression of internal object relationships experienced externally in the therapeutic relationship" (Scharff & Scharff, 1995, p. 52). Therefore, maternal transference is a description of the type of role placed upon the therapist and/or music during the therapy process. One example of this maternal transference was when Elana directed the therapist to manipulate one of the bird puppets, but transferred the role back to the "real" mother when she was available.

Awareness of countertransference issues increased the therapist's ability to understand what Elana was communicating dynamically, i.e., it was a nonverbal indicator of what was occurring between the therapist and the patient. One of the early countertransference reactions involved feelings created by Elana's repeatedly leaving the session to find her mother. She appeared to be seeking out her mother for help at a time when the therapist did not seem to meet Elana's needs. Reinforcement of this idea occurred when Elana requested the therapist's help in fixing a toy. The therapist responded by stating that she had to bring her instruments inside first; however, her mother came and fixed the toy instead. During other similar situations, the therapist became aware of feeling inadequate and unable to meet Elana's needs, in comparison to Elana's mother. When Elana ended an interaction using puppets with the therapist, she often took the puppet from the therapist and left the session to give it to her mother. The residual feeling was one of failure to comply with the responses that Elana sought. Even though these experiences with Elana exacerbated feelings for the therapist about motherhood and potentially being able to be the "good enough mother" for Elana, they really reflected Elana's feelings about her need to depend on her mother.

A significant transference-countertransference issue involved the structuring and setting of boundaries for the music therapy sessions held in Elana's home. Setting limits in regard to the participation of other family members and establishing spatial boundaries for the session in an open space led to an unavoidable focus on resolving these problems in establishing a consistent frame (Langs, 1973) for the therapy to take place. These problems contributed to unanticipated splitting by Elana between the mother and the therapist (maternal transference), and the switching of good and bad mother roles. This situation frequently interfered with the establishment of a consistent relationship with the therapist and in creating a structure for the sessions. Countertransferentially, the therapist felt the pull to move away from the nurturance role to the protector of the therapy frame or space. Of course, this raised not only strong concerns about accomplishing goals within a therapy process, but it also raised personal issues around family relationships.

Using Music to Describe Object Relationships

The initial dialogue about birthdays led to a repetition of different ideas that Elana had about being special. It is an example of how Elana was communicating, symbolically, the therapy issues of concerns about separation, which would require a feeling of specialness (autonomy and ego functioning), and acknowledgment from others of her uniqueness (i.e., using examples of people, like Santa Claus, who are always special to everyone and are celebrated for their uniqueness every year—like a birthday). It should be noted that most of the barking occurred when she was away from her mother while she attended someone else's party.

Once rapport was established, Elana began to use these symbols with greater frequency, until the therapist was able to understand the connection between the symbols and make the appropriate interpretations. Once this was done and the actual issues were being addressed directly, then Elana did not bring in these symbols to the session unless she needed to work through issues of separation and autonomy at a different time.

Elana used song material to explore and express feelings about the relationship between herself and the world. She specifically focused on the lack of a celebration of her birthday, a need to feel special (like people who have birthday parties for only them, and a desire to be seen as worthy of this tribute). She introduced a strong need to sing the songs: "Rock-A-Bye Baby," "Old King Cole," "The First Noel," and "I Just Can't Wait to be King." (Fox, 1985a, p. 229; Fox, 1985b, p. 221; Traditional, 1962; and Disney, 1996, band 9). Other combinations also included: "Brahms' Lullaby," "Away in a Manger," and "Silent Night" (Dallin & Dallin, 1966, p. 222; Anonymous & McFarland, 1962; Gruber & Mohr, 1962). The latter combination centered on a baby sleeping; a baby that is the center of attention. The former progression of songs includes this idea, as well as an emphasis on a person who is important and very special to the people around him, i.e., a king. These songs were introduced during the sixth month of treatment with her requesting them by singing them. As this use of music occurred prior to the Christmas holiday a latent meaning was not considered until the songs continued following the Christmas holiday. She brought a book of carols to the therapist and insisted that the therapist "sing with me." She often opened the book to a song that she was not singing, or held it upside down, indicating that she realized the songs were in the book, but she was not reading them. Initially, it was thought that Elana favored singing this music. However, as the songs were requested during consecutive sessions, the therapist and supervisor began to explore the possible meanings behind these combinations of material. Her methods of attempting to communicate her desire to feel as special as the baby whose birthday is celebrated at Christmas, varied. During one session that followed the Christmas holiday, she actually sat on a chair that was designed to be the throne of a character that was a queen in a movie. Thus, she was actually able to become the queen.

Birds, especially in a cage, were frequently used as ways for Elana to describe her changing perceptions of her object relations. She would name them in couples (dyads) such as, "Pretty Bird and Tweety Bird." During the second year of therapy "Tweety Bird" flew away and was replaced by another bird, which she named "Sarah." Sarah is also the name of the youngest child in a family of friends. Elana knew Sarah mainly as an infant. Symbolically, it increased Elana's ability to allude to an infant who received a great amount of interest and attention from significant others. Elana frequently referred to the birds as representing different types of dyadic relationships, e.g., friends, mother and child, and parents. This reference would often be followed by a more personal communication related to her thoughts about that particular relationship.

Music as a Transitional Object

Children use transitional objects to offer a soothing substitute for the mother figure during initial separations. Elana created transitional objects using musical instruments and/or musical dialogues and songs to express her feelings toward her mother and to express her present emotional state. One use of music as a transitional object was her readiness to work through the increasing separations from her mother and the resulting feelings of loss.

In verbal therapy, the therapist is often used as the transitional object, which increases occurrence of a maternal transference. In music therapy, the use of music materials as transitional objects (such as lullabies) precludes the need for the therapist to serve in this role. This frees up the therapist to interact with the patient in other roles, such as supporter or confronter, without threatening to eliminate the object that is containing the person's anxiety.

Furthermore, Elana used her birthday flute to begin the process of learning to say to her mother, "I miss you." First the dinosaurs missed the flute, then their mother. Elana missed the flute, through the dinosaurs and flutes, then missed the mother flute. Finally, Elana expressed her accurate feelings through the words, "Mommy! I miss you!" This is an example of transference to the music, rather than the therapist.

Musical Holding and Containment

Examples of creating a holding and secure environment are demonstrated by the structure provided by a greeting and closing song. This consistency offers familiarity and, thus, security for the child. This security provides a safe place to express emotions or ideas that are considered to be risky or dangerous to express. An example of how this structure provided a place for Elana to contain her anxiety was demonstrated in the lack of the barking behavior during any music therapy sessions. Despite the therapist's attempts to offer opportunities to exhibit this behavior, her responses to songs including dogs did not include "barking." This indicated that Elana could address feelings without the need to act them out with the "barking" sound.

An example of Elana's use of musical structure to contain negative feelings included her use of the keyboard as a battleground on which to "fight." As the time to close the session neared, the therapist stated, "I think it is time for us to sing the good-bye song." She was able to put down the instruments and join the closing song. Her use of the session to cathect her aggressive feelings enabled her to contain the residual aggression and control her behavior until the next opportunity arose. Furthermore, the therapist provided the opportunity for Elana to experience someone who could be in the maternal role and increase her tolerance for separation. The use of the "good-bye song" increased Elana's tolerance for separation with a meaningful other. It should be noted again that Elana is now able to say "good-bye" to her mother with less panic by singing this type of song to her mother.

CONCLUSION

While this is an example of one case, the authors have also observed these results with other individuals with autistic spectrum disorder. We believe that this approach is not only useful in individual music therapy, but is also effective in a group and/or family therapy setting. We hope this case will clearly demonstrate the viability of using this approach with children who are diagnosed with autistic spectrum disorder.

REFERENCES:

Abram, J. (1996). *The Language of Winnicott*. Northvale, NJ: Jason Aronson.

Anonymous, & McFarland, J. T. (1962). "Away in a Manger." In R. Olson (ed.), *Hymns and Songs for Church Schools*. Minneapolis: Augsburg Publishing House.

Benezon, R. (1991). *Music Therapy Manual*. Springfield, IL: Charles Thomas Publisher.

Brumley, A. E. (1992). "I'll Fly Away." In Y. Anderson (ed.), *Songs*. San Anselmo, CA: Songs and Creations.

Butcher, J. N., Carson, R. C., & Mineka, S. (1998). *Abnormal Psychology and Modern Life* (10th ed.). New York: Addison Wesley Longman, Inc.

Dallin, L., & Dallin, L. (1966). *Heritage Songster*. Dubuque, Iowa: Wm. C. Brown.

Diaz de Chumaciero, C. (1995). "Lullabies are 'Transferential Transitional Songs': Further Consideration on Resistance in Music Therapy," *The Arts in Psychotherapy*, 22 (4), 353–358.

Diaz de Chumaciero, C. (1992). "What Song Comes to Mind? Induced Song Recall: Transference/Countertransference in Dyadic Music Associations in Treatment and Supervision," *The Arts in Psychotherapy*, 19 (5), 325–332.

Disney, W. records (1996). *Hero Songs*, Volume 3. ABC Records Inc.

Epstein, S. (ed.) (2000). *Psychoanalytic Inquiry: Autistic Spectrum Disorders and Psychoanalytic Ideas: Reassessing the Fit*. Vol. 20, No. 6, Hillsdale, NJ: The Analytic Press.

Fox, D. (1985a). "Old King Cole." In W. L. Simon (ed.), *The Reader's Digest Children's Songbook*. Pleasantville, NY: The Reader's Digest Association, Inc.

Fox, D. (1985b). "Rock-A-Bye Baby." In W. L. Simon (ed.), *The Reader's Digest Children's Songbook*. Pleasantville, NY: The Reader's Digest Association, Inc.

Fox, D. (1985c). "Oh Where, Oh Where Has My Little Dog Gone?" In W. L. Simon (ed.), *The Reader's Digest Children's Songbook*. Pleasantville, NY: The Reader's Digest Association, Inc.

Garrett, L. (1992). "This Is the Day." In Y. Anderson (ed.), *Songs*. San Anselmo, CA: Songs and Creations, Inc.

Gruber, F., & Mohr, J. (1962). "Silent Night." In R. Olson (ed.), *Hymns and Songs for Church Schools*. Minneapolis: Augsburg Publishing House.

Hart, J. (ed.) (1982). "Where Is Thumbkin?" in *Singing Bee!* New York: Lothrop, Lee & Shepard Books.

Langs, R. (1973). *The Technique of Psychoanalytic Psychotherapy, Vol. I & II.* Northvale, NJ: Jason Aronson, Inc.

Lecourt, E. (1991). "Off-Beat Music Therapy: A Psychoanalytic Approach To Autism." In K. E. Bruscia (ed.), *Case Studies in Music Therapy.* Gilsum, NH: Barcelona Publishers.

Priestley, M. (1994). *Essays on Analytical Music Therapy.* Gilsum, NH: Barcelona Publishers.

Santrock, J. (2000). *Children*, 6th edition. New York: McGraw-Hill.

Scharff, D. E. and Scharff, J. S. (1995). *The Primer of Object Relations Therapy.* Northvale, NJ: Jason Aronson.

Schore, A. (1994). *Affect Regulation and the Origin of the Self.* Hillsdale, N.J: Lawrence Erlbaum Associates.

Traditional (1962). "The First Noel." In R. Olson (ed.), *Hymns and Songs for Church Schools.* Minneapolis: Augsburg Publishing House.

Traditional (1992). "O Christmas Tree." In Y. Anderson (ed.), *Songs.* San Anselmo, CA: Songs and Creations, Inc.

Winnicott, D. W. (1971). *Therapeutic Consultations in Child Psychiatry.* New York: Basic Books.

Winnicott, D. W. (1972). *Holding and Interpretation.* New York: Grove Press.

Part Two

Adolescents

Case Ten

"PROMISE TO TAKE GOOD CARE OF IT!": THERAPY WITH IRA

Viola Schönfeld

ABSTRACT

This case study describes the six-year-long music therapy of an adopted child. The therapy began during a phase of an acute, life-threatening somatic illness. It focused on the treatment of early childhood trauma mainly caused by incest and neglect. A complex process of psychological development within the therapy is described. In the course of the therapy, a growing resistance developed against the music. Nevertheless, a remarkable maturation and healing process took place.

INTRODUCTION

I am a music therapist and music is my most important therapeutic instrument. With my ear I tune into my client, becoming aware of his/her personal music, his/her self-hood and his/her vulnerability, his/her ideas. Within the scope of music I let myself be guided by the creativity of the client and then my response is guided by my own inspiration. This form of dialogue represents the client's psychological state and also reflects his/her relationship with me, the music therapist. In some cases, it can even be understood as a model of the client's social relationships in general, more or less as a portrayal or the reconstruction of a former relationship. The music may even show the way to a new beginning of social relations. Improvised music always depicts the state of mind. In any case, these experiences are included in the therapeutic work.

For this reason I kept asking myself, regarding the book in hand, why I chose to write a case study that clearly proves that working with the above-described ideas is not always possible. In this case study, sometimes the music is used under conditions that are different than usual and it seems only in a very secondary way. Undoubtedly my professional qualifications as a music therapist were indispensable to becoming the therapist of this child, but I have to admit that it challenged me over and over again to accept the fact that my specific element, which is music, was barely called upon. I write about the case of a girl, aged nine at the start of the therapy, who from the very beginning led me through her own therapeutic process and who finally convinced me that she herself knew the right way to her recovery. My role was to accompany the process and help her shape her psychological development, using the trained ear of a musician and my therapeutic faculties—but following her ideas. In my capacity as a music therapist, I write about a case in which my specific musical skills were more or less not wanted or needed. However, an extremely ill child taught me that we, the therapists, are very lucky when our clients are able to open themselves up and when they manage to look together with us for ways that bring them farther. This might even involve tools previously little known to us: therapeutic play with puppets and role-playing in this case. This child convinced me that we as music therapists can—and even must—deviate from our established therapeutic techniques and from the phenomenal possibilities provided by musical improvisations, if it turns out that music is not as beneficial as another therapeutic tool in an individual case. However, if our senses of hearing and of understanding are wide awake and if we can react in a flexible and creative way to what is happening, and what is displayed by the client, then we are of help.

BACKGROUND INFORMATION

Ira's Biography

The biological father impregnated his stepdaughter, thus begetting his grand-daughter whom he impregnated as well, thus begetting his great-granddaughter, my patient.

1985–Birth
The mentally challenged mother of the child had to move out of her grandparent's house after testifying in front of the youth welfare office that her grandfather was the biological father of her child and that he had raped her. She moved back to her grandmother half a year later, when the biological father began serving a three-year prison sentence.

1987–20 months
Due to continuing bloody diarrhea, the child was brought to a hospital. A severe form of ulcerative colitis was diagnosed. Surgical removal of the entire colon with the creation of an external stoma (artificial intestinal opening to the exterior of the abdomen) was followed by three months in the hospital. The patient was in a very serious general condition.

1988–3.5 years
The child told odd stories in kindergarten. The great-grandfather/father, in the meantime released from prison, was suspected of sexually abusing the child.

1989–4 years
Integration in a foster family occurred; the foster parents adopted the child in 1993.

1994–9 years
Through surgery, an ileoanal pouch (a v-shaped intestinal reservoir that is attached to both the small intestine and the anus) was created. In the following months a pouch training was carried out at home: a certain amount of water was filled into the pouch via the stoma or the anus and a specific training for the sphincter was practiced. This opened up the possibility of retransferring the stoma later on.

Late 1994
An intestinal obstruction caused by scar tissue necessitated emergency surgery. The music therapy begins.

First Contacts in the Hospital—November 1994

In November 1994, I was introduced to the nine-and-a-half-year-old girl, Ira. The music therapy began during the first weeks of a hospital stay, where she had to recover from intestinal surgery. The surgery, performed at the "Medizinische Hochschule Hannover" (Medical University of Hanover), had to be carried out to remove an intestinal obstruction caused by deformed older postoperative scar tissue (from a previous intestinal resection). The ileoanal pouch had been installed surgically in June 1994. It can be assumed that this surgery caused enormous mental strain for Ira. First, the prospect of normally functioning bowels involved the weakest part of her body. Second, it brought up the incest that had been going on for several generations in the family and awakened the experiences that the child herself presumably had with her great-grandfather as a four-year-old. At this time, Ira wore diapers that she used intensively. She received extensive medical care. Both the foster parents and the nurses worried about her physical condition, while at the same time being helpless and angry about the difficulties in dealing with her.

I met Ira for the first time in the children's ward in the company of her adoptive mother. During that meeting I experienced Ira as limitless in terms of keeping distances around her. She spoke loudly and fast with a piercing voice and she exclaimed simultaneously: orders, complaints, enthusiasm, the result of destructive behavior be it from torn clothes or feces, angry refusal of oral food intake, sharp-tongued remarks for close family, and charming and winning words for strangers. In regard to the adoptive mother, the fluctuation between a regressive-symbiotic and coarsely rejective behavior was striking. Everything in the entire palette of affective expression seemed to be available at the same time; for outside observers it was also clear that fear or depressive emotion were not present. Others, though, expressed these feelings.

Ira sat cheerfully on her adoptive mother's lap; the less willing she was to adjust socially, the more attention she got. At this time, everybody obviously had a hard time loving the child. Three personal music therapy sessions per week were planned. We used a gymnastics room in the basement of the hospital for the therapy, where I had to reinstall my musical instruments at the start of every session. The therapy room was not very cozy and there was no piano. The expectations upon me, the music therapist, were very high as was the emotional chaos of the child and that of the people relating to her. Although I had not even started my work, I felt exhausted. I also become aware of so many unanswered questions in me. I had a strong wish to better understand this girl and to find a way to make things right. I found myself facing specific expectations on the part of the children's hospital regarding the improved handling of this extremely difficult child. My position as a newly employed music therapist made it impossible for me to reject the case. But these circumstances created an awkward situation and this was why my initial motivation was rather cautious.

TREATMENT

The Music Therapy Begins

Ira explored the musical instruments enthusiastically and arranged them all around her. The instruments' singular brief performance then followed. Ira created sounds with each instrument. She gave me clear signals that I should not touch the instruments. I listened and watched. She discovered the hand puppets that from then on served her as the instrument to express her inner psychological problems. At the beginning, Ira played on her own, but she knew exactly how to manipulate my inner presence and attention for her playing. During the first sessions many of the subjects that were to accompany us for a long time appeared in extremely compact and distinctive sequences. It was within this chaotic and strenuous setting that the whole concept for our therapeutic work process was designed.

Seen from her point of view, the reason for this compactness and the exclusion of the instruments, which apparently did not directly and realistically enough present what she wanted to express immediately, could well have been the subjectively felt immediate threat of physical and psychological vitality. Furthermore, she might have realized that I could become very competent and superior when playing the instruments whereas her desire was the exact opposite: soon I was supposed to be a dependable partner in terms of listening when she was playing with the puppets. (Before Ira, at the age of twenty months, was brought to the hospital due to bloody diarrhea, she had been malnourished by her grandmother and her mother. This malnourishment continued after the surgery.) Music is often experienced as a feeding, oral gesture. Ira wanted me to be silent, to provide a holding environment and resonate empathically, according to the needs of a newborn child. In her psychological development, Ira restarted at the very beginning and made sure that everything was done exactly the way she needed it/would have needed it. She also took control of everything regarding food and communication. She played being bottle-fed and while she sat on my lap, she also spoke in the role of her ideal mother, absorbing the entire goodness coming from the close human contact. In February and March, two more intestinal surgeries followed.

The following scenarios came up when playing with the puppets:

Scenario 1:

Doctors as male destructive castrating force
Men being catheterized
Men being castrated
Male infants who are killed

Ira, when playing with the hand puppets, tortures men, makes them sterile by castration and eliminates all potential men by killing male babies.

Music:
Ira improvises songs and performs solos with a very sharp, high-pitched, and hard voice. Her lyrics are scornful including numerous swear words. She sings with great pleasure, thus the whole scenario is somewhat grotesque.

Scenario 2:

The puppets represent bad and good mothers. Ira arranges them and sorts them out. She identifies one good mother and separates her from the rest. The others are put into homes and hospitals. For a short period, Ira lets one puppet act as the mentally challenged mother having a helpless and weak character. The uncaring and indifferent grandmother is also portrayed.

Music:
Again, Ira improvises songs but performs them with a soft, very high-pitched voice and tender timbre showing the infant's affection for the mother.

Scenario 3:

Being reborn, starting life anew, growing up under better circumstances.

Scenario 4:

During the period of the second and third intestinal surgeries in February and March 1995, Ira reflects on her inevitable death in role-plays not using the hand puppets. She includes higher authorities like Santa Claus and God. Her own death becomes a subject; either as something that can be prevented through the goodwill of some higher forces or as an order from God above to which one has to resign. At the end of March 1995, Ira was discharged from the hospital with an infusion apparatus. With this, she could get additional food and her food intake could be controlled exactly.

During these months, my therapeutic activities were aimed at following Ira in her wishes to play, being a caring counterpart for her, supporting her ego, and being a steadfast witness of all the horrific events revealed through the puppet and role-play. During this phase of severe object-oriented aggressions that become clear through transferring them on me, I felt myself almost being tested as a therapist: if I passed, I might well become the longtime therapist of this child, accompanying her on a very long, often arduous and painful road.

Outpatient Therapy—March 1995

This phase began with a change in the form of therapy from inpatient to outpatient music therapy. From then on, the therapy took place in my private practice rooms. Ira's physical state became stable, yet taking care of her at home was rather difficult. Care of the stoma and continuous control of the food intake completely dominated the everyday life of the whole family. The situation became even more tense with four hours daily in school. An almost constant struggle for power developed between the adoptive mother and Ira. From then on, the mother and I met regularly in order to help her cope with the acute difficulties. We tried to find ways for both Ira and her mother to get along with each other. Our talks helped strengthen the adoptive mother, who cared for this extremely demanding child with immense intensity.

Changing the location of the therapy also changes the therapy in itself:

The first outpatient session

Ira plays some instruments and wants me to do the same. It seems as if she sees the instruments as mechanical toys and enjoys the technical usage rather than the sound experience itself. My attempt (and my faint hope) to now become more active in my role as a music therapist turns out to be contraindicated and clearly not wanted.

The theme of dying continues. In role-plays, we mourn Ira's death. She plays that she is reborn as a wanted, healthy child of happy loving parents. While doing so, she tells me exactly who I am supposed to be (mother, grandmother, father) and what I am supposed to say and feel. When my words differ too much from her ideas, she corrects them. She brings Christian songbooks to the therapy sessions. We celebrate a religious service; we sing a funeral liturgy that I am supposed to accompany on the piano. She strikes up hymns and distributes the verses to each of us. She sings with a serious well-balanced voice. Ira is a child with religious interest. She creates her own relation to the heavenly father who gives and takes life. God is not always of immediate importance within the therapy, but unlike all the other authorities, he is never dethroned during the plays. Now it becomes clearly observable that Ira is putting the things she suffered from in her small world, the experiences she had in her role as a baby, into a greater context. I still listen and hold. As the piano accompaniment, I temporarily serve as her instrument. At the end of the session, she seems at ease with herself and relaxed.

The hand puppets

The hand puppets are distributed and for a long time remain with the same player and take the same roles. These roles change over a long period of time as the child develops psychologically.

Ira plays the role of the puppet Annegret, representing Ira herself—a nice and lovely creature. She also plays the father, a policeman, as a fatherly and grandfatherly authority and aggressor.

I get to play the role of the puppet Punch, a diminished man, who is the brother and weak enough to serve as a perfect target of the father's aggressions; plus he is no threat for Annegret/Ira. Furthermore, I play the role of the grandmother who is at the same time the mother of Annegret and Punch. My own approach to the role of the grandmother/mother is that of a benevolent motherly listener. I hold and give comfort and I am always there. Sometimes I side with Annegret and sometimes with Punch. Sometimes this situation is difficult for Annegret and makes her jealous.

Summer 1995

During this period, Ira concentrated on forming relationships between the mother/grandmother and daughter in the puppet play. For a few weeks, a new musical part was introduced to the setting: the *Klangbad* (sound bath) at the end of the session. For the beginning of the therapy session, we agreed upon a short exchange of news and ordinary occurrences. From my therapeutic point of view this is a good way to learn to perceive reality and play as two separate entities in general and within the therapy sessions in particular. And although she often rushed rather reluctantly through the first part, Ira adopted a relaxed posture during the *Klangbad* at the end. If she felt like it, she closed her eyes and listened to the music that I improvised. The music had a calm rhythm and a meditative character. Afterward she sometimes described pictures that she imagined during the music. Ira enjoyed the *Klangbad* very much. She opened herself to a sound experience previously unknown to her. That was a symbol of what I could give to her. So here was a real person, I was allowed to be a good mother and give her something real. Through this, she entered the following phase.

Symbiotic stage and gradual detachment

Ira brings her doll to the session. We play quiet cozy scenes: she either lets me care for her as if she were my baby or plays the mother herself and takes great care of her own baby doll. She creates the scenes; gives me instructions that I follow strictly. Thus, I become a mother who can neither do anything wrong, nor disappoint, nor hurt, nor abandon the child. In the sense of a narcissistic personality development, Ira changes from auto-communication to communication. The good symbiotic cocoon with its soft tones and its, symbolically speaking, sweet smell of baby milk now widens and makes way for the view to the outside world, to the "other." Interacting with me, she starts to differentiate between introspection (perceiving herself as a separate entity) and the perception of the others and trains both perceptions transitionally.

Ira's adoptive mother reported that she enjoyed playing at home, much more than she used to, and that she had developed an independent interest in learning to read. On the whole, Ira seemed to be a lot more open to new experiences. Only her eating behavior was still problematic, as Ira had no great interest in eating. The pouch training was very hard work for everybody involved.

At this time, we used both role and puppet plays in parallel: she played herself in role-plays to test and internalize new experiences. If, however, stronger emotional contrasts were involved, such as revenge and love or longing for death, if the playing referred to fantasies her conscience objected to, she preferred to use the puppets as instruments. The killing and dying scenes, for example, took place parallel to Ira's phase as a baby when, held by me in the function of the caring and loving mother, she started a new and better life and was in an early developmental and psychological stage. It seemed as if the presence of the father/grandfather/great-grandfather had to be prevented over and over again, in order for her to be able to thrive as a human being. Obviously she had to repeat the killing of the complicated and complex father figure, who destroyed several generations, in order to have a positive outlook on life and to reexperience her own growing up undisturbed. In this phase of the therapy, she developed a new interest in the musical instruments. As they were formerly completely banned, I kept asking myself why. A possible explanation could be that, to Ira, her release from hospital meant triumphing over her own death. The fact that she was at home, surrounded by her family, and went to school— instead of a teacher and her family coming to see her in the hospital—let her feel a higher degree of autonomy. She bicycled to therapy on her own and there she experienced the growth of a stable relationship, thus gaining self-security and self-confidence. So maybe this was why she allowed herself to be curious for the first time. She felt less threatened than before. Ira sang for herself, communicating only with herself, thus going through an auto-communicative stage. Later on, she included lyrics in her songs that she wrote for me. Thus, she began communicating with "the other."

December 1995

Ira's digestion was so weak that she had to be hospitalized. A sepsis, caused by bacteria penetrating via the port, was diagnosed.

In January 1996, the port was removed surgically and the planned retransfer of the stoma was carried out. From then on Ira digested normally.

The shocking gift

Regaining the ability to digest normally and to flush the toilet instead of changing a bag must look like a wonderful healing process to outside observers. And what indeed seemed like a miracle when looking at Ira's biography was actually a shock for her. She was now forced to deal with her abdominal functions and needed to come to terms with the multigenerational incest on which her existence was based. What was controlled passively through her intestines since her twentieth month of life, due to the ulcerative colitis, now confronted her as something less salutary than threatening, and needed to be treated actively. At the age of twenty months, when the anal stage of a child normally begins, Ira got the artificial intestinal opening and so she neither had toilet training nor experienced anality. She now had to pass through this missed anal stage in her daily life and within the therapeutic process.

The family complained about the chaotic circumstances at home. Ira spread her excrements everywhere. She boycotted the care of her highly inflamed anus and hid dirty diapers. She refused to take over responsibility for her bodily functions and her diet, for cleaning up, hygiene, school, and her general tasks. Fighting over limits and rules became part of the daily routine. Ira's adoptive mother again proved to be a self-assertive and reliable mother. During this time the adoptive mother herself needed constant support in order to preserve her own health and to help her cope with the extremely difficult daily life with Ira. We talked a lot together.

King and queen—Omnipotence and impotence

By taking over the role of both king and queen, Ira placed herself in an omnipotent position, which was further strengthened by playing both of them at the same time. To me, she delegated the roles of the servants and other courtiers. At the king's court there was an abundance of everything: plenty of chambers, thousands of servants, tens of thousands of soldiers, large gardens, millions of roses, huge kitchens with a lot of cooks, and so on. The spectacular, omnipotent setup surrounding the king, warded off the helplessness and impotence embodied by the queen. Ira played both roles, though granting the king more care and power in the beginning. Most of the time, he was a despotic, unjust character humiliating and offending others. Only occasionally did he try to let justice rule. The people and the servants started getting nervous and the queen began to reject the injustices done by the king. Conflicts increased between the royal couple. The queen wished to protect the people and herself. By proving her willingness to make good compromises in favor of the weak, she gained more and more authority and respect. When the role of a princess was added and thus a royal family was formed, Ira passed the role of the king to me. From then on, she played the parts of the queen and the princess, who was of the same age as Ira. From the material point of view, this princess had everything she wanted. But she intervened when the mother gave orders to pull down the houses of impoverished people. The queen remained strong. In my new role as the king, I played a rejected and disgraced man. The status of the queen, who also became the mother in the course of the play, had to change within Ira's imagination, showing the analogy to her psychological state. Only when the mother was strong and not helpless anymore, could Ira identify with her. Later on, she, the mother, also proved to be an aggressor who deprived the most destitute of the little they have. She pulled down their houses—taking away shelter. It became obvious that Ira was working on her early traumas: the violent biological father/king, who, godlike, gives and takes away life (an uncle, also the outcome of a rape, has committed suicide) and an only seemingly capable grandmother/ mother/queen, who did not protect the child from abuse and was not able to nourish her. With the help of her imaginary playing, Ira reduces the aggressor king/father through the rational queen/mother. From the moment that he could not threaten her anymore—I had him well under control—the true character of the queen/mother was revealed and could be identified as something evil. The child of the queen had the chance—being an older child now—to think and act independently. She could try to convince others, and so look after her interests on her own. In the meantime, this child had developed mature and reasonable views. Intensively playing so many different roles had helped Ira to acquire a quite precise idea of the concepts good and bad.

During this time, musical elements were banned from our sessions. She did not sing either. She loved to work with clay and modeled many different meals for huge banquets prepared for unbelievable masses of people. It seemed as if she wanted to satisfy oral needs that were denied to her over many years and that she could never happily enjoy.

After gaining the ability to digest independently, Ira began having higher expectations from her social environment in terms of performance at school and keeping contact with her biological mother. These sporadic contacts with the biological mother were very strenuous for Ira. The generous, magnanimous adoptive mother allowed the biological mother to visit the family, where the latter temporarily found a new home just as if she were an additional child. In my opinion, this strongly irritated Ira and had to be avoided so that her own mental work, the self-analysis of her past, was not interrupted or disturbed. It was important not to overwhelm her with aspects of her former living conditions from which she had been deliberately removed. After several talks with the adoptive mother, we decided that meetings with the biological mother should be arranged outside the family home and only if Ira agreed to them. Furthermore, we decided it would be good to respect Ira's extreme fluctuations in schoolwork as a barometer of her mental state and not to confront her with exaggerated expectations.

1997/1998

Ira is twelve years old. I move my therapeutic office.

During these sessions, Ira now preferred role-play to puppet play. Most of the time, she came to therapy with matters that were very important to her and she had prepared her own playing plans. Then she urged me to begin role-playing.

The setting of role-play

Ira now often chose different female roles and left the roles of men and the grandmother to me. My opportunities to act more independently during the playing increased. We had arguments and sometimes fought over solutions. Toward the end of the sessions, the situation often escalated dramatically and then Ira ruthlessly had to find a solution, often disregarding the borders of the other player. Forgiving, accepting the opposite, showing mercy and thus saving someone from death were typical scenarios for those solutions that she would develop shortly before the session's end. These scenes showed behavioral patterns that were not common for Ira before this point. The theme was often the escape from a conflict into a somatic symptom. The autonomy as a role player that I was granted, and that had grown within the therapeutic process, allowed me to work with Ira on the fact that psychological experiences often hide behind organic symptoms and that we could now confront ourselves with these experiences. During the playing, the strength of our relationship was put to a test, because despite massive pressure and dramatic physical disorders, I strictly followed my personal ideas of how a relationship is to be formed. Relying on positive transference and the long therapeutic process with its stabilizing effects, I decided to approach Ira in a more confrontational way. Having to decide whether to prevail or to relent was a new situation between us—Viola and Ira. For Ira, this also meant she had to come to terms with closeness and distance. The therapy was now very difficult for her; she experienced disappointment and that I was not an ideal person any longer. Now and then, the sessions became quite heated and vivid, with Ira investing an immense amount of energy. To me, the sessions sometimes seemed like Olympic games during which we did not leave out a single discipline.

Music:

There were days when Ira came to therapy and wished to sing. She herself chose songs from a songbook. She preferred traditional folk songs. For some time, the following song was important to her: "I am looking in vain for the reason/That I am so sad and distressed/A tale known for many a season/Will not allow me to rest."[1]

On those days, she was in a less agitated, rather serious and calm mood. Her voice sounded well-centered, enriched by resonance and fervor. In the past, the chosen pitch often seemed too high and the voice less stable, whereas now it was obvious that it was really she who was singing. My accompaniment seemed to inspire her and she expressed joy. When singing, her intonation was absolutely flawless and the rhythm precise. The musician in me felt both happiness and lament at the same time, as the moments of joy to experience music with this musically talented child were so rare.

---

[1] Translator's note: Famous German folk song "Die Loreley"; lyrics based on a poem by Heinrich Heine, music by Friedrich Silcher in 1838 and by Franz Liszt in 1841.

An even older subject—the mentally challenged biological mother

A role-play performed in a calm and matter-of-fact atmosphere dealt with the mentally challenged biological mother. Ira played that she worked in a retirement home that also houses mentally challenged people. She asked me to play the roles of the elderly people. After some attempts, she took the roles of the mentally challenged people away from me. (Maybe I performed too well.) In this caring and helping role, she was very convincing and seemed extremely professional. I found it striking that she classified the mentally challenged mother as an elderly person. Perhaps in this way Ira released her mother from the general responsibility for taking care of her, which would have actually been the mother's natural role. She assigned her mother the status of a person nobody expected anything from, a person who was not blamed for not performing: the status of an old person. And in this way she could hide the narcissistically hurtful fact of being the child of a mentally challenged mother (as old people often cannot take responsibility for themselves due to their age or their health condition). Ira rarely spoke about her mother: she could neither take care of her mother in reality nor identify herself with her.

Menstruation first occurs at the age of thirteen.

1999/2000

The now fourteen-year-old only lost control of her bowels in very stressful situations, for example, during trips with her school class when the fear of being left alone and abandoned became immense. The adoptive mother reported fast mood swings that seemed to control the child. One minute she was gentle and sensitive, the next she was extremely aggressive and destructive. Unconsciously Ira expended a lot of psychological energy to maintain a split that safeguarded the achieved good and the developed positive self that were still threatened by former desires, fears, and aggressions. It seemed to be the right decision to let the girl finish school but not to force her to earn a diploma, although her development was good and her intellectual abilities promised more than she actually managed to achieve due to her psychological instability. In general, her psychological stability improved when things were made easier for her.

The last cycle of role and puppet plays—To establish and keep order

Ira played a senior police officer and my task was to play her colleague. One job after the other was assigned to us: we had to sort out many different types of crimes with mostly women and children being the victims. Every criminal was caught and they all got their just punishment. Uncompromising and stringent trials took place. Our mission was to eliminate all criminals in the world and make the world a safe place to live in. We retaliated against evil and maintained order among the people. During the plays our relationship as colleagues/partners proved that Ira strove to work on an equal basis with me, but that her need to be reassured that someone is caring for her is still stronger. In the role of the police officer, she was often worn out and needed me to support her. But at the same time, she was not willing to give up the position of the indispensable executor of the law (demanding omnipotence—fear of losing control). In regard to her psychological development, we experienced the stage of detachment. Within the context of our play as police officers, for instance, I had clearly different interests than her. I insisted on my well-deserved breaks and was not willing to sacrifice myself for my job. Subsequently I finally dropped out and became sort of a *Lebenskünstler* (survivalist), whereas Ira became a "normal" police officer, had a husband and children. She got spoiled at home and strictly kept to her working hours. During this phase of the role-play, we prepared our parting. The occasional meetings of the two ex-colleagues not only gave room for friendly gestures and exchanging familiarities but also provided the opportunity to complain about things and talk about the fear of being left alone. Over a very long period, Ira was thus able to playfully try out scenarios that she actually needed in her everyday life. She herself always knew what was most important to her during each stage of her development. She suggested and laid down the—absolutely reasonable—chronology of events.

Music:

For almost a year, we had not included musical elements in our sessions. Ira did not want to listen to music nor did she want to improvise it. Not on her own nor together with me. She felt no desire to use sounds in order to express symbolically what was going on inside her mentally. The urge to play and use words in order to express directly and verbally what was going on in herself was much stronger. She joined a folk dance class and her parents told me that she sings along loudly during church service.

The parting

We had twenty hours left to arrange our parting. The sessions now often began with longer conversations during which Ira talked about her everyday life. During some of the sessions, these conversations occupied the largest part. Seen from the angle of her psychological development, Ira had arrived at her verbal self. This grown verbal (and real) self-awareness enabled her to face me as Ira herself, talking about her current everyday life. She was no longer in the grip of older traumas, with their own momentum.

She was annoyed at the long and strenuous drives to the therapy and suggested longer intervals between the sessions. Now and then, she took up the police theme, but the situations were less dramatic. Ira also talked about her job as a baby-sitter, which she seemed to enjoy a lot. She told me that she would soon become an aunt.

One of the questions she often asked was: "How long will I be allowed to come to your music therapy?" My constant reply to it was: "As long as you wish to do it!" And to the following question: "Will I still be allowed to visit you as a grown-up?" I kept answering: "Yes." I believe that this certainty was very good for Ira. She was constantly reassured that there would be enough time to catch up with everything. Enough time to nurture herself as much as she needed and as far as it was possible with me. Finally, she indicated that she considered herself as matured and nurtured enough to prepare the end of the music therapy and to part with me, her music therapist.

To the last session, she brought along a potted plant and put it gruntingly on my kettledrum (which is thus temporarily put out of order!). At the end of the session she handed it over to me and said: "Promise to take good care of it!" A tiny rose was starting to blossom in the potted plant.

DISCUSSION AND CONCLUSIONS

What can a music therapist do upon suddenly realizing, right in the middle of the therapeutic process with the client, that the therapy developed in another direction than the one intended? How should he react if a therapy originally planned to be music therapy turns into play therapy? In this described case, the music therapy can be characterized in the beginning as a supportive therapy. It was supposed to accompany and stabilize a somatically ill child during a life-threatening phase of her disease. But the girl somehow knew for herself that she first had to resolve her early traumas and live through all the delayed developmental stages that she had never come to experience, before being able to recover physically. Six years of continuous therapy were needed to accomplish this process. In as much as the child passed almost without pause through all the stages of psychological development, it would have been fatal to stop this therapy at any time: from the oral to the anal phase, from the point of developing a "no" mentality to detachment until the time the adolescent is open to communication and can determine the end of the therapy herself. If I had decided to break off the therapy within this process, the process itself would have stopped and most likely, a repeated regression would have been induced. A halt could well have meant an acute life threat for this child. As the symptom carriers, her extremely weak and only pathologically trained intestines would not have tolerated more psychosomatic stress.

Maybe the fact that Ira takes guitar classes today can be ascribed to the music therapy that in fact was play therapy—surely not to the credit of the music itself, but rather to my willingness to widely abandon musical elements in the therapy in order to accompany the child on her very own path.

REFERENCES

Asper, K., (1991). *Verlassenheit und Selbstentfremdung.* Munich: DTV.

Canacakis, J. (1991). *Ich sehe deine Tränen-Trauern, Klagen, Lebenkönnen.* Stuttgart, Germany: Kreuzverlag.

Decker-Voigt, H. H. (1991). *Spiele der Seele-Traum, Imagination und künstlerisches Tun.* Bremen, Germany: Trialog Verlag.

Decker-Voigt, H. H. (1992). *Aus der Seele gespielt—Eine Einführung in die Musiktherapie.* Munich, Germany: Goldmann-Verlag.

Decker-Voigt, H. H. (1993). *Pummel-Entwicklungpsychologie am Beispiel einer Nilpferd-Kindheit.* Bremen, Germany: Trialog Verlag Liliental.

Decker-Voigt, H. H., Knill, P., & Weymann, E. (1996). *Lexikon der Musiktherapie.* Göttingen, Germany: Hogrefe.

Freud, A. (1983). *Einführung in die Technik der Kinderanalyse.* Frankfurt am Main, Germany:

Hoffmann/Hochapfel. (1991). *Einführung in die Neurosenlehre und psychosomatische Medizin.* Stuttgart, Germany: UTB Schattauer.

Klein, M. (1972). *Das Seelenleben des Kleinkindes*. Reinbeck, Germany: Rowohlt.

Kohut, H. (1990). *Narzismus—eine Theorie der psychoanalytischen Behandlung narzisstischer Persönlichkeitsstörungen*. Frankfurt am Main, Germany: Suhrkamp Verlag.

Niedecken, D. (1988). *Einsätze*. Hamburg, Germany: VSA.

Niedecken, D. (1989). *Namenlos, Geistig Behinderte Verstehen*. Munich, Germany: Piper.

Priestley, M. (1983). *Analytische Musiktherapie*. Stuttgart, Germany: Klett-Cotta.

Stern, D. N. (1992). *Die Lebenserfahrung des Säuglings*. Stuttgart, Germany: Klett-Cotta.

Winnicott, D. W. (1973). *Vom Spiel zur Kreativität*. Stuttgart, Germany: Klett-Cotta.

Winnicott, D. W. (1983). *Die therapeutische Arbeit mit Kindern*. Munich, Germany: Kindler.

Case Eleven

THE KNIGHT INSIDE THE ARMOR: MUSIC THERAPY WITH A DEPRIVED TEENAGER

Simona Katz Nirensztein

ABSTRACT

Eli is a fifteen-year-old boy, who arrived at a boarding school for maladjusted teenagers, after an attempted suicide. At his arrival he refused to speak to anybody. Due to a premature birth and to a deprived family environment, Eli's Self was fragile and not coherent. Anxieties, splitting, and emotional isolation made it impossible for him to adapt to normal life. The present chapter describes how Eli's Self was "restored" during the process of music therapy he went through at the boarding school. Improvising in a holding environment, experiencing a continued "affect attunement" with his therapist, and being mirrored in an empathic way allowed Eli to get in touch with his feelings, to express them—in music and in words—and to feel the vital sensation of being understood. Finally, some ethical/theoretical issues about the pros and cons of the depth of this kind of intervention in such a limited setting are considered.

INTRODUCTION

The case study that I am about to describe has as its protagonist a fourteen-year-old boy who arrived, one cold December, at the boarding school where I work. This is a hostel for maladjusted teenagers; the boys, aged between fourteen and eighteen, can be classified as deprived and with an anti-social tendency. The life of these boys is marked by deprivation, both material and affective. Their parents did not know how to, or could not, provide them with the experience of growing up in an adequate holding environment, nor did they protect them from traumas linked to material poverty, exclusion, drugs, violence, or sexual abuse. Many of the boys have serious learning problems, some of them have a psychiatric history. Their attitude toward other human beings and to their environment swings between violence and avoidance.

D. W. Winnicott (1956), in his article on the antisocial tendency, stresses the fact that the antisocial act is an expression of hope, a plea to the environment to provide what is lacking. But he himself tells of the difficulty of taking up the role of providing a therapeutic response for these deprivations. It is not easy to have stones thrown at the windows, to have to interrupt a client that strikes with such violence as to tear the drums or burst the therapist's eardrums, nor to face endless silences that express total void.

But Eli, the subject of this case study, was not at all a typical personality within the school. His frail and introverted look made him seem younger and more fragile than his companions. The violence of the environment represented a further threat to him. His success in his school studies accentuated his dissimilarity. Upon his arrival at the school, he closed himself inward and seemed determined not to open up either with his peers or with adults.

BACKGROUND INFORMATION

Eli came to the boarding school after six months in a psychiatric day hospital, where he had been admitted because of a suicide attempt. He had locked himself in his home with a brother two years younger than he, and had threatened to jump from the fourth floor. Police came to avert the tragedy. In the hospital, Eli had been diagnosed as suffering from "Dysthemia. Primary type, early onset."

The family did not provide an environment suitable for dealing with Eli, so the psychiatric and social services decided to permanently separate him from them. Eli's father suffered from a grave form of progressive muscular dystrophy that contributed to making him unstable, even from a psychological point of view, subject to frequent attacks of anger and violence. Even before his illness he had not held a permanent job. In his past he had had another family, wife and children, with whom he had no contact whatsoever. Eli's mother, a woman with a weak personality and physically fragile, bore the economic and practical burdens of the family, working for a cleaning company. Eli had two older sisters and a brother two years younger than he, who all had serious behavioral problems. The family lives in great economic hardship and need the help of social services.

During her pregnancy with Eli, his mother had suffered from preeclempsia (pregnancy poisoning); Eli was born prematurely at the seventh month, weighing two kilograms, and was in danger of dying. His mother tells that while he was in the incubator she prayed continuously. She made a vow that he would be given a name, which, in Hebrew, means "God has helped." From that moment on, she says, Eli was her only hope, a hope that had not sufficed to give the child a happy childhood.

The parents did not provide information on the first years of Eli's life—his development is defined as normal in general terms. His school and social services had long realized that the boy was suffering—isolated at school, distracted, physically restless, and afflicted with facial tics. His scholastic performance had deteriorated visibly during the year preceding his hospitalization. Efforts were made several times to distance him from the family, but a complex bond of mutual dependence with the mother made this impossible.

A report from the psychiatric hospital defined Eli as a boy with grave emotional problems:

> Where there is a need for emotional involvement there is a decrease in its potentiality reaching the loss of reality judgement. Painful emotions, such as depression, anger, and boredom, tied to thoughts of death, impose an enormous effort of containment, and threaten to overwhelm him and provoke anxiety attacks. In the effort to defend himself, Eli uses primitive defense systems, such as denial, repression, emotional insulation, isolation and splitting.

Both the hospitalization and his admittance to the boarding school for maladjusted boys were carried out against his will. Eli refused to open his mouth in the presence of the psychologist, which was the main reason he was referred for music therapy. The psychologist, being worried, asked for my help, but at the same time he told me, "Be very careful, his defenses are impenetrable and hard, but as fragile as a ceramic tile; if you touch it, you risk breaking it."

THEORY, METHODOLOGY, AND TECHNIQUES

Working with adolescents whose life experience is one of severe deprivation has helped me to identify the influence of what is missing in the relationship with parental figures on the very early development of the self. In particular, I am convinced that much can be done by means of a psychodynamic approach within a music therapy setting. Music has, in fact, a series of characteristics which make it most adaptable for creating a type of therapeutic relationship whereby the client can express his own needs and what is missing and, at least in part, regain the use of psychological patterns that have atrophied or have never existed. According to D. W. Winnicott, "a good enough environmental provision in the earliest phase enables the infant to begin to exist, to have experience, to build a personal ego, to ride instincts, and to meet with all the difficulties inherent in life"(1956, p. 304). What is missing for the boys at the boarding school is, first of all, that "good enough environment."

The concepts of "mirroring" and "holding," as expressed by Winnicott (1960; 1971), are instrumental in my approach and have accompanied the entire therapeutic process with Eli. In Eli's own story the holding was missing as much in the physical sense as in the psychological one, because of his premature birth, together with the extremely difficult family situation.

We shall see how the sensation of having to, and wanting to, "hold" and "see" Eli was an integral part of the countertransference and his need to be "held and seen" constituted the transference. The "arms" and "eyes," no less than their object, were created by the music: to listen and be heard, to express and be understood, even without words, was the backbone of the process. The music, and the silence as its alternative and container, permitted the creation of an unconditional holding that was adaptable for the various phases of development of Eli within the therapeutic process. The experience of merging with a maternal figure was the basis for the creation of the "transitional space" (Winnicott, 1971) where Eli could experience the feelings of creativity and omnipotence. Here, thanks to the presence of the therapist, he could feel his Self as an existing, significant, and valuable entity.

The ability of the infant to participate in an interpersonal relationship from the very first days of life, according to Daniel Stern's (1985) theory, is by its very essence amodal (without structure). All the senses are involved in the creation of a channel of communication between the personal experience of the child and the person who is taking care of him.

The nonverbal character of music, the complexity of its components (united in their primordial character), its unavoidable physical counterpart, its capacity to address itself simultaneously to various senses, makes it an ideal medium for re-creating conditions comparable to the constitutive experience of the self. Music allows the therapist to provide a closeness that is suitable for the client at that given moment of his experience, without going through the process of symbolization and, in certain ways, of alienation of the experience in its totality, which is intrinsic in verbalization.

Stern's theory gives a central place to nonverbal communication as a basic element in the creation of a relationship. The fundamental concept of the "vitality affect," as the quality of the affective experience arising from the meeting with the other as early as the age of two months, in the sphere of the "sense of an emergent self," (Stern, 1985) supports the basis for using a music psychotherapeutic approach, particularly because the feelings expressed are not verbalized and categorized in order to obtain a legitimization and a curative validation. On the contrary, the function of the music therapist becomes accentuated through the definition of one who can accomplish "the affective attunement," the kind of act which is nonimitative, but absolutely regulated to the affect that lies behind the infant's action. This process permits the sharing of the baby's affective state and, consequently, the intersubjective exchange, which is indispensable for the construction of the "sense of subjective self." One must keep in mind the fact that in the case of deprived teenagers the experience of affective attunement on the part of the adult is very often missing throughout the course of the entire life.

In my work, I have been guided by the principle—which is more and more accepted by self-psychology (Kohut, 1984) and the intersubjective approach (Atwood & Stolorow, 1979)—that the mutative element in the therapeutic process is the relationship with the therapist, the therapeutic act, even more than the verbal interpretation. "'Something more' than interpretation, in the sense of making the unconscious conscious is needed" (Stern et al., 1998). In my understanding, music has all the characteristics to make it the vehicle for that "something more." I have found the concept of the importance of "now moments" (Stern et al., 1998), those moments of authentic encounter connected equally to the life experience of the therapist as to those of the client, and which are capable of "modify[ing] the structure of the implicit relational knowing between the client and the therapist," very illuminating. Furthermore, this is an experience that can, in turn, modify the "client's implicit procedural knowing, his way of being with others" (Ibid., p. 903).

This is a situation in which the therapist must be in deep contact with his/her own countertransferential reactions, especially those that pass through and express themselves in such a way that they interfere with the client's music (Bruscia, 1998, pp. 51–120).

Therefore, in my approach the energy is directed to be in maximum attunement with the client in the here and now. Through this particular type of attention, it is my intention to allow the client to integrate his experience and to insert it within the more complex framework of the bonds that tie the past to the present.

The method in this case study, therefore, was absolutely nondirective and concentrated on the construction of a relationship that would allow for experiences that were lacking in Eli's repertoire of intersubjective encounters. Free improvisation was the main musical vehicle, but other experiences included music listening and dance. Words and music alternated in a natural manner and, as far as possible, one that suited the needs of the client. The meetings, lasting fifty minutes each, took place once a week. The duration of the overall therapy was one year and seven months.

THE TREATMENT PROCESS

Daring to Be in the Presence of "An-other"

I must admit that the psychologist's warning had alarmed me; I had an ambiguous mission—to create a contact, but without cracking the flimsy porcelain layer that separated Eli from the dangers inherent in any relationship. To be in touch with him without touching him. . . . But Eli helped me. Right from the first session, he defended himself and opened up at the same time.

He entered the room almost without looking at me; mumbling a greeting, he sat down next to the electric organ and began to play. A flow of sounds from his bony hands, the look on his face sharp, concentrated and intense, his body wrapped in a shapeless coat. From his hands came snatches of melodies that ran into one another; he liked to start from the high notes, to reach, descending progressively in thirds and fourths, to the low ones. Soon he moved over to the piano. He kept the right-hand pedal down, blurring and attenuating the limits of the melodic ideas that were taking shape. From time to time he played with both hands, creating hints of polyphonic dialogues. I listened and watched him with absolute intensity. Through the senses, I could perceive his existence and the obscure, confused, and painful nucleus from which that flow of music sprang. I could perceive the empty spaces. I could sense that nobody had ever looked at him this way, in an effort to reach his core-self. I perceived that music was an expression of something very authentic and very deep. Rich. I was struck by images of maelstroms, indistinct movements of dark and intense colors. The word "unintegrated" came to my mind. Speaking of the very first phases of development, Winnincott (1945) refers first of all to the process of integration and says "the tendency to integrate is helped by two sets of experience: the technique of infant care whereby an infant is kept warm, handled and bathed and rocked and named and also the acute instinctual experience which tend to gather the personality together from within" (p. 150).

Perceiving Eli's music as linked to a phase of integration, I felt I was providing him with a symbolic "infant care" by my looking and listening, while he dared to experiment and express his "acute instinctual experiences." It seemed quite clear to me that my role should not be an active one; my listening and presence allowed Eli to exist and to begin to feel his existence in an environment that did not compel him to any act of change or adaptation, that did not threaten him in any way. His readiness to let himself go with the flow of the music can be seen as a demonstration of his life force, of his not giving up to the looming disintegration.

During the second session, while I listened, I heard a fragment of melody that kept returning more and more insistently; I took some paper and noted the melody. Eli turned his head and asked for an explanation. I explained that I felt something taking shape and I did not want it to be lost. He nodded, satisfied. What reached through to Eli was an act of mirroring: I see you, therefore you exist, your music is noted down by me, I want to understand it and remember it; therefore, you exist. In a certain sense I offered him a mirror. Eli began to check whether my look continued to accompany him.

"What does the baby see when he or she looks at the mother's face? I am suggesting that, ordinarily, what the baby sees is himself or herself" (Winnicott 1971, p. 112).

Daring to Be with "An-other"

That fragment of melody developed into a real *leitmotiv*. In its structure there was something mirrorlike, or, at any rate, in the nature of a dialogue, both in its rhythm and in its melodic structure. To a theme based on a descending third, responded another, based on an ascending third. To the high C responded a low C that ascended gradually and attained it. All this at the very abyss of the end of the keyboard, toward the highest part, or, more rarely, at the lowest. One could suppose that Eli was expressing, through the very structure of the melody, his need for mirroring and relating. And also his desire to bring the abysses of his anxieties into therapy. What was certain was that this melody became our common playground. The structure of the *leitmotiv* and the persistence of its regular reemergence, gave me the feeling that Eli had already been born in the relationship and was ripe for a musical interaction. Timidly, I began to play a sort of countermelody to his music, without trying to imitate it, but rather adapting my response to his proposal, in an effort to provide an experience of affect attunement. He replied to me. A wave of emotion engulfed us. I did not try to explain to myself in words what Eli was saying to me with his melody, or to categorize the feeling that he was expressing. I tried to "match" his melody and, above all, the affect that was behind it. In our musical dialogues, that from that moment on developed with ever greater freedom on both sides, we passed through a vast gamut of what Stern defines as "vitality affects." "A quality of experience that can arise directly from encounters with other people. . . . These elusive qualities are better captured by dynamic, kinetic terms, such as surging, fading away . . . explosive, crescendo, decrescendo, bursting . . ." (Stern, 1985, p. 54). Not only did Eli have the sensation of "existing," but in addition to this was the sensation of "co-existing" with someone who adapted her own vitality affect experience to his, rendering it a common one. Someone who accompanied him within his dark maelstroms—those which may gradually be faced. The ceramic tile was not impenetrable any longer.

Daring to Communicate with "An-other"

One day, after some improvisation together, Eli turned toward the stereo, looked at the discs, asked to hear a Mozart symphony, and began to talk. His words gushed out also in a "sottovoce e prestissimo" flood. It was difficult to understand him. To do so I had to bring my ear close to his mouth, at times asking him to repeat. I was very moved. The quality of my listening and also my state of mind were complementary to those provoked by the music, but the introduction of words into our space had signaled another step toward "togetherness." "In fact, every word . . . is the product of uniting two mentalities in a common symbol system, a forging of shared meaning" (Stern, 1985, p. 170). From then on our sessions assumed a structure. Eli would begin to play and sometimes I would join him in a shared improvisation. His *leitmotiv* would always appear and would at times undergo development and variations. The music helped him to get in touch with himself, reestablishing secure boundaries for our transitional space. My musical "arms" kept him warm and safe from the threat of disintegration, provoked by his own thoughts and feelings. But the music had another, and not less important, function: to preserve the globality of Eli's emotional experience, without submitting it to the inevitable fragmentation that language brings with it. As Stern (1985) states, "language is a double-edged sword. . . it drives a wedge between two simultaneous forms of interpersonal experience: as it is lived and as it is verbally represented" (Ibid., p. 162). The music also reappeared at the end of the session. In the middle there gushed out the flow of words with which Eli invited me to get to know his existence more objectively, more categorically. His life was presented from two deeply split angles: On the one hand, there was the home and a greatly idealized family, full of every kind of material good and affection without limit from parents, always full of goodness, obliged to send away their adored son against their will. The idealization made the reality bearable, altering it substantially, and it also expressed a need that had remained unresolved during Eli's development. On the other hand, there appeared small episodes that spoke of sensations of abandonment, loneliness, boredom, desires that were not met, and unrealizable dreams. I interacted briefly, asking for clarification, pointing out connections, making comparisons, and, above all, expressing my presence which was authentic and felt.

My presence, my listening, gave Eli a container, an "envelope" (Anzieu, 1989, p. 157) that embraced and united all the different parts of his self. Truth together with lies, desires together with disappointments, thought, and narrative. And, in this way, I felt myself to be a container ready to receive his words and his sounds.

He began to take off his inseparable coat, in which his body was kept always hiding, and passed to a more symbolic and less cumbersome and less crushing protection—a pouch tied to his waist.

Daring to Show Himself to "An-other"

We were drawing close to the end of the school year. Seven months had elapsed since the beginning of the therapy. When there were four encounters left before the vacation, on a hot day we began our session with a lazy improvisation on the metallophone. He began to sway to the rhythm and then, suddenly, he began to dance. His movements were surprisingly decisive, acute, and sharp—an orderly and very rapid sequence that certainly required some skill. He looked for highly rhythmical music and began his dancing anew several times. Every now and then he would glance my way to make sure that I approved. I was, more than anything else, stunned. His dancing did not resemble anything at all that I had shared with Eli until that day. From a certain point of view, I was amazed by the display of coordination and glad about the sudden involvement of the body in therapy—something I saw as a new important step. On the other hand, I felt very uneasy: There was something grotesque, exaggerated in that dance—a lack of vitality, flexibility. Observing him, I had a feeling that resembled shame. He told me, with a certain pride, that this dance was the fruit of hours and hours of hard work in front of the TV. He had been rehearsing it from the age of seven. Instinctively, I encouraged him to repeat it. I helped him find the most suitable music. But it was only later, and with the help of supervision, that I understood its significance. After seven months of therapy, Eli emerged from his coat with his "premature," "inadequate" body, just as, after seven months of pregnancy he emerged from the poisoned womb where he began his existence. My bashfulness was a reaction to the inadequacy of his appearance. But, at the same time, I was deeply willing and happy to receive and accept him the way he was. On another level, Eli was showing me something very intimate, a picture of a child who, being totally deprived of models to follow, searched on the television screen for something to learn and with which to confront the world. It was not surprising that that "something" was grotesque, especially now that that skinny body, already on the road to adolescence, performed it. The first to feel it, albeit unconsciously, as such, was probably Eli himself. In a certain sense I felt the shame for him. What, in another theoretical context, would have been called projective identification, I would define here as a "resonance with his unconscious feelings." Only in our transitional space, suspended halfway between his internal world and a relationship with another human being, Eli the dancer could show himself and survive.

At the end of the last session before the vacation, Eli also removed the pouch at his waist and forgot it in the room. Later, he showed his dance to his companions as well, eliciting admiration and amazement.

Daring to Be Angry

During the summer, I often thought about Eli and I wondered if our special atmosphere would survive the separation. Thus, I felt relieved when we met after the two months' holiday and he began playing as though we had parted the day before.

He immediately returned to his *leitmotiv*, but it soon became clear that the separation had left its mark. The soft minor third was transformed into a biting tritone. The sound, from being muffled, became percussive. My every intervention was refused and left outside his music; my questions remained unanswered. It was at the end of the first session that he told me simply, categorically, "I am angry." The all too obvious explanation that the first object of his own anger was I myself, who had left him in his private hell for two months, was refused in words, but explored through the music; the percussive theme and the recurrent tritones became the *leitmotivs* for that period. Soon, another reason for anger was added: his sister, two years older, had been sent to the same boarding school. Eli was embarrassed and burdened down: He felt responsible and vulnerable. Most of all, he was concerned that his home had followed him here and he felt threatened that it could invade our private space. Parts of these feelings were expressed in words, parts I could feel between the lines, between the notes. In fact, the front of the idealization of the family was broken.

The ceramic tile had cracked. One day, Eli did not find me in the room because of one minute's delay: his anger imploded. Refusing my apologies, he started rehearsing his dance, but he was blocked after every two steps like a puppet whose strings had been cut. It was a despairing scene. Looking at me like a wet kitten he said, "I've forgotten how to dance." The contact with his own feelings, which my lateness had "triggered," had brought him close to a feeling of disintegration; the difference resided in the fact that now he could express this threat in therapy. A progress, in therapeutic terms, that had, however, a regressive character: the forgetting of the facade built over so many years of work. He tried and tried again, asking my help in finding the music that would enable him to re-create his dance. I felt that he was asking me to help him to be, even now that he felt his defenses were crumbling. I mirrored the anguish in not finding something so precious, I tried to be with him in his search. I also tried to encourage him in looking for a new dance, suitable for the Eli of the present. I tried to imbue him with my deep trust that he could find it. But we had to face the fact that this was not true. The music for Eli's dance did not exist. He was not ready.

Contact in Absence

Eli did not come for the next session—he was not even in school—nor the week later or the week after that. He refused to come back to school. The explanations I was given by the social worker were connected with a worsening of the situation at home and some negative episodes with his peers at school. The tension was dramatic because the parents, unable to force him to return to school, were also incapable of coping with him, together with the younger brother. Episodes of domestic violence happened day after day. At the same time, a court order calling for his compulsory removal from his home was hanging over his head, a removal which meant the risk for him of being held in a reformatory. But Eli seemed willing to fight the court order, and kept speaking of the school as a prison. I was pained and confused. I felt the void due to his absence and I realized that there was a message here also for me—the changes that Eli had confronted in therapy also threatened his relationship with external reality. His tendency toward self-protection forced him to slow down. If I wanted to give Eli a sign of the existence of our relationship in spite of his absence, and this was the only way I had to help him, I had to go outside of the setting and call him at home. To communicate, giving him a signal of the reality of our relationship, even giving up the transitional object provided by the music. I decided to do it. To telephone him at home gave me, at any rate, an important sound input. I heard the music in his house while I was calling him. I heard the sharp voice of his mother, the dominant television background, a fragment of rude and aggressive conversation. I imagined the unpleasantness on the skin of a "sound envelope" of this kind for a musical soul such as Eli's. Our conversation did not tell me much. Eli was embarrassed and ill at ease on the phone. I confirmed to him that I was expecting him and that I would keep the hour free for him in the hope that he would come. He came the following week when I, alas, was ill. They told me that for a long time he sat, disconsolate, in front of my closed room. The week after, I called again and this time things were different. "The difficult thing for me," Eli said, "is not so much facing life in the boarding school, and it is not as though being home is so pleasant, after all. What I can't manage is to get away from here." I felt that he was telling me something important about his tie to his mother, the dissolution anxiety that was hidden behind the act of separation. An aquatic image came to my mind and I told him about it: "It's like being on the point of plunging into cold water, knowing that it will bring relief from the heat, but it gives you an unbearable shiver." I felt through the telephone receiver Eli's relief at being understood. Perhaps because the association emanated from my subjective life experience (my body, my hate/love for cold water), I believe that this was a "now moment" as defined by The Process of Change Study Group (Stern et al., 1998, p. 903).

A week later Eli returned to the boarding school once and for all.

The Return: Daring to Be "Real" in the Relationship

Our telephone encounters had had an effect on the atmosphere of our meetings; they had imparted an acknowledgement of their link to reality. They had made our meetings more important and less magical at the same time. "After all, what are you?" Eli said, "You are a psychologist who works with music." Not only had he uncovered my real identity, but also shreds of his true home were revealed to me.

Music, however, remained the backbone of our meetings. First of all, through the improvisations Eli re-established his presence in the room and he let me understand his mood, his deepest feelings. The "vitality affects" were released by his notes: rhythmic, biting, and obsessive repetitions, outbursts of rage, diminutions, and minorizations that pointed to thoughts of melancholy; the confluence of the two hands telling me of his longing for loving dialogues. And at times words, whispered and rapid, were introduced into the flow. Words speaking about the inhospitality of the school, its unsuitability to give him the feeling of a real home. Words speaking about sudden fantasies around death; cutting pictures of the father who raises his invalid's cane to hit out, and the children who mock him, a grotesque Rigoletto, stealing the cane away from him, in order to threaten him in their turn. At times the vitality affects received a characterization:

"What do you feel today in your music?"
"I feel anger, sadness, boredom"
"Anger towards whom?"
"Towards mother, her voice that never stops, that gives me no peace, that follows me everywhere."

And, once again, we would enter the river of notes, to face together the unconfrontable.

We reached the sixteenth month of therapy. The anger took the form of percussion. The piano was abandoned for the darbouka and later for the drums. There were two drums in my room: one beautiful and new, and one old and incomplete. He went to play sometimes on the one and sometimes on the other, giving me sometimes an accompanying role, and, at times the role of guiding him or even expressing, in his place, the fullness, the force, the anguish of that anger that he carried within him, also his repressed energy that was confined in the great overcoat of his defenses. On the old drum it was the little Eli, inadequate and too thin, who leaned on someone else to express himself. On the new one was big Eli in the process of becoming a man, who had the strength to face his own feelings.

The last month of school came all too soon, after which we would have to part. We both realized that the longed-for release from the "prison" of the boarding school was accompanied by having to leave my musical arms. Eli, at first, denied this. It did not seem possible to him; it was too soon. And then, when he understood, he defended himself in his own way, turning away sotto voce, closing his coat slowly, button after button. He brought me a cassette to listen to together, so as not to have the time to play; he came late and even forgot our next-to-last session, for the first time in two years. For our last meeting he was not in school. Our real good-bye was over the telephone, emotional and almost silent. Diminuendo. Pianissimo.

My own act of separation was later, painful and outside the setting: I met the social worker of his place of residence to stress the urgent need for continuing to provide a therapeutic connection for Eli, possibly with greater frequency than the one provided by the school, and possibly music therapy. I stressed that Eli's chance to continue to reconstruct his own self lay outside that particular school, together with youngsters whose problems were more similar to his. Eli was born, but he needed holding arms to continue his growth. Afterward, I felt as empty as an empty container, but with the feeling that I had done the right thing.

CONCLUSION AND DISCUSSION

A process that had been so involving, and a finale in pianissimo! It would have been more satisfying to have had a beautiful cadence of twenty-four beats of dominant and tonic chords, with some drums and trumpets. . . .

We know full well that the finales in pianissimo are sometimes accompanied by an indication of morendo (dying out), while others, on the other hand, by the moving sensation of something that had touched the soul and the results of which are unknown and laden with future. In asking ourselves into which category the finale of this story belongs, the question arises as to the validity and ethical quality of a therapeutic process that, in a certain sense, has brought the client to regress, relying on a relationship that contained its finite nature within itself.

Some could say that having created such closeness, having brought Eli to lowering his defenses, only to abandon him to his fate may have had the opposite of the desired effect, recreating for him the sensation of abandonment and disintegrating loneliness. In order to confront this question I must, first of all, deal with my countertranference sensations connected with the end of the therapy. From the subjective point of view this separation was a real collision with the recognition of the inexistence of omnipotence on my part. In fact, I will go further, with the existence of my impotence. In the negotiations that I had to carry out with myself, I went through moments of pessimism, bordering on a sense of guilt; I then had detailed fantasies of adoption. It is from this point of view that the conclusion at which I arrived must be seen: the need to give up a future for therapy with Eli, which I wanted very badly, and the expulsive push I had given him toward a more all-embracing accompaniment in a less threatening environment.

At the same time, if I ask myself the question as to whether I would do again what I had done, my answer is an unequivocal "yes." First of all, for the simple reason that I could truly not have done anything else: The particular relationship between these two people, he and I, with our particular music, in that particular spatiotemporal context, could only be what it was and none other. And this, not anything else, was the context in which Eli was able to touch and share those dark maelstroms that threatened his integrity as a human being. It is my understanding that this type of relationship experience represents for Eli the indispensable basis for reconnecting with his own strengths and to set in motion blocked or atrophied mechanisms of psychological development. Only by being seen and accepted, and, let us say it, *loved*, in his entirety, can bring a human being as wounded as Eli had been, to want to live, confronting also his own dark feelings.

It is true that experimenting with one's own continuity of being within a relationship necessarily means exposing oneself to the dangers of suffering its disruptions, but the alternative can only be one of nonbeing, depression, void. A first sign of reconnection with his own strengths can be seen in the gradual way with which Eli was able to turn away from me, without drums or trumpets, and without allowing this umpteenth deprivation to shock him more than his defensive forces could bear.

This faith in the person's intrinsic capacity to develop and cure himself, given proper relational conditions, I also find in the most varied theories. One of Heinz Kohut's central points in his theory of self states that the essential element in psychoanalytic treatment "is the opening of a path of empathy between self and selfobject, specifically, the establishment of empathic in-tuneness between self and selfobject on mature adult levels" (Kohut, 1984, pp. 65–66). John Bowlby's theory of attachment, which reexamines the central role of attachment to the mother figure in the formation of the self, reconfirms the importance of providing in therapy a relationship that constitutes a secure base as an indispensable starting point for the restructuring of one's own representational and relational models (Bowlby, 1988, chapter 8). Then there is the transpersonal approach that stresses the curative value of the unconditional presence (Welwood, 2000). From another direction, the "music child" of Nordoff and Robbins also expresses, in an adequate musical environment, the tendency toward self-actualization through the reactivation of ego-functions, this in spite of the most serious handicaps (Bruscia, 1987, p. 57).

To come back to Eli, I am convinced that the process I have just recounted was able to provide this for him—let us call it "good enough environment," or "empathic response," or "secure base," or "unconditional presence"—without which a wounded self cannot be cured, just as our body can close wounds only in the presence of such basic conditions as hygiene and nourishment. For Eli, among other things, one of these basic conditions was represented by the music. I should like to stress that there is an intrinsic importance in the fact that Eli was able to discover the power of music as his personal transitional object, capable not only to unify his internal world, but also to serve as a communication bridge to another human being. His music, and ours as well, stays with him, together with the feeling of having been understood.

The gist of my thinking is well summarized in these sentences, taken from David Grossman's "Words into Flesh" (1998): "Nobody had ever spoken to him this way. It is not only what you have written him, but the way you did it. Because this child was the object of attention, he had also received maternal care and tenderness . . . but only rarely had he experienced this pleasure: being understood. What a relief. The lifting of the armour that reveals within it the knight, still alive" (letter dated the fifth of August).

REFERENCES

Anzieu, D. (1989). *The Skin Ego*. New Haven and London: Yale University Press.

Atwood, E., & Stolorow, R. (1979). "Faces in a Cloud: Intersubjectivity." In *Personality Theory*. Northvale, NJ: Jason Aronson.

Baker, S., & Baker, N. (1987). "Heinz Kohut's Self-Psychology: An Overview," *The American Journal of Psychiatry*, 144:1.

Bowlby, J. (1988). *A Secure Base*. London: Routledge.

Bruscia, K. E. (1987). *Improvisational Models of Music Therapy.* Springfield, IL: Charles C. Thomas Publisher.

Bruscia, K. E. (1998). *The Dynamics of Music Therapy.* Gilsum, NH: Barcelona Publishers.

Grossman, D. (1998). *Shetehi Li Hasakin* (Words into Flesh). Tel Aviv: haKibbutz haMeuchad.

Kohut, H. (1984). *How Does Analysis Cure?.* (Edited by A. Goldberg in collaboration with P. Stepansky). Chicago: University of Chicago Press.

Stern, D. N. (1985). *The Interpersonal World of the Infant: A View from Psycho-Analysis & Developmental Psychology.* New York: Basic Books.

Stern, D. N., Sander, L. W., Nahum, J. P., Harrison, A. M., Lyons-Ruth, K., Morgan, A. C., Bruschweiler-Stern, N., & Tronick, E. Z. (The Process of Change Study Group), (1998). "Non Interpretive Mechanisms in Psychoanalytic Therapy," *International Journal of Psychoanalysis,* 79:903.

Welwood, J. (2000). *Towards a Psychology of Awakening.* London: Shambhala.

Winnicott, D. W. (1956a). "The Antisocial Tendency." In *Through Pediatrics to Psychoanalysis: Collected Papers.* New York: Basic Books.

Winnicott, D. W. (1956b). "Primary Maternal Preoccupation." In *Through Pediatrics to Psychoanalysis: Collected Papers.* New York: Basic Books.

Winnicott, D. W. (1960). "The Theory of the Parent-Infant Relationship." In *The Maturational Processes and the Facilitating Environment: Studies in the Theory of Emotional Development.* London: The Hogarth Press and the Institute of Psychoanalysis.

Winnicott, D. W. (1971). *Playing and Reality.* London: Tavistock Publications.

Case Twelve

"MUSIC SPEAKS OF A STORY": THE VOCAL UNIVERSE OF AN ADOLESCENT

Gabrielle Fruchard and Edith Lecourt

ABSTRACT

This case study takes place in a special home for teenagers with social difficulties, in Paris. Etienne likes to play guitar. But it is through receptive music therapy that therapeutic work was done with him. In receptive music therapy, the fact that the pieces of music proposed are exterior both to the therapist and to the client, and offered as a support that mediates the relationship (between adult and young, therapist and client), is especially useful when insecurity has been experienced early on. Etienne's remark "Music speaks of a story" refers to the way, during these sessions, an unconscious accord between him and his therapist was created to "not speak directly of his personal story, but to substitute a musical discourse."

This is also an original methodological experience of an analysis of a case study, which is not supervision, but a double analysis of clinical material: one from the adolescent's music therapist, the other from a researcher (music therapist and psychoanalyst).

INTRODUCTION

In receptive music therapy, reactions to vocal music are very often more direct, emotional and personal than to instrumental music. We are generally sensitive to vocal timbres. For each one of us, some voices are unbearable and others touch us very profoundly. This peculiar sensitivity can make the choosing of musical pieces in receptive music therapy difficult, and creates the trend to stay in very conventional forms (classical or romantic music). But, in some cases, as with Etienne, the adolescent we will present in this case study, it opens up a dynamic relationship.

This case study takes place in a special home for teenagers with social difficulties, in Paris. Twenty-four boys live there. Their personal stories are characterized by a succession of ruptures, including abandonment. The result of these situations can be observed in their daily relational behaviors, in the way they try to communicate.

Due to educational deficiencies that these boys have suffered, they neglect words as a tool to communicate; their use of verbal language is reduced. As a consequence, they have difficulty accepting and pursuing verbal therapy. This is why other therapeutic tools are used in this institution to help them. Music therapy is one of these "mediations" used to introduce the boys, through a qualitative relationship (e.g., through confidence, responsibility, etc.), to the work of psychoanalysis.

Music is spontaneously adopted by teenagers to express themselves in groups and individually. Such is the case for Etienne, who likes to play guitar. In receptive music therapy, the fact that the piece of music proposed is exterior to both the therapist and the client, and is offered as a support that mediates the relationship (between adult and young, therapist and client), makes it especially useful when insecurity has been experienced early on. Music organizes a common space of emotional and corporal reactions, thoughts, images, etc., in which the psychic suffering is not directly focused on: it is present, recognized, but remains in the background. We can argue that music acts as a "detour" to introduce the client to a therapeutic process. Inside this detour, Etienne will give an important place to voices.

BACKGROUND INFORMATION

Etienne is a quiet boy who stays alone, looking for an alter ego. He is convivial. He entered the home in September 1998. At this time, he was sixteen years old, and could not stay with his foster family where he had lived with his brother Martin, who is two years older than he, since his infancy.

Even with the help of social services their very young mother was not successful in taking care of her children and that was why it was decided to find a foster family for the two boys. Etienne was a baby of four months when he was placed. The father of the two boys is German. He gave his name to the oldest boy, Martin, and Etienne received the name of one of his mother's boyfriends whom she considered as forgotten. The father returned to Germany soon after Etienne's birth and, since that time, the mother has had no more contact with him. The only information she has held onto is the address of the German grandmother. So, Etienne had very little information about his father. Etienne says that his father has now become "somebody serious and steady." He imagines that his father has a new family and is well established. He decided not to disturb his father by trying to get in contact with him: "He would have scratched out the past, so I would complicate his life. . ." (Etienne seems to adopt here the advice given by the people in his environment).

The relationship with his mother was not very regular, but was maintained over time, and Etienne was very attached to her, even though he commented on her lack of organization and her particular difficulty in taking care of young children (i.e., to answer their needs). After his stay in the "boys' home," he returned to live with her while he finished his studies.

In the foster family, the mother was attentive to the boys, but the father seemed to be concerned essentially with conformity: order and a traditional way of life. Etienne summed it up: "Tonton is Tonton." In this context, the transformation of Etienne's personality, due to adolescence, was not tolerated. Etienne was said not to care about his appearance, and his artistic interests were not understood in this environment. In contrast, his brother Martin was well adapted, more controlled, and had scientific interests. Etienne said, "He is my brother. I can't lose him, but we were always lonely, each on his own side." An educator, who had known the boys for a long time, said that they were very different, showing no complicity but joint responsibility. Etienne received visits from his brother while at the "boys' home," but the comparison with him was always negative because Martin was seen as a model: intelligent, serious, well adapted, recognized, and accepted.

Comment: We observed that, as is frequently the case in foster families, the manifestations of adolescence are even more difficult to support than in original families, because there are no natural filial links to help this passage. In many cases, it is the moment of a rupture. In Etienne's case, this situation may be seen as a repetition of the lack of his father's recognition, reinforcing his feeling of being a disturbance in a "good ordered situation," and making it impossible for him to identify with a father figure. The projective test (Murray's Thematic Apperception Test) showed this need for recognition, and his trend to seduce, in order to express himself. However, globally, his performance was logical and well structured.

At the time of his admission in the home, Etienne began studies in graphic art. However, he was not successful on the final exam, and in September 2000, he changed to the profession of horticulture, which involves a relation to nature and flowers. Thus, we observe a special link to aesthetic interests through graphic art, flowers, and music. Etienne likes music. He plays guitar—a common interest with his brother. He was given guitar lessons for one year. In the "home" he sang traditional French songs ("Chanson Française") with the guitar, with the help of his teacher. Etienne compared his need for music to drug addiction and said: "If I didn't play music I'd go crazy!" (In French: "Si je ne jouais pas de musique, je pèterais les plombs!" (I'd blow my top!). When asked, he said that in music he is looking for "a lot of things": "to speak with sounds, without limits, approaching wholeness." He finds "a sort of awakeness," "rediscovering everyday life through music."

METHOD AND TECHNIQUE

In this section, we will describe the music therapy sessions and the research methodology used in preparing this case study.

The Music Therapy Sessions

In November 1998 (two months after his admission), in response to Etienne's need for music, the team decided to recommend him for individual music therapy. The treatment lasted for two school years, with a total of forty-five sessions.

When asked, Etienne agreed to the recommendation for music therapy sessions, one forty-five-minute session weekly. The music therapist (Gabrielle) asked him to commit to a period of three months followed by a common evaluation, with the possibility to stop or to go on for a new period (he renewed each time, during these two years). This type of contract is a good protection against trends of impulsive ruptures due to the first frustrations experienced in therapy.

The sessions were organized into three sections, each one followed by a moment of free verbalization. The first and third sections were receptive: listening to recordings. The second section offered the possibility of an active musical answer to the first listening, through free improvisation. The third section was listening to this recorded improvisation.

Our study focuses on the first section of the sessions in which the music therapist chooses a piece of music, about three to five minutes long, to listen to. The therapist asks the client "to be attentive to the evocations that arise during the listening, such as thoughts, images, memories, and emotional and corporal reactions, and then to talk about this material."

The first goal was to facilitate the therapeutic relationship; the second was to help to create an articulation between external and internal worlds, and, inside the psyche, between the conscious, preconscious, and unconscious. This work develops a preconscious "space" (offering a place for fantasies, dreams, etc.). In receptive music therapy, the choice of pieces of music to listen to, by the music therapist (at least in the first phase of the therapy) is of particular importance. Different positions help to orient this choice: references taken from statistical studies on reactions to various types of music, thematic choices, choices with reference to precise aspects of the musical structure of each piece of music, etc. (See Gabrielle Fruchard's music therapy thesis on this subject [1994]). The music therapist in this case study, Gabrielle Fruchard, personally chooses to allow herself to follow her feeling from one session to the other; her musical choice reflected her process of becoming conscious of her countertransferences, her understanding of the relationship (pieces of music she likes and associates with what she perceives).

Methodology Used for a Four-Hands Case Study

We worked at two times and in two phases: Gabrielle Fruchard, Etienne's music therapist, collected the clinical material gathered in the forty-five sessions. Edith Lecourt made an independent reading of this material. Finally, both reconsidered the text.

The first phase was the selection of the clinical material. Reading her observations, Gabrielle discovered, afterward, the importance given to the voice throughout this treatment. Following this observation, she decided to focus our common reflection on the vocal material of the sessions. She collected and organized this material into three main categories: Etienne's reactions to chorus, to the male voice, and to the female voice. Her search was primarily oriented to the question of identification. In these three categories she observed various themes such as differences, strangeness, limits, corporal reactions, etc. This analysis of her clinical work brought her to the discovery of the part of her countertransference linked to vocal music (her musical instrument being the voice).

The second phase: This clinical material was communicated to Edith Lecourt who used it as associative material. She took for granted (as a hypothesis) that the material said something about the relationship between the music therapist and her client.

From this perspective, it appeared that this therapeutic work was based on an agreement about the creation of a common space between the music therapist and Etienne: the individual face-to-face relationship was opened to a third element, music. Music is part of culture and thus a common external background for both therapist and client. Furthermore, vocal music appeared to be a common object, partly internal, partly external, as both Gabrielle and Etienne liked to sing. These two points bring to mind Winnicott's concepts of transitional space and the transitional object. These two points are situated at a conscious level, being part of the setting.

But two other points appeared with the distance of a new reading of the material:

- Gabrielle discovered the extent to which her countertransference was used in regard to the importance progressively given to the voice in her choices of pieces of music (twenty-eight pieces of forty-five were vocal pieces, which was unusual in her practice). Furthermore, she realized her sensitivity to the quality of Etienne's voice (smooth, subtle, rich in harmonics). This could be seen as the seductive part of this relationship.
- Through her personal reading, Edith made the hypothesis of the presence of an "unconscious tuning" between Gabrielle and Etienne about the place given to his preoccupation about his story and origin. This "unconscious tuning" could be summed up in these words: "We better not speak of that."

In fact, Gabrielle considers that music therapy, in the case of such adolescents, is a sort of "detour," in comparison to verbal therapy. In other words, music therapy is an indirect way for Etienne to "speak" of himself using a different level of expression, without focusing on his story. This is a good argument, indeed, for the choice of music therapy in this case. In parallel, we observed that Etienne, speaking of his father, considered that it was better not to disturb his new "well-ordered" life by reminding him of the existence of his son.

René Kaës, a French psychoanalyst, considered that relationships—individual and group—are generally based on the unconscious level, on a "denegative pact," which ensures the solidity of the relationship. This is an unconscious agreement on a denial. The content of this pact is negative: it is an agreement on what should not be said, or acted, or what should not be disturbed. The positive face of this unconscious process is, in Etienne's case, the support given to the acceptance of what remains as "enigmatic," as unknown. But another aspect is the reinforcement of the process of idealization about his father's life. Music takes place in this double process: the enigmatic message about Etienne's story, and the idealization. Etienne seemed to create a musical idealized vocal portrait as a figure of identification.

Finally, this reflection brought us to organize the clinical material in five sections, as follows:

1. About music: proximity—distance
2. Voice and sexual identity
3. Voice and origin
4. "It speaks of a story"
5. Idealization.

TREATMENT

In the following sections, sessions are referred to by number with the corresponding pieces of music listed at the end of the case study.

About Music: Proximity—Distance

Etienne's reactions to music manifest his particular interests through two main distinctions: vocal/instrumental, and with/or without movement.

Vocal/Instrumental:

Etienne reacts first to vocal music and, in vocal music he generally focuses on one voice (male or female), which he characterizes. In vocal music, Etienne does not make associations with musical instruments (present in many of these pieces). He does not try to understand words, which sound "strange" for him, even if they are in English, a language he studied at school. He seems uninterested in words, preferring the quality of voice and melodies.

With/Without Movement:

Generally speaking, there are two sorts of music in Etienne's musical universe: one with movement, and one without. Popular music in festive environments and music for dance are of the first category. They are more related to the male voice (Sessions 4 and 9), than to the female voice (Session 8), but in each case they are associated with memories of Celtic festivals he attended, as a child, with his mother. These musical selections produce direct and global reactions; they invite participation. On the other hand, religious music (and some classical pieces) is generally "flat" and "without movement." Even if such a piece of music modifies his perception and his morale, as in Session 37, the musical pleasure is lost when this "dark atmosphere" takes place, and even "the very sympathetic male voice which was telling something" is covered by this new mood: "This music breaks the good mood."

If there are some "older" or "younger" musics, for Etienne music is not linked to generations, it is a transcendental means of expression, answering to many different needs. Martin, his brother, is a model for that, because he likes both old and new musics.

Voice and Sexual Identity

Focusing on voices, individual voices, Etienne tries to characterize them. This interest is manifested in his preoccupation with his own identity. The terms used very often evoke the sexual organ, the phallus: force (anxiety to get that force), power (those who do not have it are " ridiculous"), having or not having a voice (male as female), size ("big voice"), etc. He is curious about the way the singer pushes his voice out, etc. For example, in Session 36, Etienne comments on the male voices: They "tear up," "enter something" and then "flow inside the ear." These sexual preoccupations are natural for adolescents and the musical "detour," and, more precisely, the vocal detour is a good way to share it. In this perspective, one can speculate whether the silence about musical instruments is not linked to a too risky sexualized associative fantasy.

During the sessions, Etienne focused sometimes on a female voice, sometimes on a male voice, even if there were other voices and instruments in the music. Female voices were distinguished into two categories: "sharp" or "big." In Session 2, he associated paradise with a very sharp female voice. During Session 11, the music offered what he perceived as "a profound female voice" which provoked a thrilling state with a global corporal reaction. This reminded him, on the other hand, of the emotion provoked by "a sharp, intense and very well-tuned female voice." These are the two polarities. Listening to a Viking song (Session 8) he spoke of a female voice which imposed herself with power, willingness and passion: "She pushes her voice as much as a man" . . . "It is impressive." It reminded him of his mother and her Celtic origin.

As with female voices, male voices were perceived in two categories as expressed in Session 4: One is basic, the second is more melodic and beautiful. In another session (Session 9) a man, with "his beautiful big voice," alone created an ambience of festivity, through a music of movement. It seems that, for Etienne, the male voice pushes out from immobility to movement.

Female voices, as with male voices, are felt to "speak of a story" even when the words are not understandable. The difficulty of language is noted in some cases of female voices (evoking strangeness), but never with male voices, which seem to be essentially appreciated for musical qualities.

In the last phase of the therapy, Etienne focused his attention on differences between male and female voices (Sessions 31, 35, 36, etc.). For example: "What I didn't like was the male voice, I would have liked the woman to go on singing further and not the man. The female voice was beautiful. . . . Sometimes when a male voice entered something was broken . . . at the end it became ridiculous." Etienne commented further: "It is always treating this important thought as a banality, a commonness. . . . As with everything, men are null . . . so are women!" At the same time (Session 36) Etienne discovered a model of the male voice "great, wonderful" and "moving by its power." But he considers that this piece of music misses the presence of a female voice, "a big female voice." This reflection leads us to the next theme.

Voice of Origin

Three sorts of reactions were gathered on this theme: the whole and confusion, evocations of the past, and "the big female voice."

The Whole and Confusion:

The place of the chorus is very low in Etienne's associative material. He spoke of a chorus that lasted more than six minutes (Session 42) without evoking voices, speaking of "sounds," or "they say." When he did not comment on the presence of the chorus, he focused his interest on one voice, as if it was alone.

Religious choruses are "flat and without movement," with one exception being the Sanctus of "Missa di Gloria" (Puccini), which provoked a rich comment: "The greatness of earth, the human fate, something evoking the universe, our spirit, our capacity to dream, and many other things." In this sort of music he says he is looking for wholeness (the whole).

As mentioned earlier, instrumental music, present in seventeen sessions, seems to usher a sort of indifference—he cannot distinguish a part, a melody, etc. We have already made the hypothesis of a defense mechanism to avoid sexual fantasies; in the same way, it could also be a longing for regression.

But through the sessions, Etienne became more and more interested in the differentiation between voices and in a search for individuality. The two last sessions contained pieces of instrumental music, which Etienne appreciated for their own sake.

The Origin:

As we have seen, Etienne considers that music transcends generations. Therefore, it is a good medium for addressing the question of the origin. And although religious music is generally perceived as being "without movement and sad," it also addresses "unanswered questions." In Session 2, in response to a chorus with male and female voices, evoking death, hell, and paradise (female voices), Etienne spoke of death associated with "a music that speaks of things we cannot touch," with religion and with the next world.

The "Big Female Voice":

This case study invites us to go back to this peculiar "big female voice" on which Etienne repeatedly focuses. This "big" grave voice evokes his mother's Celtic origin, and it seems to be, for him, like an archetypal representation of mother and origin (his birthmother, but also the foster mother who educated him). Moreover, the continued association with this quality of voice may be a transference aspect of this therapeutic relationship. Gabrielle's voice may be representative of and support this peculiar link to mother and origin. As M. F. Castarede (2000), a French psychoanalyst, wrote: "The voice of origin, lost, the definitively lost object, searches for deferred experiences through love and through musical enjoyment."

"It Speaks of a Story"

Etienne presented himself as having an inaccessible story. It was as if his existence was the origin of the rupture of the family, of the abandonment of the father, of something wrong, the origin of his troubles. After that time, the father began a new adapted, serious life; and a new family, the foster family, was given to the boys. But what about "that" time? What was before the rupture? What sort of unity, of wholeness, existed? The foster family could not speak of "that," they did not know, they did not want to be troubled with "that." His foster mother said it was forgotten. It was as if everybody commanded him not to ask, not to try to find his father, not to disturb the society. Martin was the model to follow.

What about music? Music "speaks of a story." This was repeatedly seen in Etienne's associations. Even when it was something strange that we could not understand precisely (as with foreign languages), music was another language, with sounds, which spoke of "that" which we could not speak: moods, origin, death, heaven, and feeling of wholeness. Music gave the moods of the story, without the words. Music was the way to approach the story with the guarantee not to succeed in the search, not to disturb others, and not to be disorganized by a revelation. For instance, an English song in Session 3, sung by a woman, produced a feeling of strangeness: "Like somebody in front of us that we do not understand; she surely says a lot of things. It is speaking of a story." Etienne, who had learned English at school, and whose father's language was German, reacted particularly to these two languages with this feeling of strangeness. (It is noticeable that Gabrielle was interested and sometimes disturbed by the way Etienne's associations were differently focused on the musical material than those of other adolescents of the "home.") Where to speak with the right words would be dangerous for him (to be crazy) and for the environment (to disturb)— music was the only way to maintain the contact with this story and his internal life. Music was part of the German culture of his father, and music was the principal thing shared between the two brothers.

Idealization

Ideal unity, wholeness, and harmony are how Etienne described the actual father's imagined life, and were seen in Martin as a model. Music offered a common, communicative, accepted and valued space of expression. It gave Etienne a valued place inside the "home." The cultural and aesthetic dimensions of music were related to his professional choices: graphic art, flowers. This claim for beauty, good form, and harmony was an aesthetic transposition and a substitute for the inaccessible model of adaptation (idealization of conformity through father, brother, foster family). At the same time, as seen before, it protected him from his real story. In this case the idealization was an attempt to repair the lost love object of the origin, and reach an imaginary original wholeness. But we can also imagine the intensity of the repressed aggressive-ness against what he had to suffer. And the idealization is a defense mechanism against destructiveness.

Music therapy could have reinforced this defense mechanism, and the avoidance of conflict and depressive feelings (Lecourt, 1998). But it seemed the only possibility at this moment of his development, to open a space of sharing and analysis.

Finally, Etienne's acceptance of this study (his letter of consent) brings, for him, the value of recognition.

CONCLUSION

This example of receptive music therapy illustrates the way that shared music can, for an adolescent, be a way to create a new confident relationship with an adult, respectful of his defense mechanisms. At the same time, all of these sessions "speak of *his* story," his anxiety about sexual transformation, and sexual identity, about the unknown and strangeness of his story, and his problems of identification. We have seen how the therapeutic relationship was based on a "denegative contract," which is supposed to say, "We agree not to speak of the real story," of Etienne's story. And we discovered how this contract reappeared throughout Etienne's associations about the different pieces of music, within which voices "speak of a story": Music was the way, the detour, to "speak" of what could not be said. And this was also part of the contract.

REFERENCES

Castarède, M. F. (2000). "Voix de la passion et passion de la voix." In Vrait F.X. Dire la voix, *approche transversale des phénomènes vocaux*, Paris: L'Harmattan.

Fruchard, G. (1994). "Enregistrer des cassettes, outil thèraputique auprés d'adolescents, mèmoire du D.U." *Art en thérapie et en psychopédagogie*, Universitè Paris 5.

Kaës, R. (1989). "Alliances inconscientes et pactes dènègatifs dans les institutions," *Revue de Psychothérapie Psychanalytique de Groupe*, 13, 27–38.

Lecourt, E. (1998). "The Role of Aesthetic in Countertransference: A Comparison of Active Versus Receptive Music Therapy." In K. E. Bruscia (ed.), *The Dynamics of Music Psychotherapy*. Gilsum, NH: Barcelona Publishers.

Winnicott, D. W. (1971). *Playing and Reality*. London: Tavistock Publications Ltd.

Pieces of music of the sessions cited:

Session 2:   Vivaldi, Magnificat: Et misericordia, 4:00
Session 3:   Laurie Anderson, Strange Angels: Strange Angels, 3:51
Session 4:   Musique du monde, Les Nyamokala du Fouta Djallon: Munny'ré, 4:11
Session 7:   Puccini, Messa di gloria: Sanctus, 3:14
Session 8:   Garmana, Le mystère des chants vikings: Herr Holger, 4:30

Session 9:   Iggy Pop, Brick by Brick: Home, 4:00
Session 31:   Musique du monde, La squadra, chansons génoises: Strasetti d'Arba, 4:02
Session 35:   Stravinsky, Le Rossignol: Rossignol et le Pécheur, 4:15
Session 36:   Brahms, Un requiem allemand: 1ère partie du "Denn wir haben die keine bleibende Staat," 6:30
Session 37:   Britten, Curlew River: Near the black mountains there I dwelt, 5:52
Session 43:   Couperin, Leéons de Tènébres pour le mercredi: beginning of the third Lesson, 4:00

Part Three

Adults

Case Thirteen

THE SIGNIFICANCE OF TRIADIC STRUCTURES IN PATIENTS UNDERGOING THERAPY FOR PSYCHOSIS IN A PSYCHIATRIC WARD

Susanne Metzner

ABSTRACT

The significance of triadic structures is shown with the example of a young schizophrenic patient undergoing psychodynamic therapeutic treatment. The author presents a triadic structure model that serves as the basis for theoretically reflecting upon a multilateral transference situation in a multidisciplinary treatment team of a psychiatric ward.

INTRODUCTION

In psychodynamic psychiatry, music therapy is one component of the clinical treatment concept fitted to the personal needs of each patient. This coordination occurs in the interplay between what the multidisciplinary treatment team offers as therapy, on the one hand, and the use of this by the patient who shapes his or her therapeutic environment and forms therapeutic relationships, on the other hand. Therapy, following a psychodynamic approach, pays special attention to this interrelationship and the resulting social network in the ward, because it is seen as a reenactment, which provides insight into the intrapsychic and interpersonal real-life situation of a patient. An understanding of this can help to locate and activate resources as well as to treat disorders.

Dyadic and triadic structures comprise the smallest components of this complex social network. In this chapter, I will focus on the significance of triadic structures in the inpatient treatment of individuals with psychotic disorders and illustrate these structures with the help of a case vignette.

My presentation begins with the description of my first encounter with this patient. This is followed by a theoretical introduction to the triadic structure model, which I have developed. Finally, I will analyze a significant musical scene, taken from individual music therapy with this patient in the context of the hospital treatment, in relationship to the biography and present life circumstances of the patient and the psychotic symptomatology. My descriptions and interpretations, which are of a rather subjective nature, are written in italics.

BACKGROUND MATERIAL

Casuistry: My First Encounter with Ms. K.

I make an appointment with Ms. K., a twenty-three-year-old, much younger and quite girlish-looking patient with long blond hair, for Friday, which I write down for her on a note. Ten days ago she was admitted to our psychiatric ward in an acute psychotic condition. She had the delusion that her father had been shot by her ex-boyfriend with whom she had broken up a couple of weeks before. During the first few days after admittance she was in a condition best described by the old-fashioned term "mentally deranged." For four or five days now she has been more responsive with the help of neuroleptic treatment. In the meantime, she takes part in the day-to-day routine of the ward. The patient is now offered further psychotherapeutic help through individual music therapy. The fact that I have the time to take on another patient fits nicely with my spontaneous interest in this young woman.

As I enter the patient's room on the Friday in question, her mother quickly moves away from her and says: "Oh, music therapy, I already thought that was some kind of mistake." Everything goes so fast that I don't even have time to say hello and introduce myself.

It seems to me that the patient leaps up from her bed very suddenly in order to follow me to the music therapy room, which is located on the first floor of the building. I am worried about her circulation because she looks very pale. However, Ms. K. says that everything is okay and starts to walk off.

She hesitates at every door through which we must pass. At the door to the ward she says that this must be a mistake, she doesn't want any music therapy after all. I am surprised, pause for a moment, and wait for the patient to move either in one or the other direction. Forward or backward? She goes forward and comes with me to the music therapy room.

In this first session, I confine myself to giving the patient information about music therapy. It seems to me that this rather objective level of communication gives the best support to this hesitant patient who is still in danger of regressing. Although I act very cautiously, the situation between us remains depressingly nontransparent. The sluggishness of her verbal, as well as gestural-facial, reactions makes me feel as if I were in a dense fog which swallows up everything. The only thing that is clear, in the end, is the patient's declaration that she does not want any further treatment other than medication. I tell her that I respect this decision for the moment and that I will ask her next week again in case she changes her mind in the meantime. So there doesn't seem to be anything left to discuss, and it seems to be time to part. But all of a sudden it is difficult to end the session. The patient finds it difficult to part? detach herself? And I have the feeling as if I have to break off something by force.

After the session, I become aware of a very unpleasant, all-embracing feeling, which I cannot put into words. It is not easy to get it out of my thoughts.

At the beginning of the following week, I want to address the music therapy question once more, as promised. However, during the doctor's rounds the patient is so sleepy that I am not able to reach her on this occasion, nor am I able to do so on two further attempts. A few days later, my student, doing practical training, runs into the patient's father in the ward by chance. He mistakenly takes her to be the responsible music therapist and asks her about music therapy for his daughter. My trainee doesn't know how to react because she is not informed about the current state and, in particular, because she is interested in conducting the treatment herself. She puts him off until later, which does not leave him in too happy a state.

Nothing seems to be alright anymore. Nobody knows who wants what from whom, and I have the desperate wish to be able to start over from the beginning.

At this stage of development Ms. K. is willing to begin music therapy.

Where do we meet if we do not meet? With this ambiguous question, Deuter (1995) pinpoints the predicament which seems to be so typical of the treatment of psychotic patients. This does not only concern the meeting between patient and therapist but also a disturbance in interpersonal contact, in which the concerned persons either are unable to reach each other on an emotional level or meet each other in a state of high vulnerability, which leads to fear and defense reactions. In our case, this concerned more than two persons, for example, different members of the treatment team and/or members of the family.

In not all cases are the latter involved as strongly as in the case of Ms. K. From her family we obtained a wealth of information—some of it was given intentionally and some unintentionally—about the relationship structures in the family, to which I will refer later. This is not typical of our therapeutic work: What happens more often is that our psychodynamic understanding, as well as what we do in therapy, must rest solely upon the conclusions we draw from the reenactments in the ward and our own countertransferences.

TREATMENT

Excursus: On Multidisciplinary Teamwork

In the multidisciplinary, psychodynamic treatment of psychiatric patients in general, and psychotic patients in particular, each team member involved in the treatment relates not only to the patient concerned, but also to the other team members who all have equal rights. Thus, multidisciplinary teamwork is not simply based upon the sum of different therapeutic processes, rather it involves the use of a specific method which places particular emphasis on working on, and with, the relationships of the concerned staff.

Although I let the term "equal rights" slip into the above formulation in passing, I am not denying the fact that there is a hierarchical structure that has evolved over time in the hospital workplace. Neither do I want to deny that there are differences in qualifications and competencies between staff members. Multidisciplinary teamwork in a psychodynamic treatment concept, where members enjoy equal rights, means that one must be willing to reflect upon the relations within the team and, among other things, to think about one's own use of power.

Therefore, the interdisciplinary treatment of patients in a psychiatric hospital is more than the sum of various therapeutic processes. It encompasses the work on and with the relations of the professional staff. Thus, the mutual task is to examine the emerging constellation of multilateral relations with the patient. In this connection, attention is paid not only to the transference relations between the respective patient and the individual team members, but also to the relations that are transferred to other team members. What is so special about this perspective is that whatever happens in the team, or between different therapists, during treatment is taken into account to the same extent as whatever happens during the different therapeutic sessions. To formulate this in somewhat stronger terms, this means that the team lets the patient have an influence on the relations between the team members.

From what has been said so far, it follows that I, as a clinical music therapist, relate not only to the patient, but also to my colleagues who are involved in the treatment of this patient. In this process, I pay close attention to how our professional relationships are influenced by the mutual treatment of a patient. This approach is based upon a triadic structure model, which I have developed for the systematic analysis of multiperson relationships and for the formulation of hypotheses about possibly disturbed triadic relationship experiences of a patient, who—through his or her reenactments—asks us to help him or her come to terms with these problematic experiences.

The Structure of the Triad

In the attempt to examine the structure of the triad, the first important thing to do is to free oneself from thinking in dyads, for example, considering a triad either merely a dyad plus another interaction partner (AB+C) or a series of three dyads (AB, BC, CA). Rather, a triad has a structure that is produced by triadic interaction forms. Although quite a large number of such interaction forms exist, they can be reduced to three triadic interaction modes. These three interaction modes together make up the internal structure of the triad. Thus, triangulation— understood as both an intrapsychic and interpersonal triad-forming process— does not take place by extending a dyad by a third interaction partner nor by joining three dyads, but in multiple interrelations between three interaction partners. In the following section, I will describe the three main triadic inter- action modes in more detail.

Triadic Interaction Modes

Triadic Interaction Mode I:

Each Interaction Partner Relates to Two Objects.

This interaction mode is acquired during early childhood and consists of various elements. Prerequisite for this interaction mode is that the subject is able to relate to two distinguishable objects. Already, a newborn baby is able to differentiate between his or her mother and other persons. As if to express this relatedness, the subject uses eye movements: This is connected with casting one's eyes in the direction of one person and looking away from the other, with an alternation between foreground and background. In the course of time, representations are formed on the basis of the experience that an object, which momentarily is not in one's field of vision, has not really disappeared. This interaction mode is different when, for example, the voice or—at a later point—words are used. In his or her imagination a subject turns to two or more objects simultaneously and connects them, joins them together. A conversation between three individuals is a highly complex phenonemon: Because each person relates to both of the others, looks and words between the involved parties wander back and forth, overlap with each other, and sometimes proceed in opposite directions. The basis for this is a psychic structure which comprises the "either-or" and the "both . . . as well as. . . ."

Triadic Interaction Mode II:

Always Two Objects Together Relate to a Third One.

This statement expands upon what has already been said above and describes a triadic interaction mode in which the elements' mutuality (self with other) and counterposition (self versus other) are combined with one another.

The experience of mutuality includes the subjective experience of the individual that another person shares the contents of his or her feelings. Stern (1986, p. 179) believes that the first signs of this ability in the development of the child become evident starting in the seventh month. If an individual is certain that the other person feels, thinks, or acts the same as him or her at a given moment, then he or she experiences both himself or herself as a perceptual unity and the "we" as such a unity. In a triadic interaction, two who are united together in a "we" relate to a third. They confront a third with their mutuality, who, alone from this opposite position—merely by his or her presence—shapes the interaction process and influences the mutuality of the two others. In a well-functioning triad, the mutuality of two against a third party is not structurally fixed. However, changes do not occur very quickly because this second interaction mode needs some time to become established. It has a certain tendency to perpetuate itself, as shown by the results of social research.

Triadic Interaction Mode III:

Each of the Involved Relates to the Relation Between the Two Others.

The statement made here refers to a triadic interaction mode, which was already mentioned before in connection with the influence of a third on the mutuality of two others. This is now extended and put into more precise terms, because the relation between two encompasses more than the aspect of mutuality. The kind of relationship between two objects influences the position that a third party can take toward it. Abelin (1975) describes that the young child initially experiences him or herself as being between the parents and internalizes the relationship between the parents in the course of individuation.

If the relationship between two persons is disturbed, then a third person has only limited possibilities to take a position toward it. The interaction attempts he or she undertakes, which do not meet with a response, must be defended against. Consequently, such forms of interaction appear as a substitute, which are geared toward maintaining the defense reaction.

On the Developmental Psychological Prerequisites

Father, mother, and child—these three terms first of all indicate biologically-based positions in a triangle. Triad and dyad develop from originally biological basic prototypes of relationships between parents and children. The formation of a dyad is preceded by the physical connectedness of mother and child during pregnancy. The triad, on the other hand, has its origin in the act of procreation, which marks the beginning of parenthood for a man and a woman. Before a child is born, structural preforms of relationships between parents and child already exist. However, the individual developmental course of these three positions is inextricably linked with unconscious fantasies, prescribed role expectations, and socially determined evaluations. Triadic structures are also relevant if a child does not grow up in the traditional nuclear family, which is more common nowadays.

Whereas the parents or, as the case may be, the respective adult significant others use their ability of triangulation in their relation to the child right from the start, the child develops this capacity only in the course of his or her development. This means that the child grows into already existing structures. In this process, dyadic and triadic structures become superimposed and influence one another.

Already during the first year of life, the developing child finds out how it is to experience him or herself in relation to two objects which have something to do with each other. In the course of the further development of self and object representations (via transitional objects, Winnicott, 1971), the child also experiences that a third person relates to the relationship between him or her and another person. At that moment, when he or she understands what it means to have the feeling "both of us," the child also recognizes the dyad's boundary. Consequently, the development of the dyadic relationship depends upon this close interaction process with a third person. In other words: The existence and relatedness of this third person, which has a counterposition to the dyad or which surrounds the dyad from the start, induces the development of interpersonal abilities in the dyad.

This approach has a direct influence on the concept of the so-called "early disorder" and its treatment. In the case of a disorder which is rooted in disturbed early relationships, the influence of the mother cannot be considered as a singular force, but must be seen and analyzed in the context of the triad.

Triadic Disorders in the Development of Schizophrenic Illness

From the viewpoint of the psychology of self and object relations, psychotic disorders can point back to deficit situations and disturbed interactions experienced very early in life. The clinical manifestation almost always indicates the inability to triangulate, which stems from a fragmentation of the triad or a specific form of splitting of the triad. It is not always the case that the family situation is extremely burdened, marked by deficits, or perhaps even hopeless, in which the child has been neglected with respect to his or her mental, physical, or social well-being. Even in the seemingly intact families of schizophrenic patients, one can very often find a triadic structure characterized by a relationship between the parents which left no room for the child. The parents live in a relationship in which they are not able to mutually relate to the child. One example is a relationship characterized by extreme dependency: If both parents are constantly fighting with each other, they do not relate to two objects at a time, rather, they ignore the needs of the child. If they live in a symbiotic relationship, then they reciprocally gratify their dependency needs and shift their hostile impulses from the relationship between themselves to the one with the child. Under such circumstances, the development of the dyadic mother-child, and the respective father-child, relationship is disturbed as well.

The triadic structure model provides information about the extent of the disturbance. The child is not able to relate to two objects either because the objects are not sufficiently distinguishable or because they are incompatible. The parent, in most cases both of them, does not relate to two objects, namely the other parent and child. Moreover, the parents do not mutually relate to the child. On the other hand, the child cannot experience a mutual relatedness with one parent toward the other parent, because neither parent would be able to form a mutual relationship with the child without seriously threatening the adult relationship. As a consequence, the child cannot relate to a (mature) parental relationship. He or she is forced to internalize a parental relationship which is characterized by dependency and open or latent destructiveness.

Sometimes these pathological structures in the primary family become virulent only in the further course of development of the child. I am talking about that point in time when the main focus no longer is solely on the needs of the child and their satisfaction (as during the first months of life), but when the child's own will starts to emerge—when he or she has to reconcile his or her grandiose ambitions with the perceived limitations of the real world, both his or her own and those of his or her objects. The stubborn child, who in the crisis of the "rapprochement-phase" (Mahler, 1975) is clinging at one time and domineering at another, no longer meets the ideals of his or her parents. This, in turn, taxes their ability to deal with ambiguous feelings toward their child. The less successful the parents are in smoothing out these conflicts in their relationship with one another and maintaining their confidence in the mental healthiness of their child, the deeper the parents get into a crisis with their child. If they are not able to accept the narcissistic defeat, and bear the disappointment of not having a perfect child and not being able to create a perfect world for him or her, interpersonal constellations evolve in which the integration of omnipotence and powerlessness, and the development of more mature object relations, are blocked.

Especially if the relationship between the two parents is dominated by the myth that aggression is destructive, retaliation is unconsciously demanded of the child. A child in this position draws the conclusion that his or her developmental needs are destructive and that he or she is responsible for preventing the emotional breakdown of his or her parents by attempting to compensate for the retaliation wishes (Benjamin, 1990). In extreme cases, the child needs a justification for his or her mere existence.

The failure of the process of individuation in early childhood is reactivated during adolescence, when the already existing psychic structures are reorganized once more. In particular, events such as final examinations, moving away from home, and similar experiences make great demands on mental stability, which can trigger the initial manifestation of a psychosis.

Casuistry: Multidisciplinary Psychodynamic Therapy of Triadic Disorders

In a psychodynamic approach to therapy, the aim is to reconstruct the disturbances that are responsible for the symptoms and reenactments of the patient and to restore interaction forms. If, in this process, triadic interaction forms are also considered, a certain therapeutic perspective will result, in which there is room for a third party in one's imagination, in other words, for persons who also have contact to the patient. This means, as already explained above, the willingness to closely examine the relationships between the involved individuals and to also consider one's own emotional feelings in reference to the third party in the countertransference analysis.

With help of the example of Ms. K.'s treatment, I will show which position I, as music therapist, took in the social network which the patient set up around herself, and illustrate what value music therapeutic material has for understanding the patient. But first I must mention the fact that Ms. K. broke off the treatment so that it was not possible to bring therapy to a satisfactory close.

A Scene from the Music Therapeutic Process with Ms. K.

In music therapy, I work with free improvisation and verbal discussion. The only therapy session during which we played music was the third one (of a total of five). At that time I made the following notes:

(. . .) In the music therapy room we soon start playing. A few plucked notes on a one-string Indian instrument, the gopiphant, come from the patient. After a while I find a heartbeat rhythm on a low register clave and am inwardly happy about it, because it provides such an unobtrusive support for her and for me. But suddenly the tables are turned, and I have the feeling that the heartbeat is dissolving. It is both an unpleasant and inexplicable feeling. How can a heartbeat be dissolving?

Then, in our mutual playing I have the feeling as if a chick were hatching out of its egg. Mother hen answers from outside the eggshell. But the short dialogues quickly cease. Afterward, the patient tells me that at this moment she was afraid of doing something wrong.

Ms. K. tries out some other string instruments and eventually returns to the gopiphant. She has not yet found out how to modulate the notes on the single string. I am on the cello. A soft, enchanting, but icy music emerges, which I find fascinating. Like frost patterns in a window.

If one assumes that schizophrenic illness is the result of a dyadic relationship disturbance, then one would not spontaneously think that a triadic disturbance comes to light in the musical interactions described above. But the expression "the heartbeat gives support to her and to me" implies that there is a third entity which could provide support to both, if only it had not dissolved. The whole thing becomes clearer if one imagines that the expressions refer to an early developmental stage, in which mature representations have not yet been formed and the "other" is perceived not so much as an object than a living substance. This living substance is disintegrated. In other words, it is as if the emerging relatedness, or even the core relatedness, as described by Stern (1986), was being dissolved once more. After this, it seems for a while that patient and therapist go on in a more reassuring manner with this interaction between unhatched chick and hen. But only for a short period, then this attempt to get in touch with each other fails as well: The patient develops fear.

What exactly could be so threatening in this scene? Apparently the eggshell does not provide any protection for further development. Further, it is not a symbol for the stabilizing third entity in the relationship between hen and chick. Rather, it is the fear of doing something wrong which at least saves the fragile self from dissolving or from being disintegrated. The price which has to be paid for keeping up the self-feeling is that the interaction, and its further development, freeze, in other words, come to a halt.

Despite this freezing, I, as a therapist, have the feeling that I am on the right track in the therapy with this patient. My colleagues share this feeling. The assistant medical director and the ward doctor have family discussions together with the patient and both of her parents. This triggers numerous dynamics in the family situation. Many members of the nursing staff devote a lot of attention to the patient. One staff member helps the patient write a curriculum vitae consisting of several pages. In art therapy, a number of interesting works are produced that provide valuable information, such as a fragile, weary-looking chicken made of clay and a picture of the patient's name, hardly discernible from a background of curlicues and floral patterns of creeping and climbing plants.

All staff members had a special interest in the patient, all had "adopted" her, and all had the feeling that they were doing everything really well. It would have been only natural for rivalry to come up in our team. But this did not happen; we were hardly aware of one another. A relationship situation developed in which rivalry was completely missing and in which we were more or less content with filing away our detailed reports in the records without exchanging any information with one another. We did not personally meet with each other, neither in the concrete nor in the figurative sense. The knowledge of the patient's biography and the careful analysis of the therapeutic scenes helped us to understand the reenactment of the patient as well as our countertransferences.

The Patient's Biography—Facts and Interpretations

Ms. K. was an adopted child. Her birthmother was twenty years old and single when she became pregnant. She only noticed that she was expecting a child when she was seven months into the pregnancy. What a diffuse body feeling this woman must have had. The only explanation is that she must have misinterpreted the movements of the baby as digestion problems. Referring back to the music therapeutic scene, one can say, "The chick in the egg could give as many signs as it wanted, these expressions of its existence were simply misunderstood." The birthmother was pressured by her mother to give the child up for adoption because she had not yet finished her vocational training. One week after birth, the baby was already adopted by the K. family, which is unusually fast under German law.

Mr. and Ms. K., both teachers, already had a biological son and wanted to adopt another child because there are so many unwanted children in the world. The parallels to our behavior in the treatment team are obvious. On the basis of these countertransferences one could suppose that the adoptive parents were driven by the desire to improve the fate of another person with all their might, and so to become the better parents.

The child was difficult right from the start. As a baby she cried for hours, and it was not possible to soothe her. As soon as she was able to talk, she asked her parents if they really loved her. She was still a bed wetter as a schoolgirl. In spite of all these difficulties, her parents did not stop trying to give her their best and also to seek therapeutic help. Everything indicates that the parents tried as hard as they could to reject the narcissistic defeat in connection with the fact that they were not able to create a perfect world for their child. So, the ambiguous feelings—more than understandable for parents in this situation— had to be split off. It seems that this inevitably resulted in the parents not being able to give their daughter one thing, namely a secure feeling of belonging. She saw her existence altogether as a big mistake, and as a little girl she never ceased asking her parents if they truly loved her. This must have hurt the parents very deeply because they really loved this child. But in view of their ideals of good adoptive parents, they could not allow themselves to be "hit" by this question. The little girl was not able to develop a feeling for the reality of this parental love and had to feel guilty because of this.

After finishing school, our patient contacted the adoption agency in order to obtain the address of her birthmother, which she received. She met her birthmother and hoped to find a good friend in her. However, she was forced to realize that her birthmother saw her as the lost daughter and—much too late— tried to bind her too closely to herself. Ms. K. wanted to get out of this situation, but she was afraid of hurting this mother and so she made no decisions—neither for nor against this relationship. This was the situation at the time of treatment. However, almost two more years passed before the first manifestation of psychosis. During this period, the patient had started to study teaching in order to take up the same profession as her parents. She had also moved into her own apartment, but she did not manage very well on her own, became more and more isolated, and neglected herself.

DISCUSSION AND CONCLUSIONS

I already mentioned that a striking feature of the multidisciplinary treatment of Ms. K. was that no rivalry existed. In discussions with the family it became apparent that rivalry was also missing in the relationship between the adoptive parents. They gave the impression of being a harmonious married couple, who not only had the same occupation, but also had dedicated themselves to the same goal of becoming adoptive parents. From the perspective of another person they merged to form one whole, in which there was no room for anything that was different.

Especially for the adoptive daughter it must have been difficult to find herself as a different person. On the one hand, she was the planned baby of the adoptive parents; on the other hand, she had originally not been expected by her birthmother, who was not even aware of the fact that she had started to exist, and was exceptionally fast in giving her consent to the adoption. Therefore, the adoptive parents had all the more reason to feel that they were the better parents. From the beginning, doubts, contradictions, and a latent rivalry between birth and adoptive parents hovered over the child's existence. All of this did not get any more concrete when the now grown-up daughter expressed her wish to contact her birthmother. The adoptive parents did not only approve of this undertaking, they even arranged to meet with the birthmother themselves. They described this as being a harmonious meeting, but this harmony seems to have been icy. In this, we saw the repeated failure of the patient to discover the reality of the relationships. As in the music therapy session, the dialogue ceased, and everything remained undecided. The relations in the parent generation did not give the teenage daughter the support she needed—they did not serve as a springboard from which she could take the crucial step toward individuation. It was not possible for her to create her own individual life, the same as in music therapy where she did not find out that it was possible to modulate the note on the string of the gopiphant.

In a situation characterized by separation, namely breaking up with her boyfriend, the patient decompensated psychotically. Various things come together in the delusion that her ex-boyfriend had shot her father: the desperate search for the missing father, the desire to get out of an unresolvable relationship situation with the help of a third person, and the latent fear of her own destructive anger.

This is how far we had gotten in understanding the psychodynamics of the patient. We started to question the one-sided success of the pharmacological and sociotherapeutic treatment and to exchange our thoughts about the interaction process in the team. This evoked the resistance of the patient. To get out of this dilemma she followed the strategy that attack is the best means of defense. After two and a half months she was well enough to have herself discharged from the hospital against the doctor's advice. She argued that it would be better for her to continue therapy in a day clinic. Unfortunately, she never appeared there.

Although I referred to this end of therapy before as the breaking off of treatment, I would like to suggest a different interpretation, although it cannot be confirmed without the help of the patient and information about her further development. The analysis work in the team, which had just started but was quickly increasing in intensity, brought the reality of relations into play, so that the patient was able to use them as a springboard to find her own way. We, who had been used by her as parent figures, were simply left behind together with our relations.

REFERENCES

Abelin, E. L. (1975). "Some Further Observations and Comments on the Earliest Role of the Father," *International Journal of Psychoanalysis*, 293–302.

Benjamin, J. (1990/1993). *Die Fesseln der Liebe*. Frankfurt, Germany: Fischer TB-Verlag.

Buchholz, M. B. (1993). *Dreiecksgeschichten*. Göttingen, Germany: Vandenhoek & Rupprecht.

Deuter, M. (1995). "Beziehungsformen in der musiktherapeutischen Arbeit mit psychotischen Patienten." Unveröffentl. Manuskript, 22 Seiten.

Heltzel, R. (1996). "Der psychoanalytische Beitrag zur stationär-psychiatrischen Versorgung," Vortrag vom 27.1.1996 in Berlin, unveröffentl.Manuskript.

Lempa, Günther (1995). "Zur psychoanalytischen Behandlungstechnik bei schizophrenen Psychosen." *Forum der Psychoanalyse* 11, 133–149.

Mahler, M. S., Pine, F., & Bergman, A. (1975/1996). *Die psychische Geburt des Menschen*. Frankfurt, Germany: Fischer TB-Verlag.

Metzner, S. (1999). *Tabu und Turbulenz. Musiktherapie mit psychiatrischen Patienten.* Göttingen, Germany: Vandenhoeck & Ruprecht.

Stern, D. N. (1986/1992). *Die Lebenserfahrung des Säuglings.* Stuttgart, Germany: Klett-Cotta.

Winnicott, D. W. (1971/1985). *Vom Spiel zur Kreativität.* Third edition. Stuttgart, Germany: Klett-Cotta.

Case Fourteen

THE CASE OF MARIANNE: REPETITION AND MUSICAL FORM IN PSYCHOSIS[*]

Jos De Backer and Jan Van Camp

ABSTRACT

The significant aspect of our work is the finding that, in the treatment of psychotic patients, music is especially relevant in creating a psychic space. Since the psychic space originates from the transformation of sensorial impressions into a form or a representation, and since we know that the capacity to make representations is seriously affected in psychosis, there is a need to find out by which means this capacity can be reestablished. Working with such patients in a music-therapeutic context, we encounter the phenomenon that they often repeat the same musical pattern. In their musical improvisations, they constantly repeat a specific rhythm or a small melodic sequence. It becomes an endless iterative playing, a kind of musical rocking. From our research, we describe this repetitiveness as the presence of the psychotic "experience" of the world. Psychotic patients, from their pathology onward, do not dispose of a psychic space to reach symbolization, which means, in music-therapeutic terms, that they are not able to create a musical form in which they can exist as a subject. Therefore, the therapeutic transition from sensorial impression to musical form (protosymbolization) is a basic condition for the treatment of the psychotic patient regardless. In this case study of a psychotic woman involved in a music-therapeutic treatment, we explore and describe three important levels or moments of the music-therapeutic process (synchronization, development of a musical form, and the musical ending of an improvisation).

[*]Acknowledgment: This article is based on a more extensive research study (Ph.D. Program: Aalborg University, Denmark). The authors would like to acknowledge the research supervision of Pr. Dr. Tony Wigram.

INTRODUCTION

Psychosis and Music

The world of the psychotic patient is often unknown and inaccessible. Many years of experience with psychotic patients has convinced us that through music we cannot only find a gateway to the amazing world of the psychotic subject, but that we can also develop the means to give a certain shape and termination to the disintegration and timelessness of the psychotic world. It is not the first time that it has been shown that music moves on the same level as where the central problem of psychosis is located. This relationship between music and psychosis gives music therapy and "the thinking from music"[1] a crucial place in the treatment of psychosis.

The psychotic subject lives in a world of presence. He is the defenseless prey of thoughts and sensorial impressions, which haunt him continuously. The frontiers between the inside and outside world are so unstable and transparent that it often seems that his psyche finds itself outside rather than inside. The world and the internal movements of drives are not represented in an inner space, but they are characterized by an immediate and brutal presence. Because they can no longer fulfill their representative activity, even words are treated as meaningless things, as pure sound objects.

It is more than a metaphor to assert that the psychotic patient lives in a purely musical world. If we assume that the musical element is what is left of the voice when it is deprived of sense, one can, in many ways, assimilate our relationship with music to the relationship of the psychotic subject to the world. Neither the voice nor the music can be said to find itself inside or outside the subject. Its presence, which cannot be located, makes it a fusional object. This means that we are related to the music like a baby is initially related to the voice of its mother. Thanks to the fact that her voice has not yet disappeared behind significance, it has an immediate impact on the child. Just like a dancer starts moving immediately and simultaneously as soon as the music sounds, the child responds immediately and simultaneously to the appeal that comes from the voice of the mother. Coming into the cadence of the voice of the mother is the first affirmation of a signifier that has not yet acquired meaning at that time.

Because of the fundamentally dissonant relationship of the psychotic to the signifier, psychoanalytic theory asserts that the problem of psychosis should be put in terms of this primarily synchronic affirmation of the signifier or, in

---

[1] We believe that the inquiry of the relationship between music and psychosis is not only relevant to music therapy *stricto sensu*, but can also contribute to a broader understanding and a more appropriate approach of psychosis in general.

Freudian terms, of primal repression (*Urverdrängung*). The latter—as the form-ation of the very principle of repression or of the capacity to repress—is the foundation of the constitution of the unconscious, which not only functions as an explanatory principle for symptom formation in neurosis, but much more gen-erally as the anthropological category which is responsible for the appearance of human desire. As psychotic phenomena are traditionally attributed to the failure of the work of repression, psychotherapy should focus on the very conditions that make for the possibility of repression. Clinical observation of music therapy with psychotic patients shows enormous resistance against musical synchron-icity in the first stage of therapy.

Music is not only a fusional object that inspires the body spontaneously and immediately and brings it consentingly into motion. Insofar as the specific musical characteristics progress, music also has a linear and narrative form. The musical events do not remain in an endless repetitive play, but they develop themselves, via a play of variations and repetitions, to a totality, a synthesis. Within this development, the successive musical events lose their independence and they are functionally integrated into a whole. Each sound and each movement refers to what preceded it and to what will follow further on, although no one knows exactly what the continuation will be. Fundamentally, one may consider the development of the musical form as a play of loss and the reappearance of the losses in a new shape. It is a constant process of substi-tutions that takes place within a space, which Winnicott called the "transitional space." Winnicott does not describe the play within this space as symbolizing in the full sense of the word, but only as a "transition" to symbolization, because, just as in music, the concreteness and the irreplaceability of the substitutive object remains in the foreground. The transitional object is truly a signifier, but not an "open" signifier. The meaning remains fixed on the object and the latter is not open to other meanings. In that sense, the development of the musical form takes a step further in the symbolization process than the transitional object. In spite of the concreteness and the irreplaceability of the musical event—we had better mention the meaninglessness of the musical event—it is still integrated in the time-bound process, which makes an essentially endless variation possible. Finally, the process of symbolization takes its full shape at the moment at which the concrete object has been completely lost in speech.

The unique place of music in the treatment of psychosis therefore lies in the fact that it presents two logical times in the symbolization process, both of which are of crucial significance in the constitution of the psychotic psychopathology and which can be approached much less directly within an exclusive verbal psychotherapeutical setting. We believe, nevertheless, that the "thinking from the music" is—also outside of the music therapy room—important for the comprehension and the treatment of psychotic phenomena.

The case below illustrates our theoretical position, but it was, naturally in the first place, just like all other therapeutic experiences, the source of inspiration for the theory.

The Clinic of the Sonorous Object in Psychosis

Marianne, a young psychotic woman of twenty-five, plays on a metallophone of her choice. She sits motionless, bent over, without facial expression, her elbows pressed against her body, only her underarms move in an alternating automatic motoric way. Is she aware that she plays a metallophone and produces a series of sounds? The music is endlessly repetitive, boundless, without phrasing, without any form of dynamics or nuance, without interaction with oneself or with the therapist. The therapist experiences this music as insusceptible, as grains of sand that slip through his fingers. The therapist does not succeed in coming into contact with the patient or her musical play. Marianne does not allow him into her sensorimotor music.

She plays completely turned in on herself. The autistic and automatic character of her music blocks the therapist. There is no way for him to succeed in giving himself over spontaneously and freely to the musical play. The repetitive sounds appear as a dead thing that brings nothing into motion, fits in nowhere and—as an isolated object—seems to belong to nobody. The patient is absent in her play. Though it is she who comes into motion and plays the metallophone, the sounds remain totally strange to her, as if she were dissolved in the sound object. The object does not affirm her in her function as subject, but it is handled in such a way that the subject loses herself in it, is "dissolved" in it. The stereotypical play gives only sensations which, by their assured reappearance, have a reassuring effect, but without creating an imaginary world.

What strikes us in the first place in this musical play is its high degree of repetitiveness. However, let us specify that repetitive music is spontaneously associated with its hypnotizing, ecstatic, and discharging capacity. The obsessive repetition we find for example in house music, in new wave, or in the whipping rhythms of ritual music lead, just as in Marianne's play, to a certain undermining of the subject function and to loss of identity. Still, there exists a difference with the psychotic sonorous object, a difference which often appears audibly in the musical play, but which is especially experienced in the countertransference. The inability of the therapist to be in resonance with his patient is in sharp contradiction to the irresistible and immediate appeal, which comes from a hypnotizing rhythm. In contact with his psychotic patient, the therapist experiences a constant subtle defaced rhythm or a continued "dis-harmonization" which excludes him from playing together with the patient. Sometimes these disruptions are so barely objectively detectable that they also can barely be imitated. We are therefore able to assert that this sound object is not *erogeneized*, not involved in an exchange with the other. It remains caught within an autoerotic circuit. This refers to the failing construction of an unconscious body image, owing to the absence of the primary narcissism of the psychotic patient. The primary narcissism only develops through the labor of representation, which is produced by the *erogeneization* of the body zones which are initially involved in the satisfaction of needs. At this stage, it is important to refer to the crucial significance held by the disruption of the pure repetitiveness by surpassing the sensory level of the satisfaction of needs. A mother gives her child true contact and exchange when she does not remain equal to herself and when she brings all sorts of subtle variations (deprivation) in the way in which she meets the demands of her child. The rhythmization of presence (satisfaction) and absence (privation) can convert the sensorial impressions into drives, and by so doing brings them into mentalization. Speaking about the psychotic sound object, we shall use the terms "sensorial object" and "sensorial play" to denote that this object is not integrated into a movement of drive and *erogeneization* and as such, remains locked up in its quality of real, unimaginable, and indivisible substance.

The isolation of the sound object, however, can also be the result of the fact that it is not part of the psyche of the subject itself, but that it is an extension of the psyche of another, namely one or both of the parents. In this context, we should speak of an *incorporated object*, or, in the terminology of Abraham and Torok (1978), of an object that has not been introjected but rather "included." The status of this object reflects the fate of having to undergo a trauma when it could not be coped with in a former generation and so was transmitted to one or several following generations. As this object is not imaginable (the "thing-presentation" remains absent to the subject itself), it stays subjected to the principle of repetition. That means that the object is only present when it is made present in the most concrete manner and namely in a corporeal-sensorial way. Peculiar to this object is, contrary to the purely sensorial object, that it has been subjected to a (transgenerational) displacement and because of this acquires a psychic character and thus a form. The therapist is often amazed to see the appearance of a musical form which is significant to him, whereas it remains meaningless to the patient and cannot be integrated psychologically by the latter (Van Camp, 1999). The repetitiveness and the character—often experienced as strange by the patient—of a musical sequence, signals to the therapist the possible psychotic status of the sound object. Here, the inability to have the musical sequence take place in a musical thought is as strong as in the purely sensorial play.

Sometimes, the psychotic sound object has the shape of a "passionate" object. We sometimes notice in the music therapy session that psychotic patients can be passionately seized by the musical improvisation or by listening to music to such an extent that they lose themselves totally in it, get confused, and even are driven to psychotic decompensation. The object comes to the foreground so prominently that the patient goes into a state of being defenselessly delivered to it, possessed by it, even to the extent that the boundary between subject and object disappears completely. Contrary to the neurotic overinvestment or idealization of the object, there is no symptom involved of something the patient does not want to know and therefore displaces to an object containing the psychic elements of what has been suppressed and in which he get passionately involved. In psychosis, such a displacement (*Verschiebung*) does not take place, because there is nothing about not wanting to know. His investment can therefore fix itself on everything, with the most embracing arbitrariness. The passion for music or for a concrete musical object is nothing more than this passion itself. It does not refer, or cannot potentially refer, to a certain object of his desire, which can possibly be raised alongside the musical play.

Finally, the musical object can also become part of a delusion or it can constitute itself as such. Freud describes the delusion as an attempt to heal (*Heilungsversuch*) and the most evident model of this is naturally the auditory hallucination.[2] The object is made present by having it "take place," not as a form of imagination, or of recalling, but by having it accomplish itself in an original manner. This phenomenon is closest to what characterizes the music when we deprive it of its form or its "thought." Music can only exist within this specific modality in which a succession of sounds, intensities, and harmonies "occurs." Hence, we say that music cannot be remembered; it can only be repeated. The delusion possesses the same eventful character. At the same time, there is more adrift in the construction of the hallucination than purely having new events take place which relate to the subject. The events are also inter-related with one another by a causal band, by which the subject creates itself an alternative history and gives itself an origin. This surpassing of the traumatic-sensorial level by the development of a synthesizing history also makes us understand why Freud could see the hallucination as a "Heilungsversuch." The conception of a new reality and the telling of a coherent and explanatory story about what goes on in this reality truly draw the object out of a psychic isolation, but alienate it at the same time in the exchange with others.

---

[2] We used the terms of delusion and hallucination interchangeably because, in this context, the stress is put on what they have in common: the experience of some events *taking place*, apart from the initiative of the subject, but dictated by persons and destinies in the outside world. Those events are always seen as involving the subject himself.

It remains an undecipherable hieroglyph; an imposing certainty which cannot be shared with others as being a truth.[3] If the musical object obtains a hallucinatory character, it equally becomes the prey of this intrasubjective isolation. In spite of the fact that it has taken a certain form, which extracts it from pure repetitiveness, it still functions as an idiosyncrasy, which cannot be integrated in the musical play. If the therapist does not succeed in breaking through this delusive character, and in getting in musical line with that unimaginable sensorial level upon which the trauma finds itself, the musical play continues to turn aimlessly round in a circle, in spite of its form. Indeed, it is typical of the delusion that it is perfectly unequivocal and allows no new meanings and developments.

The common characteristic of the different modalities wherein the musical object appears in the psychosis is its repetitive character. Although the repetition cannot be immediately discerned on the level of the phenomenal appearance of the musical product, it is as a principle always at the basis of the psychotic sound object. It follows that the psychotic sound object is isolated and un-imaginable, bearing testimony to the impossibility for the patient to symbolize.

Working on a music therapeutic basis with psychotics, we regularly encounter the same musical pattern. Many psychotic patients start their musical improvisations by constantly repeating rhythms or small melodic sequences. It is an endless iterative playing, a kind of musical rocking. Clinical supervision and a review of the literature, mostly Ogden (1986, 1992, 1994), Tustin (1981, 1986, 1990) and Van Camp (2000, 2001), has made it clear that this sort of playing is characteristic of the psychotic's sensorial impression. They cannot experience this music as something from themselves; there are only sounding sounds in which they are not implicated. They are not "inspired" by the music. That means that music playing is not really an "experience" for them. We learn that psychotic patients, from their pathology onward, do not tend to have a psychic space for symbolization by which they could appropriate the musical object. In music-therapeutic terms, that means that they are not able to allow or to reach a musical form.

The capacity to have an experience can be seriously disturbed and even destroyed in psychopathology. Therefore, it is extremely important that the music therapist can find out how the transition from sensorial impression to musical form can happen. Therefore, it is essential that we verify to what extent there might be a correspondence between the obvious, empirical changes on the musical level, and the subjective experience by the patient.

---

[3] Lacan (1981) makes a clear distinction between "certainty" and "truth." The truth can (in principle) always be shared with others, while the "certainty" of the psychotic is imposed on the subject, which does not have the need to verify his content with others.

Therapeutic Framework

Music therapy is part of the psychotherapeutic offerings in an analytically oriented residential facility for young psychotics. Most of them meet the diagnostic criteria for schizophrenia (DSM-IV R). Bipolar psychotic problems of mood, schizo-affective pathology, and serious disturbances of the personality occur. Symptoms such as hallucinations, thought and perception disturbances, hypochondriac and grotesque interpretations, disturbances in body functions, autismlike or extreme regressive behavior, and serious contact disturbances spring to mind.

The music therapy work within a facility with a broad array of therapists of verbal and nonverbal therapeutic approaches puts entirely different demands on the procedure of the music therapist than within a private practice setting. The mechanisms of denial and splitting in the patient often cause incompatible contrasts between the experiences of the different team members with the patients, and require continual synthesis on the part of the treating staff. Furthermore, because of the specific character of this psychopathology, the "thinking from the music" takes a central place in this synthesis work. Music happens to possess the quality to be able to address the traumatic sensorial level directly, and, seeking a form, allows the birth of representations.

From this privileged access to the psychotic world, the music therapist also has the task to suggest that the patient continues to explore the possibilities of the presented material in the verbal psychotherapies.

BACKGROUND INFORMATION

Anamnesis

The patient tells that she has been confronted with attacks of undifferentiated fear for about five years. The reason for admission, however, was a vital depressive image. The patient described that she had had communication problems and that she lead a very solitary lifestyle with few social contacts. Marianne is very suspicious toward her parents. During the acute psychotic phase, she is firmly convinced that her mother continually persecutes her, which excludes any further contact with her. However, this continual persecution is experienced only as the point of culmination of an old situation in which the mother was perceived always as overcontrolling and inhibitive to her development.

The patient is the youngest from a family of three children. The father is retired and, according to the patient, rather aloof with regards to family life. The mother is the housekeeper.

After her secondary education, the patient started to study literature at the university. She was passionate about literature and wrote a great deal of poetry and stories. Owing to the many "literary encounters" in pubs/bars, she concentrated little on her studies and did not succeed. After this year, she had a short but very intense relationship with a man.

She finally chose another area of study, but also gave this up after two years. At this time she is unemployed.

The patient situates the beginning of her troubles around age twenty, when her relationship ended. She started to suffer increasingly from feelings of fear, which did not allow her to lead an independent life. More and more, she was convinced that she was being controlled by her mother and that her mother even hired other people to control her.

Situation at the Moment of the Admission

The patient came across as reserved in the contact. Her facial expression was flat and she had a staring look on her face. The patient seemed to be cut off emotionally. There were a few depressive complaints: sad mood, adynamics, anorexia, sleeping disorder, "anhedony" and fear outbursts. She expressed a passive longing for death and depicted herself in a self-deprecatory way. She spoke of being overtaken by crying fits and how she had the tendency to regress. The patient did not report any hallucination. There were no disorders of formal thinking, although she had heard a voice in her head once in the past.

Conclusion

A twenty-five-year-old woman was admitted because of a vital depressive situation, functioning on a psychotic level. The depressive complaints cleared up gradually under an anti-depressive treatment. The patient was referred to our department for young psychotics, for a psychotherapeutical treatment of the underlying psychotic problems.

Psychodiagnostic Research

Marianne is a talented woman with a general IQ of 126 (W.A.I.S. test), with a big difference between the verbal IQ of 133 and the performant IQ of 112. The balance between the "hold" and "don't hold" tests indicate deterioration on the organicity scales.

The patient has few complaints and does not have an expressed request for aid. Formally viewed, there is a protective shield, especially in terms of her emotional life; she cannot let herself be touched. She tries vehemently to give an answer at the expense of the reality.

The theme of her relationships is receiving. There are many conflicts and quarrels. Aggression and sexuality obviously do not have a specific place in her life. She is a very independent woman who functions on a psychotic-like level. There is nothing that is manifestly psychotic to be seen, but her cutting off and apathy can be read as negative symptoms. The patient especially has a consumer's question. She wants information. She has unrealistic goals and has little self-reflection.

TREATMENT

Marianne and Group Music Therapy

Marianne regularly participated in group music therapy, twice a week for eight months. Marianne's image was that of a withdrawn woman, choosing the same instrument, namely the metallophone, over and over again. Her posture was always the same: bent forward, with a staring glance, withdrawn in herself, always playing in a sensorimotoric way, her arms pressed against her body. She did not have any contact with the other group members or the music therapist. We could say that she was not able to create a psychic space.

In verbal psychotherapy she expressed her wish for individual music therapy. This was started two weeks later. She did not take any group music therapy after that. A combination of individual as well as group music therapy, though, was allowed in clinical psychotherapy. Here, multilevel therapy is part of a multidisciplinary treatment.

Marianne expressed the demand for individual musical therapy in the following way: "I am blocked in my creative possibilities. There are a lot of bottled-up feelings inside of me, but the moment I want to express them, I just can't. What can I do? I would like to work on that." She wrote poetry prior to her admission. Also, she used to play the guitar as an amateur.

How does Marianne present herself musically in the group music therapy sessions? She plays purely physically, in a constant repetition, in a kind of ostinato. Although she expressed, in a manifest way, her wish to escape from her blockade, the ostinato is a testament to the paralysis of her psychic life. It is a form of musical concretism. The musical elements cannot be taken up in a movement of displacement (*Verschiebung*) and substitution, because her psychic life does not allow for any displacement. It is the therapist's task to experience and come into contact with what this ostinato playing means.

Individual Music Therapy

First session: "The inability to play music."

Initial situation

Marianne enters the music therapy room, shuffling her slippers as she walks. She carries a plastic bag, which contains some of her personal belongings. She arrives punctually. She gives the impression of being worn out: a woman who is completely exhausted and who has nothing more to say. The therapist experiences a certain dryness and emptiness when he greets her and shakes her hand. Her handshake does not make contact, without any counterpressure or dynamics. It feels like the therapist is just shaking a rubber hand. Her voice is without intonation. The therapist tells Marianne about the music therapy framework: Sessions last for forty-five minutes and consist of active improv- isation. She will decide whether the session starts with a verbal part or with an immediate improvisation; after each free improvisation there can be verbal reflection. Furthermore, she chooses the instruments, for her and for the therapist, and decides if he plays with her or not. This opportunity for her to make her own choice is important in the context of transference and countertransference. (In certain therapeutic situations it could make sense that through projective identification the therapist makes a choice about the instrument, or because of the psychohygienic nature—see Session 2—he plays along.)

Progress of the session

Marianne chooses the metallophone, the same instrument that she had been playing for eight months in group music therapy. In this choice, she shows her emptiness, the necessity for security and the inability to bring variation in her contact with herself or the therapist. She also chooses a metallophone for the therapist.

Marianne places the two metallophones facing one another. She im- mediately starts to play. The music is as sensorimotoric as during the last eight months in the group music therapy. In an endlessly alternating motorical movement, her arms go up and down along the metallophone. Musically there is no phrasing, no dynamics, and no accentuation. Her improvisation is comparable with "musical rocking":

This musical fragment is an interesting example of the formlessness in the expression of psychotics. Its analysis shows this clearly. When studying the series of tones for the first musical fragment, the movement direction of the melody seems to be arbitrary. One cannot directly recognize a pattern. However, there are a number of musical structures, such as a series of parallel thirds, fourths and fifths. Moreover, there is musical pedal point. We notice that both hands stagnate in turn, while the other (especially the left hand) further steers the play. At one place/point, however, both hands stagnate: four times the same bar/rod is being hit. It is a musical rest point, a not yet voiced phrase. We can consider these structures as unintentional. They originate rather coincidentally. We can conclude that music searches for structures by itself. The empathic listening stance of the therapist is being illustrated by his musical play, in which he plays almost an identical melody line with the base line of the patient. This happens intuitively and is definitely not consciously mirrored. The instruments are opposite one another, so that it is out of the question that there is a direct imitation of the hands.

In the beginning, the therapist explored her meter and tried to get into contact with her. But the problem is that the patient's music is not addressed to someone else. The pure successiveness of time, so typical for psychosis and trauma, does not allow it. Her noncommunicative playing refers to the non-

subjective character of the repetition. Therefore, there is no other for the therapist either. In the beginning, there is only music. The therapist is focused only
on the musical part, the sound.

Intuitively, the therapist knew that he would only be able to communicate
if there were this psychic space. In trying to create such a space, the therapist
introduces a musical form, namely a "bourdon," and after that, a melody, and he

repeated it a few times. To recapture means to create the possibility of having
memories. Repetition means to take up something again, to vary, to do
something with it, to elaborate on it. If nothing can be remembered, one cannot
imagine something. To remember something creates the necessary psychological space for imagination. The therapist tries getting out of the pure repetitiveness and coming to a kind of psychological space with her.

In this psychological space the therapist imagines the other for himself. By
doing this, he plays himself into the position of being a witness of the traumatic.
He tried to stop the endless play by announcing an ending via the introduction of
a musical form. The patient did not seem to notice this, and kept on playing in
the same repetitive way. With a verbal intervention, the therapist tells her to
finish her music. She stops immediately and puts the little hammers down on the
metallophone.

The improvisation lasted for about twenty-five minutes. During the entire
time there was never one single appearance of contact. For the therapist it is
dramatic: it brings him to a level of impossibility to improvise, to make music.

So begins a silence that is as regressive as the music. Again, the therapist
experiences her emptiness. He gives her the chance to verbalize something, but
she only succeeds in answering the therapist's questions with yes and no. We
make a next appointment, after which she takes, without showing any emotion,
her plastic bag and leaves the music therapy room shuffling her feet, just like
she entered the room. It seemed as though nothing had happened during the
forty-five minutes of the session, as if the therapist does not exist for her. You
could not see any resonance. The sounds that chimed were almost nonexistent,
similar to a landscape that is covered in mist and where one cannot see any
contours, points of reference, or colors. Is there something behind that cannot be
seen?

Listening attitude of the therapist

What strikes us while watching the video fragments of the first session is the therapist's manner of listening as well as the way he is sitting: the therapist has assumed the position of the patient. Bent over, hands pressed against the body, having a rather melancholic facial expression, the therapist looks as depressive as the patient. This is an illustration of a perfect empathetic form of listening. Music situates itself at the level of the body, the sensorial. The body posture of the listener adapts to the music. It is a sort of physical dialogue toward which psychotic patients are very sensitive.

Posture of the patient

The music of the patient is characterized by aleatoric and repetitive sounds. There is no representation, no musical form. Also, there is no intention to build it up starting from a memory, from psychic space. Everything is moving on the traumatic level. The image that we get from the patient is one of an abused, traumatized woman.

Second session: "The traumatic instrument, a new melody."

Marianne enters the room punctually, again shuffling her feet. Just like the previous session she has a plastic bag with her, this time with knitting. Marianne says that she has high expectations of music therapy and that she has started to knit and to crochet. It is interesting to see the parallel between the knitting and what is happening musically. Knitting is an autoerotic, and turned into itself, repetitive occurrence, in which no disturbing object appears. To start knitting again, therefore, only confirms what is taking place musically: Her whole being is incorporated into an ostinato. To start knitting again is the confirmation of her emptiness.

Progression of the session

Marianne chooses the metallophone again. The choice of the therapist's instrument happens to be more difficult. She shows a complete indifference toward the instrument choice for the therapist. The therapist encourages her to choose an instrument for him and goes over the possibilities with her: a string-, wind-, or percussion instrument? Finally it is the calimba that is chosen, an instrument that she knows from music therapy, but has not yet played. The calimba is an archaic instrument, with a rather rough and physical sound. Compared to the first session one can notice a variation. Cautiously the variation is still placed with the therapist. He has to present the roughness. She still opts for the metallophone.

Marianne starts her sensorial music again. The therapist tries to get into contact with her, but he feels rejected again in the emptiness of her being. Whatever he tries, the therapist stays in an isolated play on his own. He is struck by a number of thoughts. Why should he still try to get into contact with her? Maybe she wants to maintain her regressive music, on her own, without allowing anyone in. Maybe she only wants him to listen receptively to what she has to say. He concluded intuitively not to play any longer with her, but solely to listen to her music, and to wait to see what could originate.

But, Marianne endlessly keeps on playing the same pattern. The style is purely impressionistic. She plays for example a high tone but does not repeat it. There is no structure in it, no phrasing. She is not developing anything and, therefore, is not able to repeat anything in a reprise. She probably hopes that a melody would originate, but that does not happen. Also, she does not integrate anything from the previous session into her music. For instance, she could have integrated the bourdon of the music therapist, but obviously she is not able to do that. The only change is an acceleration of the tempo. But in the end nothing happens.

Through Marianne's accelerando a certain tension in the musical play is born. "You left me to fend for myself" hangs in the air. Marianne seems to plead to the therapist. He has to create space. She cannot create this space by herself yet; it can only come from the therapist. She totally depends on him as a therapist.

The therapist lets the sounds come to him completely. He experiences something unbearable, something has to happen; she makes an appeal to him.

The patient plays for about eight minutes by herself until he moves himself intuitively toward the piano, which is at the left side of him. Without having to move the chair he starts to play a simple melody. The timbre and the volume are amazingly equal with that of the metallophone. One almost cannot distinguish his melody from hers in regards to timbre, tempo, and volume. They are completely at the same level. The therapist puts his psyche in the service of the psyche of the patient.

The beginning is almost a shock: Suddenly there is this melody. Somebody says: "Here I am." The "unbearableness" of nonexistence finishes. Suddenly, the therapist poses subjectivity. Suddenly, a clear melodic line originates; a kind of anti-poison. The melody evolves into a harmonic entirety, a chorale. The therapist embraces the patient's sensorial music, even though he does not experience getting into contact with her. He continues playing because he wants himself to be heard as a subject. After about five minutes, the therapist plays a definite cadence, to which the patient does not react. She continues playing on her own. Again, after a subverbal intervention she stops her music.

From the short verbal reflection that follows the improvisation, it is obvious that the musical part does not penetrate her. She did not even notice the therapist's piano playing. Just like the previous session she leaves the music therapy room shuffling her feet.

Does the musical play even make sense? At this moment one could wonder whether it ever did make sense. Does it have any significance in this therapeutic context? Diagnostically, it definitely does. This playing is a perfect illustration of how music can enter the traumatic level. The musical play is a purely successive sound, without any form. There is only repetitiveness, without reprise.

The choice to play the piano (the therapist's favorite instrument) becomes obvious to him through countertransference. It is against the therapist's music therapeutic attitude that he does not play the instrument that has been chosen by the patient for the therapist (the calimba). For Marianne, there was the desire to be able to exist as a subject and, intuitively, the therapist felt that he could only represent this through a musical form, through a melody. At this point the calimba was not form-giving enough for him. Only rhythmically could the therapist offer an eventual form, but this was too far away from Marianne's successive sounds, and also from his.

Third session: "The projected provocation."

Marianne again enters the music therapy room shuffling her feet.

First improvisation

Marianne takes a place at the metallophone and asked the therapist if he wants to play the calimba again. It is the first time that she, consciously, points out an instrument for the therapist and involves him as a subject in her music. It is interesting to note that she keeps the same instrument with the angelically, heavenly sounds, and that she delegates the rough, traumatic sound of the calimba to the therapist.

The patient plays her sensorial music again, monotonously, without any dynamics. The therapist provides support and structure but at the same time he tries to provoke the patient rhythmically. The whole time she plays "syllabic-ally," the therapist starts to play more "melismatically." Marianne, however, does not react to any provocation. There is no single variation. She never uses phrases.

The therapist experiences a projective identification. Anything Marianne cannot bear, she projects to him. Because it is the therapist who is playing the calimba, it is also him that has to bear the roughness; a comfortable situation for the patient. She leaves the expression of her traumatic psyche to the therapist. She can keep on pretending that nothing happens. The therapist takes it upon himself to continue playing.

For a moment Marianne comes a little closer. From time to time she is tempted to take over something from the tempo or dynamics, but it stays at the level of exploration.

At a certain point she has the tendency to play in a defensive way. She makes the distance bigger again, the need for projection increases again. After a somewhat more melodic piece, she continues playing in a heavenly, sensorial way. Each time he provokes her, but she covers it up with the cloak of charity. Nothing happens to her.

Marianne coughs when the therapist plays a cadence at the end. However, she does not stop at the same time with him, but only (and abruptly) because of his verbal intervention.

She coughs as a reaction to his intention to stop. The therapist interprets this cough as a signal to round off the improvisation. So, she notices that he would stop, but she does not do anything with it. She does not have any autonomy, she cannot decide for herself to stop as well. She therefore needs a verbal prompt. She is completely dependent. There is a "fusional" connection between the patient and the therapist, yet without any dialogue. Her defenselessness makes the therapist think about a baby that after being fed has been put back into the crib.

There is something strange about it: a patient that takes up therapy because she is traumatized, but only plays heavenly music and leaves it up to the therapist to take up the traumatic part. At a certain point she follows a little bit, takes something over, starts varying on the basis of the temptation of his music, seems to make the projection less great. But then she withdraws.

The therapist experiences that he does not break, or play phrases, or take space in the music. It is as if it is not possible yet. That would come later on, when a real dialogue is formed.

Marianne still experiences her music as something that stands apart from herself. Nevertheless, she recognizes in the music of the therapist on the calimba something of her previous aggressive side. The rhythms on the calimba correspond with the rhythm in the poems that she wrote before her illness. Rhythm as aggression against the outside world, that she could not display directly because such aggression was not expected from her, was not allowed or was even denied in her family. In the rhythm of her poems, she made an attempt to shock the outside world. It was traumatic for other people; she was repeating the aggression from which she was previously the victim. Spontaneously, in the therapist, the image arises of a battered child. In his provocative playing, something of this image appears unconsciously.

She expresses the hope to continue with this experiment with rhythms, even though she is aware of not being able to do that at this moment.

Second improvisation

In a second improvisation, that we later called "The preparation to become autonomous," the therapist invites Marianne to improvise on this theme. She surprises him by consciously choosing the calimba, and by asking the therapist to play this instrument as well. It is interesting that they play the same instrument and that by doing this she increasingly gets the feeling that she has more space for herself.

The improvisation on the calimba takes a very interesting turn. In a shy way, Marianne starts to play, with the same motor alternating movement as she played on the metallophone. The therapist takes over the musical rocking. By reflecting her, he creates a possibility to "reflect." He hopes that an image can originate from this, but the therapist-patient relationship remains purely fusional, just like the mother-child relationship when the mother rocks the child to the rhythm of his crying.

The therapist starts to play off beats. With this he starts to differentiate himself from her. They are no longer one but two. It is a kind of individualizing, the basis of a dialogue. The complexity of this situation lies in the fact that even though there are two individuals, the therapist is simultaneously sounding the other in a projective identification. The therapist takes a part of the patient upon himself. Detaching from each other is a deprojective movement. So, Marianne takes a part again upon herself. The therapist increasingly experiences a dynamic movement in her music. He brings on rhythms and she tries to vary. She becomes increasingly distant from the bright and heavenly and moves to the rough and rhythmical.

In the improvisation, more cathartic elements are now present. Marianne is more able to present unbearable things. The therapist experiences that she starts to take initiative. She plays fragmented rhythms that she cannot hold conceptually for some period of time yet. Each time she breaks off the rhythms; she does not allow for musical cells to develop. By this, the therapist is led to feel, again and again, that a real dialogue is not yet possible.

By the choice to play the same instrument, Marianne chooses the fusional bond between therapist and patient, as if there is no difference. Paradoxically enough, this situation made it easier to present difference, to start differentiating. And it made it easier for the patient to come into contact with her own aggression.

In addition to this, she specifically chooses the calimba, the instrument that she first pointed out for the therapist and on which the therapist played her aggression, or projected the denied feelings. She puts herself in the therapist's place by choosing his instrument. Through this choice she identifies with the therapist, or better: with the projected part in the therapist. She can now play more easily the rough, the aggressive. At that moment, it is the patient who appropriates the projected and, as a consequence, can play autonomously. She probably would never have been able to do this by herself.

This identification with this split part of the therapist is a remarkable psychic phenomenon. The patient takes from the therapist the expression of her own aggression. In this way, the therapist becomes autonomous, he has freedom, but at the same time the projection must continue to exist. Because only through the projection can she come into contact with this part of herself.

The therapist is autonomous, but at the same time he is not. The therapist makes a new appointment with the patient. This time Marianne gives the therapist a rather strong handshake and leaves the music therapy room with more dynamics.

Fourth session: "The musical form 'Lieder ohne Worte.'"[4]

Marianne looks more refreshed and dynamic. The dull glare in her eyes and glassy look, has disappeared. Also, she is no longer wearing a plain shirt with a neutral color, but one with colorful figures. There is a longing for the therapy, a longing that the therapist cannot understand. This makes him really curious.

Marianne sits down and starts to talk immediately. She tells him that during the last week she was haunted by several rhythms and series of sounds. "These are sounds that came repeatedly to my mind, but I could not do anything against them, I could no longer find any words or . . . I also found it difficult to write them down. I tried to write them down but . . ."

Therapist:	Rhythms and sounds . . . You tried to write them down?
Marianne:	Yes, they were irregular rhythms, they were rhythms that you also find in language.
Therapist:	Were you able to do something with them?
Marianne:	I don't know if I could, because yesterday they disappeared and also today they didn't come back yet. Since yesterday however I have felt tension.
Therapist:	Could you play these rhythms?
Marianne:	We [sic] could try.
Therapist:	Could you imagine on what instrument you could play these rhythms?
Marianne:	Maybe that thing from last time. (*Marianne points to the calimba.*)

In this new improvisation that we later called "Lieder ohne Worte," Marianne and the therapist play the same calimba. In the quietness that precedes the improvisation (the face of "Einstimmung") the therapist experiences certain autonomy from Marianne.

---

[4] "Lieder ohne Worte" is German for song without words.

From her first tone, he knows already in which direction the improvisation will develop. She plays the rhythmical figures that the therapist directly recognizes as the ones from the previous session. Unconsciously, she repeats and integrates them. Immediately, the therapist experiences her rhythms as a musical form. A phrasing is noticeable, a tension that is building up. It is authentic music; it is her poetry. "Lieder ohne Worte" comes to his mind spontaneously. It is a story, an image from which the therapist is allowed to be a witness. He is searching for a meter that will allow him to be present in an active way, although he remains a neutral listener at the same time. The improvisation develops in a mutually interactive play, whereby rhythmical themes are being developed and integrated. The "making autonomous" of each other's space is put first. The therapist feels entirely free in this, taking initiative and taking over her rhythmical proposals. The specific timbres of the calimba are showing up extremely well.

MARIANNE'S MUSICAL FORM "LIEDER OHNE WORTE"

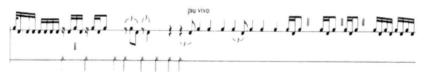

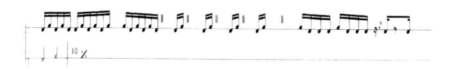

Marianne:	This is the ideal instrument to do something like this. It approximates the rhythms that I heard the previous days.
Therapist:	They are very dynamic rhythms, not so calm.
Marianne:	It was very restless like I experienced them.
Therapist:	What did you experience when you played your rhythms?
Marianne:	What I experienced was that . . . what I always experience when I come here. That is that lots of myself comes to the outside, that otherwise would stay covered up.
Therapist:	It was your music.
Marianne:	Yes, it is not just hitting a bar, it is . . . really coming to the outside with what lives inside of me. . . . I let something from myself be heard.
Therapist:	Did you also experience a dialogue in the improvisation? A question and answer; that is something new, isn't it? It is the first time that this has happened.
Marianne:	It certainly has a significance, it has a . . . it is . . . a way of living and surviving. When you have at one side the society and at the other side the poet, who doesn't fit in with society, and reacts to that society. Because he does not fit in with that society he is almost doomed to be a poet, but it is also thanks to that society that he is a poet. And that I can react to that as a kind of seismograph.
Therapist:	You definitely let yourself be heard.
Marianne:	. . . Yes, it is . . . it is more the restlessness that lives in me and the aggression that is in me . . . and . . . feelings, contradictory feelings . . . that are in me. . . but feelings that are withdrawn in me, my being introverted. . . .

As soon as Marianne came to her musical form, the whole relationship and our position changed. The transition was much more present. The next step toward the elaboration of her problems was obvious. How important the symbolization was, her musical giving form was, was shown by the fact that she integrated elements from this musical form in all of her later improvisations. She varied these and developed other musical forms from fragments that she integrated starting with what she adopted out of the central form. The musical and therapeutic interactions were sometimes very dynamic and radical, emotionally empathizing.

Marianne was released from the hospital about four months after the start of her individual music therapy sessions and left her therapist in a very touching way. She knew that she was not ready yet, but because of her release from the psychiatric center it was impossible to continue the individual music therapy treatment.

CONCLUSIONS

We can observe three phases in the music therapy process that were also present in the treatment of Marianne.

1. The moment of synchronicity or resonance between the therapist and the patient. This is the particular and sometimes laboriously achieved moment on which one makes music together. The occurrence of this moment is being signalized to the therapist by the appearance of the feeling that he can freely make music with the patient. Where, initially, he was searching for a sound that appealed to the real or traumatic part of the patient, suddenly in a liberating manner it becomes apparent that the music takes over. Two bodies dancing on the same rhythm, spontaneously and immediately being moved by the un-expectedly appearing music. An important part of the therapy is devoted to manage the resistance to the appearance of this moment, especially with the more severe psychopathology. The analysis of the fears of being captured or possessed by the "Spirit" of the music is the crucial task for the music therapist.

2. The second moment is the moment of the development of the musical form. Once the moment of loss of one's own identity in music has been reached, it depends on the subject—being within this synchronicity—to abandon the musical phrase that brought him to the loss of him/herself. In the same way the infant is confronted with the interruption of the drive by motherly deprivation, the music-making patient is being forced to break away from the purely repetitive, circular character of his musical phrase. At this moment, the therapist is a kind of Winnicotian "good enough mother." The feeding breast of the mother is not always as soft or as hard, her look is sometimes directed at the child and sometimes distracted by something else, her voice sounds sometimes sweet and reassuring, then again insecure and full of sorrow. This whole play of variations

of a mother which is not always similar to her forces the child to develop the capacity to recognize the same mother in all these different forms of appearance. This preverbal internalization of an image—what we call "recognition"—is originally very similar to a hallucination. The hallucination is being constructed as a way of resisting this play of variations and of guaranteeing the nonvariety of the object in the outside world. The recognition, on the other hand, accepts the variations in the outside world thanks to the construction of an original inner space. Finally, between hallucination and recognition there is still a transitional space in which one still frenetically clings to the musical phrase, but at the same time without coinciding with it any more. These different modes of relating to the absolute repetition of the phrase can also be recognized in the different forms of popular and art music. The capacity to abandon the ecstasy of the repetition and the analysis of the resistances against it, form, in our opinion, the most essential, although sometimes hardly manageable, tasks of music therapy.

3. When the work of variation and development—which can be considered as a form of primordial mourning—is completed, the patient is also able to finish his improvisation musically. If everything is all right, the traumatic affect and speech are no longer disassociated. In his speech, the affect can be heard. Like a tragic actor the patient has now broken away from the ecstasy of the Dionysian choir and he is now able to speak for himself.

REFERENCES

Abraham, N., & Torok, M. (1978). *L'Ecorce et le Noyau.* Paris : Aubier-Flammarion.

De Backer, J. (1993). "Containment in Music Therapy." In T. Wigram & M. Heal (eds.), *Music Therapy in Health and Education.* London: Jessica Kingsley Publishers.

De Backer, J. (1996). "Regression in Music Therapy with Psychotic Patients," *Nordisk Tidsskrift for Musikkterapi*, 5 (1), 24–30.

De Backer, J., & Van Camp, J. (1996). "Muziektherapie in de behandeling van psychotische patiënten." In M. De Hert, en E. Thys (eds.), *Zin in waanzin. De wereld van schizofrenie*, Amsterdam: uitgeverij EPO.

De Backer, J., & Van Camp, J. (1999). "Specific Aspects of the Music Therapy Relationship to Psychiatry." In T. Wigram & J. De Backer (eds.), *Clinical Applications in Music Therapy in Psychiatry*. London: Jessica Kingsley Publishers.

Lacan, J. (1981). *Le Séminaire, Livre III, Les Psychoses (1955–1956)*. Paris: Texte établi par J.-A.Miller, Seuil.

Ogden, T. H. (1992). *The Primitive Edge of Experiences.* London: Karnac Books.

Ogden, T. H. (1994). *Subjects of Analysis*. Exeter, U.K.: PBC Wheatons Ltd.

Ogden, T. H. (1986). *The Matrix of the Mind: Object Relations and the Psychoanalytic Dialogue*. Northvale, NJ: Jason Aronson Inc.

Tustin, F. (1981). *Autistic States in Children*. London: Routledge.

Tustin, F. (1986). *Autistic Barriers in Neurotic Patients*. London: Karnac Books.

Tustin, F. (1990). *The Projective Shell in Children and Adults*. London: Karnac Books.

Van Camp, J. (1999). "Musique, répétition et affect," *La Revue de Musicothérapie*, 4, Nov. 1999, Association Française de Musicothérapie, Paris.

Van Camp, J. (2000). "Musik, Wiederholung und Ritual," *Musiktherapeutische Umschau, Band 21*.

Van Camp, J. (2001). "De muzikale vorm," *Tijdschrift Beroepsvereniging Muziektherapie*, Leuven.

Case Fifteen

PROTECT THIS CHILD: PSYCHODYNAMIC MUSIC THERAPY WITH A GIFTED MUSICIAN

Louise Montello

ABSTRACT

A gifted musician (former child prodigy) with a history of childhood abuse reconnects with her essential musical intelligence (EMI)—the innate capacity to use music as a self-reflecting transformational tool—during a four-year engagement with psychodynamic music therapy. The musician, plagued with a false-self personality constellation and symptoms of post-traumatic stress disorder, is guided in using her own music (instrumental and vocal improvisation and songwriting) to facilitate the expression of her authentic self and to discover her true purpose in life.

INTRODUCTION

Gifted musicians usually work until they break down. Witness the growing number of well-known musicians who end up in rehabilitation centers with psychological and/or physical maladies. It is obvious to me that show business is not for the faint of heart. However, it is this very personality—the fragile artist—who is often thrust into the spotlight by power and money-hungry parents, teachers, managers, etc. to become, as one client described, a "dancing clown," competing with other "dancing clowns" under the strictest media-imposed rules and regulations for achieving success. It is hard enough for normal talents to play this fame game. Prodigies, however, have several strikes against them to begin with:

1. Often they grow up too fast, having been given demanding adult responsibilities at a time when they should be exploring their inner and outer selves through that remarkable invention called play. This inappropriate "fast lane" orientation to life results in a product-oriented, often perfectionistic individual who is unable to relax and smell the roses.
2. Prodigies are typically used by narcissistic adults, who project their own frustrated desires onto their young charges. In this way, the young gifted musician develops a "false self" and lives an "as if" life, relegating their true self/destiny to the back burner.
3. By nature, many prodigies live on the razor's edge between fantasy and reality and, more than anything, need compassionate and wise mentors to help them in navigating their journey through life. Many prodigies do not receive this kind of nurturance and care and are instead robbed of their innocence and childhood.

The musical prodigies with all three of the above strikes are the ones who eventually break down and disappear from public view, only to reappear in some new improved version after a quick fix and a new manager appears—that is, if they are lucky—or are they?

What follows is a case study of my work with an accomplished musician whose prodigious talent was both a gift and a curse. She was drawn to music therapy because of her ambivalence around her relationship with music. Through psychodynamic music therapy, she was able to connect with what was real about music and to use it to transform her life.

BACKGROUND INFORMATION

Jennifer, a gifted thirty-two-year-old professional jazz pianist, was referred to me by a physician who worked with injured musicians. She was suffering with severe tendonitis in her left forearm, along with extreme performance anxiety. Both disorders had reached the stage where they were beginning to interfere with Jennifer's performing obligations. Jennifer originally came to see me for a series of stress-management sessions to deal with her anxiety. One of the first techniques that I usually teach musicians for stress reduction is breath awareness and diaphragmatic breathing. While practicing these breathing exercises during our second session, Jennifer became aware of her tendency to hold her breath. I also noticed that her diaphragm was rigid and that she was physically unable to take a full breath. As she began, with some coaching from me, to let go and allow herself to breathe into her belly, Jennifer experienced what she described as waves of anxiety and terror, coupled with flashbacks of being chased and physically abused by her mother when she was a child. These feelings/flashbacks motivated Jennifer to begin individual psychodynamic music therapy with me (once a week) during the periods of time that she was not touring.

Jennifer was the only child of parents who were both gifted artistically, but at the same time frustrated and unfulfilled. Her mother had been a successful opera singer who was now teaching singing full-time at a neighborhood music school. Jennifer's father, a gifted painter, was, in Jennifer's words, forced to teach in the public school system to provide for the family. She described her father as being severely depressed for most of her young life. Jennifer characterized her mother as being angry all the time. She never knew when her mother would fly into a rage and become verbally and physically violent. Jennifer was not allowed to be angry or act out herself because, according to her mother, it might cause her father to have a heart attack and die.

Jennifer was a musical prodigy who excelled not only in singing, but also on clarinet and piano. Her father delighted in her talent, while her mother was controlling and, at times, envious and abusive. She was primed from a young age to be a diva—taking lessons from her mother and other distinguished teachers, going to the opera almost every weekend, etc. Although she loved to sing pop music (i.e., Joni Mitchell, Steely Dan) her mother discouraged her from pursuing it. She had disdain for the "natural" voice.

Jennifer's earliest memory of music was of being the center of attention while making up her own little songs with her father. Another fond memory was of her toy opera theater. As a young girl, Jennifer would regularly retreat to her room and create her own musical dramas for hours with paper dolls, as a way of coping with difficult feelings and desires. Her most traumatic memory as a young child involved the destruction of her beloved transitional object by her mother. Jennifer described this scenario to me as being a significant loss that left her feeling completely betrayed and alone.

> When I was around three years old, I had a favorite stuffed animal, "Tony the Tiger" that I carried around with me everywhere I went. He was so worn and dirty and smelly and I loved him more than anything. One day, my mother was cleaning the house in her usual frenzy. I was playing in the kitchen with Tony as usual. Mother was in a foul mood and told me that Tony was disgusting. She grabbed him out of my hands and tossed him into the incinerator. I just remember screaming and shouting until I passed out. When I came to, I realized that Tony was gone forever. I was devastated for days and felt like I just couldn't go on living. Mother didn't understand. She said it was just a smelly old toy and wanted to buy me a new one. I don't think I was ever able to trust anybody in my life since then.

From that point on, Jennifer reported that she was repeatedly abused, both emotionally and physically, by her mother—a large, rageful woman. She remembered a particularly shocking experience that occurred when she was approaching puberty. Her mother was a fan of romance novels and devoured them one after another. When she discovered Jennifer masturbating one day, she shamed her mercilessly and then proceeded, in Jennifer's words, "to instill the fear of God" in her with regard to sex. Jennifer was confused—she was aware of how much her mother enjoyed her romance novels, and yet she [Jennifer] was not even allowed to entertain the thought that sex could be pleasurable. Her mother had also disclosed to her around that time that she and her father did not have sex. This was similarly perplexing for Jennifer, particularly when she was often placed in the role of "surrogate spouse" to her father.

All through school, Jennifer was a brilliant student who was easily bored by her teachers, both academic and musical. According to Jennifer, teachers started to resent her precocity and arrogance from an early age. Her first piano teacher was abusive and mean. Her band teacher humiliated her in front of her classmates. In response, she began to develop a "false self"—a compliant, yet arrogant, "holier than thou" persona—and relegated her true self to the back burner. Her goal was to impress people as opposed to expressing her truth. In Jennifer's words, "I was like a dancing clown." She resented the fact that she had been deprived of having a real childhood. At the same time, she also felt an overwhelming sense of entitlement. Around this time she developed a perfectionistic attitude where she would have to be the best in order to win her teachers'/parents'/friends' approval. This desire to be perfect occasionally backfired, creating more and more tension in the young prodigy. Her final blow came from a famous opera singer who mildly criticized her singing when she was fourteen years old. Jennifer immediately decided to give up singing and to pursue something where she could be the absolute best and become famous. She was convinced that this would free her from the abuse and abandonment that permeated her world.

In order to separate completely from the world of opera (and her mother), Jennifer decided that she would become a famous jazz pianist. She thought this would be easy and it was—up to a point. At age sixteen, she attended a noted jazz summer program where she excelled as usual. She became the center of attention and, finally, began to achieve a sense of self-worth. At the same time, however, she repeatedly experienced frustration and humiliation in her teenage sexual encounters. She explained that boys looked up to her as a role model, but did not desire her. She grappled with feelings of guilt, shame, loneliness, and grief associated with rejection. She dealt with her depression by working harder, again feeling that if only she was the best she would finally be loved. She also saw herself as the rescuer of her family. If she could become famous, then maybe her parents would finally have money and esteem.

All during her years at a famous conservatory, Jennifer excelled. She spent eight to twelve hours a day practicing and was very competitive with other students. Her self-esteem came only from her achievements. Her sexual life continued to be skewed in early adulthood. She connected with men who were needy and less talented than she was, which eventually led to envy, conflict, and then abandonment, mirroring her relationship with her mother and father. She had conflicts around her sexuality, and was unable to let go and enjoy sex. Jennifer could only have an orgasm when she thought about violent things in advance. Trauma literature (Davies & Frawley, 1994; van der Kolk, et. al., 1996) suggests that when a child is physically and/or sexually abused by a parent, she becomes sexually fused with that parent and tends to seek out similar relationships as an adult. Or, she may choose the extreme opposite—for example, a man who is not interested in sex and/or is impotent. Jennifer would grapple with this dynamic for years to come.

After conservatory, Jennifer's career as a jazz musician took off. When I asked her about her experience recording her first album, she replied, "I wrote music that sounded like someone great . . . something that people would think was intellectual." She explained that it was all about getting the deal, not the music. At the age of twenty-five, Jennifer still maintained her student mentality: "I'm gonna die if I'm not the best. Everything I did was geared toward survival." Jennifer came to New York from Chicago and got a tour with a successful smooth jazz artist. When his record went gold, it triggered in her the desire to become a star. She told me, "The only thing I've known is to scramble for gigs—but I hated them all—especially being on a tour bus with a bunch of guys." She then joined a more mainstream jazz band. She enjoyed the fact that the music was more intellectual. This band felt like family. She explained that the leader and she had become competitive. She wanted it to be her band. She continued, "He beat me into submission and became an evil mentor like my piano teacher." While she was playing with this band, Jennifer felt like she had to work harder because she was a girl. She practiced eight hours day. She started holding her breath. "I couldn't relax," she told me, ". . . it wasn't safe . . . the drummer and the bassist wanted a guy pianist." She continued, "Women in jazz are blown off constantly . . . I was so egotistical . . . I had no center. Being blown off was like being shot."

MUSIC THERAPY ASSESSMENT

Before I began to see Jennifer for individual psychodynamic music therapy, she had asked me to hear her perform with her band at a local jazz club. While watching Jennifer play, it was clear to me that she was experiencing both physical and psychological tension. Jennifer was holding her breath much of the time while playing. She also held tension in her arms, hands, and jaw. I observed the group dynamics of the musicians on stage; there was an air of competitiveness among the players. Jennifer seemed to be playing defensively, pushing away the other musicians with her improvisations, as opposed to welcoming them in. The music was loud, driving, filled with tension. Jennifer seemed nervous, frightened, and angry at times on stage. She often pounded the piano throughout the set. Jennifer's music displayed technical prowess, but not much emotional expression. Her true expression seemed to be swallowed up by her defensiveness.

In processing the assessment the following day, Jennifer described her feelings about the performance. "I was feeling a lot of anger and rage. I felt like I had to be better than everyone else in order to survive. I just deal with it [the tension]. I was thinking—you should be grateful you have a job." In talking about the roots of these beliefs, Jennifer related them to early childhood experiences that were uncomfortable. "I had to be the best in order to gain my teachers' favor and be deemed worthy. Physical abuse was not uncommon. I felt like I would have to take tough love in order to be worth anything. Musicians—like children—have no choice but to take it. It's like the 'be-bop' mentality—shut up and take it and get your training—you don't know anything, so just shut up and pay your dues so you can play with pain and suffering, because there's so few crumbs to go around. Musicians need to work together to advance our artistry rather than keep self-esteem poor so just a few can benefit."

Although Jennifer was intrigued with the concept of using music as a healing modality within the therapeutic context, she was, at first, frightened of revealing herself through music. During our first few music therapy sessions, Jennifer had extremely mixed feelings about clinical improvisation. She resisted sitting at the grand piano, saying that she hated music—that it had destroyed her life. Still, when I asked her to just play what she was feeling inside, she complied. Her improvised music, however, was intellectually driven—elegant, with dark tonalities. She told me that she felt uncomfortable playing with me. Upon processing these feelings, Jennifer realized that she was seeing me as a music teacher who would possibly judge and abuse her. This brought up tremendous sadness and anger. As she began to trust that I was not her prototype of a music teacher, she began to relax a bit. I suggested that Jennifer simplify her improvisations and play more from a feeling level. At first, allowing herself to really feel what was going on inside was terrifying for Jennifer—it was as if all of her true feelings were dissociated and frozen deep inside. I was surprised that as a jazz musician, her improvisations lacked a bluesy, funky quality. Though beautiful and intriguing, her music was devoid of sensuality and joy. This seemed to confirm for me the aphorism—"as in life, so in music." She soon caught on through our musical interactions, however, that she had to know what she was feeling in order to create a life that worked. She later told me, "Before therapy, it was just about being the best—being perfect, not feeling pleasure in living your life."

Clinical Diagnosis

Jennifer was an extremely gifted young woman with a strong capacity for psychological insight. Narcissistically wounded from an early age, she developed a "false self" persona that kept her from acknowledging her real feelings and desires. She felt the need to rescue her parents through achieving her own fame and fortune through her musical career. Because she was separated from her real self, however, she allowed others (managers, agents, producers, etc.) to decide the course of her career. This left her feeling powerless and continually frustrated. She was living an "as if" life—at the top of her game, yet deeply depressed and anxious.

Because of ongoing sexual and physical abuse throughout her childhood, Jennifer learned to dissociate her feelings and experienced fragmentation within her personality development. The only feeling states that seemed acceptable to Jennifer were those of superiority and accomplishment. When she was not achieving, she was depressed. At the same time, she experienced entitlement rage when she did not get the recognition that she desired. Her sexuality was frozen. She engaged in codependent relationships with men whom she thought would rescue her. These short-lived relationships would inevitably end in fits of rage, violence, and heartbreak, leaving Jennifer in a suicidal state. Because of her extreme dissociation and proclivity to live an "as if" life, it was clear to me that connecting with her real self could bring up tremendous feelings of rage, grief, and loss. Finding true happiness would require a complete transformation of character. Was she strong enough to do this? Was I a good enough therapist to help her in achieving this psychological make-over?

METHODOLOGY AND TECHNIQUES

My therapeutic approach is eclectic, drawing from my training as a musician/composer and music therapist, psychoanalyst, and practitioner of yoga therapy. I also have advanced training in working with victims of trauma. While the therapeutic relationship is key to facilitating change in patients with early abandonment and abuse issues, I believe that the most significant catalyst for transformation is actually the client's relationship with the "self" through music.

Early on in my work with "normal" adults, I discovered that, at the core of our beings, we each have a powerful source of healing that can be tapped, through our engagement with music. I call this source *essential musical intelligence* (EMI)—our innate capacity to use music and sound as self-reflective, transformational tools in integrating spirit and matter—soul and personality – within the healing context. Although all human beings have access to EMI, most do not comprehend its value and, thus, do not use it as effectively as they could. EMI is our ability to perceive the voice of truth—the "will to be" (life force) that informs our beings through the archetypal language of spontaneous sound and music-making. This innate "will to be" is naturally perpetuated through the expression of human desires and emotions that must be acknowledged, processed, and integrated into the whole of our beings before total health can be achieved. Music is the most natural conduit for the expression of these desires and emotions, especially the ones that, for some reason, are hidden from ourselves, or repressed. From the perspective of EMI, music acts as a mirror of the inner life. By tuning in to the deeper meaning of music in our lives, we naturally begin to understand ourselves, and others, better. Thus, the music that we listen to and/or create can foster self-awareness, emotional intelligence, transformation, and, ultimately, deep healing of the body, mind, and spirit.

The first step in accessing EMI is witnessing—to be able to step aside and become the observer of thoughts, feelings, desires, and actions as opposed to being caught up in and controlled by them. The following steps comprise the process of using EMI for self-transformation and healing:

1. Identify the problem through witnessing.
2. Remember your EMI (your innate ability to transform pain into power through engagement with music/sound) and trust that you are safe and secure no matter what the outcome.
3. Ask for help from your EMI.

4.   Connect with your center of creativity (throat chakra).
5.   Allow a solution to the problem to unfold through your engagement with music.
6.   Give thanks for the gift of your EMI.

Jennifer described EMI-based therapy as "a transformational twelve-step program that uses music to directly access the Higher Self." Most renowned musicians/composers have naturally tapped the power of EMI to inform their creative process. These inspired individuals probably spent a lot of their time in the consciousness of the throat chakra (the energy center associated with receptivity/surrender to a Higher Power for inspiration/expression). Unfortunately, when looking at the numbers of creative/inspired musicians who have succumbed to serious pressures of the music industry, it is obvious that there is more to being healthy and whole than just being a channel for higher consciousness. All creative people need a safe, secure foundation upon which they can build their "castles" of light.

This brings me to the next structure that informs my therapeutic stance. Drawing from yoga science and philosophy, I find that the system of understanding the different levels of consciousness and how they interact as described in the treatises on chakra psychology is quite useful. According to yoga science, the chakras represent seven levels of consciousness that are associated with the nerve plexus located along the spinal cord. Each chakra reflects certain developmental/archetypal realities that need to be experienced and integrated into the self in order for us to become whole and achieve the highest levels of human functioning. The following chart (Table 1) presents an overview of the chakras and the dramas that unfold at each level.

The goal of yoga science is to assess which chakras are active and healthy in the client, where there are blockages and/or developmental delays/arrests, and to help the client to fill in and/or work through areas of weakness/dissociation/trauma so that she can move up the ladder of consciousness toward more health and wholeness. The techniques of assessing the distribution of a client's chakra energies are beyond the scope of this chapter. Please refer to my book, *Essential Musical Intelligence: Using Music as Your Path to Healing, Creativity, and Radiant Wholeness* (2002) or *Anatomy of the Spirit* (1996) by Carolyn Myss.

TABLE 1
Chakras and Archetypal Themes

Chakra	Mode of Experience	Ideal Representations	Polarities Experienced
7 – Crown	Unitary Consciousness	No representations; beyond form	None
6 – Third-Eye	Insight, witnessing	The Sage	Sage/fool; objective observer/deluded participant
5 – Throat	Devotion, receiving nurturance and unconditional love, surrender, trust, creativity, grace, majesty, romance	The Child	Object of devotion/devotee; mother/child; found/lost; trust/distrust
4 – Heart	Compassion, generosity, selfless loving, service	The Mother	Rescuer/rescued; liberator/liberated
3 – Solar Plex	Mastery, domination, conquest, competition, inadequacy, inferiority, pride	The Hero	Gain/loss; success/failure; dominance/submission; blame/praise
2 – Sex	Sensory pleasure	The Hedonist	Pleasure/pain; male/female
1 – Root	Struggle for survival	The Victim	Predator/prey; life/death

From the perspective of chakra psychology, Jennifer's core consciousness seemed to be centered at the level of the heart chakra. This was reflected in her desire to give service to humanity through her music and to rescue her parents from mediocrity/poverty. Most of her struggles in the beginning of therapy involved ego/power issues (third chakra) associated with perfectionism/identity.

A developmental arrest at the level of the sexual chakra interfered with the natural flow of nurturing energy that is usually available at the throat chakra. This prevented Jennifer from enjoying pleasurable feelings and the experience of union—both physically and aesthetically. Jennifer was also arrested developmentally at the level of the root chakra. She was never able to integrate feelings of security and safety with respect to her relationship with her parents (a common issue in victims of abuse). Through her spiritual practice (Nisherin Shoshu Buddhism) and in her relationship with music, she experienced glimpses of insight and clairvoyance (sixth chakra—third eye). This would prove to be helpful to her in understanding and utilizing the symbolic material that emerged during the course of therapy.

In my clinical approach, there is no particular therapeutic agenda. I am keenly aware of where the client's energy is focused at the moment. From that place, I endeavor to provide a creative framework where the client can connect with her EMI and enter into corrective emotional/ somatic experiences which ultimately lead to self-awareness, insight, catharsis, and transformation.

The following are the developmental stages of Jennifer's psychospiritual transformation, with EMI as the central motivating force.

Phase I

1. *Creativity/play*—Jennifer began the process of uncovering her true self. From the time her original transitional object (Tony the Tiger) was destroyed by her mother when she was a young child, Jennifer's capacity to play was thwarted. She became hypervigilant, externally-oriented, and disconnected from her inner life. It took some time for Jennifer to let down her guard within the therapy context, to connect with her EMI, and to use her sessions to play and be nurtured by our interactions. During the first few sessions, Jennifer was terrified of sitting with me at the piano. She would cry and could not understand why. When we began to process her feelings, she realized that being with me at the piano brought up excruciating memories of her childhood piano lessons—subconsciously, a part of her was just waiting for me to criticize and abuse her.

Although Jennifer was a consummate improviser, it was difficult for her to let go and allow deeper feelings to emerge through the music. A breakthrough happened about three months into therapy, when I asked her to improvise the "music" of her father at the piano. Breaking from her usual elegant improvisational style, the music at once sounded raw and filled with conflicting emotions. This was the first time that Jennifer had connected with her deeper self while improvising—her first *conscious* experience of her EMI. She later told me, "I realized that I had been playing patterns—what would sound good. . . it was the first time I actually *heard* what I was playing." With regard to her own jazz playing, she continued, "I never thought—what is the *feeling* of the song, for example, "All the Things You Are." I was just concerned with impressing people with my virtuosity."

During a series of free piano improvisations that followed, Jennifer also realized that finding her true voice was compromised by her codependency with narcissistic men. She called this her "love addiction." Jennifer explained, "More women have love addictions than men—it's related to perfectionism; we need to fill the emptiness inside us with another person."

Much of the work during our initial sessions focused on my mirroring and holding the feelings that came up for Jennifer both verbally and in the music. Because of the extreme splitting and dissociation related to early abuse and betrayal, Jennifer's feelings seemed overwhelming and terrifying. This created a lot of resistance early on in the treatment. Jennifer explained, "It [the music] had to be pretty; I couldn't let go and play from my body—it was either all rage, or all pretty." Jennifer had created a wall built by perfectionism to protect her from the devastation of her true feelings—both her pain and her glory.

2. Jennifer completed her second album, a musical tribute to powerful women through the ages, during her first stage of treatment. The album received four stars in a popular music magazine. It was touted as superior, intellectual music. After returning from her tour to promote the album with an all-woman band, she told me that she finally started to feel something in the music this time around. She became a little more connected to her inner life. She felt safer playing with women as opposed to men, and was feeling more physically connected due to the influence of a new supportive piano teacher who helped her to inhabit her body by making her count (rhythms) out loud while practicing.

In summary, during Phase 1 of treatment, Jennifer learned to express dissociated feelings related to early trauma/abandonment through musical improvisation and worked toward achieving trust within the therapeutic relationship. Once Jennifer acknowledged, felt, processed, transformed, and integrated these feelings, she was able to give birth to her real self. "I had to first put down the drug—my rageful interactions with others and my addiction to power and fame" (first and third chakra issues). She learned to discriminate between her own personal needs and what others expected from her. Musical role-playing was the most effective way of learning how to discriminate between roles and behaviors that are true to the self, and others that were introjected from dysfunctional others. Jennifer and I engaged in what she called "struggle" exercises at the piano (role-playing—exploring the music of "what is you" and "what is introjected") and finding the core of self within that struggle.

Phase II

As Jennifer began to realize the split between her real self, feelings, and desires and the false reality she had created, she entered into the second phase of treatment—what she called her "dark night of the soul." She realized that she was usually dissociated while performing and that she most often resented the audience. She used dissociation as a way of coping with overwhelming feelings of responsibility. "I wanted more from the audience than I was willing to give," she explained, "I really hated what I was giving—my music wasn't authentic. And because I didn't want to give my music, I didn't get much back in return" (heart chakra issues).

During this phase of treatment, Jennifer was dealing with feelings of alienation from her body, heart, and soul. As a way of making contact with her deeper self, I encouraged Jennifer to engage in vocal improvisations with me at the piano. She was terrified of opening her mouth and singing. In a playful way, I demonstrated my own style of vocal improvisation. "Why are you having so much fun?" she asked me. She could not imagine just having fun with singing. She hated the sound of her voice, which, at first, had a strained and pinched quality. She did not find it at all expressive. With time, Jennifer realized that she could just play with singing, that she did not always have to be so serious. We imitated the likes of Aretha Franklin and James Brown together, often breaking down in laughter. Later we would explore difficult issues through a kind of call-and-response style of vocal improvisation that I call "musical dialogue." At first, Jennifer was resistant and embarrassed to be so vulnerable and open in the music. But it seemed to me that the "child" in her was awakening, and this child part truly enjoyed our vocal interactions. I asked her to continue creating musical dialogues at home. Jennifer took this very seriously and proceeded to "sing her truth" at the piano daily. She recorded every session. "After freely singing at the piano," she shared, "I heard my true voice for the first time. I didn't realize how much tension I held around my throat, neck, and jaw. I spent a lot of time every night singing and then listening back. I was amazed at what came out—it was frightening at times—but I was speaking my truth."

At first, most of her improvisations focused on exploring her feelings about her addictive relationship with a narcissistic, emotionally unavailable lover (second chakra issues). She tried to create some distance between her dependency on this man by developing a more intimate relationship with her own creative process. She worked on her music every day and by the end of a month, her at-home improvisation sessions turned into fourteen new songs. In addition, during this phase of music therapy, Jennifer started to listen to music that truly moved her, music that appealed to the adolescent in her who had never had a chance to thrive: Joni Mitchell, Alanis Morissette, Tori Amos, Smashing Pumpkins. A transformation was occurring where Jennifer was now alive in her adolescence for the first time. She had unleashed a hidden desire to become a rock-oriented singer/songwriter—to simplify her music and finally express her heart (true self).

As Jennifer progressed in therapy, she became aware of her inner emptiness. She was prone to addictive behavior—bulimia and codependency. I encouraged her to use toning to "fill her up" energetically. She particularly liked chanting the chakra sounds on a daily basis. She told me that she used the sounds to get Gordon (her narcissistic lover) out of her body, and to help her to remember that she exists as a separate whole person without him. Right around that time Jennifer wrote a song about saying a prayer that she could stand alone, without her codependent relationship. She later told me that the song, along with weekly twelve-step meetings for people with "love addictions," had truly freed her from her codependency. (The whole process of using vocal improvisation within and outside the music therapy context and attending recovery groups took about a year.) Her recovery plan included the following goals: "To be a rock singer/songwriter and create the true music of my spiritual path." In moving into this new genre of music—and a new professional identity—Jennifer explained that she had to defend the music all the time, ". . . this made it [the music] more real, more precious." Jennifer was using the therapeutic relationship, along with her relationship to her own music (EMI) to separate from her dependency on her introjected mother and from her parasitic producers and managers, who, up until now had dictated the course of her career. She was rebelling like a teenager, belatedly entering the stage of separation and individuation.

Opening the throat chakra:

Jennifer experienced tremendous resistance related to singing during this phase of treatment. "I had issues with protecting that voice," she told me. She typically experienced tightness/tension in her throat. When we began to explore the underlying causes, Jennifer began to have flashbacks of her mother hitting her on the back of the neck. The pain was overwhelming. It was difficult for me to witness the heartbreak associated with Jennifer's resistance to singing. Yet I proceeded to focus on her relationship with her voice and singing during these sessions. Occasionally I was cast in the role of the abusive mother. In working with the transference, Jennifer was finally able to express threatening feelings that were previously disowned (murderous rage, shame, guilt) lest she summon additional abuse from her out-of-control mother. With time and patience, she was able to work through some of the pain. (See Jennifer's Therapeutic Song Cycle, pp. 316–317.)

One day, after twenty years of estrangement from the opera world, she was compelled to sing again. She brought in one of her favorite arias to her session and sang for me. Immediately after singing the last note, Jennifer broke down and sobbed from the depths of her being. I, too, mesmerized by the intensity of her musical gift, began to cry. After some time passed, I asked Jennifer if she could talk about her feelings. She told me that she realized that this (her voice) was a gift from God and that she had rejected it. She felt that the gift had required too much responsibility. Jennifer was overcome with grief. For me, these feelings signaled the opening of her throat chakra—the realization of her connection with divinity through her creative gift, and, finally, her willingness to receive and cherish this gift and be nurtured by it. Jennifer had never integrated the experience of being truly nurtured. Because of this, she had to rely only on herself and felt either omnipotent or powerless, nothing in between. "If I really did sing well," she told me, "my mother/Harold (her producer) would be jealous."

This was a difficult, heavily charged period for Jennifer—full of pain and confusion. I encouraged her to integrate EMI into her life on a daily basis. In Jennifer's words, "Music therapy was the only sane place; it provided proof that I am insane. It's the only place in the world where I am doing something that is real—so it can't be real. . . . You (Louise) were very persistent." It was difficult for Jennifer to hold the gift (her intense spirituality) and her very real pain/suffering (due to past abuse/false self) together at the same time. Engaging with her EMI was the only way that she was finally able to do that. As she called upon her EMI more often in times of need, she was able to disengage with the "false self," illusory world that she had created and take baby steps toward manifesting her true purpose in life.

Tools of EMI

The following EMI techniques were used to help Jennifer to release the shackles of perfectionism; transform her love addiction; and find her "true self."

Spontaneous song writing as a mode of problem solving:

Jennifer explained, "I wrote fourteen songs to break through the love addiction. You (Louise) asked me to sit at the piano and to sing how I felt. I had never done that before." Jennifer was asked to do daily vocal improvisations to tell her life story through music. She was also asked to sing about what was going on in the moment. She recorded these sessions and used a lot of the improvisational material in her compositions. Her treatment also included yoga breathing techniques for anxiety reduction; chakra tuning for emotional balancing; and, Guided Imagery and Music (GIM) (Bonny & Savary, 1973)—a way for Jennifer to explore her inner world through recorded music and then externalize the images/symbols found there through mandala drawing. According to Jennifer, "GIM helped to melt frozen feelings."

I encouraged Jennifer to take voice lessons. This gave her more confidence as she began to create a new rock-oriented band where she would be the lead singer. She took a hiatus from her own jazz work, and to make money, became a sideman with what seemed to me to be one sadistic band leader after another. Here she was reenacting the past trauma of her early family dynamics (emotional abuse). Jennifer was working twelve-hour days; her defenses were down and her "shadow" side was escalating. In her very real pain and suffering, Jennifer started to get in touch with a formerly dissociated, destructive child part who was wreaking havoc in both her professional and personal relationships. "She (the six-year-old) was really pissed," Jennifer told me. "She didn't want to be suppressed any longer" (third chakra: identity/power issues).

Jennifer was also manifesting her inner conflicts in the therapy room. She had deep-rooted issues around giving and receiving, and was occasionally hostile and arrogant. It was my guess that this issue was popping up in her sidemen gigs as well. For example, Jennifer had been running up a huge therapy bill, promising to pay, but consistently forgetting her checkbook. Up until this point, analyzing her resistance to pay had not been effective. During one particular session, she had again forgotten her checkbook. At the same time she was boasting about how much money she had just invested in the stock market. I had been role-playing her mother in a particularly intense vocal improvisation that day, and as she was leaving the session, I succumbed to my own countertransference and teased, "You better pay me soon or I'll get the goons out after you." (When I processed my feelings later on, I realized that I was really annoyed and angry with her. I felt that she was devaluing me but I was not able to analyze this with her because the session had already ended.) Immediately, Jennifer cast me in the role as her abusive mother. She experienced this as a reenactment of past abuse. She immediately sent me a check and notified me that she wanted to take a break from therapy.

I apologized over the phone and encouraged her to come back to talk about the painful interaction. Jennifer made a tentative comeback. She told me that she did not know if she could trust me. After this interaction, Jennifer began to become aware of how much she hated the "little girl" part (subpersonality) who was so needy, angry, and destructive. I suggested that Jennifer get to know the "little girl" instead of pushing her away. The "little girl" began writing angry letters to Jennifer in her journal. Jennifer responded by saying, "You little bitch—shut up and die." Jennifer had become the mother who ignored, rejected, and abused the innocent "divine child" who simply wanted to play—to love and be loved. We engaged in musical role-playing to explore this dynamic. I played her out-of-control mom and she would defend herself. It was helpful for her to have a chance to fight back. I was moved, however, to take care of the "little girl." During one session when Jennifer was loathe to listen to her "little girl" part, I played her role and during a vocal improvisation, sang, "You're using me, you never let me have any fun. . . ." Jennifer was touched by my words.

As the "little girl" subpersonality was slowly welcomed into Jennifer's life, she realized that she did not have to do things that she did not enjoy. She explored the masochistic statement: "You have to suffer and sacrifice in order to make it." She realized that it was better to suffer to find truth as opposed to the suffering it took to climb the "show biz" ladder. This realization gave her the strength to leave her current abusive working situation.

As she worked on making the transition from jazz to rock, Jennifer often lost her center when dealing with record companies, producers, etc. She realized that, because she had given all her power over to her producers/ managers, she felt like a slave. She harbored so much bitterness with respect to giving—her heart was closed. I encouraged her to take time to commune with her EMI. I knew that this is where her real self existed. Jennifer wrote a song for the "little girl" part. She called the song, "Protect This Child." The lyrics were quite moving:

> She didn't know why she was silent . . . show me the way to free myself to be myself . . . the diva dies, the scene is through, now it is I that must be true.

Jennifer told me, "The music showed me how to heal the child—I was given an outlet and acknowledgment and I was able to forgive this child [for sabotaging her attempts to become famous]." She realized that this child part had been frozen early in life because it was not safe just to be a child and to create without feelings of responsibility. Essentially, the child had been bound and gagged for many years. It was time now to free her and allow her to enrich Jennifer's world.

Around the time that the child part was awakened, Jennifer also began to get in touch with her submerged spirituality. As a child, she had been deeply connected to the Catholic Church. She told me that when she had become increasingly dismayed due to parental/teacher abuse (at around age eleven), she turned to God for help. When none came, she felt betrayed. It was important for her to talk about these "irrational" beliefs/feelings within the therapy context. In my experience, many musicians (and creative people in general, for that matter) are deeply spiritual, but are apt to suppress this particular passion because it is not "cool." I encouraged her to explore these feelings through her music. She wrote a new song for the child within where she worked through her "Catholic stuff." She discovered that her inner child was split into two opposing self states: the part of her that she called the "demon child" (". . . the presence that makes my life crazy") and the other, the "divine child" (". . . because I believe in the power of you"). In this song, she allowed the "demon child" (who had once been the innocent "divine child" before she was ravaged and suppressed) to creatively express her rage. This was the first time that Jennifer had used the full force of her voice in one of her songs. It was fascinating for me to watch that as the "demon child" was given a voice through the song, it actually transformed itself back into the "divine child." They truly were one in the same energy (third eye chakra: dualities are melting—approaching unitary consciousness)!

At this point, Jennifer became very aware of the inner conflict between these two sides of herself. She realized that she had a choice between suc-cumbing to the negative spiral of the "demon child" (hopelessness, inability to trust, feeling unworthy/bad), and the upward moving spiral of the "divine child" (optimistic, able to receive and give love, trust). Jennifer used EMI as an anchor in allowing her truth to unfold—trusting, as much as possible, that she was safe and secure in the lap of the creator within.

As her relationship with me and with her own self became stronger and more committed (fourth year of therapy), Jennifer was compelled to nurture herself and to choose work that was nurturing (fifth chakra is opening). She no longer felt the need to resist facing herself in therapy. She now experienced therapy as a kind of creative partnership. She also described her new love relationship with a fellow rock musician as a creative partnership. Gone were the feelings of desperation for love that plagued her. She was now able to give and receive within this relationship and create healthy boundaries when appropriate.

Jennifer's Therapeutic Song Cycle

The following is a progression of songs that emerged as a result of Jennifer's process of exploring and healing herself through EMI-based music therapy.

1. "Shelter Me"—a safe-place song
2. "Say a Little Prayer"—favorite line, "Pray for me to fly without you." A powerful song that helped her to transform a long-standing love addiction.
3. "Walking on Water"—favorite line, "Walking on the sea of love." Led her away from dependency on narcissistic men into dependency on the Christ mind.
4. "Protect this Child"—"I was able to admit that I was afraid and needed protection from abusive teachers and others to be able to sing again."

5. "Take Your Hands Off Me"—a song of fighting back. "I was able to confront past abusers through this song."
6. "Grace and Pain"—two songs about exploring the possibility of standing alone, and the fear of being loved.
7. "These Things I Love"—"I finally had the courage to look at the good things that were happening in my life and give thanks."

DISCUSSION AND CONCLUSIONS

Although Jennifer has made a lot of progress over the four years that she has been in psychodynamic music therapy, she still grapples with some fragmentation in her personality. She now uses vocal improvisation/musical dialogue as a way of identifying and giving voice to split-off parts of the self. We also regularly use what I call the "musical tantra" exercise as a way of resolving polarities within the psyche (through improvisational role-playing, the client will explore two sides of a polarity, i.e., fear vs. arrogance and, by bringing them together musically, find the center or meta-state between them). The musical tantra exercise has been wonderfully healing for Jennifer and has created a bridge between the superior/perfectionistic self-state and the inferior, hated/loser self-state. In that centered meta-state, Jennifer can find serenity and peace—the abode of her true self.

And finally, at this point in her therapy, Jennifer has unpeeled another layer of the psychic onion and is grappling with opening herself more deeply to the experience of pleasure in her musical expression, performance, and love relationship (second chakra). For years she has been controlled by her introjected mother, feeling unworthy of enjoying her femininity and sexuality—feeling that she will be shamed, or worse, physically abused, lest she relish pleasurable sensations in her body. I am currently working with Jennifer on this issue through clinical improvisation, encouraging her to explore the piano and her voice in a sensual way—to become aware of sensual/sexual impulses that emerge through the music and to embrace them instead of pushing them away or judging them harshly. This has been a frightening and painful process, as it is bringing up overwhelming feelings of remorse for the many years that she has lived repressing and inhibiting this delightful aspect of her self. My sense is that as she reclaims her innate feminine/sexual self, along with the power that she has been reclaiming through putting out her real self through her music, she will experience the wholeness that is her natural birthright and be able to fully give her unique gift and receive her just desserts in all dimensions of her life.

REFERENCES

Bonny, H. L., & Savary, L. M. (1973). *Music & Your Mind*. New York: Station Hill Press.

Davies, J. M., & Frawley, M. G. (1994). *Treating the Adult Survivor of Childhood Sexual Abuse: A Psychoanalytic Perspective*. New York: Basic Books.

Montello, L. (2002). *Essential Musical Intelligence: Using Music as Your Path to Healing, Creativity, and Radiant Wholeness*. Wheaton, IN: Quest Books.

Myss, C. (1996). *Anatomy of the Spirit*. New York: Harmony Books.

Van der Kolk, B. A., McFarlane, A. C., & Weisaeth, L. (1996). *Traumatic Stress*. New York: Guilford Press.

Case Sixteen

THROUGH MUSIC TO THERAPEUTIC ATTACHMENT: PSYCHODYNAMIC MUSIC PSYCHOTHERAPY WITH A MUSICIAN WITH DYSTHYMIC DISORDER

Paul Nolan

ABSTRACT

Individual music psychotherapy was used with a musician for one and a half years to address dysthymia secondary to his developmental problems in object relations and in the formation of the self. Resistance was encountered in the interpersonally—avoidant use of rhythm. Therapeutic attachment occurred through the use of melody within the therapeutic relationship. The client's identity emerged as he discovered musical pauses, or breaths, as a means to achieve and maintain contact with the environment. He begins to experience pleasure in the use of his voice in musical compositions and interactions. From this, he was able to emerge as a musical leader. Reduction of depressed feelings, interpersonal tension, and authority conflicts resulted from the discoveries in his music psychotherapy experience.

INTRODUCTION

This chapter will address some of the concepts and processes of music psychotherapy as a psychodynamically-oriented psychotherapy. For the purpose of description of the clinical style presented in this case study, the basic assumption of psychodynamic music therapy is that music invokes our primitive constitutional, as well as our environmentally acquired, responses to sound. These responses serve affective and cognitive functions. The affective qualities, in particular, are fused with our interpersonal life. Hence, the psychodynamic focus of music therapy in this case study includes the invocation of mother-infant interaction, through the use of music, to activate early modes of sensory and cognitive styles (Nolan, 1994). Music serves as a means for the client to develop a therapeutic attachment with the therapist. Within this adaptive relationship, problems with self-image and interpersonal functioning are able to be addressed as the music therapy relationship evolves. In this case study, the role of the therapist defines the psychodynamic approach in two ways. First, the music therapist allowed for the therapeutic relationship/environment to change in response to client growth. Second, the music therapist based clinical decisions upon interpretations of: 1) the dyadic musical relationship; 2) the client's and the therapist's music; 3) the transferential and countertransferential forces; and 4) the real relationship.

Music and the Therapeutic Dyad as Objects

Some music therapists refer to music itself as a transitional object (Nolan, 1989) and as an object. David John (1995) suggests that music has, as one of its uses, to function as the transformational object, a concept developed by Christopher Bollas, a British psychoanalysist. The concept of the transformational object describes the infant's experience of the object as a process of alteration of the infant's self experience. It is as if the transformational object is the infant's other self, in that the mother transforms the infant's internal and external environment. According to Bollas (1989), the transformational object "refers to the mother's function as a processor of the infant through her continuous action that alters the infant's psycho-somatic being" (p. 213). From this experience of the mother as a process of transformation, a trace remains in adult life as the person seeks out others for their function as a signifier of the transformation of being. John (1995) believes that this transforming quality is at the core of music "in that we expect music to do something to our self-experience" (p. 161). The process of seeking out music to organize, or transform our experience, as when a teenager looks for a particular song on the radio, contains a trace of the search for the transformational object. John again relies on Bollas when he compares music with "a particular object relation that is associated with ego transformation and repair" (p. 161). I agree with John's conception of the music therapist, as one who develops a relationship with the client in a similar way to what Bollas describes as the transformational mother, as the infant's "other self." In the case example that follows, this stage represents the very beginning of therapy. Change is seen and influenced by the client "using" the music therapist and the therapy experience. This use not only facilitates the transformation of the client's immediate world, or self-experience, but eventually makes possible contact with the other, transforming the self in relation to the other, thus achieving some level of adaptation.

The Evolving Therapeutic Relationship

I have found that the music therapy relationship, including the client, the music therapist, and the music, within a long-term psychotherapeutic relationship can be conceived as a gestalt. This gestalt consists of identifiable factors, or forces, which change over time. The client and therapist dyad function as two objects (as in object relations) held together in changing ways by the forces they exert upon each other. The music serves as both a process and an object. The development of the music over time exerts an evolving force over the dyad. Likewise, the evolution of the therapeutic relationship results in change in the function, as well as the content, of the music. Thus, the gestalt changes as the forces within redistribute their energies. In the beginning of treatment, a greater emphasis is placed upon the music, something shared by client and therapist. As in a gestalt, the music may be seen as a figure and the beginning therapeutic relationship serves as the background. As therapy progresses, the healing emphasis often shifts as the dyad becomes more of the figure, held by the music as more of the background. In the early stages of therapy, where the role of the music is so important, I see music serving the function as the transformational object. In the case which follows, and as seen quite regularly by music therapists, transformational experiences, such as moments of deep rapport experienced with the music, and the experience of fusion, or of being held by the music, are experiences of being rather than of mind. These "music as therapy" moments, especially as part of an aesthetic occurrence, are experienced as such "because they express that part of us where the experience of rapport with the other was the essence of life before words existed" (Bollas, 1987, p. 32). These inarticulate contents of psychic life are termed the "unthought known" by Bollas, in that they are recognized from a time when the infant experienced the illusion of deep rapport between subject and object, both in the primary transformation experience of emptiness, rage, and agony becoming fullness and contentment, delivered by the mother's aesthetic style of handling, and in the creating of Winnicott's "facilitating environment." In the music therapy relationship, especially early in treatment, these experiences of transformation are identified with, and attributed to, the music. As therapy progresses, these experiences are increasingly identified with, and attributed to, the relational aspects of the creators of the music (the dyad). It is through this representation of music, early in treatment, as the transformational object, that the music therapy experience can create the environment (initially internal) necessary to strengthen attachment capabilities in the client. As the therapeutic relationship develops, transformation occurs in the external environment. Change can begin in terms of how the client experiences the self in relation to others as true object relations.

Interpretations of the Music

One of the main processes used by the music therapist that separates psychodynamically-oriented music therapy from other music therapy approaches is the interpretation of the music by the therapist and the client into nonmusical realms. This is also one of the least developed areas in our profession due to a lack of a shared, agreed upon, empirically derived data base which reliably demonstrates the relationship between music behaviors, non-music behaviors, and mental processes. However, my belief is that most music therapists make at least some interpretations regarding a client's musical expressions. Music therapists should continue in the development of methods of clinical musical interpretation. There are two reasons why a music therapist is capable of, and should develop, clinical interpretations of the music, the client, and of the music relationship. The first is that the music therapist has been a musician for a great deal of his or her life and has developed sensitivities and intelligences pertaining to musical expression and communication. The second reason is based upon the premise that within normal development, all people should be able to identify and reproduce rhythms and tonal arrangements with some degree of accuracy. The normal development of music cognition allows for all music listeners to make at least some degree of interpretation that relates music to mood states, levels of tension, and good gestalt qualities, such as the laws of proximity and good continuation. All listeners are generally capable of identifying some culturally congruent connotations in music. These sophisticated cognitive processes are so well ingrained in humans, beginning in utero, that music cognition seems to be preserved even in the presence of cortical dementia. This ability of the music therapist to perceive and understand affective, cognitive, and interpersonal nuances within a musical interaction can integrate with the therapist's psychological mindedness, personal history, and clinical education/supervision to produce some ability to form hypotheses (through a process of interpretation) about possible relationships between a client's musical behavior, his or her internal world, and extramusical life. The therapist uses interpretations as one of the determining factors in making clinical decisions. As illustrated in the following case example, my use of musical and verbal interpretations served as a guide through which I developed clinical hypotheses. My interpretations develop into increasingly more specified questions. The interpretations do not become set facts.

In the case which follows, I will demonstrate how a psychodynamically-informed model of music therapy allowed for the client to experience developmental growth, thus limiting the level and effect of depression in his life.

BACKGROUND INFORMATION

The client, Rick, was a thirty-three-year-old man with one older male sibling. He experienced a normal birth and the early developmental years were, according to Rick, normal, in terms of physical, cognitive, and social development, although it was difficult to get a report on his emotional development. There were no reported events of physical or psychological trauma. Other than a brief psychiatric hospitalization for depression, his medical history seemed to be unremarkable. Shortly after the beginning of treatment, he informed me that he had been involved in treatment with various alternative medical specialists for a variety of medical issues involving his back, stomach problems, and a spastic colon. His mother and father were alive at the time of therapy. He lived with his dog in a house that he owned.

Education

In high school he was an average student where he reportedly developed the role of the "jokester." Following graduation, he attended two years at a community college where he began to use marijuana, but no other drugs. He denied the current use of drugs.

Current Occupation

He worked for his parents' floral business, mostly as a driver, transferring materials between stores and making deliveries. His older brother served as his boss and seemed to have all of the success between the siblings. They had a very uncomfortable relationship. The older brother seemed to view Rick as not being serious enough with the family business, while Rick believed that the older brother was overzealous, too driven, and competitive. Rick was certainly no match for his brother in terms of gaining parental approval in relation to the family business. Rick was not able to commit to the business with the intensity of his brother, yet was unable to consider alternatives for an occupation. During treatment he described a wish to be able to make a living from his music in some way, as in being able to bring people together through music-making. I thought of this as indicating, to some degree, a positive transference.

Eventually, during the later stages of treatment, he was able to develop group music-making into a much larger part of his life, often as a facilitator of drum circles and other musical gatherings. He was also later able to develop as a professional accompanist for dance groups.

Musical Experiences and Interests

Rick was interested in playing music and was a self-taught percussionist. He enjoyed hand drums and slit drum, but stated that he had a hard time playing with others. Although he had no formal training, Rick possessed a fairly sophisticated level of musical ability. Over several years, he had acquired a vast collection of African and Middle Eastern percussion instruments. He spent many years playing hand drums and regularly sought out opportunities to play music with others in various forms of drum circles and jam sessions, usually related to variants of what may be called "world beat" styles (combinations of non-Western and Western musical styles). He never joined with other musicians in a band, which would develop repertoire and work toward giving performances, although this was one of his wishes. He regularly attended a weekly community improvisational dance at a dance studio. This was his primary social exposure and most of his acquaintances were met through this setting. Rick's role was a drummer, as part of the musicians who played music for the improvisational dancers, although occasionally he would also join the group dance. The leader of the music group was a man who Rick described as a rather powerful, authoritative leader. Often the group's musical direction was chosen and directed by the leader. Rick's role in the music seemed peripheral in that he seemed to be allowed to play along with the musicians. He usually played African drums. Rhythmically, Rick would choose to play complex subdivisions of the basic pulse of the music, using sixteenth and thirty-second notes. These subdivisions would be broken down into repeating patterns with subtle changes in accent and grouping. There was very little use of rest or sustain, in that all temporal space was filled with fast subdivisions, regardless of the tempo.

Prior Psychological Treatment

He reported entering into mental health therapy on ten different occasions, each time at the suggestion of his rejecting and "domineering mother" and his brother's wife, with whom he did not get along. He reported that his prior therapy experiences included group therapy, bioenergetics, gestalt therapy, and cognitive therapy. He was currently seeing a therapist for transitional analysis for four weeks prior to our initial meeting, lasting for a few months. He reported that the longest he remained in any therapy was for four to five months. He reported one psychiatric hospitalization, four to five years ago, for depression, following the break up with a girlfriend. He stated that his depression began at around the age of twenty, at the end of another relationship. His current interest in receiving music therapy began when his former girlfriend entered an expressive therapies education program and began to describe to him connections that she was able to make between her dreams and her artwork. Since that time, he again experienced a loss when she ended the relationship and he again felt more depressed. He stated that "the end of that relationship helped me to see." Although I was not sure what he meant by this, and he did not elaborate, I generally understood this statement, and his entering into therapy with me, a music therapist, as his seeking a means to elaborate upon his internally activated quest or "vision" to stop this repetition of failed relationships.

Clinical Impression

Interpersonally, Rick seemed to be preoccupied with his problems and with his negative self-appraisals that he described as "the knives I throw at myself." The experience of growing up with an emotionally unavailable parent can result in the child, and later the adult, developing a complementary model of the self as unlovable, and as the other to be unloving (Bretherton, in Dozier, Stovall & Albus, 1999). Although he longed to be a part of a community, to have a relationship, and to have a meaningful occupation, he regularly distanced himself from any situation that would require ongoing responsibilities and he generally avoided conformity.

Rick had an odd way of initially relating when standing face-to-face with another person. He would appear to have a questioning, slightly disoriented facial expression. He seemed as if he was awaiting instructions. He reported that when he met someone, typically a woman, he would at first see the experience as an opportunity to guess what type of man the woman would like him to be. This would lead to ruminations and staging of affected personality traits in an attempt at impressing the woman. He reported that he was regularly criticized for not showing an awareness of others. This was a frequent complaint of the women with whom he had attempted to develop relationships.

Clinically, Rick's symptoms and complaints seemed to fit the description of dysthymic disorder (formerly referred to as neurotic depression). This disorder is defined by Cameron and Rychlak (1985) as a mood disturbance in which "tension and anxiety are expressed in the form of dejection and self-depreciation, somatic disturbance, and repetitive complaints of feeling inferior, hopeless and worthless" (p. 296). Using diagnostic categories from the *Diagnostic and Statistical Manual IV*, dysthymic disorder seemed to describe

Rick's history and current state, in that his depressed mood seemed to be more often present than not for at least two years, accompanied by difficulty in making decisions, low self-esteem, and frequent complaints of fatigue, low interest, and consistent self-criticism. There was no history reported of manic episodes or any other psychotic episodes. The mood disorder contributed to a distorted self-perception and to his ongoing interpersonal problems. His symptoms did not meet the criteria for major depressive disorder. In the description of a person who experiences Dysthymic Disorder, Cameron and Rychlak (1985) described many of the maladaptive outcomes that were reported or presented by Rick. His continual need for "reassurance and his complaining is the chief defense against the internal assaults of his destructive superego attacks" (p. 297). He regularly "reaffirms his dejection and self-depreciation, which in turn encourages others to try more assurance and counterclaims" (p. 297). Considering the length of time that Rick experienced his symptoms, and the similarities of his symptoms to the known clinical descriptions of dysthymic disorder, I approached his clinical problems with this diagnostic category in mind. Rick was not under the care of a psychiatrist and his prior psychiatric medical records were not available, therefore this diagnostic impression could not be confirmed. He was not taking medication for depression throughout music therapy treatment. He was receiving medical attention for a spastic colon throughout the first half of therapy.

Methods and Treatment

Music therapy treatment took place for one and one half years on a weekly one-hour basis at a university-based music therapy studio. Treatment occurred on a fairly regular basis without major disruption. Most of the sessions used clinical musical improvisation approaches. The instruments used differed over the course of treatment and serve as indicators of the phases of treatment. Initially, Rick relied upon various drums that were within the collection of the studio. Over time, he expanded his instrument use to piano, xylophone, tone bells, voice, and finally voice with drums.

Usually the sessions began with Rick entering the studio followed by a brief greeting and updating about events of the week. Following this, a musical experience would emerge from either Rick or myself in a number of ways. Rick may have been holding an instrument, quietly, half consciously, playing while talking. In this case I would encourage him to stay with, and focus upon, his musical expression. I would then choose an instrument upon which to join his music. In another session, I would choose a musical experience, including instruments for both of us, based upon what Rick verbally expressed and, to some degree, based upon what had transpired in prior sessions. In yet another bridge between discussion and music, Rick would pick an instrument without making a verbal statement about the music and begin playing. I would then choose an instrument and join in with the music.

The music served varying functions within the sessions. Most of the time it served nonreferential purposes, where the musical process had no stated specific purpose other than itself.

Therapist's Roles in the Music

During all of the musical experiences, I took various positions as accompanist, co-creator, and/or initiator, in different musical pieces or within the same piece, while maintaining my role as therapist. Sometimes, especially in the early stages of treatment, my musical presence functioned in a similar way to Bollas's description of the transformational mother, in shaping or exerting musical structure in the form of style, and in the determination of many musical elements. Other times, I provided a support by accepting whatever expression in musical sound, "spoken word," or chanted formats, emerged. Musically, I matched the energy level and "fanned the flames" of primal musical expression, or confronted/challenged Rick's various efforts and expressions directed toward the object of transference, or at the "real musician" (during late stages of therapy) who was his therapist. At times, my musical function was influenced by my imagined manifestation of what he was attempting to create through me. At other times, my role reflected where, developmentally, he needed, and seemed equipped, or capable, to go.

During our music therapy sessions we used improvisational styles that were structured by Western music styles, tonalities, and meters. We also used free, atonal improvisational models. Sometimes the music served as a backdrop of sounds for Rick's "spoken word" monologues. (This is my own loose description based upon the contemporary art form that includes nonrhyming prose dramatically recited over a musical, or sound landscaped, background.) During these times he would pace and hit a drum as an effect to emphasize a complaint regarding his current unfavorable interpersonal status. Outside of the context of the music therapy relationship, these events may be seen as a type of patient acting out, or exhibitionism. However, within our sessions, I felt that it was important for Rick's self-esteem to allow him to communicate his sense of being a part of the nonconservative, postmodern, or avant-guard, artistic community. By posing no resistance to the apparent exhibitionist qualities of Rick's "spoken word" events, we were both able to broaden the expressive range of therapy and yet maintain a therapeutic alliance. In this way, I believed that it seemed to be always understood that Rick's expressions were in some way linked to his chief complaint of his depressed mood, and his insecure, unfulfilling relationships and low self-esteem. By allowing these expressions in a musical medium, there remained the possibility that Rick would eventually hear and accept those aspects of the music which seemed to be creative, thus providing a contradiction to his "unloved and unlovable" self-image.

Rick was usually able to develop a rhythmic "groove" to the therapist-structured Western musical formats, and likewise, was able to invent, or produce, rhythmic dance music patterns on percussion when he initiated dyadic improvisations. He was very familiar and comfortable, from his past experiences with other musicians, with these ways of making music. The music portions of Rick's treatment sessions presented an opportunity that simulated a "real-life" social interaction for Rick.

This type of relationship requires the therapist to maintain a sophisticated level of music-making. In that level of musical play, I was able to allow myself to draw upon my own creativity toward the matching of the musical intensity and sophistication in Rick's playing. Hence, the three components of the therapeutic relationship, developed by Greenson and cited by Gelso and Carter (1994), were present: 1) the working alliance—the alignment or cooperation of therapist and client; 2) the transference configuration; and 3) the real relationship—the degree of genuineness between both parties to see each other in a realistic way. Each therapeutic relationship simultaneously contains some ratio of these three types of relationship. Depending on the style of therapy and the current stage of the therapeutic progress, one of these relationships will be prominent with the other two having lesser, but identifiable, roles. For example, the beginning stages of therapy will demonstrate a greater transferential, but less of a real, relationship. This balance will probably change near the ending of therapy, with a greater emphasis on the real, and less of a transferential, relationship. In the give and take of two musicians exploring musical styles, musical problems, and musical solutions together, it would seem that the real relationship would be prominent early in therapy. Also, it is both impossible, and countertherapeutic, for the music therapist to maintain distance from the music while engaging in the aesthetic and creative field of music improvisation. This inevitably invites therapist disclosure in the way one organizes the self in the music, preferences, roles, figure, and background habits, and of course, areas where there is a lacking of musical abilities. However, these issues can also heighten the transference/countertransference relationship, largely, I believe, due to the self-consciousness of the music therapist regarding musical abilities. This was the case on those occasions when I had to reach into musical resources and take musical risks that were not typical in my work with lower functioning clients. This level of playing together brought up feelings in me about the music and about the way we would play together. Staying in touch with these feelings was very important for me within my role as his therapist. It allowed for an awareness of what Rick is like in a musical relationship (or, a real relationship) both in terms of his tendency to disengage through an overuse of rhythmic subdivision and in terms of his potential to recognize his creativeness as a contributor in building a musical relationship with others. It was through this awareness of his musical and relational potentials that I hoped to move his self-appraisal from the distortions that he created and through which he lived ("the knives I throw at myself"). These types of musical experiences in therapy can blur the real with the transferential relationship. In order to maintain the necessary boundary within these relationships, it was helpful for me to remain focused upon the therapeutic alliance component of the relationship. This perspective helped to maintain an awareness of Rick's experience of our relationship. Although often our music playing was very "together," Rick was still experiencing transferential issues with me being a male authority figure. Suppressing this component of the relationship would have limited the therapeutic benefit of therapy because Rick's basic problems were manifested within his relationships.

TREATMENT

Music Assessment and Overview of the Therapy Process

The therapy progression seemed to occur over three stages, although material and processes from each stage were also observable in the other stages. The first stage included the acceptance of, and working with, Rick's persistent rhythmic subdivision on percussion instruments. I made an interpretation that this musical behavior was a compulsive defense in an attempt to bind the anxiety that he felt in interpersonal experiences. This quality of his playing, and my response, will be described in further detail later in this chapter. Sometimes I allowed him to maintain his distance with this rhythmic behavior, to let him know that it was accepted in our relationship, and other times I would musically confront him and go "toe to toe" by providing syncopations against his subdivisions in an attempt to learn how fixed Rick was with his interpersonal positioning. Also, modeling musical figure/ground roles seemed important in demonstrating other ways that we could relate musically. Even though parts of the second stage of treatment were clearly apparent in the first stage in Rick's melodic inventiveness, I felt that I had to support what I identified as Rick's rhythmic defense while encouraging his melodic exploration, which is where I heard his potential for ego flexibility. It was through Rick's explorations in creating a melodic figure in the second stage of treatment, supported by a responsive background (therapist), that he began, over time, to stand alone with confidence and with a greater sense of himself as a complete person. Musically, this seemed to occur in a developmental process whereby he began to co-create melodic phrases with me, moving toward the creating of his own melodic fragments. Then he would trade, mirror, and vary the melodic material with me. Following these melodic improvisations he seemed to experience relaxation and pleasure from the music. He verbalized that he was becoming aware of his musical role as a figure, in a figure/ground relationship, with support from the ground of musical structure, and was better able to notice and accept his creative strength. Within melodic improvisations, I encouraged his use of motive development and "breathing" between phrases. I believed that when Rick engaged in his rhythmic subdivisions that he was, in a sense, not breathing. He was not experiencing a neutral space in his music, for which a breath would allow. In this space of a musical breath, I believed that Rick could begin to increase his awareness of the musical relationships.

The second stage also brought with it Rick's interest in using piano. Although he had no prior training on piano he seemed less defended and more open for interpersonal relating on this instrument. Rick began to use the piano to develop a compositional base for our improvisations. During his piano playing, I would stay away from harmonic instruments and use drums or the tone bells in order to encourage his feeling, and experience, of control. I believed that he was ready to accept that his musical creations could be felt as the source for his felt transformations. During these pieces, Rick would occasionally give me solos. He would communicate this by dropping his volume and by removing any melody, limiting the right hand to open intervals in an accompanying style.

The third stage was a period where Rick was encouraged to use his voice for chanting and singing. This was a continuation of his using his breath for a way to maintain awareness of his musical expression, the musical field, and on my presence within that field. It was in this stage that he began to develop "his own voice" as a leader, and he began to hear himself in a more self-expressive way. Also, in this stage his depression seemed to have less of a negative effect upon his self-image. He reported that he began to establish more comfortable relationships with men and women. Within these relationships he reported less of a tendency to ruminate and was more able to focus upon the matter at hand.

The following seven subsections include specific clinical interpretations, therapist responses, and key areas of focus in the therapeutic process that describe how a psychodynamic music therapy approach was able to address Rick's depression and interpersonal problems.

Early Stages

Rick's musical productions were at first guarded, self-conscious, stifled, and relied upon rather conventional rhythm patterns. However, as what I believed were his communications to me that he was different from others, he would occasionally leap into somewhat impulsive flurries of sounds of an arrhythmic, convulsive quality. I sensed that Rick was attempting to convey to me that he was familiar with the avant-garde world of music, although I also held onto the possibility that these were impulsive discharges of his anxiety and, in a way, communicated his issues with authority. During the improvisations in this first stage, my countertransference became conscious as memories and images of my past jam sessions in my personal life, where new acquaintances would "size each other up" and briefly show off their abilities. This competitiveness was expressed by me as a self-conscious disclosure of stylistic nuances, or "licks," that I could demonstrate in a "cutting session" fashion, as seen in jazz jam sessions. This sibling rivalry countertransference reaction was important to recognize. In addition to supplying a safeguard to prevent countertransference-derived destructiveness to our relationship, awareness of these feelings became an important source of information for me about Rick's tendency to use passive-aggressive behaviors in his relationship with his brother. In that relationship, passive-aggressive expressions would provoke a competitive response by his brother, as the authority in both birth order, and as Rick's boss in their family business. Rick would withdraw from aggressive responses because it fit the defense of repetition compulsion in maintaining his low self-esteem. Our therapy together was able to progress, due in part to my consciousness of his defensive use of projective identification.

Withdrawal Behaviors in Percussion Playing

When playing music together it was soon apparent that Rick would use a very intense level of rhythmic subdivision (long passages of sixteenth and thirty-second notes), grounded by accents that had an overpowering effect in both intensity and volume. Throughout the early stages, this manner of playing was pervasive, even on melodic instruments such as xylophone or thumb piano, where Rick often used similar organizing patterns. Although Rick was able to maintain the tempo and stylistic invariants of each musical piece, his frequent emphasis upon relentless rhythmic subdivision without the use of rests would eventually become autonomous, such that two-way musical communication became very limited. These patterns developed subtle accentual or note value changes, seemingly only in relation to Rick's overall music. As mentioned earlier in this chapter, I had the awareness that this pattern may have served as a withdrawal defense. I cannot say that this musical behavior was always meant to reduce anxiety, as is the purpose of a defense, although at times it was clear to me that he could use this technique to avoid having to deal with my music. From Rick's rhythmic "subdivision phases" I could imagine being imbedded in the maternal womb, a confluence of pulse and subdivisions, no need to breathe, as in distinguishing between phrases, because it is done for you. This type of rhythmic playing was like playing along with a recording, with no expectation of a response from another person. I believed that this behavior was an attempt for Rick to be in the music without having to deal with the other party making the music, hence a resistance to therapy based upon some fear. Conversely, when I would initiate an improvisation with a slower tempo, or a style which was not associated with underlying rhythmic subdivisions as part of its rhythmic invariants, Rick, while on xylophone, could become melodic in creative, playfully inventive, and much more interactive ways. It was in his melody-making that I could hear his health, and this is also where I began to encounter further resistance as I made interpretations to him about the health I heard in his music.

In later, final stages of treatment he would focus for long periods on his own creations on piano. These events involved periods of isolated creative activity, yet these experiences had a wholly different character, in that they did not serve a withdrawal function. I felt that in these experiences Rick had a need for a witness for his play, or musical composing. This type of activity always led to dyadic music-making based upon the musical material that he was composing. Other relational differences in this area will be described later in the third stage of treatment.

Relatedness Ability

From our first session, Rick demonstrated the capacity to create melodic motifs on xylophone, and to respond to musical interaction with me on piano, in ways that did not seem defensive. This tendency would emerge on occasions when his incessant rhythmic subdivision relational style was relaxed. His ability in these areas seemed counter to the clinical description of dysthymia, in that there were no displays of low energy, low self-esteem, poor concentration, inability to make decisions, feelings of hopelessness, or other signs of impairment. At other times, his musical relational style would change and he would switch instruments randomly to create sonic nonsense, although it seemed to allow him to play in very free ways, with no set tonal or rhythmic structure. There is less opportunity, within this type of improvisation, for the music therapist to use echo, imitative, and other interactive responses. Thus, there is a possibility of a countertransference response. I had to be careful to distinguish when this musical behavior seemed to serve a defensive function of acting out, or when its function was a rejection of authority to allow for the beginning of individuation as he began to develop more of a musical identity.

Verbal Processing

Following most of the music improvisations, we would discuss what affect the music, and the music therapy experience, had on Rick. It became apparent to me that although Rick could articulate various affective states and memories, verbal processing did not serve his progress. In fact, it had a regressive effect. In these processing conversations, Rick resorted to complaints about his depression and would tend to use overly dramatic, exhibitionistic enactments of recent events in his life. In this case, these regressive behaviors, associated with the symptoms of dysthymia, served as a defense to diminish the anxiety associated with the affective descriptions of his life. Although he certainly was expressive, these affected techniques never allowed him to cross the gap between subjectivity and objectivity. He was not able to experience himself in an authentic and integrated way. I realized that one function of his behavior, during this verbal processing, related to his conflicts with authority. For no matter how well we were able to construct a positive musical relationship, Rick, in his apparent image of my role, saw me as an authority and persisted in his projections of authority anxieties. For me, these situations allowed me to experience Rick's interpersonal behavior when he was anxious. He would resort to behaving like a clown, again, in an attempt to frame an appearance of himself in terms of his interpretation of how he could be liked by the other, seemingly based upon past successes in this role. When these behaviors were not supported or encouraged by me, or when they would not result in a transformation of his state, Rick would complain about his low mood (even if the mood of his melodic music-making clearly expressed the contrary) and refute or become unable to understand how it was possible to hear, through my interpretations, any other mood in the music other than the depressed feelings he would describe. I decided to neither confront nor support these rejecting defenses.

From this awareness, it became clear to me why past experiences in verbal therapy were difficult and unsuccessful for Rick. I began to see that the music relationship could be used for him to experience his health, as long as there was no, or very little, verbal processing of the experience. It was clear that his verbal defenses served to promote his depression and complaining-fostered oral dependency. Positive verbal descriptions of the music, in terms of their health content or health potential, were dystonic and alien to Rick's sense of self. Statements by me, such as "your melodies seemed to be very invigorated and bright" were actually experienced as confrontations to his dysthymic position that "rejects, despises, and looks down upon the self" (Cameron & Rychlak, 1985, p. 301). Therefore, I had to use caution in making interpretations about his music. However, in accepting or supporting (not confronting) his syntonic verbal expressions of low self-esteem, I believed that I was allowing him a self-injurious pleasure and was partially reenacting the role of the disapproving mother. In Rick's case, my role in the music as an occasional transformational object could provide him with a stronger sense of support from which he could then explore new ways of relating through the music.

Later Stages

During the later stages, our improvisations included mostly melodic work, through bells and xylophone and finally, Rick's singing voice. These instruments allowed Rick to further his explorations into composition, using motives and phrases, which required segments separated by breaths. This contrasted with the earlier stages where Rick's use of mallets on melodic instruments was like drum sticks. His use of the xylophone was actually a reproduction of his rhythmic, subdivision defense. Therefore, the use of bells was introduced because they produced more sustain, a greater sense of space, and their use is not as conducive to the extremely fast, rhythmically subdivided manner of Rick's typical playing. This introduction of the bells was a way of confronting Rick's resistant playing. I believed his resistance expressed a fear of his newly developing ability to meaningfully relate to another. However, it was clear that his ego strength could support experimentation in this new way of relating. Simpkins (Bruscia, 1987, p. 373), in his integrative improvisation therapy, used a similar method in handling client resistance by working in a medium where resistance could not be expressed (in Rick's case, within slower melodic improvisations).

Within our second and third stages we found a way for Rick to begin, in his individuation process, to experience mastery over his felt threat from authority, and to begin to experience his true self within a relationship.

Composition on Piano

When Rick composed on the piano, it became clear to me that he was allowing more thought and affect to emerge, as if a positive presence from an internal object was allowing this experience to be fun, rewarding, and nurturing. He was able to create edits into his compositions that I understood as allowing for a degree of healthy narcissism. He began to "own" the compositions as products from his self. Thus, he was aurally experiencing a transformation derived from his actions. This capacity represented what I had earlier heard in his melodic expressions as his health. These melodies were now becoming aesthetically pleasing to him. This use of libidinal energy could serve as a guide in his having an experience in the creation of beauty. This seemed to represent the presence of a healthy, yet still partially hidden, self-esteem. He was now able to focus libidinal energy toward a true inner representation of the self. This contrasted favorably with his former method of projecting images of himself onto others in an attempt to create a socially approved self, albeit, a false self. This same process was later transferred (in the third stage) to his voice. The breath now was considered as being part of the composition, in that it set the mark for phrase endings and also allowed for a pause. I began to see that these pauses, in contrast to incessant rhythmic subdivision, were opportunities where Rick could achieve consciousness of his creations.

Vocal Compositions

By the final stages of therapy, Rick used voice for compositional purposes, creating pieces which included scat, or nonsense sounds, accompanied by a large African drum. The drum, formerly used to distance him into a peripheral role within an ensemble, was now functioning as a sustained, supporting ground that provided a temporal setting to accompany his voice. My musical involvement now allowed for shifting between figure and ground roles in the music. There was less of a focus on my providing structure in terms of musical style and instrument selection. Rick enjoyed the experimentation in using his voice in musical leadership, and he was able to incorporate my musical input.

The idea for encouraging Rick's voice to emerge followed what actually became an informal supervision with a psychologist friend. When I described Rick's tendency for intricate, closed-off rhythmic subdivision, my friend said, "It sounds like he doesn't breathe." Not only would the use of Rick's voice allow him to breathe, but also it could allow him to listen and think. He was also able to experience pleasure through discharge and through the tension and release of singing, as well as through the gestalt qualities of melodic creation. Afterward, I noticed that his use of singing in our sessions allowed for a return to a healthier level of object relations experience. While taking a breath one can at least hear what is taking place in the environment. Thus, a relationship based upon a shared reality, in this case the music, can grow. His use of voice in our sessions may have also allowed for him to sublimate, through compositional "rules," or stylistic constraints, while allowing for the use of vocal nonsense sounds. This allowed for discharge while maintaining contact with me and with a recognizable style. It was my view that Rick's choice of nonsense sounds in his musical vocal productions was a way to bridge his transformational object desires with a developmentally more successful (for him) means of musical communication. His vocal role could move him from a diffuse background role (playing along with the music) to a position where he is heard and can interact in musical reality in a more authentic way

Now that Rick's ability at musical relatedness was developing, the "transitional space" between Rick's inner world of music and the external reality of other people in the music, could be bridged. The use of musical structure in Rick's compositions could now allow for others to enter into the music with him in a variety of ways—rhythmically, melodically, or harmonically.

Changes in Personal Life

This phenomenon of relatedness was beginning to take place within Rick's social life, on weekends during musical gatherings with friends and others at private homes. Rick was later asked by members of a band to join them as a percussionist and vocalist. This became a source of pleasure, as well as a creative outlet for him. His musical life led him to additional social contacts. These contacts and relationships began to provide a source of gratification and an improved self-esteem, as seen by fewer and fewer negative self-appraisals. The closure process to our therapy was summoned by Rick telling me to play our next improvisation "like a musician, not like a therapist." My interpretation of this statement, outside of appreciating the humor contained within, was that he had grown away from needing a source outside of himself who would adapt to his needs and to his experience in the music. He was ready to coexist as peers, maybe even allow for competition to "kill off the therapist" within the music. His medical problem of a spastic colon was no longer present and his social life was showing changes similar to those that were taking place in his music therapy. He met a woman with whom he was able to relate in a less dependent manner than in past relationships. He began to entertain thoughts of leaving his family's floral business and starting his own music merchandising business.

DISCUSSION

I believe that Rick was able to benefit from a psychodynamic form of music therapy because within the musical elements and musical structure lay both his conflict and his solution. Rick's pattern of distorting relationships, and dissecting the image which he believed that others formed of him, was expressed in his musical attempts to try to fit in rhythmically with others. His attempts at doing this were accompanied by so much anxiety that he created pseudomusical interactions that actually led him into patterns of isolation within his musical ensembles, and within our improvisational duets. These may have been linked with projections of a false self in his interpersonal relationships. By concentrating upon his voice, via melodic explorations on xylophone, Rick began to discover a true musical identity that he preferred over his defensive rhythmic musical behaviors. Rick found a way over the course of therapy to emerge as a figure or, as a true identity, from within our relationship. He was able to develop trust in his musical voice, which carried over into musical and other relationships. The music therapy relationship functioned, in part, as the maternal mother who provides opportunities for the infant to acquire experience and develop an ability to grow. Also, the transferential relationship allowed Rick to experiment with ways to deal with authority, while incorporating components of the transference to allow for the emergence of his own capacities as a musical authority. This was first experienced as a melodic figure in our improvisations and later supported by the emergence of his voice as a force within a medium where he could have influence. Rick's beginnings at mastery over his anxieties within relationships, and with authority, were derived from his experiences as a musical figure that received support from my role as a therapist. The music therapy experience provided for structure building, in that it allowed Rick to incorporate successful and fulfilling aesthetic experiences and to attribute their source to his own creative ability. Opportunities for his experience of a sense of autonomy with adaptive strengths resulted from his ability to make use of the flexibility allowed for in the musical roles in therapy.

CONCLUSION

Fortunately, I was able to come into contact with Rick on more than one occasion following the conclusion of therapy. In each situation he greeted me with an embrace and a bit of an update regarding the positive elements and processes that were current in his life. It seemed that he had not completely "killed off" the therapist, yet was able to maintain the boundary that we were no longer conducting therapy. A mutual acquaintance of ours recently invited me to a sold-out musical review produced by Rick that featured several contemporary musical acts, including Rick's singing and drumming. During intermission, Rick greeted me and upon receiving my compliments for his performance and in producing the event he replied that "therapy had a lot to do with it." Although he may experience an occasional relapse of symptoms, as is the prognosis for dysthymic disorder, Rick seems to have found, and further developed, his interpersonal strengths through his music therapy experience. Although it is not known how the therapy results will affect his later life, the self-report after more than a decade from treatment closure seems positive.

REFERENCES

Bollas, C. (1987). *The Shadow of the Object: Psychoanalysis of the Unthought Known.* New York: Columbia University Press.

Bollas, C. (1989). *Forces of Destiny: Psychoanalysis and the Human Idiom.* London: Free Association Books.

Bruscia, K. E. (1987). *Improvisational Models of Music Therapy.* Springfield, IL: Charles C. Thomas Publisher.

Cameron, N., & Rychlak, F. F. (1985). *Personality Development and Psychopathology: A Dynamic Approach* (2nd ed.). Boston: Houghton Mifflin Company.

Dozier, M., Stovall, K., & Albus, K. (1999). "Attachment in Psychopathology in Adulthood." In J. Cassidy & P. R. Shaver (eds.), *Handbook of Attachment: Theory, Research and Clinical Applications*. New York, London: Guilford Press.

Gelso, C. J., & Carter, J. A. (1994). "Components of the Psychotherapy Relationship: Their Interaction and Unfolding During Treatment," *Journal of Counseling Psychology*, 41 (3), 296–306.

John, D. (1995). "The Therapeutic Relationship in Music Therapy as a Tool in the Treatment of Psychosis." In T. Wigram, B. Saperston, & R. West (eds.), *The Art & Science of Music Therapy: A Handbook*. Chur, Switzerland: Harwood Academic Publishers.

Nolan, P. (1989). "Music as a Transitional Object in the Treatment of Bulimia," *Music Therapy Perspectives*, 6, 49–51.

Nolan, P. (1994). "The Therapeutic Response in Improvisational Music Therapy: What Goes on Inside?" *Music Therapy Perspectives*, 12, 84–91.

Case Seventeen

MEETING RICH:
INDIVIDUAL MUSIC THERAPY WITH A MAN
WHO HAS SEVERE DISABILITIES

Roia Rafieyan

ABSTRACT

Rich is a man in his mid-thirties, diagnosed with autism, profound mental retardation, and a seizure disorder. Rich has been receiving object relations-oriented music therapy for the past seven years in an institutional setting. Examples from sessions will be used to describe the establishment of a working relationship with the therapist. The process through which Rich, who does not use speech, began to use instruments, vocalizations, and songs as representations and expressions of feeling states is described. Music therapy with Rich is ongoing.

INTRODUCTION

"The trouble is . . . many people have been serving people with disabilities for years and yet have never met them" (Hingsburger, 2000, p. 20). For the first six years of my work at a state developmental center I really *did not* meet any of my clients. I had assumptions about them, and I had beliefs about what they were capable of accomplishing and what I wanted them to be able to do. But it was not until I tried a different approach, one that taught me to focus on developing relationships with the men and women I served, that I really got to *meet* some of my clients for the first time—this after having worked with most of them for years. Rich was one of the first people I met.

The following comments, made by Sean Barron, a man with autism who, unlike Rich, is able to express himself verbally, were important in helping me begin to have a sense of how Rich might experience his world.

> My attention was on what I was doing at the time: 100 percent of my focus was on that. I vaguely knew my mother was around, but I wasn't really aware of her unless she did something bad to me—like yelling or stopping me from doing what I wanted. She was not important (Barron & Barron, 1992, p. 21).

Meeting Rich would have to start with an awareness that he did not see or experience the world as I saw or experienced it.

Psychodynamic music therapy invites changes and an increased level of self-awareness not only in the client, but also in the therapist. It asks us, as therapists, to begin to question our assumptions, to really listen to what our clients are presenting to us, and to meet them, over and over again, musically and in dialogues and to make connections through those meetings.

BACKGROUND INFORMATION

Rich can be described as "determined." He is a man who, at thirt-seven, has had a number of labels tagged on him, numerous hospitalizations (since he was a baby), and who has grown up within the confines of various institutions. Rich and I met in 1994 when I began to see him for individual music therapy sessions in the state institution where I work and where he lives. Among his many labels, Rich has been diagnosed as having autism, profound mental retardation, a seizure disorder and, most recently, a hypoactive thyroid and hypothermia. My first impression of him, one that has stayed with me, was that he was "quite bright." Perhaps it was the way he kept a peripheral eye on me as I presented him with different instruments during those early sessions, with him wheeling himself just out of reach in his wheelchair. Perhaps it was the definite "f--- you" which he managed to hum at me, with great inflection and tone even though he does not use words to communicate, when I asked him to refrain from eating a piece of dust off the floor. A look behind his eyes gave me the distinct impression of something going on apart from his developmental disabilities and his medical hindrances.

In order to learn more about Rich, I went to the hospital basement where the older records are kept. I gathered from the cottage logs that he had not received visits from his family very often, if ever. The records that were in storage gave me a little more information about his family and how he had come to live at the developmental center. Although the details were somewhat sketchy, a picture emerged as I read.

Rich was born, prematurely, in 1965. He was the youngest of five children, with three sisters and one brother. His mother had a tenth-grade education, and his father had completed high school. They lived in a rural area of the state and, from the beginning, he was very hyperactive and destructive; chewing on furniture and the wood on the windowsills, and falling down stairs because he would not stay in bed at night. He began having seizures when he was nine months old and was hospitalized at eleven months because he stopped breathing after a series of seizures. He spent quite a bit of time in hospitals for various reasons, including periodic emergency visits to stitch up injuries from his many falls (he apparently enjoyed climbing up on everything and, due to his unsteadiness, tended to topple). Rich was not able to talk, and he walked with a staggering gait, but this never decreased his almost constant activity. His mother noted that he needed to be watched carefully lest he have a seizure or injure himself.

Overwhelmed by the pressures and fears of caring for him, his family decided to seek institutional placement for Rich when he was three years old. After staying in the nursery unit of a state training school for almost a year, he moved to a similar residential facility in a neighboring state in 1969. The notes from this institution indicate that Rich's medical needs were a challenge to them, as they had been to his family, and they recommended he be sent to a different placement. In 1971 he arrived at a new developmental center where he has lived ever since.

He arrived in the hospital unit (where all new admissions were sent) with notes that described him in terse terms: "deaf mute; underweight; congenital heart disease; hyperreflexia; toe-walker; spastic paraplegia; wears a helmet; seizures; no speech; destructive of toys; continually pokes self in face; drools a great deal; receptive language—none; expressive language—groaning." He was excluded from the education program. Furthermore, they felt that he could not benefit from speech therapy, but felt that he should receive language stimulation "in the hope that he may develop a need to relate and respond to people." He seemed to adjust to institutional life and was seen as being "manageable and cooperative" until he went through an "aggressive" period in 1973 (although no reason is noted). An entry in the log stated: "Rich is included in the teacher-consult program; however, he remains in the crib cage most of the time." The "crib cage" is exactly what it sounds like, a crib with metal bars and a top that looks like a cage. He was prescribed several powerful medications at this time: phenobarbital, Tegretol, Thorazine, and Valium.

Over the years, he was noted to have very serious pica tendencies (pica is a condition in which people ingest inedible items), to be self-abusive (biting his hands until they bled), and, while he was aware of his surroundings, he showed "poor interest in staff and peers." Various sources described him as someone who liked music, but did not handle rhythm instruments, and as preferring to "play by himself with toys he slams around." Rich's temperament was described as "irritable and stubborn" and he was "not sociable." The cottage logs noted that he: "bites," "is self-destructive," "damages property," "must be dressed and bathed," "is incontinent," "is unresponsive to conversation," and "receives no visitors." Through it all, he has continued to spend time in hospitals for various conditions, including recurring bouts of pneumonia, viral syndromes, and intractable seizures.

When I first met Rich, he wore a "crash" helmet most of the time because he sustained frequent injuries from falls. He loved action and exploring; he often incurred injury due to sudden-onset seizures, and also got hurt while running in his living area. The crash helmet had a metal cage in front of his face and a soft cushiony back to reduce head trauma from the frequent falls.

Psychologists had been trying to develop a behavior modification program to stop his pica behavior since 1980. His program in 1994 appeared to be somewhat successful, providing him with an opportunity to chew on various "safe" items (such as large, hard rubber rings). These items were used to "reward" him when he completed a task and given to him as something to do when he was not wearing a helmet. A containment helmet was applied when he made attempts to eat inedible items. This "pica" helmet completely covered his face with a hard clear plastic bubble with little air holes.

One of the program staff noted that receiving individualized attention seemed to have the occasional effect of reducing Rich's pica attempts. This fact, coupled with his apparent lack of interest in most social interactions and a seemingly inward focus, encouraged me to offer him the opportunity to take part in individual music therapy sessions.

METHODOLOGY AND TECHNIQUES

An object relations approach to music therapy establishes the relationship between the music therapist and the patient as the guiding force (J. Dvorkin, personal communication, August 8, 2001). My goal at all times was to learn about Rich through his use of the instruments and the music, to increase my understanding of how he experienced his life, how he experienced his relationship with me, and how he coped with what life had to offer him. Dvorkin notes: "The unique contribution of music in this overall process is to provide a concrete external expression of the client" (1982, p. 54).

Assessment was an ongoing process, and I was constantly trying to learn more about Rich and assimilating information into a clearer picture of who he was, through his interactions with me and with the music. Cashdan elaborates the basis for the importance of the relationship in this type of an approach:

> Of the various relationships that make up the human drama, perhaps the most important is the relationship with an early caretaker. . . . In most instances, this early caretaking relationship is with the mother. Because this relationship occupies so much of the early life of the child and because it is so tied up with emotional gratification (and deprivation), object relationists believe it forms a template for all subsequent relationships (1988, p. 23).

It can be seen, then, that the therapy relationship becomes a reproduction of the client's earliest relationships. As the therapist and client reflect on their current relationship, and the meanings that the client has attributed to it, the process of growth through self-awareness can begin.

My initial assessment questions were along the lines of: Would he relate to me? Who was he musically? What did "normal" look like for him? What did "upset" or "happy" or "frightened" look and sound like for Rich?

Two important tools used in a psychodynamic approach are reflection and interpretation. In Rich's case, reflection involved singing about what he was doing, letting him know that I was listening to him, that I was curious about him, that we were going to be using music to communicate in this space, and that I was going to be commenting on what I was learning about him. It also served as a way to model how he might begin to use music to communicate with me and to express himself. Interpretation involved speculating as to what his behaviors and sounds meant. This was intended to help him to attach meanings and words to his feelings, actions, and expressions. As I reflected and interpreted, I paid particular attention to patterns in his actions and sounds. I was also trying to help him make connections between the actions he chose and his past and present experiences. Reflection and interpretation served to build an empathic relationship with Rich, one through which he could begin to understand himself and his relationships with others, in much the same way as that of a parent-child relationship.

In order to learn more about Rich's early relationships, it was important to have some sense of Rich's history. A detailed description of Rich's life provided some insight as to his role in his family (and subsequently in the institution) and gave me information as to how others may have perceived him. The descriptions I had read about him indicated that he had lived a somewhat isolated and lonely life, corrected frequently and subjected to numerous, and often invasive, means of keeping him safe. In addition, I felt that his history might provide a glimpse into his sense of himself, based on his interactions (or apparent lack thereof) with the people in his life. A further reason for gathering historical information was so that I could make educated guesses as to what might be going on for Rich—linking his present to his past. Stephens (1981) gives a succinct description of the process:

> The music therapy session is a microcosm of the client's whole experience. Every aspect reveals something about the way she experiences and copes with the world: the way she relates to the room, to me, and to her music; her movement and breathing (p. 26).

I generally used improvised music in our sessions. These improvisations were based on an effort to connect Rich's actions, sounds, moods, and choices to words or specific musical sounds which could then carry specific meanings and lead to a shared means of communication. In this way, I took on, as therapist, the role of the "good enough mother," helping Rich to put sounds to feelings and to contain strong affective experiences.

In addition to improvised music, I found it helpful to include specific pre-composed songs, and some songs that I had written, at various points in the process of the therapy. These songs were used to assist Rich in expressing feelings within the context of a greater musical structure as well as to associate certain feelings (such as sadness, pleasure, and loss) with specific music. This is described in greater detail in a later section.

TREATMENT

"Nice to Meet You"

> "It is surprising how smart people become once we find ways to understand what they really mean!" (Lovett, 1996, p. 18).

Rich came with me tentatively for our first session, which was conducted in a dorm room (a bedroom) in his cottage. I had brought in two chairs and set out instruments which, given his severe reputation with regard to pica, I thought might be safe for him to handle. There were two hand drums (a larger and a smaller one), a tambourine, and a maraca. A staff person, with whom he was familiar, walked him over. It was the only session in which Rich did not use his wheelchair. I was later told that he liked whizzing around in his wheelchair, and that he might be more willing to accompany a stranger (like myself) if invited to use his chair. Using his chair also had the advantage of allowing him to be helmet-free for the session, giving Rich a chance to see more of what was going on around him.

First Impressions

The first thing I noticed about him was his almost constant teeth grinding. He actually was quite adept at it, using a variety of rhythms and dynamics. He picked up a maraca, crashed it around on the floor and headed for the window, bringing the maraca with him. I walked over to the window and sang a greeting to him, accompanying myself on guitar. He looked at me briefly and made a humming sound, which was in tune with me, and then quickly turned his attention back to the window. I continued to play, singing about his actions, extending the melody of the greeting song, and inviting him to use the maraca to play about what he was watching out the window. He gave it a very brief shake.

Rich barely acknowledged me visually, but it was pretty clear that he was listening. He settled on one of the beds in the room. When I asked him to shake the maraca to say "yes" if it was okay to sit near him, he did so without hesitation. Every so often Rich would pause, lean his head back somewhat, and hold his breath, letting it out at the very ends of his lung capacity, almost toppling over in the effort. His staff had told me that on a "good" day he might end up having a seizure as a result of this breath-holding, so I anxiously tapped his shoulder, hoping he would come back to the moment. An object relations approach encourages the analysis of the therapist's countertransference responses as a means through which the therapist might develop an understanding of the client's internal experiences in therapy. The therapist may be reacting on an unconscious level to projective identification or unwittingly participating in the client's unconscious reenactment of a traumatic event. In this case, I wondered if the anxiety that I was feeling in response to Rich might have something to do with anxiety he may have been experiencing with me.

"Is This Meeting Over . . .?"

Rich lay back on a bed, and he began to close his eyes as if he were dropping off to sleep. Sensing we might have reached the limits of his tolerance for interaction, but thinking that perhaps he needed a change of scenery, I tried to get him to come and sit in a chair. Having no luck, I reflected, by singing, on what he was doing in the session, taking guesses as to why he might be looking as if he were about to fall asleep. Still trying to get a sense of Rich, I presented him with some of my hypotheses, which were based on the countertransferential reactions I was having in the session, as well as on what I was seeing in his behavior. I wondered aloud in the music: Perhaps he was feeling anxious? Bored? Tired? When I changed the style of music that I was playing on the guitar (from a somewhat minor-based sound to the blues), Rich opened his eyes. This was short-lived, because he went back to his "snooze" mode, and after a while I managed to catch him in between blinks and offered him the drum, showing him how to tap it with his hand. He seemed willing to try this instrument, grabbing it and moving himself to the floor and out of my reach. He turned the drum over a number of times and examined it.

Rich went back to having his eyes closed, and I suggested that if he was too tired to continue I would be happy to take him back to his living area so he could rest. He did not take me up on the offer. I alternated between singing/playing about what he was doing and trying to get him up and in a chair. Being inexperienced at psychodynamic music therapy, I was still struggling to overcome my need for a session "agenda."

Endings

When it was time to go, I sang "Good-bye," recounting the ways I had seen him work to communicate with me. He seemed to be listening as I sang, because he decreased his teeth-grinding so that he could hear me and he was watching the guitar. When I offered him the opportunity to play the guitar, he turned away and would not touch the instrument.

When I finished the song, I offered him a hand to stand up (he had spent the rest of the session sitting on the floor). He would not budge. In fact, he did not budge for quite a while. I wondered if he did not understand that it was time to go, so I tried to involve him in helping me pack the instruments onto my cart.

He responded by leaning forward and seemed to want me to rub his back. I then opened the door to the room (this, I had learned, was often a good way to let people who had been conditioned to the schedules and ways of institutions know that the session was over by giving a visual cue that could be translated as "it's time to go now"). This having failed, I resorted to the probably less helpful, and definitely more confrontational, tactic of tugging and pulling at him. I was feeling somewhat panicked, because I was not sure how safe it was to leave a person—who, left to his own devices, would eat his own clothing—alone in the room while I went down the hall to ask for help. Rich finally got up and came with me, and we made it back to his living area. Once there, he promptly dashed over to the window, and I got the distinct impression that I ceased to exist for him.

What Is It about Him?

So went the first meeting with Rich. I contemplated what I had learned about this man. I wondered how I might begin to understand Rich from our initial interactions. He apparently could discern between people he knew and people he did not know—that was important. He could hum a note which was in tune with the key I played (and seemed willing to do so without any effort on my part); he gave the impression that he understood what it meant to "use the maraca," even though shaking this instrument did not seem to be his usual style. He did not seem to understand how to use the drums, as he tended to flip them rather than actually making any musical use of them. Developmentally, his music was at about an eight-month-old level.

Overall, the objects in the room and the windowsill seemed to hold more appeal to him than interacting with me. The exception to this was the fact that he could tell the difference between conversational/reflective singing and actually singing a song, responding with a more obvious form of attention when I sang "Good-bye" than when I was simply "commenting," musically, on his actions.

I was curious about his reaction to the guitar—especially since I was conscious of the fact that the guitar was attached to me by a strap. He had expressed an interest in the instrument but had been clear in his unwillingness to touch or explore it. I also considered my *own* feeling of "ceasing to exist" for Rich when our session ended. How might that connect to his experiences with his family? Did he feel he ceased to exist for them when he moved to an institution and never saw them again? Or was this more of a developmental issue and a lack of a sense of object constancy?

Oddly, for all of the warnings I received about Rich's constant need to put things in his mouth, it had not been much of an issue during this session. Maybe the person who thought individual time was helpful to Rich in terms of reducing his pica attempts was right. Of further interest was that, although he was feigning sleep through parts of the session, he showed no desire to leave at the end of our time. Perhaps transitions were a challenge for him. Perhaps he was curious, in spite of his apparent trepidation, or even surprised by the fact that I had used music in my approach. I recalled a scene described by Sean Barron:

> Once [the doctor] got down on the floor beside me—I was very shocked that he would do such a thing. I still don't know what he was doing. I was so surprised by his action that I remember actually looking at him (Barron & Barron, 1992, p. 40).

It was likely that this method of interacting with him was radically different from his usual intervention experiences. Certainly most of these did not involve "interacting with" as much as "doing to" him. And what of my feeling of panic when he refused to leave at the end of the session? What information might that feeling be giving me about Rich's internal experience of leaving?

Getting to Know Rich

I referred to Sean Barron again as I tried to understand Rich from his perspective:

> People bothered me. I did not know what they were for or what they would do to me. They were not always the same and I had no security with them at all. Even a person who was always nice to me might be different sometimes. Things did not fit together to me with people. Even when I saw them a lot, they were still in pieces, and I couldn't connect them to anything (Barron and Barron, 1992, pp. 20–21).

I wanted to get a baseline of how Rich ordinarily functioned, and in order to do that I tried to establish a sense of consistency: in our sessions, in my verbal and musical responses to him, and in my expectations. Another way of describing this period of our work is to say that I was working toward establishing myself as a constant object. As Cohen and Sherwood note:

> Constancy can be seen as a kind of emotional home base from which children may venture forth to confront the larger world. Object constancy stabilizes this enlarged world through the illusion that a familiar presence sees, defines, and validates the child's strivings and feelings. This illusion serves as an emotional bridge for children: They may travel forward to explore and be challenged by the unknown, or return for a time-out from the strains of reconciling the

familiar and the strange, the hopes and disappointments, the loving and the hating (Cohen and Sherwood, 1991, p. 13).

Object constancy, according to Mahler, Pine, and Bergman (1975), "does not seem to occur before the third year" (p. 110). Given Rich's slow development and his various sensory and neurological challenges, the fact that he left his family at three years of age, that he had experienced numerous changes in caregivers and living situations, and that he was, at twenty-nine (when I first met him), functioning at the level of an eight-month-old socially and emotionally, it was safe to hypothesize that constancy had yet to be established. By creating a space where Rich could feel safe, by mirroring him, by offering a stable environment in which he could explore and express his feelings, I attempted to lay a foundation on which I could provide an organizing presence.

Meeting Rich's Past

In an effort to maintain a sense of constancy, I saw Rich once a week for approximately forty-five minutes, at the same time and in the same place. I found it helpful to record my observations and thoughts about our sessions so that I could see a progression over time. This way I could gain a greater sense of Rich and how he organized himself. I could also begin to notice various patterns and to increase my awareness of which aspects of our relationship may have triggered certain responses on his part. It was through these observations and interactions that I began to get a sense of the emerging transference.

> From a psychoanalytic perspective, transference occurs when the client, during the process of exploring the inner content of the psyche through free association (and in the music therapy context, through improvisation, spontaneous song-writing, etc.) begins to ascribe infantile attitudes and feelings to the analyst. These attitudes and feelings usually reflect conflictual strivings of instinctual impulses related to the client's early relationships with parental figures (Montello, 1992, p. 6).

Rich's experiences with his early caregivers were characterized by inconsistency, loss, and abandonment. As noted previously, his family and support staff responded to him with a mixture of anxiety, confusion, and invasion. I had to assume that this was a response he expected from me (and from most people he encountered), and one that he would unconsciously seek to elicit in me through various reenactments. An example of this dynamic could be seen in our very first session, in which I discovered Rich's unwillingness to leave at the end our time together. As noted previously, my immediate countertransferential response was some confusion ("Does he understand me?"), which advanced to panic ("I cannot leave him here alone and get help"), which then led to my behaving in an intrusive manner and pulling at him.

Communicating in So Many Ways

In our sessions, a pattern of withdrawal in response to emotional connection emerged almost immediately. Rich usually entered the music therapy session with a great deal of energy; however, this energy seemed to dissipate after a few minutes, and he often ended up falling asleep shortly thereafter. This habit was particularly noted when I tried to engage him for any sustained period of time (in this case, for longer than it took for me to musically greet him and for him to have moved some instruments around). Several possible reasons, such as feeling tired from his seizure medications and the time of day our sessions were conducted (which was right after lunch), were ruled out. As such, it appeared that this behavior was an unconscious means that he used to defend himself against overwhelming feelings of anxiety with regard to engagement and emotional closeness. The falling asleep took on the appearance of a general state of withdrawal, which he expressed by frequently holding his breath, looking out the window for long periods of time, or simply by "tuning out" with his eyes closed.

I musically and verbally acknowledged his need to withdraw during sessions, and I interpreted the behavior by making suggestions about how his retreating might be serving him: Perhaps he had a fear of being abandoned or a belief that I would hurt him. It seemed that, once Rich had a general idea of who I was, what I was doing, and how I was responding to him, his willingness to reach out and be present in the sessions increased.

Rich began to demonstrate a sense of curiosity about me—turning from his frequent perch at the windowsill to see which instrument I was going to play next, or what my shuffling around was about. At times, Rich was playful, pulling at me, trying to wrap his arms around my head to give me a hug, alternating this with trying to get me to scratch his back or give him a head rub. At other times, he was sullen and sleepy, spending the duration of the session by the windowsill. This later variation on the withdrawal aspect of Rich's transference to me was expressed in his moving closer to me and then moving away in some manner. The moving away was enacted by actually moving himself physically away from me during the session, refusing to attend sessions at all, or attending sessions and increasing his level of nonmusical activity, specifically by attempting to ingest various items in the room, or by flatly ignoring me.

The transference was also expressed in his use of instruments. While he was unable at this time to organize himself to the point of actually playing instruments, he seemed interested in them and made frequent use of them during the sessions. We stayed for quite a while with the hand drums and the sturdy tambourine, avoiding the maraca because he tended to jam the handle into his mouth. Rich often picked up the instruments that I laid out for him on his way into the room. He would carry them with him over to the windowsill, and when he got there he lined up the drums and tambourine in various ways, going over to each and flipping it over or adjusting the spacing in between the objects.

I began to notice that Rich seemed to change the spacing between the instruments, particularly the larger and smaller hand drums, depending on the type and quality of interaction we happened to be having that day. For example, during a period of time in the session when he spent a lot of time interacting with me, the drums were placed closer together. If he was frustrated with me, it was not unusual for him to move the drums far apart from each other. He often rearranged the drums numerous times during the session, sometimes carrying one or the other, or both, on his lap.

On one particular occasion, he was moving the drums into various positions on the windowsill. I observed this and I wondered aloud which drum might be representing Rich. With that, Rich ceased all interaction with the drums for the greater part of the remainder of the session. Interestingly, he had a great deal of difficulty leaving that session and with returning the larger of the two drums.

When I tried to engage Rich musically, by picking up one of the instruments he had placed on the windowsill, he would snatch the instruments away from me and hold them just out of my reach. It seemed important to him to have a sense of control, to know what to expect and when. It was not until approximately two years after we began our work together that Rich began to leave an "unattended" drum, for me to play, on a bed. At first, the length of time he would allow for me to play the drum was very short, and he came quickly to retrieve the instrument from me. As his trust in me increased, he "allowed" me to play for longer periods. During these occasions, he watched me as I played the drum, and he listened as I sang about his apparent willingness to share this instrument that he seemed to hold so tightly and carefully out of my reach most of the time (much in the same way that he held himself far out of my reach emotionally).

The teeth-grinding had decreased and was used in a more "conversational" manner (rather than as a tuning-out device that he seemed to have employed earlier in the therapy process). His habit of holding his breath continued; however, it was now a signal to me that something was going on for Rich, and he needed me to look into what it might be.

Leaving sessions was never an easy task. He often refused to return instruments and pulled away in his wheelchair when I let him know it was time to leave. Preparing him by giving him five- and ten-minute warnings did not seem to do anything to ease the difficulty he experienced with the endings of sessions. It was also not unusual for him to refuse to attend a session or two after I had been on vacation. Initially, he was unable to express feelings with regard to my absence and would resort to withdrawal (in Rich's case this was usually by falling asleep). He alternated the withdrawn behavior with teasing in a somewhat sadistic manner (i.e., repeatedly putting instruments into his mouth and watching me for my reaction or holding instruments just out of my reach).

I wanted to offer him a means through which he could begin to identify and explore the feelings he seemed to be having about my vacations. I began to reflect his apparent distress in song when I saw that there was a change in his behavior in response to my announcing a break in our sessions. A song which Rich responded to most frequently was "Do You Have to Go?" (a song I had written). Some of the words to the song are:

Do you have to go? You know how I hate this part—
You know how I cherish the times we spend together
Why so soon? It seems like we just started—
I swear it was just moments since we said "hello."
Do you see how it matters to me that you be here?
Will you remember to come and see me again?
I wish I could be with you always and forever . . .
Don't forget me when you go. (Rafieyan, copyright, 1999)

At first Rich stopped his actions and listened to me quietly as I sang. Gradually he began to reach out and strum the guitar, occasionally even making eye contact as he played. It was in this way that he was able to begin to express his sadness, anger, ambivalence, and even outrage toward me and toward the abandonment he was feeling. My acceptance and encouragement of his feelings enabled him to begin to develop a greater sense of the consistency in our relationship. He also began to feel safer exploring and expressing feelings within the context of the session.

Where Is He Now?

Today, Rich is living in a cottage (along with thirty-one other men) that is geared specifically toward men who require significant pica precautions. He still uses the "pica helmet" on occasion, but much less frequently. He uses a wheelchair, which he is quite adept at maneuvering, so he does not need to wear the crash helmet as much as he had to in the past.

He continues to receive individual music therapy services, and he is now also a member of a music therapy group. In contrast to being seen as antisocial and unresponsive, he is now an eager participant, and he seems to enjoy playfully teasing his housemates and taking part in group music improvisations. He has given in to his curiosity about the guitar and learned how to strum carefully, stopping himself from pulling on the strings. He also has begun to use the maraca and cabassa purposefully, actually pausing and watching me, as he begins to shake or move the beads on these instruments in order to take part in a musical interaction.

Rich was acknowledged; his feelings were acknowledged; his music was heard; and through the music he was given a way to reciprocate. In other words, he had the experience of being met, musically and emotionally. Rich demonstrated tremendous growth developmentally and socially when, at an outdoor concert a year or two ago, he met a new person. The man offered him his hand in greeting, and Rich carefully, looking up and smiling, lifted his hand in response.

DISCUSSION AND CONCLUSIONS

Much of our work focused on the process of developing the therapy relationship and, through this, a sense of object constancy. Consistency was naturally an important aspect of this process. For example, sessions were held every week at a particular time, in a particular place, and for a specific duration. I prepared Rich when I was going to be away (and also let him know when I would be back) and encouraged his responses. My regular use of reflection and interpretation served as a means through which Rich and I could explore and deepen the therapy relationship.

The changes in Rich were subtle, and they occurred over a long period of time. His gradual growth took place within the context of the therapy relationship and through the transference that emerged as he related to me. As noted, Rich's initial contacts with me were characterized by curiosity as well as a great deal of caution. He had developed a defensive style that included frequent use of withdrawal. I interpreted this relational style within the context of his familial relationship history. I reflected the ambivalence with which Rich interacted with me, linking it to his apparent desire to connect with me, coupled with his fear of my abandoning him. The process of working through these feelings is ongoing. Rich, as noted above, is now able to take a more active role in that he is more apt to use the music and be responsive instead of falling asleep or refusing to attend the session altogether.

A major source of information with regard to Rich's internal experience of the sessions was my countertransference reactions. I took note of my emotional responses, questioning myself, wondering if I might in some way be enacting Rich's disowned feelings through projective identification.

The role of the music and the instruments was varied. As Rich began to make use of the organizing aspects of music therapy (especially the consistency), his musical sounds became more organized (i.e., strumming the guitar for the duration of a verse instead of avoiding the instrument), the use of the instruments became more purposeful rather than random, and there was a greater interactive quality to his music. It might even be said that he was less likely to abandon the musical expressions of his internal states as he began to feel held within the music therapy session by the therapist.

REFERENCES

Barron, J., & Barron, S. (1992). *There's a Boy in Here.* New York: Simon & Schuster.

Cashdan, S. (1988). *Object Relations Therapy: Using the Relationship.* New York: W. W. Norton.

Cohen, C. P., & Sherwood, V. R. (1991). *Becoming a Constant Object in Psychotherapy with the Borderline Patient.* Northvale, NJ: Jason Aronson.

Dvorkin, J. (1982). "Piano Improvisation: A Therapeutic Tool in Acceptance and Resolution of Emotions in a Schizo-Affective Personality," *Music Therapy,* 2 (1), 53–62.

Dvorkin, J. (2001). Personal communication, August 8.

Hingsburger, D. (2000). *First Contact: Charting Inner Space (Thoughts about Establishing Contact with People who have Significant Developmental Disabilities).* Quebec: Diverse City Press Inc.

Lovett, H. (1996). *Learning to Listen: Positive Approaches and People with Difficult Behavior.* Baltimore: Paul H. Brookes.

Mahler, M. S., Pine, F., & Bergman, A. (1975). *The Psychological Birth of the Human Infant: Symbiosis and Individuation.* New York: Basic Books.

Montello, L. (1992). "Transference in the Music Therapy Relationship." In *Proceedings Booklet: Body, Mind, Spirit: AAMT Coming of Age* (pp. 6–12). American Association for Music Therapy.

Rafieyan, R. (1999). "Don't Forget Me When You Go." On *Songs From Behind Locked Doors* [CD]. Kingston, NJ: DTC Records.

Stephens, G. (1981). "Adele: A Study in Silence," *Music Therapy,* 1 (1), 25–31.

Case Eighteen

HARMONY AND DISSONANCE IN CONFLICT: PSYCHOANALYTICALLY INFORMED MUSIC THERAPY WITH A PSYCHOSOMATIC PATIENT

Mechtild Jahn-Langenberg

ABSTRACT

In this case study, the descriptions of four sessions in an individual music therapy treatment are presented. The treatment is integrated into the setting of a psychosomatic clinic. The core of the analysis is the patient's problem with perceiving his own inner incompatibility within relationship activities and with using his affect in order to regulate his needs. The improvisatory playing activity, as well as the palpable catching up on the experience, illustrates the methodological possibilities of psychoanalytically informed music therapy. In this, both the oscillation between regressive and aggressive aspects, and transference activities, are given special attention. During the development of the therapeutic process, creative experiences with opposite poles play an important role. The opposite, the therapist who is playing along, offers both harmonious and dissonant experiences. Within the protected space of the therapeutic activity, the fear of the loss of a relationship as a result of necessary demarcation and confrontation becomes bearable and able to be processed. Work on the perception, clarification, and differentiation of affect are central to music therapy. The treatment of these psychosomatic disturbances with a portion of structural ego disturbance requires that the music therapist, as a resonance- and answer-giving instrument of treatment, suffer, as well as process, breaks in the dialogue.

INTRODUCTION

During a fight for harmony, the partner is in effect forced to do something for his own happiness. Adáptation and solidification, tension and growing aggressiveness, determine such a relationship. Experiencing these conditions together is the starting point for the therapeutic work, whose main task is to understand the individual history of the patient. The following case study presents the problem of a forty-year-old male patient who underwent treatment in a psychosomatic clinic for several weeks. During an individual music therapy session, a step in development, which made it possible for the patient to open up to perceiving his own affect, occurred as he experienced opposite poles as a challenge. The psychoanalytically informed manner of working on the specific restaging of the relationship dynamic, and the use of regressive and aggressive impulses in relationship activities, will be made clear through the presentation of extracts from four different sessions from his treatment. Furthermore, the integrative possibilities of the improvisation process, in playing activities as well as the verbal processing of what was experienced, demonstrate the work of affect perception, clarification, and differentiation inherent in the music therapy procedure.

The Problem—The Restaging of the Relationship Dynamic

The forty-year-old patient, Mr. G., underwent treatment in group music therapy, among other types of therapy, within the framework of an integrated whole treatment plan, at a psychosomatic-psychotherapeutic clinic (Heigl-Evers et al., 1986; Tress et al., 2000). Music therapy was one of a set of treatment instruments. In addition to verbal individual and group therapy, in this setting creative arts therapies such as music, art, and body therapy are allotted special significance. The common theoretical framework for all procedures within the treatment setting is psychoanalysis.

After several sessions in which he clearly put himself under pressure, Mr. G. expressed the desire to receive individual music therapy instead of having to take part in group music therapy. After careful deliberation on the indications, the therapy team decided to grant him his wish. An additional aim was that the individual music therapy sessions would serve toward a renewed diagnostic evaluation of the patient. The initial diagnosis read: presents a depressive condition with neurotic personality development accompanied by somatization. Renewed deliberation on the indications, in relation to a creative therapy procedure, should open up a space in which he can more clearly perceive his own needs.

Alongside his deficiencies in relationship regulation and affect perception came the question of whether he had a partial structural ego disturbance (Fürstenau, 1977), which, next to the neurotic symptoms, was becoming increasingly clear. The differentiated possibilities of a complementary diagnostic process in a research project conducted by a music therapist and a psychosomatic doctor are presented elsewhere (Jahn-Langenberg & Schmidt 2001). In this study, it became clear that, especially with a creative procedure like music therapy, alongside the psychoanalytical first interview two spaces for unfolding were made available to the patient. These both served the restaging of relationship experiences. Through this, the integrative function of the ego is called upon. The patient is perhaps not consciously aware of this, but, actively restaged by him through scenic and situative information, a mutual playing of emotional ideas occurs which is first integrated into a superior whole on the therapeutic level. Thus, from the beginning of the therapeutic task, new emotional experiences (Alexander & French, 1946) can promote the development of those experiences which have been lacking until then. The process of understanding occurs using a diagnostic instrument seen from two perspectives.

TREATMENT

"To come in to play" was the invitation to the first music therapy individual session. In view of the group music therapy's clearly overdemanding nature, it was necessary now to observe how Mr. G. would form a new space for playing in which he could unfold, undisturbed by other patients. Within an arm's length, a chromatic metallophone, cymbals and a drum, a basket with different percussion sticks, a psalter, a cello, a violin, and a diverse array of other percussion instruments had been made available to him. The music therapist sat at the piano where eye contact was possible.

Scene One

With two sticks, the patient begins to play on the metallophone directly in front of him. He only uses the diatonic scale, and plays in regular quarter notes, rarely eighth notes, primarily from high to low tones in 2/4 time. His playing appears to be narrow, it does not go beyond his own personal space: His facial expressions and gestures seem stiff, almost without inner involvement. His playing lacks drive; it makes a fussy, almost helpless impression. The music therapist takes up that quiet playing on the piano and supports it with various harmonies. After a short rhythm change, which the therapist also assumes, the patient falls back into his initial impulse. A short departure, a timid banging on the cymbals, has the effect of being clumsy. For the first time, his facial expression fleetingly changes; a dissatisfaction with the newly tried out sound is implied. The mood strikes me as being sad, melancholic, and triggers associations with a dream world. Increasingly, uncomfortable tension and aggression can be felt; the patient seems to be looking for a harmonious mutual playing, which he cannot find. Within this unfulfilled longing, he appears to lose more and more space for himself. Impulses toward defining borders, other sound poles such as the cymbals, for example, are broken off as if they had been censored.

In the conversation afterward, both Mr. G. and the music therapist describe that at the impulse to differentiate themselves from narrow, monotonous sounds, they immediately called themselves back, due to the need to not play something inappropriate, to avoid creating dissonance. The patient stressed how he had tried really hard to find something appropriate in order to make harmony. In this first scene, it becomes clear that each and every individual impulse toward expansion must be called back. In this sense, the playing is in and of itself unharmonic, although on a purely musical level the therapist attempts to maintain mutual tonal harmony. Dissonance, as an idea for defining borders, as a new color, as an expansion of the space, comes up during the first playing as an idea of both players. However, it is thrown out as if censored. This shaping created strong tension with physical cramping; the reduction of the playing space in an almost unbearable measure. The developing play stands in contrast to the atmosphere in the room, which is felt as challenging tension, charged energy, and aggressivity. The blending of the bass tones at the end of the improvisation, which has the effect of being broken off—at which both partners look astoundedly at each other—brings no release, instead giving the disharmony a "harmonious" end.

The Significance of Countertransference—The Resonator Function Psychoanalytical Interactional Psychotherapy

Psychoanalytically informed music therapy can utilize the method of improvisation. "We play what occurs to us, allowing ourselves to be determined by that which is inside us, putting on pressure to be expressed" (Langenberg, 1988). This analytical ground rule, expanded around the playing, determines a basic assumption between the therapist and patient: What is pictured during the interactive process of the encounter in the treatment work being created is unplanned. How this psychoanalytically modified artistic therapy form is applied can be shown through several case studies (see Langenberg et al., 1995; Langenberg, 1997; Langenberg, 1999).

Of particular significance, the importance of the resonator function (Langenberg, 1988) has been methodically studied (Langenberg et al., 1992). The music therapist makes the most important instrument of treatment, that is, her countertransference, available. In specific music therapy activities, this means bringing inner experiencing to the realm of associative fantasy, as well as bringing the realm of musical ideas into the playing. As a result, at first the music therapist and the patient experience the affective significance of the problem being treated. In the case of Mr. G., harmonic and dissonant relationship wishes already occur within the first improvisation in a conflicting manner. As will be more clearly seen, the suctionlike playing finds a counter-movement to its ever new, harmonic twists, which, alongside a strong experience of tension, keeps the session lively.

This (for music therapy) typical witnessing of the emotional qualities in the playing process with patients finds a parallel in psychoanalytical-interactional treatment techniques (Heigl-Evers et al., 1997). In this procedure, the "Answer Principle" plays the decisive role, which means that the therapist selectively-authentically makes herself available to the patient with her affective experiencing. The method has been proven to promote development, especially for patients with structural ego disturbances, because, to a great extent, it does so without interpretation. Instead, using the capacity for giving affective responses, it makes object relationship experiences from their earliest childhood moments available to the patients. This means concretely that, through the direct answer of the therapist, the patient experiences an authentic reaction to his action. The confrontative element of "the opposite" plays an important role here.

This modification was developed through psychoanalytical treatment procedures in individual and group therapy in verbal psychotherapy settings (Heigl-Evers & Ott 1994). In music therapy procedures using the method of free improvisation, the divided emotional experience of the patient and the therapist has the effect of strengthening in the playing process, so that it can be effectively applied, especially in the area of affect differentiation in psychosomatic patients (Langenberg, 1999).

Process of the Four Individual Sessions

In the first individual music therapy session, the patient stages his relationship wishes. The longing for harmonious playing together becomes clear in all its conflicting ambivalence and, alongside the wish for an expansion of movement, seems like a commission for treatment. However, the intuitive play with the instruments brings unplanned impulses to sound, which cannot be controlled in their effect and possible responsibility. Unusual tones are immediately given up again because in the patient's imagination they do not fit comfortably into his fantasies of harmony. The discovery of new sound spaces in order to expand one's self, and through this to experience the definition of borders, is withdrawn as if censored. The stiffness and physical restriction, which have already been observed in the patient, are transferred onto the music therapist. Exertion and dissatisfaction are spread; the avoidance of dissonant tension hems in liveliness, and as a direct result creates dissonance through physical unease.

In the verbal part of the session, the therapist confronts the patient with his spontaneous impulses, indicating, for example, that the sound of the cymbals, as a new element in the playing, aroused curiosity. The second improvisation, with a clear invitation to expand the space, also brings the same result of great narrowness. Although both players seem to be extremely related to each other in their attention, which becomes clear above all in a high degree of physical vigilance and in that they are playing alongside each other, it seems affectively as if no contact takes place. On the physical level, only tension is experienced.

The second music therapy session is opened by the patient with the words, "I really have a lot to work out at the moment, the weekend was very difficult, my six-year-old son didn't want to leave me." With these words, the theme of separation, and above all how it is experienced, becomes determining for this session. On the one hand, the patient describes the (for him) terrible parting from his son as he returns to the clinic again after a weekend vacation, and how the son clings to him and cries so much that he has to tear him away with violence. On the other hand, the patient tells about one of the neighboring families who have lost their small son in a deadly accident.

Scene Two

Encouraged to begin the improvisation, the patient begins with childlike melodies in the diatonic mode, but increasingly includes other instruments like the cymbals and drum. The impression he makes is a bit less frightened. The music therapist does not respond to his diatonic-harmonic playing, but instead counters it with different, layered chords. The patient also carefully feels his way into chromatic playing and maintains it. His instrumental outburst on the drum and cymbals is supported by the music therapist through more dramatic effects such as volume, more frequent changes in chords, and more vehement layers of sound. For the first time, the patient uses the metallophone at the same time as the drum or cymbals, which leads to the intensification of the musical activity. A slowing down and withdrawal of the impulses described introduces an end phase. But the patient stops playing only after he obviously feels that the music therapist is looking at him. Even though in the verbal part of his story no concrete concept of how the experience of separation feels to him is realized, now for the first time he speaks about how his heart broke as his small son screamed, releasing his earlier rather distanced reaction.

In the playing, however, strong dissonance and friction are now present; the theme's inner dynamic demands to be expressed. While the patient occupies himself with children's melodies in a regressive posture, the music therapist pushes more vehement sounds, projectively demanded through the affect of the patient, into play. These impulses, and the assumption of another emotional quality due to the atmospheric shaping, expand the playing space within this improvisation. The patient clearly gives up the more aggressive and more dramatic tones to the playing partner. Within the playing, he experiences release, which he can express in the conversation afterward.

In this session, a change happens again during the transition from playing to speaking. The reflections on experienced separations have the effect of being cool, are presented without affect, are rationally deliberated. The most impressive example is the remembrance of a longtime girlfriend who threatened suicide when he expressed his intention to leave her. Even in this case, his personal shock cannot be felt as he tells the story. So, he is invited to explore this feeling again in a new improvisation.

The second improvisation of this session has the effect of being less affective than the previous one—the patient seems resigned and he seems to guide the playing cognitively. His movements seem stiff again; the improvisation itself is like a return to the old pattern. Everything that had just become richer and more permeable seems to have disappeared again. His play is monotonous, lacks imagination, and is boring. His own involvement is not apparent anymore and in the conversation closing this session he describes his ideal as being "separation in harmony." It appears as if the wish and the idea of a harmonious separation exist in a certain discrepancy to the painful separation that he has actually experienced.

The third music therapy session clearly brings a processing step to his problem. The first session served to set the problem in scene, above all showing his defensive side (a strong affect isolation) and the sympathy of the music therapist, and initiated a first understanding. A way of saving himself from overexertion presented itself in the second session. In the form of a regression, he avoided the experience of conflicts. This was more and more clearly demonstrated audibly in the music as he engaged in the avoidance of difference, the avoidance of contrast-rich playing which differentiated itself. The affects were not felt in the sense of isolation, but were actually given up to the therapist who was also playing, and who, by way of projection from Mr. G., took on the dynamic affects that were in play for him. A specific transference constellation had been created. Typical relationship patterns, which will later be related to his particular psychodynamic, entered into the therapeutic relationship. The work in transference begins (Körner, 1989).

Scene Three

The patient expresses his desire to play something different right at the beginning. He reaches toward the string psalter, unpacks it carefully with the words "The last time I played one of these was in school." While he tries it out, the music therapist plays a few tones on the piano. The patient remarks that he is searching for a song. Carefully, the music therapist retreats; perhaps she is disturbing him. The patient denies this, and continues to explore next to the music therapist, who is present in the background. The sound space expands, and he plays the instrument with increasing security and a more powerful sound production in the shaping of his song. During the improvisation, the music therapist begins, with a deep voice, to hum an accompanying melody while she continues to play the piano. The singing opens a new space for the play.

On a playfully developed basis of understanding for his regressive need for a foothold and security, further uncertainty through exposure to the new and strange can be dared. Especially in this session, the possibility for the playful movement between regressive and progressive positions seems to stage itself more clearly. While there were phases in the second session in which it can be supposed that the patient came closer to his affective experience during the improvisational playing, this perception is much more clearly developed in the third session. Feelings of uncertainty and security are being searched for at the same time. "Furthermore, something has got to change," the patient's clearly formulated order, is stated in the verbal part of the session.

The patient opens the session with a new initiative: he wants to play the string psalter, which he remembers from his school days. Something new is being dared, within this new the long-known revisited, through which he again finds a piece of himself, something which was once a part of him. In the regression, stabilization takes place before further developmental steps can be made. While looking for a familiar melody, which in its exploratory character reminds one of church songs, the accompanying therapist retreats into a posture of listening in order not to disturb him in his search for the personal. She allows for space in her posture, erecting a playing relationship together with the patient in which, without fear, regression is allowed and desires can become free. In this affective relatedness the therapist begins to sing after a while; the atmosphere has the effect of being closed and each of the two dreamily gives into his/her fantasies. This regression in the service of the ego (Kris 1952) allows both players to stay with themselves while going into a sensual-physical level.

In the verbal part of the session, alongside pleasurably experienced sensitiveness and calming down, the patient describes how, as if exonerating himself, through old memories he is very able to influence the sounds. With urgency, the reality of many unmastered problems push themselves onto the rational working level. While the music therapist makes her fantasies of being far away in the vastness of the Norwegian highlands available, the patient poses his own problems to himself.

In real life he has to master changes at his workplace: because of the large amount of time he has been absent due to his physical symptoms, he has been demoted in his professional field, which makes him feel terrible. However, the challenge of having to feed a family of three children, and the feeling of being unable to meet the competing demands of his professional life, have left him with no other possibility than to stage breaking off his responsibility and breaking down (becoming ill). Important in this session is that the patient affectively admits to, and can speak about, his dissatisfaction and annoyance in relation to the unsolved situation. The beautiful, dreamy mood gave security as if it were a sanctuary in the face of the actual life situation, and seemed at the same time to give him strength to face it again. Together it was considered that the "inclination toward destruction," experienced by the therapist again and again as the wish to define borders, to feel contrast, and to do something differently, seems to be an important clue to the patient's desire for change. The confrontative element, to feel the presence of an opposite who is able to share his regressive wishes, for example, to offer an expansion of space through the mobilization of the voice, clearly incites liveliness. The patient seems happy that his desire for impulse within the dialogue has been understood. He wants to have his own way, and can achieve this more successfully when he has a palpable and challenging opposite.

The fourth and last session of this music therapy sequence can be placed under the heading: defining borders and dealing with conflict, obtaining clearer contours. The patient announces directly that "he doesn't feel like it today" and this is not the time for beautiful music; at the same time, he fetches various percussion instruments as if he needs to be well-equipped. As the therapist offers him the appropriate stick for the newly-chosen triangle, he accepts it reluctantly, only to immediately put it down again. The theme of defining borders hovers in the room.

Scene Four

With a chromatic scale on the metallophone, the joining in of cymbals and drums, a dynamic playing begins. First the piano plays high clusters and chords which are interrupted by pauses, and changes then to an ostinato, broken chords with a scale which slightly changes. The sounds have the effect of being glassy and release feelings of pain and aggression. A melody-like, sad music sounds on the metallophone and changes with the percussion, accompanied by a moved and dramatic play from the piano. It develops in a mutual crescendo into a climax between the players. A clear musical rapprochement takes place, resulting in a duet in which the piano spreads out the tonal carpet on which the metallophone, in more and more moving and significant figures, unfolds. The patient appears for the first time to have clearly defined his own borders within the playing, instead of sticking fast in a continual effort to play with the therapist. The more the therapist offers him a supporting base, the more lively and clearly he seems able to step into the foreground.

The patient's first reaction to the improvisation is to establish the fact that playing with several tones and instruments was fun! The therapist brings an emotional opposite into play here, and says that she found stretches of the music to be very dramatic. This aspect is taken up immediately by the patient and he connects it to his general life situation: "Life is like that, nothing is for free." The relation to experiencing (the contact to his feelings) in the improvisation seems to remain in this part of the conversation, in that the patient can refer to it. He reflects on his shy, very withdrawn posture during his first days on the ward, and compares his experience during the improvisations to it. "As soon as one breaks out of his shell, he gets a reaction." While playing, he noticed that he had come out, that he had carried the music therapist away with him, and he found that to be very good. Vitality and power were felt, the perception of vehement tones and confrontative duets is clearly experienced as a relief, and he feels himself noticed in these impulses.

The playing relationship as a continuing dialogue allows him to experience various aspects of his personality. Despite a great deal of insecurity in real life, in the therapy relationship he risks challenges and wishes that more confidence would be placed in him. In addition to his expressed longing for harmony and agreement, he seems to also have a thoroughly belligerent, very lively and lusty side to him. The opposite poles of wild and beautiful play want to be integrated into unison. The quality of liveliness is achieved by the acceptance of a playful friction between them, so that being fresh can also be fun. "I wanted to play my own music." This clear statement, and the taking of a clear personal position, shows his aggressive potential in a certain way and further development, which, for him, is constructive. Here, emotions are clearly applied to regulate relationships, and serve to carry through his needs; in this case, the needs for differentiation and independence (Langenberg, 1996).

The dramatic turnaround, experienced and formed in the improvisations, now receives a relation to his life story. His way of dealing with aggressive impulses, often experienced in the form of the breaking through of uncontrolled impulses, is dangerous for him, partly because of the nonintegrated aspects of himself. With a provocative laugh, the patient can now report how, on the super highway, he created mortally dangerous situations when passing other drivers who had annoyed him. The aggressive feelings, which suddenly break through, can hardly be controlled. With this background, it is understandable that even in relationship to the music therapist who is playing with him, he tries again and again to grab the reins and to control his own feelings, as well as those of his partner, when possible. The picture of a volcano, which could erupt at any time, comes up; the fantasy of the evacuation of surrounding villages brings the patient to merry laughter.

Behind his harmonic-friendly behavior lurks a great deal of aggressive potential, which can release itself in a destructive manner if it does not experience an understanding opposite who clarifies and integrates the context of the development of the affects with him. Within the confrontative conflict of a dialogue, where the partner who is playing with him understands his desires for expression and his ability to occupy and form space, the patient experiences respect, above all for his masculinity. In this session, it becomes clear that, within the protection of a good therapeutic alliance, the patient must experience a space free of fear in order to use his desire for aggressive conflict for the purpose of his own further development.

DISCUSSION

The Patient: From Affect Isolation Toward Opening (Regressive and Aggressive Movement)

In the course of the treatment sequence of four sessions, a specific dynamic in the relationship can be pointed out. I will now round out the picture, verifying and expanding the restaging with data from another perspective, that is, information extracted from the first psychoanalytic interview. Due to his biography, Mr. G. is extremely unsure in his behavioral role. He cannot remember his primary male caregiver/role model, his biological father, due to his sudden, early death. He could not accept his stepfather; instead a strong fixation on his mother, who seemed to see a substitute partner in him, occurred. Through this special relationship to his mother he experienced a revaluation (an increase in value), which compensated for his narcissistic illness of earlier times. On the one hand, he suffered from a lack of acceptance by a father figure: his older brother had a much better relationship with his stepfather. On the other hand, after several years, a third son was born. Within the group of his brothers, Mr. G. seemed to be the least able to assert himself, was sickly with various complaints as a child, broke off his professional training, experienced little development in his self-confidence, and, in the search for his masculine identity, cannot have been sufficiently encouraged. He idealized his mother, and he fantasized that he had a special relationship with her. Even in his current marriage, he surrenders the field to his strong wife. He also has three sons, of whom he is very proud. The responsibility for his family is a great burden to him, especially because he is frequently ill and, thus, often misses work.

The helplessness and weakness he experienced through early sickliness lead to aggression, which shows itself in somatic complaints and depressive conditions where he psychically experiences failure. His need for safety and security are in ambivalence with his desire for aggressive self-assertion. Thus, above all, the defense mechanism of affect isolation, which is so clearly palpable and releases great tension in his opposite in the first therapy session, seems to be, understandably, his protection against the all too vehement impulses resulting from his experiences of being sickly. The experience of regressive movement toward desire for harmony and the same sound as the opposite is, on the one hand, to be understood as avoidance of conflict. On the other hand, however, as can be demonstrated in the music therapy treatment sequence, it includes the possibility for recovering one's own familiar security. Aggressive movements in terms of pushing through desires, to disassociate oneself from a personal playing, expand the way to a greater perception of ones own feelings. The creation of diffuse tensions between ideas/images and desires can only be experienced in the framework of a forming relationship. In the playing relationship of a music therapy situation, the experience of a continuing dialogue, in the sense of working in transference (Körner, 1989), takes place free from fear, allowing every ambivalence and the security of not being able to lose the motherly space, while, however, wanting to differentiate one's self from it.

Restaging repeats the analytical relationship pattern that is frequently observed in such patients, which, however, shows signs of affects that are important to understand (Krause, 1988).

CONCLUSIONS

Harmony and Dissonance as Poles in Therapeutic Development Activities (Fear of Losing a Relationship during Confrontation)

In conclusion, psychoanalytically informed music therapy should once again be pointed out in a dialectic of change (Fischer, 1989). Healing can only take place within a relationship, the playing relationship of the music therapy situation, coupled with a psychoanalytical understanding and working with counter-transference. With the idea of being an instrument, the resonator function in music therapy offers, especially in the processing of psychosomatic problems, good prospects for treatment.

An oscillation between playing and speaking, primary and secondary processslike experiencing, especially challenges development by establishing polarity in the therapeutic activities. Opposites become a challenge to one's own playing levels of getting involved in, or observing, and are genuinely contained in the therapy procedures. The necessary observing distance is structurally applied by this patient, in his personality, as a survival strategy and protection against overwhelming impulses. It now prevents him from being effectively able to vibrate in relationships: to appreciate the other's close similarities as well as the differences. Harmony first seems to be a forced experience in this treatment, and leads to the assumption that the patient experiences fear of losing the relationship during confrontation. He has to control the situation and restricts the partner and himself to the point where it is physically unbearable.

Within the playing relationship, however, it is not only allowed, but desired that registered impulses toward differentiation and contrast be lived out. Opposites are not experienced as being urgent, rather as separated and at the same time, very present. Here, the patient's lack of a father figure must again be pointed out, as well as his strong fixation on his mother who, as a result of her own neediness, had indiscriminately bound him to her. This early experience could mean that he was not allowed to differentiate in relation to his mother, or women in general, because otherwise he would lose the relationship.

Mr. G. lacks experience in relation to another fatherlike object, which on the one hand, could have helped him to differentiate himself from his mother, and on the other, could have served as an example for his masculine identification. It can be read, from the vehement countertransference feelings, that first a confrontation with his own annoyed affects must take place within the secure playing relationship so that within this friction he can experience something entirely personal. This did in fact take place within the fourth session, where the patient experienced his own wild and beautiful playing in turn. Dissonance, friction, and conflict are now able to be viewed as lusty and lively potential.

Diagnostically, from a music therapy viewpoint, it can be added that the obviously oedipal level in the palpably libidinous shading of the relationship to the mother, but also deficits in his earlier experiencing of affect perception and differentiation, have become visible. Furthermore, it should be observed to see whether the patient's fear of confrontative situations points toward a lack of object constancy, thus a partial structural ego disturbance. It is encouraging and prognostically positive that Mr. G. clearly begins an expansion of his affective ability to experience within the music therapy work. The experiencing of the other, the possibility to move between regressive and aggressive needs, now allows him to pose himself problems and not circumvent them. The desire for personal assertiveness must not be censoriously denied anymore.

Music therapy offers the contrast-rich playing space required for looking for needs for safety and security, as well as for living out of dissonant impulses which do not destroy but instead, colorfully augment.

REFERENCES

Alexander, F. & French, T. M. (1946). *Psychoanalytic Therapy: Principles and Applications*. New York: Ronald Press.

Fischer, G. (1989). *Dialektik der Veränderung in Psychoanalyse und Psychotherapie (The Dialectic of Change in Psychoanalysis and Psychotherapy)*. Heidelberg: Asanger.

Fürstenau, P. (1977). "Die beiden Dimensionen des psychoanalytischen Umgangs mit strukturell ich-gestörten Patienten (The Two Dimensions of Psychoanalytically Dealing with Patients with Structural Ego-Disturbances)," *Psyche,* 31, 197–206.

Heigl-Evers, A., Heigl, F., Ott, J., & Rüger, U. (1997). *Lehrbuch der Psychotherapie. 3. überarbeitete Auflage (Handbook of Psychotherapy, 3rd revised edition).* Lübeck, Stuttgart, Jena, Ulm: Gustav Fischer Verlag.

Heigl-Evers, A., Henneberg-Mönch, U., Odag, C., & Standke, G. (eds.). (1986). *Die Vierzigstundenwoche für Patienten—Konzept und Praxis teilstationärer Psychotherapie (The 40-hour Week for Patients—The Concept and Practice of Partially Stationary Psychotherapy).* Göttingen: Vandenhoeck & Ruprecht.

Heigl-Evers, A., & Ott, J. (1994). *Die psychoanalytisch-interaktionelle Methode—Theorie und Praxis (The Psychoanalytic-Interactional Method—Theory and Practice).* Göttingen: Vandenhoeck & Ruprecht.

Jahn-Langenberg, M. (2000). "Musiktherapie als psychoanalytische Methode—Gedanken zur Entwicklung eines Spielraums im integrierten Gesamt-behandlungsplan (Music Therapy as a Psychoanalytical Method—Thoughts on the Development of a Space for Playing within an Integrated Whole Treatment Plan)." In W. Tress, W. Wöller, & E. Horn (eds.), *Psychotherapeutische Medizin im Krankenhaus—State of the Art.* Frankfurt/Main: Verlag für Akademische Schriften VAS.

Jahn-Langenberg, M. (2001). "Psychodynamic Perspectives in Professional Supervision." In M. Forinash (ed.), *Music Therapy Supervison.* Gilsum, NH: Barcelona Publishers.

Jahn-Langenberg, M., & Schmidt, H. U. (2001). "Erstbegegnung im Vergleich—diagnostischer Eindruck einer musiktherapeutischen Sitzung und eines analytischen Erstinterviews (First Encounters in Comparison—Diagnostic Impressions of a Music Therapy Session and an Analytical First Interview)." *Musiktherapeutische Umschau,* 22, 173–184.

Körner, J. (1989). "Arbeit an der Übertragung! (Work on Transference!)." *Forum der Psychoanalyse,* 5, 209–223.

Krause, R. (1988). "Eine Taxonomie der Affekte und ihre Anwendung auf das Verständnis der 'frühen Störungen' (A Taxonomy of Affects and their Application toward the Understanding of 'Early Disturbances')." *PPmP*, 38, 77–86.

Kris, E. (1952). *Psychoanalytic Explorations in Art*. New York: International University Press.

Langenberg, M. (1988). *Vom Handeln zum Be-Handeln. Darstellung besonderer Merkmale der musiktherapeutischen Behandlungssituation im Zusammenhang mit der freien Improvisation (From Action to Treatment. Presentation of Special Characteristics of the Music Therapy Treatment Situation within the Context of the Free Improvisation)*. Stuttgart: Fischer.

Langenberg, M. (1996a). "Affektivität (Affectivity)." In H. H. Decker-Voigt, P. J. Knill, & E. Weymann (eds.), *Lexikon Musiktherapie*. Göttingen: Hogrefe.

Langenberg, M. (1996b). "Psychoanalyse und Musiktherapie (Psychoanalysis and Music Therapy)." In H. H. Decker-Voigt, P.J. Knill, & E. Weymann (eds.), *Lexikon Musiktherapie*. Göttingen: Hogrefe.

Langenberg, M. (1997). "Musiktherapie (Music Therapy)." In A. Heigl-Evers, F. Heigl, J. Ott, & U. Rüger (eds.), *Lehrbuch der Psychotherapie*. Lübeck: Fischer.

Langenberg, M. (1999). "Music therapy and the meaning of affect regulations for psychosomatic patients." In T. Wigram & J. De Backer, *Clinical Applications of Music Therapy in Psychiatry*. London: Jessica Kingsley Publishers.

Langenberg, M., Frommer, J., & Tress, W. (1992). "Qualitative Methodik zur Beschreibung und Interpretation musiktherapeutischer Behandlungswerke (Qualitative Methods toward the Description of Music Therapy Treatment Works)." *Musiktherapeutische Umschau*, 4, 258–278.

Langenberg, M., Frommer, J., & Tress, W. (1995). "From Isolation to Bonding: A Music Therapy Case Study of a Patient with Chronic Migraines," *The Arts in Psychotherapy*, 22, 87–101.

Tress, W., Wöller, W., & Horn, E. (2000). *Psychotherapeutische Medizin im Krankenhaus—State of the Art 2000 (Psychotherapeutic Medicine in the Hospital—State of the Art 2000)*. Frankfurt/Main: Verlag für Akademische Schriften VAS.

Case Nineteen

THE REVIVAL OF THE FROZEN SEA URCHIN: MUSIC THERAPY WITH A PSYCHIATRIC PATIENT

Inge Nygaard Pedersen

ABSTRACT

In this case study I will share some very positive results in music therapy with an adult psychiatric male patient with personality disorders. I am working with improvisational music therapy based on a psychodynamic understanding of the process. I have chosen to frame the case study by dividing the case retrospectively into six significant phases in the therapeutic process. For each phase I will describe the most important verbal metaphors and statements the patient brings into the process, as these are used as guidelines for the aim and direction of the therapy process. I will also provide vignettes to illustrate methodology and techniques applied in the musical relationship we built up together during the treatment.

INTRODUCTION

I was primarily trained as an analytical music therapist by Mary Priestley (London) and by Johannes Eschen, Colleen Purdon, and Ole Teichmann (Herdecke, Germany) from 1978–1980. For the last twenty years I have been deeply involved in music therapy as an educator, a clinician, and a researcher. I have tried to follow the advice that Mary Priestley repeated over and over again during our training: "Take from me what you can use and transfer it into your own approach." Today, I have also almost completed my training in Guided Imagery in Music (GIM), with Ken Bruscia as my primary trainer. In my everyday work I simply call my treatment approach music therapy. I work in a context of psychotherapy treatment at the Music Therapy Clinic in Aalborg Psychiatric Hospital, where music therapy can be offered to a patient instead of verbal psychotherapy. In the following case, I only use active improvisational methods. In each session I alternate between verbal and musical interventions.

In the case I will present in this chapter, the patient was referred to the Music Therapy Clinic as an outpatient, and he refused the offer of supplemental medical treatment. So, music therapy was his primary and only treatment as a psychiatric patient during the two years (57 sessions) I worked with him. This is a rather unique phenomenon in psychiatric hospital treatment. Also, this patient allowed me to use his material (of course in an anonymous form) for whatever purpose might support the profession of music therapy. As a consequence, I asked the patient to write his own report/account of the music therapy treatment three years after the treatment was finished. The report was requested by a national medical journal that wanted to publish an article on music therapy in general that included a report from a patient's perspective.

I am ending this case study by quoting the last bit of this report, as I consider the patient's perspective of treatment as very important when documenting the process and outcome of music therapy. So, I am very aware, that what I am writing here could be called a "success story" or "successful case," usually referred to in Danish as a "sunshine story" (as the sun does not shine that often in Denmark!). Not all my clinical work results in "successful cases," and I have learned just as much from what could be called "disastrous cases."

During the treatment, I had regular supervision with a psychiatrist in a small group consisting of music therapists.

BACKGROUND INFORMATION

The patient (here called H.) was forty-one-years-old when he started the music therapy treatment. He was referred for psychiatric treatment, in the form of psychotherapy, as an outpatient on the basis of the following diagnosis: F60.8 from the World Health Organization's International Classification of Diseases tenth revision (1993): Personality Disorders with specific anhedonic and obsessive compulsive features—very intellectualizing in verbal contact with other people.

H. had been tested using the Wachler Adult Intelligence Scale, and the Luria and Rorschach tests before referral to music therapy. Music therapy was suggested as a suitable treatment instead of verbal psychotherapy because of H.'s intellectualizing use of words (he knew all the psychological/analytical theories, but it did not help him) and because of his anhedonic features. He himself defined his problem as primarily being afraid of relating to others, especially women.

Biographically, H. was the second of two children. His older sister died two weeks after birth. His father suffered from manic-depressive disorder and was pensioned when H. was seven years old. H. described him as partly violent, an alcoholic, unpredictable, and often spending long hours lying in bed. H. had no experience of a father/son relationship. H. was very close to his mother as a child and his mother gave up her career to look after him. H. described her as overprotective and dependent.

H. was hospitalized at the age of eighteen months for six weeks because of an eating disorder. He did not see his parents during this period, due to hospital practices and regulations at that time. He could hardly recognize them after this period and he more or less refused any intimate contact with them after this time. His parents divorced when he was eighteen, and H. stayed in contact with both of them. His father committed suicide two years ago. H. felt extremely insecure, diffuse, and compulsive during his teenage period. He managed to obtain a high school degree and started studying mathematics at the university, which he subsequently abandoned. Later, he completed training as a school teacher and also as a social pedagogue,[1] but he could not cope with being in contact with either children or adolescents.

H. experienced himself being pushed by his mother to take these courses and to succeed in examinations, and was often reminded that she gave up her career because of him. He reported that he was aware from the beginning of his

---

[1] A social pedagogue is someone who is involved in different practical activities with children with special needs, such as working with them to assist them to function in their homes, kindergartens, or schools.

enrollment as a student that he would never be able to use his training as a teacher because of his symptoms. He could not communicate with children on an emotional or associative level.

He had had only one long-term relationship with a girlfriend, but this ended two years before the start of therapy. He suffered deeply at that time and simultaneously ended contact with most of his friends. He himself did not connect these events with the suicide of his father around the same time.

He tried out drugs (LSD and others) between the ages of sixteen and eighteen, and experienced some very bad trips.

In the preparatory discussion before therapy started, H. was very formal in the contact, and clear in spatial orientation. He could not remember episodes and times. He himself saw his primary problem as a lack of ability to function in contact with other people. H. described that he felt like he was disappearing when in contact with others, almost phobically—and he could not think clearly. H. could not set clear boundaries and felt like withdrawing very quickly. He could not handle intimacy or closeness, from which he often had the feeling of being exposed. He reported compulsive symptoms, where he had to control opening and closing windows and doors many times on a daily basis. He only remembered one period of happiness and freedom in his whole life, during a vacation in Greece some years before the start of therapy.

We agreed that an aim for the music therapy work at the beginning would be to work on developing better contact with himself, and with others—especially women. This aim included working on establishing boundaries, and also valuing himself as a person worthy of being in a relationship with others.

TREATMENT

I will describe the treatment process, dividing it into six phases integrated with vignettes describing the methodology and techniques used. I have retrospectively named the six phases:

1. "Into concentration": Sessions 1–10
2. "Beginning of self-manifestation": Sessions 11–19
3. "Emotional fluctuations and openings": Sessions 20–32
4. "Searching for resources": Sessions 32–42
5. "Sexuality" Sessions: 42–46
6. "Stabilization and dialogue": Sessions 46–57

During the first four phases H. formulated problems in the form of identification of the self in polarities. I will use the patient's own words in defining the core polarities for each phase.

Phase 1: Into Concentration: Sessions 1–10

In this phase the patient formulated the following polarities in his perceptions and experiences:

1.   Being distant, restless, not present in reality
2.   Experiencing explosive energy, acting out, not present in reality.

During this phase, together we defined my role as being his centerpoint, both in talking (keeping us to the point) and in the musical dialogues (keeping a stable pulse).

Vignette A: From the very first session

H. had never played music before starting therapy. I asked him to choose an instrument. He chose the piano, which I have noticed is very often chosen by intellectualizing patients. They consider the piano as a "grown up," challenging instrument. I asked him to try to express "his experience of his personal space in the music" as the playing rule for the music. I instructed him to start to play by striking a key and listening to that sound and to let this sound lead him to the next sound, listen to it and so on—and if possible play with closed eyes. He started exploring how to express himself on an unknown instrument and he gradually followed my instructions. He played single sounds either in the lower or the upper part of the piano. The sounds were single sounds in the beginning, not interrelated, and he created a fragmented soundscape.

I listened very carefully to his music to sense how I could be a part of this "soundpicture" and I, playing on a second piano, intuitively placed myself as a kind of center in the picture—repeating one sound in a heartbeat rhythm, but with contrasting dynamics in my way of playing, as if coming closer and then being more distant through the sound. I chose this position, but I could not know for sure if it was meaningful for H.

Gradually, in this first thirteen-minute improvisation, H. played more related sounds—at one point playing a melody with a strong drive in its rhythm and direction. But he constantly rushed back to a more fragmented way of playing the sounds. At certain moments his differentiated sounds and my repeated pulsed sound created beautiful harmonies.

After the music finished, I was unsure whether he noticed my part in the music. He was sitting at the piano for a couple of minutes without talking and then suddenly said: "I have no words." After a long pause he continued with the comment: "But I heard some quite melancholic moods there."

I considered these brief and isolated statements as very important for a person that normally talks a lot and overintellectualizes in his way of speaking. As I felt in rather close contact with H. during some of the music parts, I asked him if he had heard my part in the music and he said: "Barely, but I had a sense of some kind of a center somewhere to which I came a little closer to and from which I also moved away."

I also asked if I had disturbed him and he responded that I had not. We reflected verbally together that he probably needed a centerpoint from outside, and we decided that this role should be my part in the music-making over the next sessions—acting as the centerpoint, holding things together, and trying to give him a free space to explore himself through sounds.

During Phase 1, the patient developed in the way that he played. At first, he often played rather predictably and in a programmatic way—associating the light sounds (upper part of the piano) as the distant, restless part of him and the darker sounds (lower part of the piano) as the explosive energy and acting out part of himself. Subsequently, he found he could move into a state of letting himself go and flow along a little more using both musical sounds. In verbal reflection he used phrases like "unknown perception," "unknown feelings," "I am wondering," "being touched," "empty in my head," "replacing my crowd of thoughts."

Phase 2: Beginning of Self-Manifestation: Sessions 11–19

In this phase, he formulated his experiences in the polarized symptoms of his problems as:

1. A need to choke all sounds around him, the experience of being constantly disturbed from outside
2. A beginning of listening to and keeping self-expressions in the music.

At the beginning of this phase, the patient allowed himself to act out chaotically on the piano (see Vignette B) and he associated these experiences with having been on drugs at the age of eighteen. He noticed that he had not had any access to such perceptions or experiences since he had had bad drug experiences. He also noticed that these acting-out experiences in the music left him full of energy and not as empty and anxious as he remembered having been after he had taken drugs earlier.

I constantly encouraged his need for acting out in the music and kept my role of being a centerpoint by sustaining a stable pulse in my left-hand ground rhythm, while, at the same time, following him into chaos with my right hand and with vocal sounds.

We defined an intermediate aim for the next phase as trying to build a bridge between the maelstrom and verbalization.

Vignette B: From Session 14

In this example, H. played the piano and I played the congas and used my voice. The playing rule was that the patient should try to allow himself to express an experience of power. I facilitated him in my playing, still keeping the centerpoint through my stable pulse-playing.

H. was acting out in this musical selection, playing loudly, chaotically, and energetically on the piano. His pulse, in the playing, was unstable. He was alternating playing very loud sounds and repeating clusters. I tried to follow his dynamic and level of energy on the drum and through my voice. At the same time, I tried to keep a stable pulse. At the conclusion of the music, we matched shortly in a soft sound and slow tempo for a few seconds, but H. immediately stopped the music as if he had burned his fingers. He told me that this energetic way of playing reminded him of taking drugs, which he did when he was younger. But here he did not feel that empty after playing the music. Taking drugs made him feel very empty and lonesome afterward.

During this phase, the patient developed a need to be creative. His experiences while playing the music moved from feeling disturbed by every sound from outside (including my music part) to being able to shut out other sounds and being totally engaged in his own musical expressions. He could now keep his concentration for a longer period and had the feeling of filling out his personal space in the music. During this period he contacted strong feelings of rage and sorrow.

During this time, he started dreaming again, which he had not been doing for years, and he recalled many childhood memories of loss and trauma, which he could now also express in the music. He started to write a diary, of his own accord, about this therapy process. He expressed constantly that he now experienced the music-making as a maelstrom (whirlpool)—but still not connected to verbalization.

Phase 3: Emotional Fluctuations and Openings: Sessions 20–32

In this phase, the patient experienced himself as rather unpredictable. He experienced large emotional fluctuations. The polarization from the first phase, where he associated light sounds with distance and restlessness and darker sounds with explosive energy, was transcended and he created another polarization where he experienced:

1. A pinned-down side, being an audience to the world
2. An unsuspecting, simpleminded side newly awakened and identified.

Many new openings to childhood memories took place and words for his musical experiences were mostly connected to "new" sensations and perceptions. He was also "better able to flow in the swing of the music." We defined the next intermediate aim as moving the inner dialogue from taking place between parental representations (concretized through light sounds being mother qualities and darker sounds being father qualities) to a dialogue between the following "inner child" representations:

1. A terrified, paralyzed inner child, and
2. A naive, but safe inner child.

H. gained and expressed more insight into the effect of his childhood trauma, and the influence that it had on him later in terms of being fragmented and basically insecure in terms of perceiving his surroundings. At the same time, he seemed to be more open to lively and playful qualities in terms of expressing himself in our joint music improvisations. I still kept my position of being a centerpoint, but simultaneously went with him in playful ideas and movements in the musical improvisations.

Phase 4: Searching for Resources: Sessions 32–42

In this phase, the patient started to bring some of the dreams from his newly revived dream activity into the music therapy work.

Vignette C: From Session 32

The patient brought a specific dream to the music therapy session which he described as follows: "I was running along—searching—climbing a fence of barbed wire and finding myself on a frozen water hole. Just under the ice I saw a fossilized sea urchin, which I recognized as a part of myself." I encouraged him to use his voice to express the quality of the fossilized sea urchin and we improvised together for the first time with unaccompanied voices. I tried to match him and our voices sounded very thin, metallic, insecure, and icy. We both experienced this as being very naked in the quality of our expressions, using a high-pitched pianissimo. Gradually, both voices grew in intensity and created more vibrations and sound waves, which can be understood as the performers becoming more and more present and related in the joint sound space. I felt almost overwhelmed by insecurity, and tried to resonate with the icy, fragile, and insecure expressions from the patient. At the same time, I tried to be encouraging with my voice by taking the lead in terms of intensity and in creating more sound waves. We were improvising standing side by side with closed eyes—sharing the atmosphere in the room. The patient was very touched by the music and, most important, he was able to show it to me afterward.

This experience created the opportunity for us to work solely with vocal improvisations, and using these improvisations to search for inner resources and to recognize how to fill oneself up from the inside using vocal sounds. H. very basically explored: "I feel myself—I am allowed to be in the world."

At that point the patient started to paint watercolor paintings between the music therapy sessions. He brought two to four paintings to each session. Each session I asked him to choose one painting that he felt was most important to him and to explain to me what it meant for him, symbolically. In the beginning an ongoing theme in the paintings was a "mask in the water"—there was something under the waterline on the paintings while at the same time the picture was full of distorted human beings and animal figures above the waterline. The mask in the water transformed into a face and his focus developed into the polarities of:

1.   An alive eye
2.   A glazed eye.

Generally the patient verbalized that he felt in greater contact with his feelings, and that he had very high dream activity, with themes of destruction, death, and new beginnings. His vocal expression developed from being thin and icy to becoming much more intense and careful, with increasingly powerful sound. During this period, the patient allowed primitive energies and emotions, like hate and rage, to be expressed. It led to a new aim for the work—the aim of sexuality and the polarities of being a boy/man.

Phase 5: Sexuality: Sessions 42–46

The aim formed in Phase 4 continued here and a new ongoing dream symbol of a black panther emerged. The patient dared to express the power of that panther, with his voice now sounding very deep and full of colors—alternating with sounds that I associated with Tibetan monks. I gradually felt free to challenge him more and our vocal improvisations grew into rather dramatic expressions. At this time, the patient also dared to express himself in the form of vocal improvisation solos without support or countermelodies from me. He talked about experiences of filling himself out from these vocal sounds, now more in the basic understanding of: "I am not only allowed to be in the world—I am proud of myself and my sounding self."

This phase was not identified by polarities by the patient, but rather through insight into his progression. H. was now able to move from being afraid of his own strength, to realizing his need for support from his surroundings, to allowing himself to integrate more primitive energies and, thus, to develop more containment. Finally, he dared not only to express the black panther, but to identify with the power of this symbol. The patient talked about an experience of a new and totally unknown energy which he could now express through a powerful and vibrating-sounding voice—as if he was developing, for the first time, a real "core sound" of his voice. The anxiety was transformed to strength and this transformation was realized, and could be expressed, through vocal improvisations.

Phase 6: Stabilization and Dialogue: Sessions 46–57

During Phase 5, and especially in Phase 6, I could begin to leave my supporting roles and also my challenging roles as a therapist. He could now both support and challenge himself. He still needed me as a careful listener and a mirror. The patient often experienced traumatic situations being repeated, and of being locked up/stuck by frustrations or anxieties, or by making decisions he could not yet handle. The important thing was that he could now contain these feelings and he did not panic by being locked up/stuck. He knew things would change. Through these experiences, much insight about his former repressive tendencies (being out of contact with emotions and fantasies—the whirlpool) and use of defense mechanisms (the need to control the surroundings) became clear and conscious, and he worked consciously on breaking through the defense mechanisms he wanted to get rid of. He repeated some of the former themes of the therapy process in our joint improvisations and I gradually felt more like an equal partner having no more countertransference feelings of "having to" hold a ground or "having to" reinforce his expressions anymore.

In his daily life he now acted out a lot, setting up new boundaries for his mother and for friends. He broke ties with friends that he felt kept him locked up/stuck and he found new friends, including female friends.

In session fifty-five, he told me that he now felt ready to leave the music therapy and to continue to exercise in real life by himself. We decided to continue for another two sessions to bring closure to our relationship.

Vignette D: From Session 57

In the very last session he wanted mostly to play—not so much to talk. He suggested that we played together on the two pianos on the topic of "leaving and future." We both used piano and voice. We played for about thirty minutes in a baroquelike style, floating rhythmically in a modal harmony, and I totally forgot that I was playing with a patient. I could as well have been playing with a colleague. I felt totally free to put myself spontaneously in the music; we took turns in introducing new musical ideas and floated with the ideas from one another. After the music stopped the patient said: "I now feel much younger, more vulnerable, and much better integrated."

After the therapy stopped he went into rehabilitation, began studying at an art college, and today he makes his living by selling his paintings. He did not know he was that skilled.

DISCUSSION AND CONCLUSIONS

I have tried to write this case study paying close attention to defining important phases in the patient's development, and the process involved, and by illustrating in vignettes the methodology and techniques used. This patient was very motivated to delve into the process, and was ready to dive into his repressed whirlpool of creativity, which he had repressed since his bad experiences with drugs between the ages of sixteen and eighteen. His inability to relate to other people, and his need to control by intellectualization, was connected to many traumatic periods and experiences in his life, but probably seeded by the age of one and a half when he was hospitalized and not able to see his parents. During the therapy process, he came to verbalize several episodes from childhood and adolescence, where he felt emotionally abused, especially by his father and also by other adults. He also realized how he had felt almost choked by his mother's care for him while, at the same time, he was aware that she wanted to control him totally in his adult life. I think in the case here, as in most cases of pathology, the patient's symptoms were the result of him being very vulnerable and, at the same time, being part of a traumatic life story. He did not have the resources to cope as a child and adolescent with the problems.

In the music therapy treatment, he used the music to contact and express emotions and dream symbols, and he used the music and me to be held, supported, expanded, and challenged in his attempts to live out these emotions and fantasies. He also used the music to gradually build up a more stable self-identity and to better integrate male and female parts of himself. His obvious artistic creativity, which was unknown to him prior to therapy, helped him to very quickly dive into a deep concentration and intensity in the musical improvisations, and our use of vocal improvisation obviously gave him a tool for self-exploration, and later, self-regulation.

I want to end this case study by providing an excerpt of the patient report that I mentioned at the beginning of this case study. Through this report, I will let the patient end the story with his own words:

Patient Report (Excerpt):

"More than three years have passed since the music stopped. Things have happened. I feel like I have partly changed and still part of me remains the same. But I have a clear feeling of being able to 'fill up' myself much better than before the music therapy.

"Earlier, I often felt like a sad, lonely, and misunderstood 'steppe wolf' (an archetype of human loneliness) sitting in a waiting room, and when with other people I felt like the 'spy coming in from the cold': I am still a 'steppe wolf' but now a far more free, unpredictable, amused, and acting one. Instead of being tacit and speculating, I am now a 'wolf' who enjoys howling with the others. I am much better at taking care of myself and I am not that scared of hurting other people. My former morning crisis—a crisis which could last for the whole day—where I felt like a catastrophe was waiting just around the corner, has almost disappeared. Even if the music therapy has officially ended, I feel as if it is still working in me. All the experiments, sounds, and motifs I created in the music, I am now using in interaction with other people and this gives me a greater feeling of freedom; freedom understood as me having more strings to play on—many more possibilities of handling different life situations. I still make sound improvisation with my voice, just to sense how I feel at certain moments deep inside myself. This gives me a useful tool to loosen up the psychological knots and tensions building up."

REFERENCES

Bonde, L. O., Pedersen, I. N., & Wigram, T. (2001). *Musikterapi: Når ord ikke slår til. En håndbog i musikterapiens teori og praksis i Danmark. (Music Therapy: When Words Are Not Enough. A Handbook on Theory and Praxis of Music Therapy in Denmark)*. Aarhus. Denmark: Klim.

Bruscia, K. E. (1998). *The Dynamics of Music Psychotherapy*. Gilsum, NH: Barcelona Publishers.

Pedersen, I. N. (1998). *Indføring i musikterapi som en selvstændig behandlingsform. (Introduction to Music Therapy as a Primary Treatment Form)*. Musikterapiklinikken. (The Music Therapy Clinic). Aalborg University/ Aalborg Psychiatric Hospital.

Pedersen, I. N. (2002). "Analytical Music Therapy (AMT) with Adults in Mental Health and in Counseling Work." In Johannes Th. Eschen (ed.), *Analytical Music Therapy*. London: Jessica Kingsley Publishers.

Priestley, M. (1975). *Music Therapy in Action*. London: Constable.

Priestley, M. (1994). *Essays on Analytical Music Therapy*. Gilsum, NH: Barcelona Publishers.

The ICD-10 Classification of Mental and Behavioural Disorders: Diagnostic Criteria for Research. (1993). Geneva: World Health Organization.

Case Twenty

HEALING AN INFLAMED BODY:
THE BONNY METHOD OF GIM IN TREATING
RHEUMATOID ARTHRITIS

Denise Grocke

ABSTRACT

This chapter will describe the psychodynamic features of the Bonny Method of Guided Imagery and Music (GIM) therapy with a forty-three-year-old woman who, at the start of GIM therapy, had a fifteen-year history of rheumatoid arthritis (RA). The psychodynamic aspect of the study is based on the concept of physical illness as a manifestation of unresolved issues in the client's life, and that the symptoms of the illness depict the client's pschoemotional needs.

The case study will illustrate how GIM sessions over five years allowed the client to relive events from childhood, and to express emotions relative to those events. The client's imagery was symbolic of the manifestation of the illness and she frequently had imagery relating to her blood stream, joints, and cells, and learned quickly that she could enter the imagery of the body as a means of engaging the precipitating cause of the irritation.

The issue of countertransference will be discussed with respect to two significant sessions in which the client was in extraordinary pain. The countertransference issue was whether the choice of music (which exacerbated the pain) made her condition worse, or whether the pain she was suffering was a necessary process of working through the disease.

INTRODUCTION

The Bonny Method of GIM is a specialized area of therapy in which clients listen to prerecorded classical music in a deeply relaxed state and in which visual imagery, changes in mood, and physiological effects in the body are experienced. GIM was developed by Dr. Helen Bonny, a music therapist at the Baltimore Psychiatric Institute, USA, in the 1970s.

The method is based on the principles of psychodynamic therapy, where unresolved psychological issues in the client are brought to the surface and may be resolved. In GIM, the clients' issues are represented in symbolic form in the visual images, feeling states, and body responses.

The music programs used in GIM were designed by Bonny, and each incorporates selections from the classical music repertoire. The music contour of the program is designed to have a beginning piece which stimulates imagery, a middle selection to deepen the experience emotionally, and a final selection which returns the client to a nonaltered state of consciousness. A section of a large music work (e.g., a symphony or concerto) may be programmed alongside a work of another composer or another stylistic period. The choice of music for each program is made according to the potential for inducing imagery and deepening emotion.

A GIM session lasts approximately two hours. There is a period of discussion (of approximately fifteen minutes) in which the client and therapist decide together on a focus issue for the session. The client moves to a relaxation mat and reclines with eyes closed. The therapist provides a relaxation induction which is individually tailored to the client's energy level and to the focus issue for the session. A focus image is given to stimulate the commencement of the imagery process, and the music program is chosen (by the therapist). As the music plays, sequences of images unfold, and these are verbalized by the client. The therapist makes interventions which are designed to bring the client closer to the image, and to notice any feelings or emotions which are associated with the images. The therapist also takes a transcript of the imagery sequence. At the end of the music, the therapist helps the client bring the imagery to a close, and a reorientation to the nonaltered state of consciousness is given. The client processes the meaningfulness of the imagery in relation to their daily life issues. This processing is done through verbal discussion or through free drawing or mandala drawings.

Only one study has been done on the efficacy of GIM in treating patients with RA (Jacobi, 1994; Jacobi & Eisenberg, 1996). Twenty-seven patients with RA received ten individual sessions of GIM, and data were collected on medical measures (including walking speed, joint count, and perception of pain intensity), and general psychological status (including mood, symptoms of distress/anxiety, and "ways of coping"). Statistically significant results were found for lower levels of psychological distress and subjective experience of pain. Statistically significant differences were also found for walking speed and joint count. There were no statistically significant results, however, in disease status, and it was argued that a longer period of treatment with GIM may be indicated for changes to occur in disease indicators.

In working with clients who have physical illness, Short (1990, 1991) noted that images emerging during GIM sessions may be physical markers of the illness. She found further that the marker could be useful in diagnosis. The image may be directly similar to the diseased body part, or may be an image of the fight against disease.

BACKGROUND INFORMATION

Sandra referred herself to GIM at the age of forty-three. She came from a large family of eight children and was the third daughter. She had married in her early twenties and given birth to three children. Her husband was frequently relocated by the company he worked for, so that Sandra lived in various houses throughout the marriage. After one such relocation, she was diagnosed with rheumatoid arthritis (RA). The psychodynamic features of this disease are fascinating. One of the group of autoimmune diseases, RA affects women more than men in a ratio of 3:1, with the age of onset being between twenty to fifty years. The etiology of RA is unknown, but there is evidence of genetic predisposition to the disease (Akil & Amos, 1999, p. 40). The onset of the disease is thought to take place when an antigenic stimulus activates the components of the immune system. The antigen is picked up by a cell of the body, activating the secretion of antibodies. The antibody then binds to the antigen. Once the immune system has detected foreign antigens, this is communicated to other systems within the body, thus complicating a vicious cycle—the body detects the antigen, produces antibodies, and these may be deposited in tissues, joints or blood vessels causing inflammation (Morrow, Nelson, Watts, & Isenberg, 1998). In essence, the body "turns upon itself."

In the acute stage, symptoms include painful joints, accompanied by a low level fever, fatigue, weight loss, and anemia. In the advanced stage there may be severe muscle wasting and deformity of joints and loss of movement resulting from contractures. In the acute phase, rest and analgesics are required for the pain and immobilization of the joints. A wide range of medications is used, particularly anti-inflammatory drugs and gold salts (Collins Concise Medical Dictionary, 1986, p. 326), and these are potentially toxic.

A condition associated with RA is Sjögren's syndrome, a key symptom of which is dry, gritty eyes, which may appear to be inflamed (redness), although vision is normal. The progression of RA is one of "flare-ups" and periods of remission. It is interesting to note that symptoms of RA disappear during pregnancy, but flare up after childbirth, indicating that hormones may play a major role.

Since there is no cure for the disease, patients frequently turn to complementary medicine for relief of pain through diet, gentle exercise, and other forms of treatment. Naparstek (1995) uses Guided Imagery (without music) in treating patients with a range of conditions. In relation to RA she comments: "Generally speaking rheumatoid arthritis erodes the bone at the joint and swells the soft tissue surrounding it. . . . Corrective envisaging includes 'filling in' the bone at the eaten-away points. . . " (p. 60).

The key symptoms of RA lend themselves to symbolic interpretation. Inflammation suggests heat, fire, and anger, and the term "flare-up" suggests a spontaneous rapid increase in these symptoms. The "dry, gritty eyes" of Sjögren's syndrome suggest the need for fluid to flush out the residual grit, and this fluid can be found in tears. Interestingly, at the start of GIM therapy Sandra was wearing plugs in her tear ducts in order to keep her eyes moistened. From a psychodynamic point of view, the eyes could be better lubricated by naturally formed tears.

In the process of GIM therapy it is common for therapists to look for symbolic associations between the symptoms of disease and the psycho-emotional needs of the client. For Sandra, it appeared that her therapeutic needs might include an exploration of feeling inflamed (angry) and expression of tears (possibly of grief or hurt) that would moisten her eyes. In addition, the concept of flare-ups suggested that her symptoms and her progression in therapy might wax and wane, particularly her experience of pain, stiffness, and fatigue. And it was probable that, as GIM therapy progressed and unresolved issues came to consciousness, those symptoms might be exacerbated before they were ameliorated.

Sandra responded extremely well to the Bonny Method of GIM. Initially she had monthly sessions, but these increased in frequency during times when she was dealing with an issue from childhood, or an issue evident in her current life situation. She had always enjoyed music, had been involved in musicals as a child, and loved to sing. She also played the guitar. She recalled childhood experiences where she had felt overlooked in the large family—her mother was constantly busy with many children and the needs of an aging grandmother and a busy farming business. From early childhood, Sandra had learned to be the peacemaker in the house, repressing her real feelings in favor of keeping the peace. Several of her siblings, however, were very vocal in making their needs known, so that Sandra developed a fear of speaking up in the presence of strong, authoritarian men and women. She was a qualified nurse, and often had found it difficult to assert herself in the presence of authoritarian charge nurses and medical doctors.

This nexus of issues was evident in the symptoms of her illness. Her difficulty in expressing anger, and in asserting herself, had led to the development of an illness in which the joints and tissues were periodically inflamed and painful. As a peacemaker, her tears of grief and disappointments from childhood had been blocked, and this was manifested in the plugs in her tear ducts which were necessary to keep the moisture inside her eyes.

In GIM sessions, Sandra would often have imagery associated with water. In her early sessions she had the opportunity to swim in water, sometimes naked, and other times supported by key people in her life. She had imagery of significant animals, particularly a black snake. One of her most reliable sources of strength, however, was the image of a school friend, an Aboriginal girl whose name was Miriam. Miriam frequently appeared as a welcome face with a "huge smile."

TREATMENT

In order to explain the elements of psychodynamic therapy with Sandra, three GIM sessions using the same music program will be discussed.

In Sessions 38, 45, and 57, the program entitled Body Program (Bonny, 1987) was used. The Body Program comprises music mostly written during the twentieth century, including:

Shostakovich: Allegretto, from the *String Quartette #3*
Shostakovich: Allegretto, from the *String Quartette #8*
Nielsen: Andante un poco tranquillo (excerpt), *Symphony #5*
Vierne: *The Chimes of Westminster* (a solo work for organ)
Beethoven: Largo, from the *Piano Concerto #3*
Prokofiev: Larghetto, from the *Classical Symphony*

The prominent features of the Shostakovitch selections are dissonant harmonies, short, angular melodies, and dancelike tempi. The music programs often chosen for Sandra in previous sessions had featured consonant harmonies and music with lyrical melodies, and so the decision to use more dissonant, angular music was a significant one.

In Session 38, Sandra had presented for the session describing a flare-up of her arthritis. A measure of the activity of the illness is the erythrocyte sedimentation rate (ESR). The normal range is 4–19mm; Sandra's level was 80. She described two issues that she felt contributed to this: her work environment, where she was required to take on more demands, and ongoing health problems with one of her children. She complained of pain in her head, shoulders, and neck, and that the sensation of the pain was "nagging." As I mentally considered the range of music programs available, the Body Program seemed to best fit the sensation of "nagging," and so I chose this music for the session. I asked Sandra to designate a color for the "nagging pain," and she chose "dull dark blue." I suggested she breathe this color through her body as a means of strengthening her awareness of her body. I then started the music.

As soon as the music began, Sandra's face changed. Her brow became furrowed, and her face was distorted with pain. She began to report what was happening in the imagery: "someone has a paintbrush, painting my joints with blue" When I asked how that felt for her, she said, "Slapdash, a bit rough, grating." I asked if she could see who was doing the painting. She said, "It's a big hand, a man's hand." I asked if she had something to say to him. She replied, "You don't understand how painful it is, I need something smoother, the bristle is too rough, it's making the pain worse instead of better, it's really irritating."

In the Bonny Method of GIM the therapist may change the music if it seems inappropriate to the client's experience. In this session I was ambivalent about what to do. Sandra's imagery suggested she wanted something smoother. Her words "you don't understand how painful it is" I took to be directed to me, and my countertransference was activated. On the one hand, I felt I had made her pain worse. By choosing the "wrong" music I was inflicting greater pain on Sandra, rather than lessening it. On the other hand, the pain she described was a "nagging" pain, and the Shostakovich was a good match to the quality of the pain. In addition, I felt somatic changes within my own body—my heart rate had increased, and I felt stiff throughout my chest as I wrestled with what to do. My inner voices also clouded the decision: "This was a terrible choice of music," and "I'm causing her pain." Finally, I changed the music to a different program in which the music of Vaughan-Williams was gentle, calming, and consonant. The imagery then changed to images of her as a child with her hair in two long plaits. She ascended a castle staircase and was taken into a room where the young girl was gently massaged. Something was burning up inside her, like a fever, and the girl in the imagery began to cry. Sandra then recalled that her mother had said that when she (the mother) died, Sandra would be the one to ensure that the family stayed together. Sandra felt this was too big a responsibility, and that it was not fair for her to carry that responsibility.

At the end of the music, and once Sandra had returned to a nonaltered state of conscious, she began to talk about the session. I commented that I noticed that the music at the beginning had made the pain worse, and apologized to her for exacerbating the pain. But Sandra commented that the music had forced her to feel the extent of the pain, and that it had opened up the insight into taking on the responsibility of keeping the peace. On reflection, I was uncertain whether Sandra's reassurance was to placate my concern or whether it had been as helpful as she described. In my notes of reflection after the session I had written,

"Had I taken on the role of peacekeeper, and placator in the session by changing the music?"

Bruscia (1998, p. 76) has written about the aspect of choosing music in GIM as a point at which the therapist's countertransference can be activated. When Sandra described the "nagging pain," my choice for the music was influenced by my own experience of "nagging pain." Thus, when she stated "you don't know how painful it is" I felt responsible for causing the exacerbation of the pain and therefore decided to change the music to something more gentle.

Some weeks passed, and in Session 45 Sandra presented with low energy. She had resigned from her demanding job and was preparing to start a new business from home. She was physically tired; however, she stated that her tiredness was also due to the domineering women at her workplace, who had in part influenced Sandra's decision to resign from the job.

As Sandra settled on to the mat, she spoke of an image of two domineering women pushing her in the back, and this was irritating her. As I considered all of the music programs available for the session, I again felt the Body Program best matched the irritation of being pushed in the back. As the first of the Shostakovich selections began, Sandra had an image of witch's hands—they were long, thin, and pointy. Sandra was irritated by the witch and wanted to be rid of her. This could only happen if she confronted the witch. During the Shostakovich piece, Sandra started to develop a body shape the same as the witch—her breasts became matronly, her bottom developed a wiggle, and she developed an authoritarian "strut." "When I am sweet and docile, she walks all over me. I want to be her equal, meet her where she is at. I want her out of my body" Sandra reported. "She is like the music—powerful, with an authoritarian look. I don't have to feel her power over me, I have to get rid of her, she's not going to attack my back any more. The energy is coming out of my hands—I'm challenging her to a fight." At this point I offered Sandra a high-density foam pillow to pound. This type of physical intervention can be helpful for clients in GIM in order to release pent-up emotion. After Sandra had pounded as much as she needed, I asked how her hands felt. I was concerned that the physical pounding may have hurt her arthritic hands. She commented that her hands were "relieved," they had been "niggling and frustrated" and the pounding had done them good.

In this session, I did not experience any of the ambivalence felt in Session 38. Sandra seemed to be empowered by the music and I did not take on any imagery experiences at a countertransference level.

In Session 57, Sandra had presented with problems with her eyes. She had new plugs inserted in the tear ducts. Her eyes felt irritated and sore, and she had a visual image of a black zigzag across her eyes. The back of her head felt heavy, with a dull ache. Since Sandra had worked well with the Body Program in Session 45, I chose it again. Initially, she stated that the music corresponded with her head, and she was irritated "everywhere." Her eyes were gritty and sandy, like sandpaper. It was like being in a dark room "not knowing where things are." Small darting animals appeared, and then birds like magpies started pecking at her. While she was experiencing this imagery, she was "ducking" her head on the cushion, as if to protect herself from the attacking birds.

At this point in the session I felt the same feelings of doubt that had emerged for me in Session 38. This music exacerbated her pain, but I thought it could also give her clarity about being "pecked" if she could explore the imagery further. Was the music I chose helping or causing more pain? If she was in greater pain, should I intervene by changing the music? Yes or no?

Before I could act on this dilemma, Sandra's imagery quickened—the magpies took on the faces of three domineering women in her life: They were "so quick, say things so quick, they go through you, so irritating right through my body, everywhere, my arms, head, shoulders, and eyes. I try to open my eyes slowly, to mesmerize the magpies, but the eyes are too irritated to open." My countertransference was enacted again—perhaps I was one of the domineering women, in choosing this music for her. Perhaps not opening her eyes was a form of resistance? I had written "resistance" (with a query sign [?]) in the margin of the paper used to transcribe the session. The music changed to the Nielsen selection of the Body Program and Miriam, her Aboriginal childhood friend, appeared in the imagery. "She'll bathe my eyes with healing waters—the waters are cool on my eyes that feel SO hot. Miriam's eyes are so beautiful, and she puts her fingers over my eyes, saying I should also put my own hands there. I can feel my own strength coming into my eyes."

During the Beethoven selection (the slow movement of the Piano Concerto #3), Sandra commented, "All the meanness I felt toward them, but not saying, was in my body. It's all out now, I don't want to feel mean, I don't want to feel irritated by them, I don't want to fight fire with fire. I want to see them clearly, hear them clearly, then say back to them what I want to say. I've been scared of people all my life." And later in the Beethoven: "There are electric charges going through my body, I am becoming more alive." Miriam appeared once more in the imagery, saying, "You have your own strength."

By not changing the music in this session I allowed Sandra to bring about her own resolution to the irritating magpies. Her resolution was to invoke the image of Miriam, the Aboriginal girl, who healed the burning of Sandra's eyes. Miriam could be seen as an archetypal figure, or as a projection of Sandra's feminine identity. The important point, however, was that I did not act as peace-maker (as I had in Session 38) by changing the music to something more gentle. Instead she enacted her own inner strength to resolve the unpleasant imagery.

DISCUSSION

Part of the process of the Bonny Method of GIM involves the client bringing to the surface images and associated feelings that have been repressed or un-resolved in the unconscious. The music plays an integral part in bringing these memories to the surface so that they can be resolved in the imagery. The choice of music is therefore pivotal. Some aspects of the GIM session involve input from the client—in deciding on the focus issue for the session, in the imagery that comes forth, and in processing the meaning of the imagery at the end of the session. The one major decision in which they have little or no influence is the choice of music. Clients may infrequently request gentle music, or strong music, but they do not choose the program. This decision therefore depends on the therapist's knowledge of the music, and an informed calculation of how well the music of the entire program (of 30–45 minutes) will relate to the issue brought by the client to the session. Should the music be inappropriate it is possible to change to another selection of music, or another program altogether, but such changes themselves involve a therapeutic decision made by the therapist.

Countertransference may be operating as the therapist makes these choices. Priestley (1994) discusses different types of countertransference, including e-countertransference, in which the therapist "becomes aware of the sympathetic resonance of some of the patient's feelings through his own emotional and/or somatic awareness" (p. 87). This was certainly my experience in all three sessions mentioned above.

However, Summer (1998) has stated that "in all music therapy techniques there is a triadic, not dyadic relationship" (p. 433). That is, there is potential for the client to have transference to both the therapist and the music. Within the Bonny Method of GIM, Summer argues that transference may be a "pure music transference," when "the music serves the essential therapeutic function" (p. 434). The client's transference may also be split between the primary music stimulus, and the verbal interventions of the therapist. In Session 38, for example, Sandra's experience of "someone has a paintbrush, painting my joints with blue" was influenced by my subsequent intervention—"How does that feel for you?" Although we argue that GIM therapists do not direct the imagery per se, the direction inherent in this intervention is to focus Sandra's attention on her feelings about being painted, rather than, for example, the size of the paintbrush, or who might be holding it. Each intervention of the therapist, therefore, has a propensity for countertransference. Likewise, when Sandra reported the feeling was "slapdash, a bit rough, grating," my intervention was to ask if she could see who was doing the painting. "It's a big hand, a man's hand" prompted me to ask if she had something to say to him. And this intervention evoked the response "you don't understand how painful it is, I need something smoother, the bristle is too rough, it's making the pain worse instead of better, it's really irritating."

From a psychodynamic perspective, both transference and counter-transference are operating interactively. Sandra's transference is operating toward the music, but influenced by my interventions. My countertransference was operating toward Sandra's exacerbated pain, and also to the music.

THERAPEUTIC GAINS

Each of the three sessions described above were pivotal sessions for Sandra. In each case, the sessions following unearthed memories of a significant event that needed to be reexperienced from her adult perspective in order to gain insight into the meaning of the event.

After Session 38, when her ESR count was 80, Sandra telephoned for an extra session. The precipitating cause was the ongoing illness of one of her daughters. In this session, I used the program entitled Mostly Bach, a program comprising works of Bach orchestrated by Stokowski. Typically, this music program is used for sessions requiring strong music, to match an issue of similar content. Sandra's imagery covered a range of hurtful events from her life—she recalled memories of the daughter (currently sick) as a baby; that soon after the birth her husband had been transferred by the company he worked for to a new location, and Sandra packed up the old house and moved once again into a new home. She recalled being overwhelmed by the physical work involved. In addition, her husband was working late into the night to acquaint himself with the new job. It was at this point that she received the diagnosis of arthritis. She was placed on medication, but one of the side effects was lockjaw. She recalled the terrifying feelings of not being able to move her mouth, or speak, and feeling a lack of control over the situation.

The session following Session 45 also unearthed significant and traumatic memories. She recalled being a very small child, and being unnoticed by everyone around her. She had a profound feeling of not being wanted, or not belonging. She recalled slinking out of the family house and not being noticed, and she experienced grief over her father's illness and subsequent death, recalling vivid images of him dying in hospital, an ashen gray color.

Imagery Related to the Body

After Session 45, Sandra began to use imagery to explore within her physical body. In Session 54 she arrived for her session describing her body as very tense and sore. During the relaxation induction she chose the color "electric blue" to illustrate the feeling within her body, and she imaged a gentle blue color to take into her body to relieve the pain and soreness. To the music of Vaughan-Williams (*Fantasia on a Theme of Thomas Tallis*), she found herself underwater. Initially she was weighed down with heavy armor, and instead of removing the armor (her defense), she decided to leave it on and journey inside her body to find the answers. At first, she explored her heart, which was a brown-red color, then she found tentacles growing in her body—in her bones, muscles, joints, and the cells. As she looked closely at the tentacles they transformed into vines of ivy, twisting through her body, like poison ivy. I asked her to look to the roots of the ivy vine. She found herself inside a house, as a small child, aged seven. Her energy had been "zapped." The girl was crying "burning tears" and the tears began to burn down the ivy. Later the armor fell off her body.

In subsequent sessions, Sandra recalled hurtful events from her childhood, growing up in a household with seven other children and the challenge to be seen and heard. She recalled crying herself to sleep at night. She also recalled hurtful events at school where she was singled out for ridicule. In Session 56, a masculine figure appeared in her imagery with the same color hair and eyes as Sandra. She named him David. In Jungian theory this image represents the internalized masculine. But one week later she suffered a flare-up of the arthritis in her spine, sufficient to put her to bed for a period of four weeks. In the next GIM session she experienced quite grotesque imagery—a black spider with red stripes appeared, but the legs of the spider transformed into tentacles of burning hot coal. A red lump started to get bigger and bigger, ready to explode. An image of her domineering sister appeared. She was holding a thorn and was pressing the thorn into the lump. As Sandra screamed at the woman—"Don't do this anymore"—the pain subsided. The spider reappeared with the message "speak the truth."

At this point in Sandra's therapy there were visible signs of change. She had her hair cut short, and she felt she was becoming more assertive with her domineering sister. In Session 71, she reexperienced the onset of lockjaw, in which the jaw was rigid, unable to move. She was terrified by the sensation of having no control over her mouth.

In Session 72, Sandra's imagery returned to an exploration within her body. She was experiencing pain in her sternum, and as she imaged the pain, she found the ribs on either side of the sternum involved in a fight. The sternum was "caught in the middle." This image was the catalyst for exploring further childhood memories where she was caught in the middle, and she would shut herself away from the family when others were arguing.

In the ensuing months Sandra was faced with two significant losses—the death of her mother (which was expected) and the death of her youngest daughter (as a result of an accident, and unexpected). At a time when she expected her RA to reappear, it did not. Over several sessions, Sandra was able to mourn, and in one session found a place within her heart to rest. She imaged a seat where she could sit within her own heart and grieve for her loved ones.

Her heart featured again in Session 84. The music program "Peak Experience" was used during the session, and during Wagner's *Prelude to Act 1 of Lohengrin*, Sandra's heart began to expand. Her heart became so enlarged that her body could fit inside it. A red and gold glow, like the sanctuary light in a church, filled the heart, and she felt enormous energy radiating from it. Sandra called this image of the heart the "core" of herself, and from this session on she frequently entered her heart to sit on the seat and rest there. In one session (98), she maintained a dialogue between her mind, body, and spirit, recognizing the "wise woman" within her and the "anxious woman" who disturbed the harmony of the mind-body-spirit connection. She felt she was beginning to recognize the different aspects of herself, and this was helpful when faced with stresses and demands.

After a break over the Christmas holiday period, Sandra commented that she had not experienced a flare-up for more than a year, and that she was no longer taking medication. We were fascinated that there had been no flare-up given the traumatic year she had experienced with the death of her mother and her daughter. It was as if the profound grief had brought the mind, body, and spirit together, and in that deep connection the RA had gone into remission.

Most recently, Sandra has changed her focus of work, choosing to conduct grief counseling through her local church. She continues to be free of symptoms of RA, and has been off medication for three years. She believes that the Bonny Method of GIM completely changed her life.

SUMMARY

In this case study, the Bonny Method of GIM was effective in many ways. It helped Sandra to confront the acute pain of arthritis, and via the imagery to find the root cause of the inflammation. This process of exploration, however, initially exacerbated the pain, and once this had occurred several times, I became more aware of her capacity for engaging the imagery and invoking images to help herself. Because the pain was heightened, Sandra was able to see clearly some of the childhood issues that had caused her to develop a pattern of repressing emotion, hiding from conflicts, and hiding disappointments and grief.

Later GIM sessions allowed her not only to explore the very core of her body, but to find a sanctuary deep within her own heart where she could sit and rest. This sanctuary became an essential inner place during the profound grief she suffered over the loss of her mother and her beloved youngest daughter. That she is currently free of symptoms and medication is testimony to the capacity of the Bonny Method of GIM in bringing about life-changing transformation.

REFERENCES

Akil, M., & Amos, R. S. (1999). "Rheumatoid Arthritis: Clinical Features and Diagnosis" (Chapter 10). In M. L. Snaith (ed.), *ABC of Rheumatology*. Second edition. London: BMJ.

Bruscia, K. (1998). "Signs of countertransference." In K. E. Bruscia (ed.), *The Dynamics of Music Psychotherapy*. Gilsum, NH: Barcelona Publishers.

Collins Concise Medical Dictionary. (1986). London: Collins.

Jacobi, E. (1994). *The Efficacy of the Bonny Method of Guided Imagery and Music as Experiential Therapy in the Primary Care of Persons with Rheumatoid Arthritis*. Unpublished doctoral dissertation. Union Institute. Cincinnati, OH.

Jacobi, E., & Eisenberg, G. (1996). *GIM in Medicine: Enhancing the Quality of Life in Rheumatoid Arthritis*. Presentation to the AMI Conference, Vancouver, BC, Canada.

Morrow, J., Nelson, L., Watts, R., & Isenberg, D. (1998). *Autoimmune Rheumatic Disease*. Second edition. Oxford: Oxford University Press.

Naparstek, B. (1995). *Staying Well with Guided Imagery*. London: Thorsons.

Priestley, M. (1994). *Analytical Music Therapy*. Phoenixville, PA: Barcelona Publishers.

Short, A. (1990). "Physical Illness in the Process of Guided Imagery and Music," *Australian Journal of Music Therapy*, 1, 9–14.

Short, A. (1991). "The Role of Guided imagery and Music in Diagnosing Physical Illness or Trauma," *Music Therapy*, 10 (1), 22–45.

Summer, L. (1998). "The Pure Music Transference in Guided Imagery and Music." In K. E. Bruscia (ed.), *The Dynamics of Music Psychotherapy*. Gilsum, NH: Barcelona Publishers.

Case Twenty-One

A WOMAN'S CHANGE FROM BEING NOBODY TO SOMEBODY: MUSIC THERAPY WITH A MIDDLE-AGED, SPEECHLESS, AND SELF-DESTRUCTIVE WOMAN

Niels Hannibal

ABSTRACT

This is a case study describing the developmental process of a woman called Lise. She wanted to develop and change, but could not use language therapeutically. This was why she was referred to music therapy. In the follow-up session three months after termination of the therapy, she expressed that the musical interaction and playing had made it possible for her to express herself. The music, and the interaction in the music with me as her therapist, had been a key factor in the development of her ability to communicate and interact. In this case study, I shall focus on the way her transference relationship with me emerged in the relationship both within and outside the musical context, and how it changed.

INTRODUCTION

I am a music therapist trained at the University in Aalborg, Denmark. In 1995, I began a Ph.D. research project, completed in 2001, entitled "Preverbal Transference in Music Therapy." This was a qualitative investigation of the transference process in musical interaction, and "Lise" was one of the case studies in this project. The kind of music therapy I practise is analytically oriented, similar to the concept of "*music in psychotherapy*" (Bruscia, 1998). In this therapeutic approach, the therapeutic issues are accessed, worked through, and resolved through musical and verbal experiences. The music and the verbal discourse are used to explore, transform, and develop the client's ability to relate to his/her self and the "other person." Often I use the musical interaction to enhance, work through, and resolve conflicts in the client's relationship patterns that emerge in the verbal discourse. This is important because the relationship between the therapist and the client contains the same transference patterns whether they unfold in music or in the verbal dialogue (Hannibal, 2001). Thus, both music and verbal interventions are used. The therapeutic focus is on investigating, developing, and transforming conflicts and deficits, both in the client's self-experience and in the way the client relates to other people. In this case, I used the concept of transference synonymous with a subjective, present experience, where a replication of implicit early relational patterns and experiences with significant others and things from real-life situations emerge in the therapy situation and/or in the relationship with the therapist (Bruscia, 1998). Transference relationship patterns can also be seen from the perspective of Luborsky and Crits-Christoph's (1998) concept of *Core Conflict Relationship Themes* (CCRT-method). Here, the transference pattern emerges in client narratives of relationship episodes. These narratives of real-life relationship episodes include three discrete elements: the client expressing an explicit or implicit wish, a response from others, and a response from the client. The CCRT-method reveals central conflict patterns that are similar to the transference relationship. In my Ph.D. research, I used the CCRT-method to identify Lise's transference relationship patterns, and I refer to Lise's wish (need), her experienced or expected responses from others, and her experienced or expected responses from her self, when talking about transference patterns in this case.

The media for interaction is both verbal and musical. The client and therapist identify a topic, a feeling, or a condition and investigate it through musical improvisation. It is a kind of dynamic intersectional spiral where the flow of the experience, the content, and interaction mode changes and develops.

BACKGROUND INFORMATION

Lise was admitted to music therapy because verbal psychotherapy was not prescribed, due to a reduced ability to verbalize and because of her problems with containing conflictual emotions. She was the second of two children. From childhood, Lise had received treatment for a chronic somatic disease. She described her mother as a person that kept/held her back, and who was over-protective and controlling. This provoked outbursts of anger. Besides this, Lise felt that her father was more fond of other people than of her. Lise completed school and became a gardener. At the time of therapy, she had a protected job because of her psychical illness, which means that she did not have to work full time. She has had one long-term relationship with a man, but this relationship ended a few years before therapy started. At present she lives alone.

Initial Condition

Her psychological condition was as follows: Lise described herself as having a negative self-image, low self-esteem, and low self-confidence. She thought that she was to blame for everything and her mood was typically depressed. She revealed self-mutilating behavior in relation to emotional distress and a lack of ability to recognize her own emotions. Lise experienced inhibition in her relationships with other people in general. She was never right and whatever she felt, said, or thought was always less important or meaningful than what the "other" felt, said, or thought. Therefore, Lise had severe difficulty in protecting herself, and standing up for herself. She was self-blaming and thought that she was guilty and to blame for her own situation. This made her feel angry toward herself and often led to her acting out and being destructive toward objects or toward her-self. It was very difficult for Lise to keep and maintain positive relationships with other people.

Besides music therapy, Lise also took antidepressive medication (Cipramil), which had a positive effect, reducing her tendency of being self-destructive.

From a diagnostic point of view, she was classified in the World Health Organization's International Classification of Diseases tenth revision (1993) as F.60.30: Emotional instability personality disorder of impulsive type. Outside the therapy, Lise had a tendency to act impulsively and to suffer from affect liability and unstable mood. During the music therapy assessment phase, she showed a different side of her personality that corresponded more with the evasive and anxious personality disorder. She was very uneasy and tended to experience overwhelming feelings of inferiority. She often felt rejected and criticized, and she withdrew from contact because of her fear of rejection. She was described as a person with a self-mutilating superego.

TREATMENT

Assessment Phase

The conclusion of the assessment phase was that Lise could identify the following psychological problems: She experienced insecurity about her own worth and abilities and she felt a general mistrust toward what her surroundings offered and, furthermore, a lack of autonomy in relationship with others. She was ambivalent about her need for recognition and affirmation from others and her need for respect from others. This appeared both in relation to keeping her boundaries and in relation to expressing aggression. Lise was afraid of rejection and she often responded by acting out when she experienced emotional stress.

She was accepted for music therapy because she was compliant and capable of keeping the therapeutic contract. She showed motivation to work with her psychological problems. In the beginning, she had difficulty in achieving insight through verbal dialogue because her self-image was so overwhelmingly negative, but she could reflect and work with herself through musical improvisation.

The goal of the therapy was to support Lise's sense of her self, to develop the therapeutic alliance, and to develop her ability to establish contact. The goals were also to develop her ability to express herself in relation to others, both verbally and musically, and to explore her malfunctioning way of expressing her needs and emotions.

The Transference Relationship

The analysis of Lise's core conflict relationship themes (Luborsky & Crits-Christoph, 1998) showed that her wish for being respected as an adult was very central, and that she wanted autonomy and independence, as well as to help to change and generally improve herself. She expected and experienced that other people responded to these wishes by being unhelpful and critical. This confirmed for her that other people did not like her. She responded by feeling unloved and helpless. She became angry and turned these feelings toward herself. This showed two major conflict themes. The first theme was concerned with contact and relationships toward other people; that other people were "above" her in the contact. Lise was an "inferior" person. And she dared not challenge this hierarchy because of her fear of being abandoned. The second theme was concerned with her sense of herself. Lise experienced a feeling of being worthless and blamed herself for this. This low self-esteem resulted in rage and anger that she turned upon herself, both in her thoughts and in her actions.

The Frame of Therapy

Because of Lise's relatively weak ego, the therapeutic frequency was two times a week for forty-five minutes. The intention was to build the alliance and avoid malignant regression. However, after twenty-two sessions she was admitted to the psychiatric ward for a short period, to support and stabilize her because she showed regressive behavior with more acting out. She had suicidal thoughts and desires for revenge. She was caught up with her aggressive feelings. After this hospitalization, the therapeutic frequency was changed to one session a week and pharmacological treatment was initiated. In these later sessions there was less of a focus on expressing her aggressive feelings. After some months she was able to work more directly with frustration and Lise continued in therapy without further need for hospitalization.

The entire therapy period is divided into four phases. Each phase has retrospectively been given a title that describes the central theme in this part of the therapy process:

Phase 1: Establishing alliance and how to involve other people in her experience.
Phase 2: Support for self-action.
Phase 3: To stand up for herself.
Phase 4: The fear of standing alone.

Phase 1: Establishing Alliance and How to Involve Other People in Her Experience

This phase was from Session 1 to Session 25. In this phase, Lise had extreme difficulties in expressing herself verbally and musically—a condition that often led her to a feeling of inadequacy and defeat. When she tried to speak or to answer a question, she typically stopped or interrupted herself and stalled. This also happened in the music where she tried, but often stalled. Therefore, Session 1 to Session 25 focused on using the music to find a way for her to express herself. In the beginning of therapy, the negative transference showed itself both in the verbal and in the musical contact. Lise quickly judged her music as something that would never be good enough.

Vignette A: From Session 4

In this session, we are talking about her experience of a previous musical improvisation. She describes that it gives her a tense feeling. The improvisation is about trying to find her "size" in the music, but she cannot concentrate on her feelings and her size at the same time. I ask if she needs more time, which she does. We sit quietly, but then I pick up an unpleasant feeling that I am not sure that the relationship will be able to contain. I suggest that she tries to find "a nice place" in the music. Lise gets confused because I have just suggested that she could sit quietly, but she accepts to play a cellolike instrument called a grotta. Her music is characterized by phrases of tones on the open strings. They are without metrical pulse. Starting in the low register, she intensifies the melody by doubling the number of tones. She reaches a tonal and dynamic "climax" of the phrase and descends to the low note again. These phrases are quiet and last ten to fifteen seconds. She repeats this pattern for a minute. I am even quieter than her, matching her tempo and trying not to overpower her dynamic. After a minute, she introduces a new note and I engage in the change by becoming dynamically and rhythmically more clear. She responds to that by using this new rhythmic pattern for a few seconds, whereafter she returns to her original way of playing and stops.

I ask her what she thinks of her music. She tries to say something, but stops, and says, "I am not very good at this." I can still feel the tension growing; this is not helping her. Then she finally says that she is afraid of being rejected from music therapy and starts to cry. I tell her that I have no expectations of her music, and that my impression is that she seriously wants to work with herself. This calms her down though she does not recognize being serious.

This example shows two important things. First, it shows that Lise was able to create structure in the music. She produced something recognizable that, though it was weak in structure, represented her. She was there. It also showed that whenever the "surroundings" became "hearable" Lise would immediately turn her attention toward the other person and lose her sense of her self. The negative transference was her experience of being inadequate and her fear of being rejected. The surprise was that she was more coherent than I expected.

It is also positive that although her negative self-experience was very present, she tried and continued. She was also able to receive verbal feedback that she did not have to perform anything, and what she had just done was sufficient, because it showed how seriously she was working. It calmed her down to experience the sharing of feelings with me, and that I thought she was serious. The themes in the therapy were how to make a choice, how to move and hold on to something. This also increased her contact with conflict material, which led to her acting out and subsequent hospitalization.

Phase 2. Support for Self-Action.

From Session 26 to Session 36 the focus was on identity, which included meeting, contributing something, and moving. Because of her recently regressive episode, the conflict material was approached in a dissociated manner, which meant that she worked with her aggressive feelings by "watching" them from "the outside" instead of trying to contain and express them directly—verbally or musically. All her conflict work was explored indirectly in the musical interaction.

One important part of this process was her recognition of the conscious and unconscious demands on herself, her ever-present and judging "superego."

Vignette B: From Session 33

This session starts with an improvisation. Lise's drumming is energetic and expressive, and I follow her dynamics and participate in her creation of a pulse. She stops and changes instrument, still playing with occasional short increases and decreases in intensity. At the end, we are floating together where she controls the tempo and dynamics. It ends in an intense dynamic climax. She explains that the music expresses impatience. We talk about the experience, but she quickly gets frustrated, and starts to blame herself for not "giving a clear message," and not living up to my expectations. The conflict is between her expectations of herself and her feeling of not fulfilling these, and the ensuing fear of being rejected by me. Despite this conflict, she is able to recognize the music as expressing, and identical to, her feelings. Her frustration is also related to the feeling that, in general, whenever she tries to express herself in words, she stalls and has to back out. She is seldom the one that is proven right. Her feeling of impatience is related to her feeling of not progressing in the therapy. I focus on her ability to move and separate from others, and we work with this issue in the music. After the music, Lise thinks the music was messy, and she is disappointed that she did not find the right notes. This point of view is different from my experience and therefore she is in conflict with me. We end the session talking about the possibility that her experience is as legitimate as mine, and she seems to accept the fact that only she felt the music was wrong.

Seen from a transference relationship point of view, this example showed that Lise had developed the ability to use the music and the instruments as expressive tools. The music could enlarge/enhance her feelings, but also made her negative transference "visible." Her fear of being rejected was because she could not formulate herself verbally, and she felt inadequate because she could not live up to her own unconscious expectations. It was a sign of progress that Lise was able to recognize the consequences of her own demands, and also to start working toward autonomy.

Phase 3. To Stand Up for Herself

This phase from Session 37 to Session 62 explicitly focused on the therapeutic relationship and events in the outside world. There had been some important changes in her life situation. She had decided to quit a job because she was not happy about her work, and she was now searching for another one. Her acting out had decreased and she expressed more positive expectations of herself and her life. Lise began to work with her role in her family and began a process of separation. Her new goal was greater self-acceptance, which meant she wanted to accept herself "as she is." She wanted to disconnect more from her family, and function better socially. In the therapy, she worked more directly with conflict material without getting guilt feelings and low self-esteem.

Vignette C: From the Session 52

In this session, Lise presents a list of her explicit demands to herself. It contains thoroughness in everything, never to give up, being fair to others, being nice and sociable toward others, showing other people respect, and being able to talk and have fun together with others. I want to investigate these demands, but this activates her feeling of not being able to formulate and express herself. "It suddenly does not sound as much," she replies. Through this conversation, her feeling of frustration increases and the situation gets more and more tense. It is possible for me to interpret her unconscious demand, that she has to be able to formulate herself in front of me, but it does not help her. She is worried that she cannot change, and cannot contain the ability to be light and funny. "Why does it have to be so serious?" I ask if she would like to do something in the music that was not serious, or unserious. This she would.

The music is without structure in the beginning. We both play separately, but not isolated. The tempo is up, and there is no tonality. Lise begins playing a drum, then a steel drum, then metallophone. After several minutes, I begin to play a rhythmic structure, to contain and frame the energy. She is in charge, and

I am supporting her. There is suddenly space in her melody and the music becomes more harmonic, then it ends.

Her verbal comments on her music are that it was fun. She experimented, and feels better. My comment is that the music was floating. Finally, she turns her attention toward an important meeting she is nervous about. This is what is really worrying her.

This session showed that Lise is working explicitly with her self-image, and confronting her "superego." She quickly got in contact with the implicit and unconscious demand that she had to answer to me whenever I asked her anything and, because it is difficult for her, she felt low self-esteem and blamed herself for it. In this situation, an alternative opportunity emerged: To be unserious.

Lise used the musical improvisation to break out of her negative feeling. The fact that she was capable of doing this demonstrated her development of trust in the therapeutic relation and in herself.

Phase 4. The Fear of Standing Alone

The last three sessions focused on the termination of the therapy. Lise was worried about whether she could manage to be on her own without the support from the therapy. These sessions demonstrated that she had gained a lot. She could investigate her inner life. She could experiment with her expression, both in the verbal and musical context. This was clear in Session 63 where Lise could float in and out of contact. She could receive support and give support. She could lead the melody. Her experience was both of joy and sadness and she did not put herself down or judge her performance in the same negative manner as she had throughout most of the therapy.

Outside the therapy, Lise felt strengthened and able to cope with frustration without acting out. She was less negative in her self-conception and more relaxed toward other people, though she still worried about her social abilities. She expressed that she felt accepted and understood by me. I told her that I thought she had gained an increased ability to contain opposite and conflictual feelings and thoughts in relation to other people. She had greater knowledge about her role and conflict patterns and finally she showed less of a tendency to judge herself from statements by other people and less tendency toward self-destructive behavior. She showed an ability to transfer her experiences from the therapy into her daily life. Finally, she showed an improved ability to express her emotions and reflect verbally about these in a two-person relationship.

When Lise was asked to assess the whole process, she rated it as very good and emphased that the music "was a tool for her to express feelings, that she otherwise could not get rid of."

DISCUSSION AND CONCLUSION

In this discussion, I shall address the functions of the music in Lise's change in her ability to relate to herself and others.

It is clear that without a different medium than language Lise would never have been able to work psychodynamically with herself and make this change. Her core relational conflict was centered around a wish for respect for her as a person, her feelings and thoughts. But whenever these feelings and thoughts were in conflict with others, she could never stand up for herself, and would always lose. This prevented her from doing anything. If she defied the "other person," she would lose attachment and be isolated. If she *did not* do it, she would suppress her own instincts, feelings, and thoughts. This is what she did, and this was the reason for her low self-esteem and her acting out and self-mutilation.

So in Phase 1, this dynamic become clear. But what was also clear was that when she played and improvised there was coherence and this meant that she was present. This was unconscious to her, but it was important. From a relational point of view she was trying to fulfill my expectations and perform and produce some kind of musical material. I could communicate to her—"I hear you, I support you, I respect your music." It took a while before this experience precipitated. The function of the music in this phase was as a kind of "open space" where Lise could try herself out and begin to share what she could not say. The therapeutic alliance was formed with her, both in the verbal and the musical context.

In Phase 2, the musical space functioned both as support and as a field of exploration. In the music, she could confront her aggressive feelings and she began to recognize what she was demanding of herself. It became explicit to her, that she was judging herself and not me.

In Phase 3, the musical improvisation gave her a potential space for exploring, negotiating, and experimenting, both with her self-expression and with her relationship with me. Her judging of herself diminished, as it become clear to her that she did not have to fear my rejection.

In Phase 4, the music was now a safe environment for her. She could "play" now. This process seemed to emphasise the importance of Lise's experience of a relational space and process that was nonverbal. Here, Lise could break out of her rigid and destructive habitual way of being with other people. In this period of the therapeutic process, this is what she did. It was not the music therapy alone. Lise received pharmacological, as well as environmental, support throughout the entire process. The medicine gave her an emotional stability that was needed, and the social supporting environment gave support in between therapy. After the termination of music therapy, Lise continued to have supportive meetings for the next two years. In the spring of 2001, she terminated this contact, declaring that she no longer needed this. Today she is discharged from any further contact or treatment by the psychiatric system.

I conclude that this case demonstrates that psychodynamic work and change can be done even though the client, in the preliminary phase, shows difficulty in verbal reflection and insight. Language was, in this case, a very weak foundation on which to build a therapeutic alliance and to work with psychological conflict and deficit. Musical improvisation and interaction proved to be a significant and sufficient media in which an alliance could grow, and where intersubjectivity could emerge. This case also demonstrated that Lise's improved range of communication skills and expression capability, which developed in the musical context, was carried over to the verbal context as well, and into her daily life.

REFERENCES

Bruscia, K. E. (1998). *The Dynamics of Music Psychotherapy* (chapter 1). Gilsum, NH: Barcelona Publishers.

Hannibal, N. (2001). *The Preverbal Transference Relationship in Music Therapy.* Ph.D. dissertation. Aalborg University, Denmark.

Luborsky, L., & Crits-Christoph, P. (1998). *Understanding Transference—The Core Conflictual Relationship Theme Method.* 2nd edition. Washington, DC: American Psychology Association Publishers.

Stern, D. (1985). *The interpersonal World of the Infant.* New York: Basic Books, Inc.

Stolorow, R.D. and Atwood, G.E. (1996). "The Intersubjective Perspective," *Psychoanalytic Review,* 83, 181–194.

The ICD-10 Classification of Mental and Behavioural Disorders: Diagnostic Criteria for Research. (1993). Geneva: World Health Organization.

Index

INDEX